T0331854

Exploring the Convergence of Big Data and the Internet of Things

A.V. Krishna Prasad
K.L. University, India

A volume in the Advances in Data Mining and
Database Management (ADMDM) Book Series

Published in the United States of America by
    IGI Global
    Engineering Science Reference (an imprint of IGI Global)
    701 E. Chocolate Avenue
    Hershey PA, USA 17033
    Tel: 717-533-8845
    Fax: 717-533-8661
    E-mail: cust@igi-global.com
    Web site: http://www.igi-global.com

Copyright © 2018 by IGI Global. All rights reserved. No part of this publication may be reproduced, stored or distributed in any form or by any means, electronic or mechanical, including photocopying, without written permission from the publisher. Product or company names used in this set are for identification purposes only. Inclusion of the names of the products or companies does not indicate a claim of ownership by IGI Global of the trademark or registered trademark.

Library of Congress Cataloging-in-Publication Data

Names: Prasad, A.V. Krishna, 1974- editor.
Title: Exploring the convergence of big data and the internet of things /
    A.V. Krishna Prasad, editor.
Description: Hershey, PA : Engineering Science Reference, 2017.
Identifiers: LCCN 2017011959| ISBN 9781522529477 (hardcover) | ISBN
    9781522529484 (eISBN)
Subjects: LCSH: Internet of things. | Big data. | Convergence
    (Telecommunication)
Classification: LCC TK5105.8857 .E96 2017 | DDC 004.67/8--dc23 LC record available at https://lccn.loc.gov/2017011959

This book is published in the IGI Global book series Advances in Data Mining and Database Management (ADMDM) (ISSN: 2327-1981; eISSN: 2327-199X)

British Cataloguing in Publication Data
A Cataloguing in Publication record for this book is available from the British Library.

All work contributed to this book is new, previously-unpublished material. The views expressed in this book are those of the authors, but not necessarily of the publisher.

For electronic access to this publication, please contact: eresources@igi-global.com.

Advances in Data Mining and Database Management (ADMDM) Book Series

David Taniar
Monash University, Australia

ISSN:2327-1981
EISSN:2327-199X

MISSION

With the large amounts of information available to organizations in today's digital world, there is a need for continual research surrounding emerging methods and tools for collecting, analyzing, and storing data.

The **Advances in Data Mining & Database Management (ADMDM)** series aims to bring together research in information retrieval, data analysis, data warehousing, and related areas in order to become an ideal resource for those working and studying in these fields. IT professionals, software engineers, academicians and upper-level students will find titles within the ADMDM book series particularly useful for staying up-to-date on emerging research, theories, and applications in the fields of data mining and database management.

COVERAGE

- Database Security
- Data warehousing
- Data mining
- Web mining
- Profiling Practices
- Enterprise systems
- Neural networks
- Sequence analysis
- Educational Data Mining
- Cluster Analysis

IGI Global is currently accepting manuscripts for publication within this series. To submit a proposal for a volume in this series, please contact our Acquisition Editors at Acquisitions@igi-global.com or visit: http://www.igi-global.com/publish/.

The Advances in Data Mining and Database Management (ADMDM) Book Series (ISSN 2327-1981) is published by IGI Global, 701 E. Chocolate Avenue, Hershey, PA 17033-1240, USA, www.igi-global.com. This series is composed of titles available for purchase individually; each title is edited to be contextually exclusive from any other title within the series. For pricing and ordering information please visit http://www.igi-global.com/book-series/advances-data-mining-database-management/37146. Postmaster: Send all address changes to above address. Copyright © 2018 IGI Global. All rights, including translation in other languages reserved by the publisher. No part of this series may be reproduced or used in any form or by any means – graphics, electronic, or mechanical, including photocopying, recording, taping, or information and retrieval systems – without written permission from the publisher, except for non commercial, educational use, including classroom teaching purposes. The views expressed in this series are those of the authors, but not necessarily of IGI Global.

Titles in this Series

For a list of additional titles in this series, please visit: www.igi-global.com/book-series

Data Visualization and Statistical Literacy for Open and Big Data
Theodosia Prodromou (University of New England, Australia)
Information Science Reference • copyright 2017 • 365pp • H/C (ISBN: 9781522525127) • US $205.00 (our price)

Web Semantics for Textual and Visual Information Retrieval
Aarti Singh (Guru Nanak Girls College, Yamuna Nagar, India) Nilanjan Dey (Techno India College of Technology, India) Amira S. Ashour (Tanta University, Egypt & Taif University, Saudi Arabia) and V. Santhi (VIT University, India)
Information Science Reference • copyright 2017 • 290pp • H/C (ISBN: 9781522524830) • US $185.00 (our price)

Advancing Cloud Database Systems and Capacity Planning With Dynamic Applications
Narendra Kumar Kamila (C.V. Raman College of Engineering, India)
Information Science Reference • copyright 2017 • 430pp • H/C (ISBN: 9781522520139) • US $210.00 (our price)

Web Data Mining and the Development of Knowledge-Based Decision Support Systems
G. Sreedhar (Rashtriya Sanskrit Vidyapeetha (Deemed University), India)
Information Science Reference • copyright 2017 • 409pp • H/C (ISBN: 9781522518778) • US $165.00 (our price)

Intelligent Multidimensional Data Clustering and Analysis
Siddhartha Bhattacharyya (RCC Institute of Information Technology, India) Sourav De (Cooch Behar Government Engineering College, India) Indrajit Pan (RCC Institute of Information Technology, India) and Paramartha Dutta (Visva-Bharati University, India)
Information Science Reference • copyright 2017 • 450pp • H/C (ISBN: 9781522517764) • US $210.00 (our price)

Emerging Trends in the Development and Application of Composite Indicators
Veljko Jeremic (University of Belgrade, Serbia) Zoran Radojicic (University of Belgrade, Serbia) and Marina Dobrota (University of Belgrade, Serbia)
Information Science Reference • copyright 2017 • 402pp • H/C (ISBN: 9781522507147) • US $205.00 (our price)

Web Usage Mining Techniques and Applications Across Industries
A.V. Senthil Kumar (Hindusthan College of Arts and Science, India)
Information Science Reference • copyright 2017 • 424pp • H/C (ISBN: 9781522506133) • US $200.00 (our price)

Social Media Data Extraction and Content Analysis
Shalin Hai-Jew (Kansas State University, USA)
Information Science Reference • copyright 2017 • 493pp • H/C (ISBN: 9781522506485) • US $225.00 (our price)

701 East Chocolate Avenue, Hershey, PA 17033, USA
Tel: 717-533-8845 x100 • Fax: 717-533-8661
E-Mail: cust@igi-global.com • www.igi-global.com

Editorial Advisory Board

Akhil Khare, *MVSR Engineering College, India*
P. Premchand, *Osmania University, India*
S. Ramakrishna, *Sri Venkateswara University, India*
G. Sreedhar, *Deemed University, India*

List of Reviewers

Muhammad Anshari, *Universiti Brunei, Brunei*
Singaraju Jyothi, *Sri Padmavati Mahila University, India*
Anvita Karara, *Carnegie Mellon University, USA*
Ankit Lodha, *Amgen, USA*
Varaprasad Rao M, *Anurag Group of Institutions, India*
Gunasekaran Manogaran, *VIT University, India*
Satya Narayana, *K. L. University, India*
Rizwan Patan, *VIT University, India*
Pothuraju Raja Rajeswari, *KL University, India*
A. Prasanth Rao, *Anurag Group of Institutions, India*
Sreedhar G. Rashtriya, *Vidyapeetha, India*
Varsha Sharma, *RGPV, India*
Vadlamudi Sucharita, *K. L. University, India*
Chandu Thota, *Infosys Ltd., India*
Brisheket Tripathi, *AKTU, India*

Table of Contents

Detailed Table of Contents

Big data and cloud computing are transforming information technology. These comparable technologies are the result of dramatic developments in computational power, virtualization, network bandwidth, availability, storage capability, and cyber-physical systems. The crossroads of these two areas, involves the use of cloud computing services and infrastructure, to support large-scale data analytics research, providing relevant solutions or future possibilities for supply chain management. This chapter broadens the current posture of cloud computing and big data, as associate with the supply chain solutions. This chapter focuses on areas of significant technology and scientific advancements, which are likely to enhance supply chain systems. This evaluation emphasizes the security challenges and mega-trends affecting cloud computing and big data analytics pertaining to supply chain management.

In the field of Aquaculture with the help of digital advancements huge amount of data is constantly produced for which the data of the aquaculture has entered in the big data world. The requirement for data management and analytics model is increased as the development progresses. Therefore, all the data cannot be stored on single machine. There is need for solution that stores and analyzes huge amounts of data which is nothing but Big Data. In this chapter a framework is developed that provides a solution for shrimp disease by using historical data based on Hive and Hadoop. The data regarding shrimps is acquired from different sources like aquaculture websites, various reports of laboratory etc. The noise is removed after the collection of data from various sources. Data is to be uploaded on HDFS after normalization is done and is to be put in a file that supports Hive. Finally classified data will be located in particular place. Based on the features extracted from aquaculture data, HiveQL can be used to analyze shrimp diseases symptoms.

    V. Sucharita, K. L. University, India
    P. Venkateswara Rao, ASCET, India
    A. Satya Kalyan, K. L. University, India
    P. Rajarajeswari, K. L. University, India

At present in Big Data era mining of Big Data can help us find learning which nobody has possessed the capacity to find some time recently. There is a developing interest for tools and techniques which can prepare and investigate Big Data effectively and proficiently. In this chapter, the accessible information mining tools and techniques which can deal with Big Data have been abridged. This paper additionally concentrates on tools and techniques for mining of data and information streams. Through better analysis of the vast volumes of information that are getting to be accessible, there is the potential for making speedier progresses in numerous scientific areas what's more, making strides the productivity what's more, victory of numerous organizations. The challenges incorporate not just the self-evident issues of scale, be that as it may too heterogeneity, need of structure, error handling, protection, opportunities at all stages of the analysis from acquisition of data to obtaining to result.

    Syed Hassan Askari, National University of Sciences and Technology (NUST), Pakistan
    Faizan Ahmad, National University of Sciences and Technology (NUST), Pakistan
    Sajid Umair, National University of Sciences and Technology (NUST), Pakistan
    Safdar Abbas Khan, National University of Sciences and Technology (NUST), Pakistan

As due to the predominant money related emergency and the developing needs, Higher Education Institutes establishments are confronting challenges in giving essential information technology backing to instructive, innovative work exercises. The higher education establishment must adventure the open doors managed by cloud computing while minimizing the related security dangers to permit access to cutting edge information technology base, server farms, and applications and ensure touchy data. In this paper, cloud computing building design for higher education organization containing the different sending models, service models and client area is proposed. We at last give the suggestions to a fruitful and effective relocation from customary to cloud based framework. This research also to discover different options for the utilization of IT, while driving colleges to enhance dexterity and get investment funds. The examination system comprised in a thorough investigation of the most recent exploration on cloud computing as a different option for IT procurement, administration and security.

    Krishnaveer Abhishek Challa, Andhra University, India
    Jawahar Annabattula, K. L. University, India

Linguistic distance has always been an inter-language issue, but English being a interwoven cluster of rhyming words, homophones, tenses etc., has turned linguistic distance into an intra-language unit to measure the similarity of sounds. In many theoretical and applied areas of computational linguistics i.e., Big Data, researchers operate with a notion of linguistic distance or, conversely, linguistic similarity has become the means to optimise speech recognition systems. The present research paper focuses on the mentioned lines as an attempt to turn the existing systems from delivering good performance to perfect performance, especially in the area of Big Data.

Chapter 6

Muhammad Anshari, Universiti Brunei Darussalam, Brunei
Syamimi Ariff Lim, Universiti Brunei Darussalam, Brunei

The purpose of this chapter is to identify the opportunities of big data application that allows Customer Relationship Management (CRM) strategy to gain deeper insights into customer retention and let the businesses make innovation in term of sales, service, and marketing. This chapter is motivated from the concept of big data in CRM by proposing a conceptual model to address mobile commerce in an organization. It examines the progress of big data in creating value for m-commerce. Researchers employed thematic literature analysis and discussed broader issues related to customer behavior in using smartphone and its internet habit activities. Despite the limitation of the study, CRM with big data remains an important area for future research in mobile commerce setting.

Chapter 7

Varsha Sharma, Rajiv Gandhi Proudyogiki Vishwavidyalaya, India
Vivek Sharma, Rajiv Gandhi Proudyogiki Vishwavidyalaya, India
Nishchol Mishra, Rajiv Gandhi Proudyogiki Vishwavidyalaya, India

Recently, Internet of Things (IoT) has aroused great interest among the educational, scientific research, and industrial communities. Researchers affirm that IoT environments will make people's daily life easier and will lead to superior services, great savings as well as a nifty use of resources. Consequently, IoT merchandise and services will grow exponentially in the upcoming years. The basic idea of IoT is to connect physical objects to the Internet and use that connection to provide some kind of useful remote monitoring or control of those objects. The chapter presents the overall IoT vision, the technologies for achieving it, IoT challenges and its applications. This chapter also attempts to describe and analyze threat types for privacy, security and trust in IoT as well as shows how big data is an important factor in IoT. This chapter will expose the readers and researchers who are interested in exploring and implementing the IoT and related technologies to the progress towards the bright future of the Internet of Things

Chapter 8

Pallavi Khare, Matrusri Engineering College, India
Akhil Khare, MVSR Engineering College, India

The Internet of Things (IoT) is a system of interrelated computing devices, mechanical and digital machines, objects, animals or people that are provided with unique identifiers and the ability to transfer data over a network without requiring human-to-human or human-to-computer interaction. The Internet of Things (IoT) shall be able to incorporate transparently and seamlessly a large number of different and heterogeneous end systems, while providing open access to selected subsets of data for the development of a plethora of digital services. Building a general architecture for the IoT is hence a very complex task, mainly because of the extremely large variety of devices, link layer technologies, and services that may be involved in such a system.

Chapter 9

Internet of Things (IoT) is an evolution of mobile, home and embedded systems that can be connected to internet increasing greater capabilities of data analytics to extract meaningful information, which can further used for decision making. Billions of devices are connected to internet and soon its number may grow higher than number of human beings on this planet. These connected devices integrated together can become a network of intelligent systems that share data over the cloud to analyze. IoT is an emerging technology where several machines are embedded with low power consuming sensors that allow them to rely data from each other with little or no human intervention. Especially, PIR motion sensor plays a key role in security systems for detecting movements, intrusion and occupancy by interacting with other devices simultaneously like alarms, cameras etc. In this paper, researchers studied IoT applications using PIR motion sensor and proposed architecture and algorithms to be implemented for better development of security systems.

Chapter 10

The Internet of Things comprises billions of devices that can sense, communicate, compute and potentially actuate. The data generated by the Internet of Things are valuable and have the potential to drive innovative and novel applications which are one of the sources of Big Data. IoT connects real world objects to the internet using tiny sensors or embedded devices. One of the biggest advantages of the IoT is the increasing number of low-cost sensors available for many different kinds of functionalities. These sensors include a variety of devices and solutions. The trend is moving towards multi-sensor platforms that incorporate several sensing elements. In such environment, discovering, identifying, connecting and configuring sensor hardware are critical issues. The cloud-based IoT platforms can retrieve data from sensors. Therefore, IoT is a comprehensive inter-disciplinary technology, So, this chapter presents Better scheduling decisions should result in saving the time, utilization of resources and enable to meet the time constraints.

This chapter proposes an efficient centralized secure architecture for end to end integration of IoT based healthcare system deployed in Cloud environment. The proposed platform uses Fog Computing environment to run the framework. In this chapter, health data is collected from sensors and collected sensor data are securely sent to the near edge devices. Finally, devices transfer the data to the cloud for seamless access by healthcare professionals. Security and privacy for patients' medical data are crucial for the acceptance and ubiquitous use of IoT in healthcare. The main focus of this work is to secure

Authentication and Authorization of all the devices, Identifying and Tracking the devices deployed in the system, Locating and tracking of mobile devices, new things deployment and connection to existing system, Communication among the devices and data transfer between remote healthcare systems. The proposed system uses asynchronous communication between the applications and data servers deployed in the cloud environment.

Chapter 12

Smart City is the product of accelerated development of the new generation information technology and knowledge-based economy, based on the network combination of the Internet, telecommunications network, broadcast network, wireless broadband network and other sensors networks where Internet of Things technology (IoT) as its core. Traffic congestion caused by vehicle is an alarming problem at a global scale and it has been growing exponentially. Searching for a parking space is a routine (and often frustrating) activity for many people in cities around the world. This search burns about one million barrels of the world's oil every day. A smart Parking system typically obtains information about available parking spaces in a particular geographic area and process is real-time to place vehicles at available positions. In our proposed chapter, we will be discussing the advanced features of IoT in order to development an intelligent parking management system in a smart city i.e. called as Smart Parking system.

Chapter 13

The Internet of Things concept arises from the need to manage, automate, and explore all devices, instruments and sensors in the world. In order to make wise decisions both for people and for the things in IoT, data mining technologies are integrated with IoT technologies for decision making support and system optimization. Data mining involves discovering novel, interesting, and potentially useful patterns from data and applying algorithms to the extraction of hidden information. Data mining is classified into three different views: knowledge view, technique view, and application view. The challenges in the data mining algorithms for IoT are discussed and a suggested big data mining system is proposed.

Chapter 14

The growth of World Wide Web and technologies has made business functions to be executed fast and easier. E-commerce has provided a cost efficient and effective way of doing business. In this paper the importance of e-commerce web applications and how Internet of Things is related to e-commerce is well discussed. In the end-user perspective, the performance of e-commerce application is mainly connected to the web application design and services provided in the e-commerce website. A grading system is used to evaluate the performance of each e-commerce website.

Chapter 15

Rizwan Patan, VIT University, India
Rajasekhara Babu M, VIT University, India
Suresh Kallam, VIT University, India

A Big Data Stream Computing (BDSC) Platform handles real-time data from various applications such as risk management, marketing management and business intelligence. Now a days Internet of Things (IoT) deployment is increasing massively in all the areas. These IoTs engender real-time data for analysis. Existing BDSC is inefficient to handle Real-data stream from IoTs because the data stream from IoTs is unstructured and has inconstant velocity. So, it is challenging to handle such real-time data stream. This work proposes a framework that handles real-time data stream through device control techniques to improve the performance. The frame work includes three layers. First layer deals with Big Data platforms that handles real data streams based on area of importance. Second layer is performance layer which deals with performance issues such as low response time, and energy efficiency. The third layer is meant for Applying developed method on existing BDSC platform. The experimental results have been shown a performance improvement 20%-30% for real time data stream from IoT application.

Chapter 16

Ankit Lodha, University of Redlands, USA
Anvita Karara, Carnegie Mellon University, USA

The concept of clinical big data analytics is simply the joining of two or more previously disparate sources of information, structured in such a way that insights are prescribed from examination of the new expanded data set. The combination with Internet of Things (IoT), can provide multivariate data, if healthcare organizations build the infrastructure to accept it. Many providers are able to integrate financial and utilization data to create a portrait of organizational operations, but these sources do not give a clear idea of what patients do on their own time. Embracing the centrality of the IoT would relinquish the idea that provider is the only pillar around which healthcare revolves. This chapter provides deeper insights into the four major challenges: costly protocol amendments, increasing protocol complexity and investigator site burden. It also provides recommendations for streamlining clinical trials by following a two dimension approach-optimization at a program level (clinical development plan) as well as at the individual trial candidate level.

Chapter 17

Peyakunta Bhargavi, Sri Padmavati Mahila Visvavidyalayam, India
Singaraju Jyothi, Sri Padmavati Mahila Visvavidyalayam, India

The recent development of sensors remote sensing is an important source of information for mapping and natural and man-made land covers. The increasing amounts of available hyperspectral data originates from AVIRIS, HyMap, and Hyperion for a wide range of applications in the data volume, velocity, and variety of data contributed to the term big data. Sensing is enabled by Wireless Sensor Network (WSN) technologies to infer and understand environmental indicators, from delicate ecologies and natural resources to urban environments. The communication network creates the Internet of Things (IoT) where sensors and actuators blend with the environment around us, and the information is shared across platforms in order to develop a common operating picture (COP). With RFID tags, embedded sensor and actuator nodes, the next revolutionary technology developed transforming the Internet into a fully integrated Future Internet. This chapter describes the use of Big Data and Internet of the Things for analyzing and designing various systems based on hyperspectral images.

The chapter investigates the scheduling load added on a long-term evolution (LTE) and/or LTE-Advanced (LTEA) network when automatic meter reading (AMR) in advanced metering infrastructures (AMI) is performed using internet of things (IoT) deployments of smart meters in the smart grid. First, radio resource management algorithms to perform dynamic scheduling of the meter transmissions are proposed and shown to allow the accommodation of a large number of smart meters within a limited coverage area. Then, potential techniques for reducing the signaling load between the meters and base stations are proposed and analyzed. Afterwards, advanced concepts from LTE-A, namely carrier aggregation (CA) and relay stations (RSs) are investigated in conjunction with the proposed algorithms in order to accommodate a larger number of smart meters without disturbing cellular communications.

Mobile cloud computing is the emerging field. Along-with different services being provided by the cloud like Platform as a Service, Infrastructure as a Service, Software as a Service; Game as a Service is new terminology for the cloud services. In this paper, we generally discussed the concept of mobile cloud gaming, the companies that provide the services as GaaS, the generic architecture, and the research work that has been done in this field. Furthermore, we highlighted the research areas in this field.

Preface

This book represents recent investigations and enhancements in the field of Big Data Analytics, Internet of Things, Web Engineering and other related areas. The growth of World Wide Web and technologies has made business functions to be executed fast and easier. E-commerce has provided a cost efficient and effective way of doing business. The Internet of Things (IoT) comprises billions of devices that can sense, communicate, compute and potentially actuate. The data generated by the Internet of Things are valuable and have the potential to drive innovative and novel applications. As everything gets connected to everything, data is the commodity being transferred between the various IoT components and attempts to store all the data being generated as a result continues to push the boundaries of Big Data. To make the Internet of Things useful, we need an Analytics of Things. IoT analytics applications can help companies understand the Internet of Things data at their disposal, with an eye toward reducing maintenance costs, avoiding equipment failures and improving business operations. This book will aim to provide relevant theoretical frameworks and the latest empirical research findings in Big Data and Internet of Things.

The book consists of various researchers' investigations and ideas in the above said fields. The book is organized into 19 chapters. The Chapter 1 demonstrates big data and cloud computing concepts and the insights of supply chain management. In Chapter 2, big data information is used as source for extracting the useful information in medical application. The Chapter 3 encompasses techniques and tools for effective usage of Big Data in data mining process. The Chapter 4 describes about cloud computing techniques that can be used as model of college information system in various educational applications.

The Chapter 5 demonstrates about computational linguistics and in this chapter with concept of Big Data on linguistics help to find and optimize accurate speech recognition system. The Customer Relationship Management (CRM) strategy to gain deeper insights into customer retention and let the business make innovation in terms of sales, service and marketing information is used as big data analytics in Chapter 6.

The Chapter 7 presents the overall IoT vision, the technologies for achieving it, IoT challenges and its applications. This chapter also attempts to describe and analyze threat types for privacy, security and trust in IoT as well as shows how big data is an important factor in IoT. This Chapter 7 will expose the readers and researchers who are interested in exploring and implementing the IoT and related technologies to the progress towards the bright future of the Internet of Things.

The Chapter 8 describes the Internet of Things (IoT) is a system of interrelated computing devices, mechanical and digital machines, objects, animals or people that are provided with unique identifiers and the ability to transfer data over a network without requiring human-to-human or human-to-computer interaction.

The Chapter 9 describes about IoT and sensors concepts for the development of remote applications.

The Chapter 10 explains the concepts of Internet of Things, Big Data and Cloud computing techniques for data generation that can be used in better scheduling decisions in time optimization, resources and satisfy the time constraints.

The Chapter 11 proposes an efficient centralized secure architecture for end to end integration of IoT-based healthcare system deployed in Cloud environment. The proposed platform uses Fog Computing environment to run the framework. In this chapter health data is collected from sensors and collected sensor data are securely sent to the near edge devices. The main focus of this work is to secure Authentication and Authorization of all the devices, Identifying and Tracking the devices deployed in the system, Locating and tracking of mobile devices, new things deployment and connection to existing system, Communication among the devices and data transfer between remote healthcare systems.

The Chapter 12 demonstrates Internet of Things (IoT) is the network of devices that are connected together and communicating with each other to perform certain tasks, without requiring human-to-human or human-to-computer interaction.

The Chapter 13 explains about Internet of Things and Data mining. The Internet of Things concept arises from the need to manage, automate, and explore all devices, instruments and sensors in the world. In order to make wise decisions both for people and for the things in IoT, data mining technologies are integrated with IoT technologies for decision making support and system optimization. Data mining involves discovering novel, interesting, and potentially useful patterns from data and applying algorithms to the extraction of hidden information. Data mining is classified into three different views: knowledge view, technique view, and application view.

The Chapter 14 explains about growth of e-commerce applications. The growth of World Wide Web and technologies has made business functions to be executed fast and easier. E-commerce has provided a cost efficient and effective way of doing business. In this paper the importance of e-commerce web applications and how Internet of Things is related to e-commerce is well discussed. In end user perspective the performance of e-commerce application is mainly connected to the web application design and services provided in the e-commerce website. A grading system is used to evaluate the performance of each e-commerce website.

The Chapter 15 demonstrates about Big Data Stream Computing (BDSC). The BDSC Platform handles real-time data from various applications such as risk management, marketing management and business intelligence. Now a days Internet of Things (IoT) deployment is increasing massively in all the areas. The frame work includes three layers. First layer deals with Big Data platforms that handle real data streams based on area of importance. Second layer is performance layer which deals with performance issues such as low response time, and energy efficiency. Third layer is meant for Applying developed method on existing BDSC platform.

The Chapter 16 provides deeper insights into the four major challenges: costly protocol amendments, increasing protocol complexity and investigator site burden. It also provides recommendations for streamlining clinical trials by following a two-dimensional approach-optimization at a program level (clinical development plan) as well as at the individual trial candidate level.

In Chapter 17 Big Data and remote sensing concepts are well described. The recent development of sensors remote sensing is an important source of information for mapping and natural and man-made land covers. The increasing amounts of available hyperspectral data originates from AVIRIS, HyMap, and Hyperion for a wide range of applications in the data volume, velocity, and variety of data contributed to the term big data. Sensing is enabled by Wireless Sensor Network (WSN) technologies to infer and understand environmental indicators, from delicate ecologies and natural resources to urban environments. The Chapter 17 describes the use of Big Data and Internet of the Things for analyzing and designing various systems based on hyperspectral images.

The Chapter 18 investigates the scheduling load added on a long-term evolution (LTE) and/or LTE-Advanced (LTEA) network when automatic meter reading (AMR) in advanced metering infrastructures (AMI) is performed using internet of things (IoT) deployments of smart meters in the smart grid. First, radio resource management algorithms to perform dynamic scheduling of the meter transmissions are proposed and shown to allow the accommodation of a large number of smart meters within a limited coverage area. Then, potential techniques for reducing the signaling load between the meters and base stations are proposed and analyzed. Afterwards, advanced concepts from LTE-A, namely carrier aggregation (CA) and relay stations (RSs) are investigated in conjunction with the proposed algorithms in order to accommodate a larger number of smart meters without disturbing cellular communications.

The Chapter 19 discusses the introduction of mobile cloud gaming which is followed by the identification of cloud gaming companies. General architecture of mobile cloud environment is discussed. Related literature work is also described in this chapter.

Acknowledgment

I am very much happy and thankful to IGI Global for giving me the opportunity to produce the book *Exploring the Convergence of Big Data and the Internet of Things*, which is very much preferred in the present scenario. I also would like to express a deep sense of gratitude to Jan Travers, Katherine Shearer, Taylor Chernisky, Marianne Caesar, Melissa Wagner and other members of IGI Global who directly or indirectly supported this book project.

I am thankful to all the authors who contributed their valuable efforts and ideas in the form of the chapters in this book. I would like to express my sincere thanks to Prof. S. Ramakrishna and Prof. P. Premchand, Dr G. Sreedhar for their continuous support and encouragement of my career.

I am thankful to the Principal, Head - CSE department and other faculty members for their support and kindness in completing this book.

Finally, I am very thankful for the support of my parents Smt. A. Laxmi Devi, Sri. A. Anjaneyulu, and the support of my wife Smt. A. Sathyavathi and my children Kumari A. Vaishnavi and Mr. A. Venkata Sai for their encouragement in achieving this target goal in my academic career.

Chapter 1
Big Data and Cloud Computing:
A Review of Supply Chain Capabilities and Challenges

Marcus Tanque
Independent Researcher, USA

Harry J Foxwell
George Mason University, USA

ABSTRACT

Big data and cloud computing are transforming information technology. These comparable technologies are the result of dramatic developments in computational power, virtualization, network bandwidth, availability, storage capability, and cyber-physical systems. The crossroads of these two areas, involves the use of cloud computing services and infrastructure, to support large-scale data analytics research, providing relevant solutions or future possibilities for supply chain management. This chapter broadens the current posture of cloud computing and big data, as associate with the supply chain solutions. This chapter focuses on areas of significant technology and scientific advancements, which are likely to enhance supply chain systems. This evaluation emphasizes the security challenges and mega-trends affecting cloud computing and big data analytics pertaining to supply chain management.

INTRODUCTION

Big data and cloud computing are technologies that continue to gain customers' attention. These technologies, provide a wide range of capabilities to numerous global clients: resources, services, applications and Internet. In recent years, vendors i.e., Microsoft, IBM, Oracle, Yahoo, Google, Amazon, eBay, GoGrid, 3Tera, Salesforce, Zoho, CloudPassage among others are leasing their cloud-based computing solutions and big data services to many organizations (Leighon, 2009). These service signatures are based on each organization's requirements, including the volume of storage capacity that is required to provision or store data. Whereas virtualization and grid computing technologies have perfected cloud and big data services. Vendors continue to refine and plan for groundbreaking IT solutions to satisfy

DOI: 10.4018/978-1-5225-2947-7.ch001

Copyright © 2018, IGI Global. Copying or distributing in print or electronic forms without written permission of IGI Global is prohibited.

customer's requirements (Gartner, 2009; Gartner, 2012). The adoption of cloud solutions and big data analytics comprises a number of business and technology factors applicable to supply chain systems. To effectively align with the adoption of cloud-based solutions and big data analytics, decision makers must first evaluate their offered financial resources as a key factor for implementing innovative products (Gartner, 2009; Gartner, 2012; Leighon, 2009). Decision makers should also view the total cost ownership, as alternate strategic factor toward the implementation of new information technology solutions. It is common for organizations to lease commodity computer system hardware and application software appliances from cloud service providers or managed service providers. Commissioning these information technology resources i.e., servers, bandwidth, storage & network systems, and applications, offers business the ability to reduce their capital and operational expenditures (Leighon, 2009).

BACKGROUND

Big data and cloud computing offer organizations relative and cost-effective advantages. Aside from cloud and big data technology continuous adoption, decision makers are concerned about user's privacy and data security/protection (Gartner, 2009; Gartner, 2012). Privacy and data protection are both vital IT solutions for logistic functions and supply chain. Any violation of business and IT infrastructures could impact an organization's productivity. High security for distributed systems in supply chain can be regarded as superior solutions for protecting the enterprise IT infrastructures that are physically dispersed in several locations worldwide. The advantages big data and cloud computing have include: cost-effectiveness, pay-per-use, rapid readiness of resources, acquiring extra bandwidth, hardware and software resource-leasing. Through proportional and economic advantages, organizations have the option for not acquiring extra IT computer system hardware and applications software. Cloud services providers or managed service providers are responsible for ensuring that scalable technology is developed that can fulfill information technology and supply chain organizations' requirements (Gartner, 2009; Gartner, 2012).

MAIN FOCUS OF THE CHAPTER

For many years, big data and cloud computing contributed for the convergence of supply chain systems. Big data and cloud computing are defined as areas the industry should research on due prevalent issues affecting a range of services associated with these technological solutions. Vendors should also give precedence to the following big data elements: data acquisition, management and analytical mechanisms (Cooper & Mell, 2012). In spite of several investigations and findings related to big data analytics, more research attention is required. Big data is still a growing area where further research must be done to attract more information technology stakeholders and supply chain organizations (Cooper & Mell, 2012). Over the course of years, several dynamic supply chain systems have converged with cloud computing, big data analytics, computational models, and cyber-physical systems (Gartner, 2009; Gartner, 2012). To deliver these augmented supply chain management solutions, vendors should adopt agile IT based solutions. Augmented challenges in the globalized financial markets encouraged many corporations, to leverage on their supply chain capabilities required to augment the way IT infrastructure and processes are being deployed (Gartner, 2012; Gartner, 2009; Buyya, et al., 2015). The introduction of big data and cloud computing is an evolving phenomenon that data scientists, IT engineers, decision makers, lawmakers, and supply chain organizations should improve in years to come. Vendors should agree on how to investigate these technologies, to foster responsive results that can satisfy customer's requirements (Cooper & Mell, 2012). Vendors view data evolution and opportunities as a model consisting of five dimensions (Gartner, 2012): volume, velocity, variety, verification, and value (Gartner, 2012; Chow et al., 2009). Whereas volume is classified by the mass of data being processed and provisioned; velocity is characterized by speed of data transported from, and to other storage systems. Variety describes an array of data categories and sources (Agrawal, Das, & Abbadji, 2011). As a result of these technology trends, organizations now are able to optimize the delivery time that suppliers used to spend in the past. These trends are designed to improve the method through which, customers and businesses in future deliver supply chain services (Chow et al., 2009). To fulfill decision makers and their organizations' business needs, vendors continue to develop technical solutions and processes to better support the global IT infrastructure (Buyya, Ranjan, Rodrigo, & Calheiros, 2010; Agrawal, Das, & Abbadji, 2011).

EVOLUTION AND GROWTH

Decision makers and their organizations rely on supply chain systems as a vehicle for delivering personal or corporate merchandise from and/or to physically dispersed locations worldwide (Leighon, 2009). Vendors, practitioners, public and private sector customers describe supply chain as continuance of logistic management focusing on the production and distribution of commodity. The following are characteristics of supply chain management (Gartner, 2012; Chow et al, 2009):

- Flow of goods,
- Services,
- Storage of raw materials,
- Work-in-process inventory,
- Finished goods transported from one location to another for the user's consumption.

Supply chain management consists of: people, organizations, activities, information, resources, etc. In supply chain, convergence is defined as a process of shipping products and/or services from the supplier to customer's destination. Supply chain management offers the public and private sector customers the premier level of e-commence: Business-to-Business, Business-to-Customer and Business-to-Employee (CPNI Security Briefing, 2010). Supply chain is a vital logistical platform that decision makers and organizations rely upon to conduct day-to-day transactions and shipment of products or services from to dispersed geographical areas (Chow et al., 2009; Ross, 2010).

THE INTERSECTION OF BIG DATA, CLOUD COMPUTING AND SUPPLY CHAIN MANAGEMENT

Studies conclude that big data and cloud computing are ubiquitous IT technologies that have spawn the public and private sectors interest. The recent adoption of dynamic and virtualized IT infrastructures is intended to offer customers the capabilities needed to support their day-to-day operational resources

(Armbrust et al., 2009). Many data experts identify big data as a technology that spins around volume. Whereas some view such technology as a platform offering huge value to enterprises and consumers (Armbrust et al., 2009).

Review of Use Cases

Vendors and customers have different technical perception with respect to how cloud computing services interact with supply chain solutions (Fawcett et al., 2011). Whereas IT and big data experts describe cloud computing an enabler delivering practical solutions, to organizations whose use is to correlate with supply chain systems (Fawcett et al., 2011). These theories are proved concepts that should be presented to supply chain domain. IT and big data experts, also recommend that to adequately attain a manageable or profitable advantage or standards, vendors should develop responsive IT solutions that can support broad-based client requirements (Fawcett et al., 2011). The introduction of IT solutions e.g., the electronic data exchange is a feasible process designed to withstand performance of platforms that are deployed on the supply chain infrastructure. In theory, this concept, should be in tandem with customer-based business and technical strategies being adopted to support the sharing of information process within the supply chain domain (Monczka, Petersen, Handfield, & Ragatz, 1998; Lee et al., 1997a, 1997b).

Reference Architecture

Lacking expertise and experience while adopting cloud solutions may conceivably degrade consumer and organization's productivity as well as increase capital and operational expenditures. IT and big data experts should be adequately skilled to challenge any technical issues affecting the overall system performance of the IT infrastructure (Armbrust et al., 2009).

CHALLENGES FOR THE FUTURE

Big data and cloud solutions are developed to support several components in the supply chain e.g., network collaboration, back-office support, transport and logistics management (Chow et al., 2009). The need for integrated, trusted, and agile IT solutions should determine the concomitance of cloud solutions and supply chain services (Gartner, 2009; Gartner, 2012). As many organizations i.e., Pfizer, eBay, Google among others are re-engineering their supply chain models, to ensure for the agile delivery of products to selected clientele, Pfizer is revolutionizing its legacy holistic IT infrastructure to converge with the company's modernized business and operational cloud solutions (Armbrust et al., 2009; Ross, 2010). In spite of these crucial upgrades, Pfizer has also encountered significant challenges while converging its traditional-based IT resources, to advance business performance and resource effectiveness (CPNI Security Briefing, 2010; Armbrust et al., 2009).

Scalability and Elasticity

Lacking scalability and elasticity in cloud solutions can alter the performance of IT infrastructures deployed on the digital supply chain domain. IT experts are confident that in the near term, vendors will develop prime solutions to properly address these technical constraints, and ensure that there is no latency between the infrastructure provisioning and information sharing. The integration of cloud solutions and big data analytics is a viable tool to moderate organizations' concerns on future IT adoption within the supply chain environment (Fawcett et al., 2011).

Use Case

One descriptive illustration focusing on the integration of cloud-based solutions and data analytics was conducted by the U.S. National Cancer Institute (Mudinuri et al., 2013). In this significant study, multi-format data from many cloud-based sources were incorporated into a prototype data analytic infrastructure. The purpose of these efforts was to draw a parallel of genetic data with cancer incidences (Uma et al., 2013; Armbrust et al., 2009). Key lessons learned in this study include (Uma et al., 2013; Mudinuri et al., 2013):

- Data consumption from multiple cloud-based sources into a centralized cloud-based repository may take a very long time
- Multi-format data sources requiring domain expertise for construal and programming skills. This expertise is required to extract and generate useful metadata needed for driving queries.
- Significant computing resources (e.g., compute and input/output) are necessary to scale suitable and produce realistic or agile querying results
- Hadoop and other open source tools were available for data analysis and query visualization

CLOUD COMPUTING

The National Institute for Standards and Technology (NIST) describes cloud computing a "model for enabling convenient, on-demand network access to a shared pool of configurable computing resources (e.g., networks, servers, storage, applications, and services) that can be rapidly provisioned and released with minimal management effort or service interaction" (Badger, Grance, Patt-Corner, & Voas, 2011; Grance & Mell, 2011; Chow et al., 2009; Gartner, 2012). Cloud computing consists of three service and deployment models that are defined by NIST (CSA Security Guidance, 2009). The below diagram in (Figure 1) illustrates the three-cloud service model.

This cloud service model includes (Chow et al., 2009; Gartner, 2009; Gartner, 2012):

- **Software-as-a-Service:** The capacity needed for supporting organizations' cloud IT infrastructure. SaaS offers a unique instance of services that can be provisioned on the cloud and adjacent services being run by end-users

Figure 1. Diagram for cloud service models
Source: Gorelik, 2013.

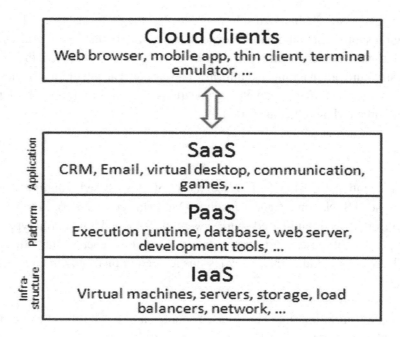

- **Platform-as-a-Service:** A crucial layer of software within the developmental environment needed to capture or render services through which high levels are constructed. In PaaS organizations have the ability to select or customize preferred applications software using several programming languages and identified tools (i.e., Java, Python, .Net) among others. Apart from customer or organization's limitations to stage-manage or regulate the fundamental cloud-based infrastructure: network, servers, operating systems, storage infrastructure, these applications software and computer system hardware can dynamically be configured and deployed
- **Infrastructure-as-a-Service:** Offers storage or computational resource capabilities to selected organizations and their stakeholders. This model also ensures for the provisioning of data through the servers, storage systems, networking equipment, data centers. These IT resources are deployed to manage diverse workloads. Organizations have the ability to lease commodity computer system hardware and application software appliances that cloud service providers or managed service providers often have at their disposal for renting

Reference Architecture

Planning architecture cloud based solutions is a top-level evaluation and prototyping of IT resources. These resources are needed to support the level of complexity that service and deployment models present. The distribution of unified cloud services or managed service providers consists of applications, information and related IT infrastructures (CSA Security Guidance, 2009; Chow et al., 2009). While the orchestration, provisioning, implementation and decommissioning of cloud solutions often determines a unique and functional model for data sharing and resource feeding cloud architecture also consist of the following characteristics (CSA Security Guidance, 2009; Chow et al., 2009; Buyya, et al., 2015):

- **Infrastructure Abstraction:** A process where an abstraction of resources from the following components: computation, network, and storage infrastructure is diverged from the application and information resources. Often this is process translated as service delivery function

- **Resource Democratization:** The abstractive process of infrastructure based assets encompassing IT resource democratization, etc. In resource democratization the infrastructure, applications software and information being processed by means of resource capability are available for machines to physically or virtually access despite their geographic locations worldwide

- **Service-Oriented Architecture:** Given its infrastructure abstraction applications and information frequently determines how inaccurately or accurately IT resources are democratized. The process of resource utilization and data accessibility in common standards, hence, allows for service-oriented architecture posture. In SOA, the delivery of service is prioritized by the management of IT infrastructure

- **Elasticity:** The process of coupling on-demand and cloud provisioning models with integrated automation, virtualization, ever-present, dependable and agile connectivity of network resources. This concept also encompasses resource provisioning for determining desired network services by utilizing assigned service models to sustain required system capacity

- **Dynamism:** The orchestration and synchronization of resources based on a multi-tier resource realization

- **Consumption and Allocation of Utility Model(s):** The process of abstracting, democratizing, service orienting and resource elasticity often provides improved data automation, orchestration, and resource provisioning. The atomic level, resource consumption may be used to render organizations unique price tag and usability model. These models are designed to orchestrate and predict expenditures that business and IT organizations may incur at the end of separable or joint payment circle

- **Additional Defining Characteristic of Cloud Computing:** Elasticity is relevant to big data analytics issues. Elasticity is the ability to expand the resources, specifically compute and Input/Out, needed to analyze large datasets. Such analysis encompasses exploiting large-scale parallelism of CPU and storage resources. The cloud model is an ideal enabling platform for big data research. The ability for moving and creating on-demand, virtualized compute environments is also a key enabler of flexible, ad-hoc, data analytics

Cloud Computing

Evidenced strategies for the adoption and deployment of converged IT resources into digital supply-based networks is critical. How organizations take advantage of these presented IT resources maybe a factor on how more customers, IT, and supply chain organizations frequently adapt to ubiquitous resource accessibilities (Gartner, 2012). Not all supply chain processes converge, when deployed to the cloud. This is due to their specifications and level of complexities. (Chow et al., 2009). Despite this degree of abstruseness that decision makers and patrons often present towards the migration of IT assets to the cloud, legacy, in-house technical computer system hardware, and application software appliances are still effective (CPNI Security Briefing, 2010; Gartner, 2009; Gartner, 2012). To avoid unforeseen complexity between physical and virtual IT infrastructures, vendors have developed agile solutions and hybrid technology that can readily be integrated with traditional systems. These IT technology processes are designed for regulating supply chain management's organizations comparative and competitive advantages. Such advantages also offer business the ability to reduce their capital and operational expenditures. To adopt hybrid cloud solutions, customers should have the right expertise, familiarity and insights of the cloud and traditional IT environment (Chow et al., 2009; Gartner, 2009; Ross, 2012).

THE IMPACT OF BIG DATA ANALYTICS AND CLOUD COMPUTING ON SUPPLY CHAIN MANAGEMENT

Since mid-20th century, decision makers and organizations benefited from computational analytics and the earlier discovery of computer-based solutions. Vendors define computational analytics a method which determines how customers and executives make informed decisions that bring enormous benefits to their organizations. Continued progresses in big data analytics have redefined the supply chain management and business landscapes (Ketchen & Hult, 2007; Buyya, et al., 2015). In spite of these advances, continuous implementation and convergence of physical and virtual computing systems into the cloud, poses significant challenges to vendors and their stakeholders (Gartner, 2012; Chow et al, 2009). In supply chain management, big data analytics is defined a computational model that is used to analyze, track, order, retain and process data. Through computational analytics, customers and supply chain organizations can benefit in the global market space (Gartner, 2012; Chow et al, 2009). Big data analytics comprise the following characteristics (Gartner, 2012; Amazon, 2012; Dastjerdi, & Versteeg, 2015):

- **Volume:** The significant volume(s) of datasets required for determent methods
- **Velocity:** The increasing speed that is required to creating, processing, provisioning, storing data in real-time. This includes the necessary amount of speed necessary for data to be analyzed by relational databases. In velocity, the data is generated and processed to fulfill the customer or user's requirements
- **Variety:** The variation of time and context required to influence data models, and workloads being uploaded, manipulated (i.e., visual data for instance photos). Entities who analyze this data processing must comply with ostensible hypotheses on attestable results to be integrated in each dataset
- **Veracity:** The means of determining accuracy or validity of data required to assist in the decision-making process. This process often takes place in autonomous machine learning algorithm. The process also includes, but is not limited to data extracted from plane text, images, audio, video, and the process of completing each activity using data fusion, etc. The quality of data being captured and manipulated may vary, which could affect the analytical processing of data
- **Value:** The process of determining values in crucial data analyses
- **Variability:** Data that its connotation is repetitively being altered, due to language processing. There are many irregularities each data set sustains, which may lead to process degradation
- **Visualization:** The process of visualizing data being processed by different computational systems. This process also is determined by a number of variables and parameters

SUPPLY CHAIN MANAGEMENT

Globalization is a paradigm that results from organizations and customers' needs, to ensure that supply and demand is a key factor aiming at global markets' gain such as comparative and competitive advantages (Gartner, 2012). Supply chain is a developing area with significant IT application resources. These integrated resources and/or solutions are the key reasons industry is committed to develop agile processes and applications needed to foster organization's day-to-day operations and increase productivity (Gartner, 2009; Gartner, 2012; Amazon, 2012). In the new era of information and communications technology such research trends emerge with many technical topics; most importantly those encompassing the supply chain management, customer relationship management to name a few. Supply chain is a keystone for generating most favorable business results (Gartner, 2012; Chow et al., 2009). Internal, external, business and customer marketing models comprise the core value of supply chain management. These models focus on offering suppliers and buyers with a business competitive and comparative advantage required to ascertain frontier markets (Gartner, 2012; Chow et al., 2009; Foster, Kesselman, & Tuecke, 2008). To fulfill these customer's requirements, vendors are developing improved solutions to adequately address their customers' needs. Further in, the strategic life-cycle model has played a major role in supply chain management. The following are characteristics of matured supply chain model:

- Agility,
- Leadership,
- Application,
- Technology,
- Reliability,
- Responsiveness,
- Cost,
- Business,
- Asset Management,
- Information/Data.

This model converges with the following core architectural concepts: business architecture, information architecture, application architecture and others. Such capabilities are designed to complement the key process integration and organizational factors (roles and functions, etc.). In contrast, data and business information models are in concert with the corporate market culture and organization drives. The process of data and protocol rules required to define business processes is vital to an organization's growth. The need for scalable capabilities: mobile, hardware, software, and network platforms to deliver optimum solutions is critical to organizations and customers' requirements (Gartner, 2012; Chow et al., 2009). In supply chain, suppliers and customers should often anticipate some business and market setbacks. These business and market constraints may conceivably impact the productivity and customer's satisfaction. The following are benefits and limitations that either party should expect in supply chain:

- Benefits:
  - Great efficiency,
  - Improved quality,

- ◦ Zero-touch integration,
- ◦ Insight and oversight.
- • Limitations:
  - ◦ Customer dissatisfaction,
  - ◦ Operational inefficiency,
  - ◦ Inability to flex.

BIG DATA

Big data is formally described as data analytics. Big data is classified as a technology with the ability to extract values from datasets (Gartner, 2009; Gartner, 2012). Data scientists, specialists, engineers and decision makers are in accord that the accuracy procedure in big data focuses on determining the level of confidence on how information is managed. How data is managed also allows decision makers, data specialists and scientists, to predict or determine a considerable size of datasets. These predictions and analytics allow decision makers to determine their operational effectiveness, cost reduction and conduct risk mitigation (Gartner, 2012; Chow et al, 2009). Big data is classified as: volume, velocity, variety, verification and value described by a variety of data assets. These data assets are described as different data forms required to enhancing or improving decision-making process amidst IT managers (Gartner, 2012; Chow et al, 2009). These assets take account of the insight discovery and optimization methods. Datasets are supported by traditional information processing applications. The following are challenges that comprise big data analytics: analysis, capture, data curation, sharing, storage, transfer, visualization, querying, updating and data privacy (Gartner, 2012; Chow et al, 2009). This diagram explains the holistic big data framework/stack (Figure 2).

Figure 2. The emerging big data stack
Source: Trifu &Ivan, 2014.

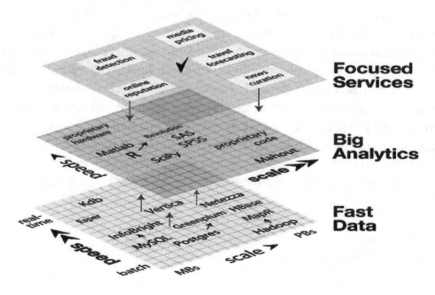

Big data platform consists of two eccentric classifications. These classifications are developed to offer IT managers, scientists, specialists, decision makers and researchers adequate data required to support their informed scientific decisions. This layered structure illustrates (Gartner, 2012; Chow et al, 2009; Buyya, et al., 2015; Amazon, 2012):

- **Application Layer:**
  - Query,
  - Clustering,
  - Classification,
  - Recommendation.
- **Computer Layer:**
  - Integration,
  - Management:
    - Filesystem,
    - SQL,
    - NoSQL.
  - Programming model:
    - Dremel,
    - MapReduce,
    - Pregel,
    - Dryad.
- **Infrastructure Layer:**
  - Computation,
  - Network,
  - Storage.

Big data analytics comprises a set of challenges that often impact the entire system performance. Adopting and deploying solutions in big data can be a complex task, which could impacts the inclusive infrastructure planning and executing phases (Fawcett, Wallin, Alfred et al., 2011). In big data, scalability defines how commodity hardware and software appliances converge. This association includes how these elements can support organizations and customers' needs. IT and big data experts recommend that the following steps be well-thought-out, during the adoption or deployment of big data solutions (Chang, et al., 2006; Buyya, et al., 2015):

- Data Representation,
- Redundancy Reduction/Data Compression,
- Data Life-cycle Management,
- Energy Management,
- Data Privacy and Security,
- Scalability,
- Collaboration.

Scientists and engineers rely on a wide range of big data infrastructures to access, provision, configure, and share information. Due to its volume, variety, and velocity, big data poses many challenges to IT experts and supply chain organizations. These challenges include (Fawcett, Wallin, Alfred, Fawcett, & Magnan, 2011; Gartner, 2009):

- Approximate Analytics,
- Connecting Social Media,
- Deep Analytics.

In data sources data generation is exemplified by its rate, which evolves a range of technology discoveries. There are three categories comprising big data analytics. Such categories are as follows (Fawcett, Wallin, Alfred, Fawcett, & Magnan, 2011; Gartner, 2012):

- **Business Data:**
  - Information Technology,
  - Digital Data.
- **Networking Data:**
  - Internet:
    - Business-to-Business Transaction,
    - Business-to-Commerce Transaction,
    - Business-to-Consumer Transaction.
  - Mobile Network,
  - Internet of Things.
- **Scientific Data:**
  - Computational Biology,
  - Astronomy,
  - High-Energy Physics.

Big Data

The evolution of digital technologies (Gartner, 2012; Chow et al, 2009): Smartphones, computers, storage infrastructure, applications, tables, scanners, shipment tracking devices, radio-frequency identification, wireless sensor networks, remote sensing and software logs have improved the way decision makers and organizations conduct daily or periodical transactions (Chow et al., 2009; Leighon, 2009). Increased IT requirements in the global supply chain network resources i.e., servers, storage infrastructure, application management, have raised/presented many challenges to decision makers and organizations (Stock, Greis, & Kasarda, 2000). To augment productivity in supply chain management, decision makers should implement organizational strategies to support their day-to-day operations (Ketchen & Hult, 2007). Due to storage and bandwidth limitations required to enhance competitive advantages, decision makers are convinced that real-time data sharing will increase productivity and customer service (Ketchen, & Hult, 2007). Research has revealed that unified supply chain practice and improved data sharing are essential components for customer relationship management (Zhou & Benton, 2007; Stock, Greis, & Kasarda, 2000). Thomas et al. (2011) points out that vendors should develop better solutions to fulfill customers' business and IT requirements (Ketchen & Hult, 2007; Stock, Greis, & Kasarda, 2000).

Security and privacy issues are major concerns for vendors, organizations' decision makers. Research has confirmed that in big data, the volume, variety and velocity pose major concerns on large-scale cloud infrastructure. When analytics detect an irregularity immediately generate outliers (Armbrust et al., 2009). These outliers could affect the cloud infrastructure, if not accurately isolated and sanitized (Armbrust et al., 2009; Lakshman & Prashant, 2010). IT managers are alarmed that data the outflow could be a fundamental challenge for the information sharing. Amassed challenges affecting the digital security realm, absence of policies, and procedures, has contributed to emerging threats that businesses are facing in the enterprise (Lakshman & Prashant, 2010). Ninety percent (97%) of organizations and decision makers have a better appreciation of the benefits big data analytics bring to their organizations. Whereas 17% of these decision makers already adopted and converged big data analytics as part of their supply chain solutions (Leavitt, 2009; Gartner, 2012; Chow et al, 2009). Advanced research in information technology resulted in the adoption of cloud computing. Cloud technology a paradigm encompassing servers, storage, application, network infrastructure and related peripherals. The services and deployment models that characterize cloud technology are i.e., software as a service, infrastructure as a service, platform as a service; public cloud, private cloud, and community cloud (Foster, Kesselman, & Tuecke, 2008; Rochwerger et al., 2010; Buyya, et al., 2015). Aside from these concerns many organizations continue to benefit from cloud computing services or capabilities (Rochwerger et al., 2009; Thomas, Defee, Randall, & Williams, 2011). Vendors are developing a number of resource-based solutions and social capital theory, as business frameworks. These resources are focal point for the integration of information technology and supply chain solutions, and yet provide the user with the quality of customer service needed (Rosenthal, Mork, Stanford, Koester, & Reynolds, 2010; Thomas, Defee, Randall, & Williams, 2011). IT and big data experts, regard cloud technology as an integral component in adopting, planning, and implementing new solutions for supply chain management. Resource-based solutions and social capital theories are conceptual models developed to provide resource scalability required to support the supply chain (Clemons et al., 1993; Lee & Whang, 2000; Sahin & Robison, 2002; Rosenthal, Mork, Stanford, Koester, & Reynolds, 2010; Leidner & Jarvenpaa, 1995; Petersen & Ragatz, 2005; Xu & Beamon, 2006). The collaboration between cloud computing and resource-based solutions focuses on leveraging information sharing in today's digital supply chain environment (Bharadwaj, 2000; Mata, Fuerst, & Barney, 1995).

TRADITIONAL VS. CLOUD-BASED SUPPLY CHAIN

In recent years, supply chain gained new trends in wide-ranging marketplace, as a result of value-added source of comparative and competitive advantages offered to various customers. Supply chain is defined as a platform that allows organizations to compete in the global market space (Gartner, 2012; Chow et al, 2009). There are two types of supply chain: traditional and cloud-based organic solutions. These cloud-based solutions, offer decision makers and organizations the ability to select perfect services, while preparing to acquire, transport and deliver their corporate goods to various locations throughout the world. Traditional in-house and cloud-based supply chain services are indispensable for the process of determining how risk and cost factor should be mitigated (CPNI Security Briefing, 2010; Ross, 2010; Gartner, 2012; Gartner, 2009). As a result of these integrated activities, resilient or applicable results on how customers and information technologists conduct their business in the supply chain management domain encompasses the following areas (Gartner, 2012; Chow et al., 2009):

- Purchasing & Shipping,
- Manufacturing Operations,
- Transactions & Order Processing,
- Customer Service & Supplier's Commitment,

- Information Flowing between Enterprise Borders,
- Trading & Supply Management,
- Inventorying & Procuring,
- Freight & Transportation,
- Warehousing & Delivering,
- Physical Distribution to Dispersed Geographic Locations,
- Industry Initiatives & Support services, etc.

Supply chain is a source for continuing business processes and technology trends developed for supporting client-based requirements. Aside from apparent economic inequity affecting many customers, financial and business, information technology experts, describe globalization a transient phenomenon that determines an organization's economic growth (Gartner, 2012; Chow et al, 2009). Such growth, is often determined by the economy of scale, and how customers should manage or market their resources (Gartner, 2012). Supply chain is also a model that organizations rely upon to import and/or export merchandiseand be able to track, manage, monitor, procure or deliver the best service to satisfy the customer's expectations (Gartner, 2012; Chow et al, 2009).

Supply Chain Convergence

Early studies validate that vendors, cloud service providers/managed service providers rely on IT and supply chain organizations' hardware and software solutions. These solutions are developed to assist decision makers and organizations, when adopting or deploying their supply chain services. As part of the supply chain management, decision makers often depend on end-to-end business operational strategies and solutions to support such a convergence (Gartner, 2012; Chow et al., 2009). This figure (Figure 3) describes cloud supply chain framework.

Figure 3. Cloud supply chain framework
Source: (Linder et al., 2010).

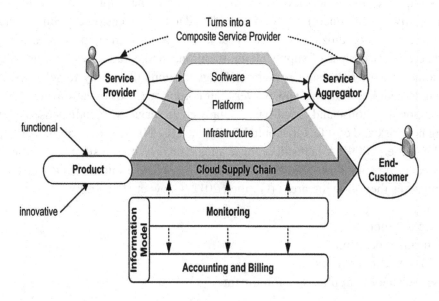

If appropriately converged supply chain portfolio and cloud solutions could adequately provide shippers and/or suppliers with an underlying ability to collaborate with their customers in real-time. This concept aims to decrease the time and resources shipping companies often allocate each day, to meet customer's requirements (Chow et al., 2009). Supply chain management processes comprise (Gartner, 2009; Gartner, 2012):

- Digital Technologies,
- Digital Supply Network,
- Business Modeling,
- Mobility,
- Information Supply Chain,
- Cloud Computing,
- Talent Supply Chain,
- Business Management,
- Social Media,
- Financial Supply Chain,
- Customer Relationship Management,
- Physical Supply Chain,
- Big Data Analytics.

Lacking IT infrastructure to support the convergence of resources may result in momentous degradation of deployed computer system hardware and applications software on the enterprise. Despite the adoption of integrated processes into supply chain, many business and technical challenges could be identified as major concerns to decision makers and organizations (Gartner, 2012). The need for state-of-the-art telecommunications infrastructure i.e., control towers and satellite systems required to connect service providers and their clients throughout the globe is paramount (CPNI Security Briefing, 2010). The maturity of supply chain model consists of four classifications: decentralization, unification, network, and orchestration. For several years, many organizations and consumers have benefited from the adoption of advanced supply chain models aimed at supporting a variety of transformational and sustainable initiatives. These models are designed to provide suppliers with a maturity model targeted at espousing customer values and business competitiveness. Supply chain management consists of two business levels: evolutionary and revolutionary supply chain capabilities. These levels of services are required to balance the competitive and comparative customer demands and organization's business values (Gartner, 2012; Chow et al., 2009). Aside from the level of sophisticated systems organization have today, vendors believe that integration of supply chain resources does not fully meet customer's requirements (Gartner, 2012; Chow et al., 2009) These standards describe diverse market segments needed to generate tenable business value (Gartner, 2012; Chow et al., 2009). These levels or elements consist of (Gartner, 2012; Chow et al., 2009):

- **Decentralization:** Defined as single process and respective locations required to optimize and provide efficiency with limited system integration. These processes emphasize each unit of supply chain management that is designed to operate autonomously.

- **Unification:** It is a process offering internal and external departments the ability to share information that is provided from a centralized supply chain unique system. This system is also designed to supply data to physically dispersed systems across the supply chain domain.
- **Network:** The integration of multiple networks designed to provide a shared repository to suppliers and customers. This repository can be described as a single point entry. All systems in the supply chain require a unique protocol to communicate.
- **Orchestration:** An end-to-end supply system is developed to support the orchestration process. In orchestration process, systems are capable to deliver, provision, share, and distribute data in real-time.

In supply chain environment, digital technology aims to improve business theories and related specifications (Gartner, 2012; Chow et al, 2009). Vendors should design advanced technology sensor devices enabling suppliers, to provide their consumers with adequate shipment services (Gartner, 2012; Chow et al, 2009). This model further provides suppliers and customers with several options to choose from to ensure goods are shipped or delivered expediently (Gartner, 2012; Chow et al, 2009).

The following are benefits that control towers could offer to supply chain and/or digitizing customer-based community of value (Gartner, 2012; Chow et al, 2009):

- **Integrated Transaction Systems:**
  - Real-time Visibility,
  - Alarms Generated,
  - Dashboards.
- **Analytics:**
  - Root Cause Analysis,
  - Simulations, what if scenarios,
  - Risk Analysis and Response Management.
- **Execution:**
  - Management Insights,
  - Executive Decisions,
  - Improved Knowledge Performance Indicators.

The convergence of cloud services or managed service providers with digital supply networks required to boost current supply chain business posture. These benefits consist of (Gartner, 2012; Chow et al, 2009):

- Intelligent systems,
- Scalable hardware and software,
- Connectivity between commodity and appliances,
- Agility,
- Cost-effectiveness,
- Speed,
- SaaS based approaches,
- Business-to-Business,
- Enterprise resource planning,

- Single source of truth,
- Business value,
- Time for action.

Logistics Management

Procurement and acquisition are integral themes that can often be integrated to the supply chain. These areas provide customers, information technology, and supply chain organizations the ability to complement their commodity hardware and software applications, by using cloud services and big data architecture for scalability (Gartner, 2012; Chow et al., 2009). Cloud and big data solutions are designed to improve the way inventories are managed or transported in the supply chain domain. This includes air, sea, and ground transportation of goods and chattels among others (Gartner, 2012; Chow et al., 2009).

INTERNET OF THINGS

For many decades, IT and supply chain customers have benefited from available opportunities to support organizations' missions and purposes. Successful IT and supply chain organizations often need integrated, automated, analytical and agile resources, to sustain their day-to-day operations. Public or private sector customers also depend on these solutions, to support their business and operational requirements (Buyya, et al. 2015; Ross, 2010). Internet of Things is defined as the process of incorporating networks (i.e., objects, things, sensors and devices). The connectivity over the Internet is established through a physical and virtual information and communication infrastructure. These IT infrastructures often are designed to provide value-added services over the Internet (Buyya, et al., 2015).

Figure 4 describes the technology mind mapping for IoT smart objects.

Figure 4. Technology mind mapping for IoT-based smart objects
Source:(Want, Schilit & Jenson, 2015).

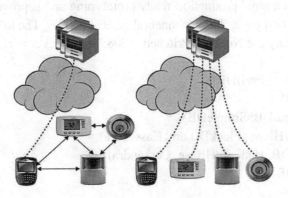

Reference Architectures

The development of programing languages i.e., java allows for the delivery of file distribution. In big data, sharing files can be labeled as a method for storing and querying data across multiple servers. This process also allows storage systems to amass and dispense structure, sim-structured, and unstructured datasets across many servers (Buyya, et al., 2015).

Use Case

Large retail companies specifically, Amazon and Walmart, along with other shipping logistics organizations i.e., United Parcel Service are taking advantage of the intersection of cloud computing services and data analytics to grow their business portfolios (Rozados & Tjahjono, 2014). These services and analytics are developed to monitor and analyze billions of product sales, consignments, and resupply centers worldwide. Such activity is intended to produce multiple petabytes of data, to be examined and allowing for appropriate response time. These responses focus on changing business conditions and customer expectations: descriptive, predictive, and prescriptive analytics. In essence, this analysis is believed to support all aspects of supply chain management: marketing, procurement, warehouse operations, and transportation (Rozados & Tjahjono, 2014).

NoSQL

A class of database management systems identified as not only SQL. NoSQL database systems are platforms that do not require classical querying language to perform their respective activities (Pritchett, 2008). NoSQL functions without a need for fixed schema formally described as structure. These systems are capable to handle very large data sets. In NoSQL database, the process of partitioning, replicating or sharing files is done through a load-balancing achieved concept. This concept, provides users with the capabilities for partitioning, replicating or sharing files in the enterprise (Pritchett, 2008; Gartner, 2012). Scaling is highly preferred in NoSQL database systems horizontally scaling is possible (Pritchett, 2008). The platform also supports a rapid production-ready prototyping and is proved to handling continuous workloads of traffic spikes (Pritchett, 2008; (Stonebraker, et al., 2007). The following are names of some organizations that extensively use NoSQL (Pritchett, 2008; Stonebraker et al., 2007):

- Google (i.e., BigTable, LevelIDB),
- LinkedIn (Voldemort),
- Amazon (e.g., DynamoDB, SimpleDB),
- Twitter (i.e., Hadoop/Hbase, FlockDB and Cassandra),
- Netflix (e.g., SimpleDB, Hadoop/HBase, Cassandra),
- CERN (e.g., CouchDB).

In NoSQL the process of scalability is achieved by the utilization of "ACID also known as Atomic, Consistent, Isolated and Durable" compatibility (Chang et al., 2006). This process, allows for constant scalability and optimized performance of NoSQL (Pritchett, 2008). NoSQL performs the "BASE generally known as Basically Available, Soft state, Eventual Consistency".

At discrepancy with ACID systems, which are designed to implement consistency on operation commit, NoSQL is designed to warrant reliability in future. ACID is a method that interacts with consistency rating at the end of each operation (Stonebraker, et al, 2007). BASE is defined by its optimistic and acceptance approach also noted as a database consistency tailored to either 'in a state or flux'. When database nodes are added to the IT infrastructure, the process of scaling is optimum, despite the need for continuous synchronization that increases. Similar to other database systems, NoSQL consists of the following drawbacks (Pritchett, 2008; Stonebraker et al., 2007):

- Lacking maturity,
- Lacking 365 x 24 x 7 customer support for enterprise commercial users,
- Lacking supportability of data analyses,
- Maintainability efforts and related skills are required, though expert database engineers and administrators are very difficult to find.

Hadoop

Hadoop is an open source big data framework. This framework also performs as a baseline for both distributed storage and processing of substantial data sets stored in many computer clusters. In Hadoop all modules are designed to satisfy a necessary hypothesis (Chang, et al., 2006). In principle, hardware degradation often is normal, though the framework is responsible for identifying and correcting any system errors, etc. Hadoop framework comprises (Fawcett, Wallin, Alfred et al., 2011; Gartner, 2012):

- Hadoop Common,
- Hadoop Distributed File System,
- Hadoop Yarn,
- Hadoop MapReduce.

The term Hadoop denotes the ecosystem unit, base segments and collection of associated software packages. These software packages are installed on the following Hadoop versions (Fawcett, Wallin, Alfred et al., 2011):

- Apache Pig,
- Apache Hive,
- Apache HBase,
- Apache Phoenix,
- Apache Spark,
- Apache Zookeeper,
- Cloudera Impala,
- Apache Flume,
- Apache Sqoop,
- Apache Oozie,
- Apache Storm.

Spark

An open source system acting as an interface for the entire cluster computing framework. This framework comprises analogous data structuring and fault-tolerance. The benefits of Spark solutions that are presented by its application program interface can be found on centralized data structure. Such structure is identified as robust distributed dataset. The distribution process can be carried out via a machine-based clustering process that is preserved by a fault-tolerant method. Vendors have developed Spark, as a replacement software that offers machine clustering capabilities to diverse systems allowing for scalable performance. Spark software is also designed to interface with the following applications (Fawcett et al., 2011):

- Cluster Manager,
- Distributed Storage System,
- Hadoop Yarn,
- Apache Mesos,
- Hadoop Distributed File System,
- MapR File System aka MapR-FS,
- Cassandra,
- OpenStack Swift,
- Amazon S3,
- Kudu.

Data Warehousing

Information systems' assets are vital components for the information and communications technology domain. Data warehouse is a phenomenon that emerged from digital datasets. Data warehouse also is defined as a technology that affords decision makers the opportunity needed for them to make informed decision in support of organizations (Gartner, 2012; Chow et al., 2009). Vendors perceive the need to develop data warehousing as business platform necessary to fulfill customer's requirements. Whereas data warehousing is regarded as a warehouse whose data is stored for future access. Software that run(s) on data warehousing is/are: SQL, database catalogs, etc. In data warehousing information is stored via an aggregated SQL query. While privileged data warehousing is designed to perform online analytical processing or online transaction processing. When data is accessed from several sources is then rearranged in data formats (Gartner, 2012; Chow et al., 2009). Data formatting is the process of converting information into more readable format, then making this data available for customer's usage. This process focuses on assisting decision makers and managers in gathering the right information to be used in day-to-day planning and operational sustainability. The process of defining, maximizing, and measuring information in data warehouse is crucial to organization's business efficiency. The following are qualities of data warehousing (Gartner, 2012; Chow et al., 2009):

- Accuracy,
- Freshness,
- Completeness,

- Consistency,
- Availability,
- Traceability,
- Clearness.

For these qualities to be introduced as part of data warehousing set of matrices are essential to support the IT and database operations. Every major industry in the world that is, banking, airline, manufacturing, governments retail chain stores, uses data house to support its everyday business and operation posture. The following model describes the types of industries and organizations that have benefited from data warehouse solutions (Gartner, 2012; Chow et al., 2009):

- **Retail:**
  - Customer Loyalty,
  - Market Planning.
- **Financial:**
  - Risk Management,
  - Fraud Detection.
- **Airlines:**
  - Route Profitability,
  - Yield Management.
- **Manufacturing:**
  - Cost Reduction,
  - Logistics Management.
- **Utilities:**
  - Asset Management,
  - Resource Management.
- **Governments:**
  - Manpower Planning,
  - Cost Control.

Security Trends and Challenges

Security and privacy require best practices and tools, to detect, isolate, and repudiate any related issues affecting organization's information technology infrastructure (Fawcett et al., 2011). Lacking suitable security solutions to encode or unencrypt data stored in the cloud may be a key concern to cloud service providers and managed service providers, IT or supply chain organizations' decision makers as well as their stakeholders (Fawcett et al., 2011). As many IT and supply chain organizations adopt digital business or IT solutions to guarantee collaboration and information sharing, it is imperative that experts and vendors are committed to support their clientele's requirements. In the absent of a collaboration between these two industry entities i.e., IT experts and vendors, data provisioning, security deportment and consumer/organization's privacy maybe compromised (Fawcett et al., 2011; Lakshman & Prashant, 2010).

Aside from client community's desire to adapt these innovated cloud solutions, deployed in support of supply chain markets, yet customers need to be assured that cloud service providers or managed service providers are exceedingly devoted to secure their data (Armbrust et al., 2009).

SOLUTIONS AND RECOMMENDATIONS

This chapter discusses IT solutions and scenarios for big data and cloud computing that can be used as basis for future studies (Gartner, 2012; Chow et al., 2009). Vendors are committed to develop solutions for stakeholders and supply chain organizations, to adopt as part of cloud technology and big data analytics business efforts (Buyya, et al., 2015). Aside from synchronicity with Hadoop and other systems, big data is still far from its maturity. Database management systems have been in business and in the industry for over four decades. To scale up to its optimum performance based stage, Hadoop was developed to produce massive data collection for delivering responsive solutions and processing batch-processing standard (Cooper & Mell, 2012; Buyya, et al., 2015; Chow, Golle, Jakobsson et al., 2009). The provision of supportable business strategies for planning and implementing proven solutions to reassure decision makers and customers is vital to protect and support everyday storage infrastructure, data centers and business operations (Cooper & Mell, 2012; Buyya, et al., 2015). Analytical methods in big data platform and processing models remains an evolving topic that researchers should commit their financial and technical resources to develop use cases that can aptly address customer's demands (Leavitt, 2009). Advanced data analysis methods and real-time processing models, should be designed to satisfy customer's requirements (Buyya, et al., 2015).

FUTURE RESEARCH DIRECTIONS

Investigations and findings in big data analytics or cloud computing have concluded that IT and vendor communities should direct their attention in further research. This will generate better strategies, techniques, and procedures required to support organization and customers' needs (Lakshman & Prashant, 2010; Agrawal et al., 2011). In future, most of the big data analytics and cloud computing issues can be adequately examined to ascertain the scientific behavior of these IT systems, scalability, sustainability, performance, provisioning, and resource usability (Lakshman & Prashant, 2010). These adoption and implementation challenges often affect decision makers' reluctance to migrate their IT assets to virtual environment (Agrawal, et al., 2011; Blaze, et. Al, 2009). Decision makers are concerned with the security and privacy of their data and yet the continued involvement of cloud services providers/managed service providers.

Lacking effective and easy to use data management could yield major concerns for vendors and organizations (Agrawal et al., 2011; Buyya, Ramamohanarao, Leckie et al., 2015). Standards and reference architectures for this intersection are evolving, which means vendors should develop optimal solutions to converge with these industry benchmarks (Cloud Standards Customer Council, 2015; Buyya, et al., 2015). The ease of analysis can be enhanced through the use of machine learning tools that can be applied to data repositories (Buyya, Ramamohanarao, Leckie et al., 2015). Vendors and experts recommend that more leading-edge interfaces parallel to database management systems, be employed to support Hadoop stage-processing. The lack of Hadoop cluster to provide infrastructure with optimum performance is paramount. IT organizations acquire commodity hardware and deploy to their unique physical locations (Lakshman & Prashant, 2010; Buyya, Ramamohanarao, Leckie et al., 2015). A sizeable amount of energy consumption is required, to power single or multiple servers in the enterprise. Whereas the adoption of Hadoop is centered on energy efficiency (Dastjerdi, & Versteeg, 2015). Aside from energy consumption or efficacy, the lack of security and privacy could raise major security concerns to IT and supply chain organizations which often benefit from Hadoop services (Lakshman & Prashant, 2010). When storing data on several storage infrastructures, a methodical approach of scanning all datasets should prevent or minimize any unforeseen system anomalies. The new pervasive processing model, when developed could decrease unnecessary capital and operational expenditures that often organizations may incur (Cooper & Mell, 2012).

CONCLUSION

Big data and cloud computing transformed how customers, IT and supply chain organizations have been conducting business. In recent years, the global supply chain has been impacted by cloud computing and big data technologies (Gartner, 2012; Chow et al., 2009). These changes, have allowed consumer and IT organization operational benefits and capacity targeted at reducing capital/operational expenditures (Gartner, 2009; Gartner, 2012). IT customers and supply chain organizations are now able to decide whether to conduct transactions by electronic means or in-house. Either process has been a significant improvement in the supply chain domain (Chow et al., 2009; Ross, 2010). The adoption of new solutions: warehouse management, transportation management, global trade management, consumer-based procurement has allowed businesses to migrate their IT infrastructure and business resources to the cloud (Leavitt, 2009; Leighon, 2009; Gartner, 2012; Chow et al, 2009). While big data analytics guarantee that supercomputers are able to process, manage, store, and protect large volumes of data acquired from various assets e.g., physical storage systems such as warehouse-to-warehouse and/or online transactions, etc). With the evolution of the cloud-based and big data solutions, shippers now are able to effectively plan, forecast, track, monitor, procure and deliver their supplies or packages without further delays (Leavitt, 2009; Gartner, 2012; Chow et al., 2009).

REFERENCES

Agrawal, D., Das, S., & Abbadji, A. (2011). Big Data and Computing: Current State and Future Opportunities. Retrieved from https://www.researchgate.net/publication/221103048_Big_Data_and_Cloud_Computing_Current_State_and_Future_Opportunities

Alliance for Telecommunications Industry Solutions. (2017) Retrieved from http://www.atis.org

Amazon S3 Availability Event. (2008). Retrieved November 29, 2012 from http://status.aws.amazon.com/s3-20080720.html

AOL Apologizes for Release of User Search Data. (2006). Retrieved August 7, 2006 from news.cnet.com/2010-1030_3-6102793.html

Armbrust, M., Fox, A., Griffith, R., Joseph, A. D., Katz, R. H., Konwinsky, A., . . . Zaharia, M. (2009). Above the Clouds: A Berkley View of Cloud Computing. Technical Report No. UCB/EECS-2009-28, Department of Electrical Engineering and Computer Sciences, University of California at Berkley. February 10, 2009. Retrieved from: http://www.eecs.berkeley.edu/Pubs/TechRpts/2009/EECS-2009-28.pdf

Association for Retail Technology Standards (ARTS). (1997-2017). Retrieved from http://www.nrf-arts.org

Badger, L., Grance, T., Patt-Corner, R., & Voas, J. (2011, May). Draft Cloud Computing Synopsis and Recommendations. National Institute of Standards and Technology (NIST) Special Publication 800-146. US Department of Commerce. Retrieved November 20, 2012 from http://csrc.nist.gov/publications/drafts/800-146/Draft-NIST-SP800-146.pdf

Baharadwaj, A. (2000). A resource-based perspective on information technology capability and firm performance: An empirical investigation. *Management Information Systems Quarterly*, *24*(1), 169–196. doi:10.2307/3250983

Bertion, E., Paci, F., & Ferrini, R. (2009, March). Privacy-Preserving Digital Identity Management for Cloud Computing. IEEE Computer Society Data Engineering Bulletin.

Biggs & Vidalis. (2009, November). Cloud Computing: The Impact on Digital Forensic Investigations. *Proceedings of the 7th International Conference for Internet Technology and Secured Transactions (ICITST'09)*, London, UK.

Blaze, M., Kannan, S., Lee, I., Sokolsky, O., Smith, J. M., Keromytis, A. D., & Lee, W. (2009). Dynamic Trust Management. *IEEE Computer*, *42*(2), 44–52. doi:10.1109/MC.2009.51

Bruening, P. J., & Treacy, B. C. (2009). Cloud Computing: Privacy, Security Challenges. Bureau of National Affairs.

Buyya, R., Ramamohanarao, K., Leckie, C., Calhieros, N., Dastjerdi, A., & Versteeg, S. (2015). Big Data Analytics-Enhanced Cloud Computing: Challenges, Architectural Elements, and Future Directions. Retrieved from http://arxiv.org/abs/1510.06486

Center for the Protection of Natural Infrastructure (CPNI). (2010, March). Information Security Briefing on Cloud Computing. Retrieved November 29, 2012 from http://www.cpni.gov.uk/Documents/Publications/2010/2010007-ISB_cloud_computing.pdf

Chang, F., Dean, J., Ghemawat, S., Wilson, H. C., Wallach, D. A., Burrows, M., . . . Robert, G. E. (2006). Bigtable: a distributed storage system for structured data. Proceedings of the 7th USENIX Symposium on Operating Systems Design and Implementation (OSDI '06) (*Vol. 7*). USENIX Association, Berkeley, CA, USA.

Chen, Y., Paxson, V., & Katz, R. H. (2010). What's New About Cloud Computing Security? (Technical Report UCB/EECS-2010-5). EECS Department, University of California, Berkeley. Retrieved from http://www.eecs.berkeley.edu/Pubs/TechRpts/2010/EECS-2010-5.html

Chow, R., Golle, P., Jakobsson, M., Shi, E., Staddon, J., Masuoka, R., & Molina, J. (2009, November). Controlling Data in the Cloud: Outsourcing Computation without Outsourcing Control. *Proceedings of the ACM Workshop on Cloud Computing Security (CCSW'09)*, Chicago, Illinois, USA (pp. 85-90). New York, USA: ACM Press. doi:10.1145/1655008.1655020

Clemons, E., Reddi, S., & Row, M. (1993). The impact of information technology on the organization of economic activity: The move to the middle hypothesis. *Journal of Management Information Systems, 10*(2), 9–35. doi:10.1080/07421222.1993.11517998

Cooper, M., & Mell, P. (2012). Tackling Big Data. Retrieved from: http://csrc.nist.gov/groups/SMA/forum/documents/june2012presentations/f%csm_june2012_cooper_mell.pdf

Distributed Management Task Force. (2017). Retrieved from http://www.dmtf.org

Ft.com. (n. d.). Don't Cloud Your Vision. Retrieved from http://www.ft.com/cms/s/0/303680a6-bf51-11dd-ae63000779fd18c.html?nclick_check=1

European Network and Information Security Agency (ENISA). (2009). Cloud Computing: Cloud Computing: Benefits, Risks and recommendations for Information Security (report no: 2009).

Fawcett, S. E., Wallin, C., Allred, C., Fawcett, A. M., & Magnan, G. M. (2011). Information technology as an enabler of supply chain collaboration: A dynamic-capabilities perspective. *J. Supply Chain Manag., 47*(1), 38–59. doi:10.1111/j.1745-493X.2010.03213.x

Foster, I., Kesselman, C., Nick, J.M., Tuecke, S. (2008). Grid services for distributed system integration. *The New Net*, June, 37-46.

Gartner. (2009). Gartner Says Cloud Customers Need Brokerages to Unlock the Potential of Cloud Services. Retrieved from http://www.gartner.com/it/page.jsp?id=1064712

Gartner (2012). Hype-Cycle 2012 – Cloud Computing and Big Data. Retrieved from http://www.gartner.com/technology/research/hype-cycles/

Gorelik, E. (2013, January). Cloud Computing Models. Retrieved from http://web.mit.edu/smadnick/www/wp/2013-01.pdf

Grance & Mell. (2011). The NIST definition of cloud computing. (NIST Publication No. NIST SP- 800-145). Washington DC: US Department of Commerce. Retrieved from http://csrc.nist.gov/publications/drafts/800-146/Draft-NIST-SP800-146.pdf

Ketchen, D. J. Jr, & Hult, G. T. M. (2007). Bridging organization theory and supply chain management: The case of best value supply chains. *Journal of Operations Management, 25*(2), 573–580. doi:10.1016/j.jom.2006.05.010

Lakshman, A., & Prashant, M. (2010). Cassandra: a decentralized structured storage system. *SIGOPS Oper. Syst. Rev., 44*(2). 35-40. doi:10.1145/1773912.1773922

Leavitt, N. (2009, January). Is Cloud Computing Really Ready for Prime Time? *IEEE Computer, 42*(1), 15–20. doi:10.1109/MC.2009.20

Lee, H. L., Padmanabhan, V., & Whang, S. (1997a). The bullwhip effect in supply chains. Sloan Management Review, *38(3)*, 93–102.

Lee, H. L., Padmanabhan, V., & Whang, S. (1997b). Information distortion in a supply chain: The bullwhip effect. *Management Science, 43*(4), 546–558. doi:10.1287/mnsc.43.4.546

Lee & Whang. (2000). Information sharing in a supply chain. *Int. J. Manuf. Technol. Manag., 1*, 79–93.

Leidner, D. E., & Jarvenpaa, S. L. (1995). The use of information technology to enhance management school education: A theoretical view. *Management Information Systems Quarterly, 19*(3), 265–291. doi:10.2307/249596

Leighon, T. (2009). Akamai and Cloud Computing: A Perspective from the Edge of the Cloud. White Paper. Akamai Technologies. Retrieved from http://www.essextec.com/assets/cloud/akamai/cloudcomputing- perspective-wp.pdf

Linder, M., Galan, F., Chapman, C., Clayman, S., Henriksson, D., & Elmroth, E. (2010). The Cloud Supply Chain: A Framework for Information, Monitoring, Accounting and Billing. Retrieved from https://www.ee.ucl.ac.uk/~sclayman/docs/CloudComp2010.pdf

Mata, F. J., Fuerst, W. L., & Barney, J. B. (1995). Information technology and sustained competitive advantage: A resource-based analysis. *Management Information Systems Quarterly, 19*(4), 487–505. doi:10.2307/249630

Monczka, R. M., Petersen, K. J., Handfield, R. B., & Ragatz, G. L. (1998). Success factors in strategic supplier alliances: The buying company perspective. *Decision Sciences, 29*(3), 553–577. doi:10.1111/j.1540-5915.1998.tb01354.x

Petersen & Ragatz. (2005). Examination of collaborative planning effectiveness and supply chain performance. *J. Supply. Chain Manag., 41*, 14–25.

Pritchett, D. (2008). BASE: An Acid Alternative. *Queue, 6*(3), 48-55. doi:10.1145/1394127.1394128

Rochwerger, B., Breitgand, D., Levy, E., Galis, A., Nagin, K., Llorente, I. M., & Galan, F. et al. (2010). The reservoir model and architecture for open federated cloud computing. *IBM Journal of Research and Development, 53*, 4–11.

Rosenthal, A., Mork, P., Li, M. H., Stanford, J., Koester, D., & Reynolds, P. (2010). Cloud Computing: A new business paradigm for biomedical information sharing. *Journal of Biomedical Informatics, 43*(2), 342–353. doi:10.1016/j.jbi.2009.08.014 PMID:19715773

Ross, V. W. (2010). *Factors influencing the adoption of cloud computing by Decision making managers. (Capella University)*. ProQuest Dissertations and Theses.

Rozados, I., & Tjahjono, B. (2014). Big Data Analytics in Supply Chain Management: Trends and Related Research. *Proceedings of the 6th International Conference on Operations and Supply Chain Management*, Bali. Retrieved from https://www.researchgate.net/publication/270506965_Big_Data_Analytics_in_Supply_Chain_Management_Trends_and_Related_Research

Sahin, F., & Robinson, E. P. (2002). Flow coordination and information sharing in supply chains: Review, implications, and directions for future research. *Decision Sciences, 33*(4), 505–536. doi:10.1111/j.1540-5915.2002.tb01654.x

Stock, G. N., Greis, N. P., & Kasarda, J. D. (2000). Enterprise logistics and supply chain structure: The role of fit. *Journal of Operations Management, 18*(5), 531–547. doi:10.1016/S0272-6963(00)00035-8

Stonebraker, M., Madden, S., Abadi, D. J., Harizopoulos, S., Hachem, N., & Helland, P. (2007). The end of an architectural era: (it's time for a complete rewrite). Proceedings of the 33rd international conference on Very large data bases (VLDB '07) (pp. 1150-1160).

Thomas, R. W., Defee, C. C., Randall, W. S., & Williams, B. (2011). Assessing the managerial relevance of contemporary supply chain management research. *International Journal of Physical Distribution & Logistics Management, 41*(7), 655–667. doi:10.1108/09600031111154116

Trifu, M. R., & Ivan, M. L. (2014). Big Data: present and future. *Database Systems Journal, 5*(1), 32-41. Retrieved from http://www.dbjournal.ro/archive/15/15_4.pdf

Uma, S., Mudinuri, K. M., Repetski, S., Venkataraman, G., Che, A., Brian, T., . . . Stephens, R. S. (2013). Knowledge and Theme Discovery across Very Large Biological Data Sets Using Distributed Queries: A Prototype Combining Unstructured and Structured Data. Retrieved from http://journals.plos.org/plosone/article?id=10.1371/journal.pone.0080503

Want, R., Schilit, B. N., & Jenson, S. (2015, January). Enabling the Internet of Things. *Computer, 48*(1), 28–35. Retrieved from http://parallelanddistributedsystems.weebly.com/uploads/7/7/0/3/77031663/enabling_the_internet_of_things.pdf doi:10.1109/MC.2015.12

Xu, L., & Beamon, B. M. (2006). Supply chain coordination and cooperation mechanisms: An attribute based approach. *J. Suppl. Chain Manag., 42*(1), 4–12. doi:10.1111/j.1745-493X.2006.04201002.x

Zhou, H., & Benton, W. C. Jr. (2007). Supply chain practice and information sharing. *Journal of Operations Management, 25*(6), 1348–1365. doi:10.1016/j.jom.2007.01.009

KEY TERMS AND DEFINITIONS

Big Data: Term that is used to describe a collection of information such large or complex datasets which are traditionally inadequate to handle. This solution was designed to analyze, capture, sanitize, provisioning, store, transfer visualize, query, update and protect the desired or identified information. The term often refers to the process of predicting future disposition of data, user's behavior using different analytics tools.

Cloud Computing: On-demand internet-based computing delivery platform developed to provisioning data to geographically dispersed computers in real-time.

Information and Communications Technology: A different term for information technology which emphasizes on integrated communication and unified telecommunications protocols, standards as well as procedures. ICT encompasses computer devices and software applications such as audio-visual, storage systems, middleware and software. These devices and applications are designed to exchange and deliver information or allow users to share, retrieve, send and process data via technology-based network medium.

Internet of Things: A global network containing physical and vertical objects: sensors, actuators, wired/wireless devices, smart homes, smart appliances, embedded electronic systems and others. In the IoT-based environment objects are capable of accessing, sharing, processing, and collecting data in real-time.

Logistics: The process of employing organization's complex-based operations. This includes managing vast amount of resources e.g., merchandise from a single to multiple locations or vice versa. In logistics, goods can be acquired, procured, and sold between parties where quality of service is retained, along with financial gains.

Predictive Analytics: A concept of data mining designed to extract data through the use of forecast tendencies and performance forms. This process also allows for score processing where customers or enterprises have the ability to analyze the patterns and conjectures affecting the data.

Security: Practice and methods of averting illegal user's access, usage, discovery, disruption, alteration, examination, recording of data within the infrastructure.

Stakeholders: Participants whose actions, objectives and/or policies are designed to guarantee for the common good. Government participants, private sector associates, single or multiple owners who have a vested stake or interest in a particular business can also be regarded as stakeholders.

Supply Chain: A single or multiple organizational entities such as people, data, resources and activities designed to serve a unique interest. The shipment of merchandise or goods from one location to another can easily be defined as part of supply chain. This includes the transformation process of natural resources i.e., fresh ingredients and components for processing as finished product which can be delivered to various commercial establishments for retailing or user's consumption.

Trade: The process of acquiring and retailing goods or services to a single or multiple entities namely organizations, governments, marketers, etc. This process can be carried on by exporting or importing raw materials, produce, and related manufacturing goods between various locations worldwide.

Chapter 2
Big Data Analytics in Aquaculture Using Hive and Hadoop Platform

P. Venkateswara Rao
ASCET, India

A. Ramamohan Reddy
S. V. University, India

V. Sucharita
K. L. University, India

ABSTRACT

In the field of Aquaculture with the help of digital advancements huge amount of data is constantly produced for which the data of the aquaculture has entered in the big data world. The requirement for data management and analytics model is increased as the development progresses. Therefore, all the data cannot be stored on single machine. There is need for solution that stores and analyzes huge amounts of data which is nothing but Big Data. In this chapter a framework is developed that provides a solution for shrimp disease by using historical data based on Hive and Hadoop. The data regarding shrimps is acquired from different sources like aquaculture websites, various reports of laboratory etc. The noise is removed after the collection of data from various sources. Data is to be uploaded on HDFS after normalization is done and is to be put in a file that supports Hive. Finally classified data will be located in particular place. Based on the features extracted from aquaculture data, HiveQL can be used to analyze shrimp diseases symptoms.

INTRODUCTION

With the quick increase of huge data there is a need of innovative analytical strategies that handles complex data. At present the aquaculture has entered into the world of Big Data. The key challenges are to be identified by analysts of Big Data that are trying to solve problems for experts of aquaculture. Due to advances in communication huge information is available. More data is generated in huge quantities

DOI: 10.4018/978-1-5225-2947-7.ch002

Copyright © 2018, IGI Global. Copying or distributing in print or electronic forms without written permission of IGI Global is prohibited.

from various sources. Big Data is defined to be the digital data in large scale which is very difficult to manage and analyze using software tools that are traditional (Chenx et al., 2014; Marx, 2013; Zhang, 2014). The data that is being generated is expected in exabytes on daily basis(Gandomi et al.,2013). There are various sources of big data as shown in figure 1. They are logs of application, streams, sensors, generated data, media, Business organizations, daily transactions, emails, mobile phones signals, twitters. Smart Phone users have been increased to 75% in USA (Huh et al., 2014). Thise kind of data can be used for sentimental analysis by which it is identified what people think about different products (Arora et al., 2015; Laney, 2001). Therefore, volume is considered to be very important here. The current meters also generate huge daily reading. This is very important to analyze this kind of data which helps to optimize the energy. Another feature of Big Data is Velocity. One aspect of the velocity is combining of different data like the data may be structured or the unstructured (Gandomi et al., 2013) data arriving very quickly. Data is generated from various sources that have different features. The importance is on the capabilities of processing or based on infrastructure that is present for processing the data in the other case it is not possible with the existing framework. Different people gave different definitions like (Laney, 2001) have given as it is the high volume, high variety information, high velocity which demand on cost effective for improved decision making which is 3V model. Later the definition was updated to 4V model and value is added for the Big Data. Then veracity is also added to Big Data and called it as 5V model. For storing and processing the data that comes from the value it required new platform. Because of the drawback in the traditional methodologies the Big Data processing comes in large volume, variety of data coming at changing velocity. To process this the scalability is required. In the processing of Big Data there will be data from various sources. The data from various sources is put into a single platform. At first the data is acquired from various sources, then processing is done. After processing visualization and finally decision making from visualization. The data from different sources like logs, streams, mails, media, phone calls are combined. Integration tools can be used to combine unstructured and structured data.

Flume is one such tool for combining the data in logs and streams (Boulon et al, 2003). Then data collected in huge volumes will be processed. These large data can be stored in node of clusters on Hadoop Distributed file system which is fault tolerant. 360 0 view will be therein visualization and finally

Figure 1. Various sources of Big Data

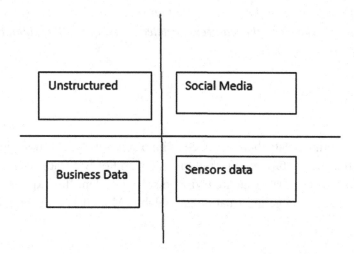

the management can make decisions based on visualizations out of analyzing big data. Aquaculture researchers are now finding new solutions for the different challengers like scalability, analyzing and management schemes. The main aim of this chapter is to find the recommendation solution for shrimp disease based on historical data which helps aqua cultural researchers or officials to take decisions. Apache Hadoop provides tools in the distributed environment as shown in table 1. Hadoop will solve the problems of aquaculture that are of scalable infrastructure (Emani et al., 2015; Zhang et al., 2015; Yuy et al., 2015; Nordberg et al., 2013). In Big Data analytics Machine learning is used to give the solutions to certain problems as it is used to find the associations and extract the patterns and trends of big data.

BIG DATA APPROACH TO AQUACULTURE

In this chapter, it is discussed about the present impact of Big Data on agriculture which motivates for Big Data approach to aquaculture. In agriculture, the Big Data is mainly focused on solving the economic prospective of management decisions. In agriculture, there is improvement in resource optimization which includes use of spatial maps, analytics on crop models (Schumachr et al., 2014). It also uses the data analysis tools for visualizing and extracting the real-time data. The impact of transformation made in agriculture also give impact on aquaculture based on sensors, computer vision, imaging, machine intelligence and big data analytics. The trends in technology also makes us to use drones, boats of driverless, Internet of things etc. Aquaculture and agriculture both of them share same objectives like optimizing the production costs. This can be done by using data analytics in aquaculture. The Recent research in aquaculture operations began to implement new technologies like computer control systems, computer vision and imaging. These are the different kinds of measurements that will allow aquaculture facilities to optimize their efficiency by reducing labour and utility costs. The advantages of aquaculture process control and Machine intelligence systems are:

1. Process efficiency can be improved.
2. Energy and water can be reduced.
3. Labour costs can be reduced.
4. Improved accounting.

Table 1. Big Data tools

Big Data Tools	Description
Hadoop	It is an Open source framework being developed for storage and processing in distributed environment.
Map Reduce	It is programming model which writes applications to process large amounts of data in parallel
Mahout	It is Open source project for implementing machine learning algorithms with scalability
Hadoop Distributed file system	It is a distributed file system that provides access to huge quantities of data on clusters
Hive	It is a open source data warehouse which resides on top of Hadoop and does querying.
Hbase	It is Hadoop database which is distributed.
Apache Pig	It is used for parallel execution of data on Hadoop.

FRAMEWORK

The objective of this chapter is it prioritize the outcomes that gives the solutions to aqua researchers, farmers that can be easily understood and helpful to recommend a solution which is based on the historic data. In the Big Data world data is collected from various data sources that are available like laboratories, fisheries department and websites. The reports of various laboratories are the main sources of data where researchers perform different tests. It will be a very important information. Website also provides useful information in the form of statistics and also data related to economic entities to various people anytime and anywhere that helps farmers for choosing new methods. Some tools are used to download these web pages related to aquaculture and save on Hadoop distributed file systems (Ratner, 2011). The Processing flow is shown in Figure 2.

Fisheries department reports give information about specific geographical area. Therefore, they are very helpful in taking decisions of particular geographical location. Then the data stores on Hadoop distributed file systems is raw which is not meaningful and full of noise. So, the first step is to remove the noise from the raw data. Then feature extraction has to be done. Where important features are taken out. After feature extraction is done the normalization id done to maintain uniformity and to remove technical variations by replacing with different values (Lam et al., 2010). Of incomplete and missing data. Next the query is to be executed on Hive which is on the top of Hadoop (Shvanchko et al., 2010) which help to analyze and take the decisions. Hive executes the query using HiveQL on the distributed environment (Thusoo, 2009). The query can be given in application interface or command line. Once the query is given the master node optimizes it and gives to map reduce which executes query on the distributed environment (Song, 2013). It identifies the similar match between the diseased shrimp features. The similarity gives the data how many are matched with those disease features based on the characteristics. After the mapping the results are combined by the reducer depending on the solution from each class and sorts the results based on the similarity and data on same location etc. It finally recommends the solution.

EXPERIMENTS AND RESULTS

The objective of this chapter is it prioritize the outcomes that gives the solutions to aqua researchers and farmers. A setup is established to perform an experiment with Hadoop 2.6 with an configuration of master node having 8 GB and two data nodes of 3 GB. The data is collected from various laboratories

Figure 2. Processing flow of Big Data

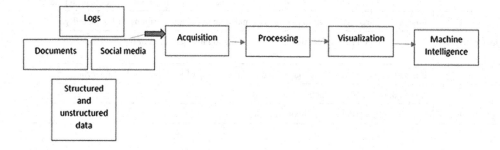

Figure 3. Feature extraction

and other websites. Then the features are extracted from the data sets which contains thousands of records related to shrimp diseases as shown in figure 3. For developing an application Eclipse Integrated Development Environment is used with Java. SQL query is generated to select a region which is specific for certain diseases from Hive server and then it is saved as text file on Hadoop server. This query will be converted by Hive to HiveQL query which will be implemented using map reduce and its returns the results that will be saved into the file. The file containing results will contain all details like disease symptoms, field, and solution. Then the mapper split this file into various parts on different hosts and calculates the probability depending on the similarity between various symptoms of the shrimp disease that are entered by the different users and the historical datasets. It finally selects the symptoms that are matched mostly from all the categories. Then recommendation solution is given. The opinions of the experts based on the recommendation solution will increase the efficiency of the system.

CONCLUSION

The objective of this chapter is it prioritize the outcomes that gives the solutions to aqua researchers, farmers that can be easily understood and helpful to recommend a solution which is based on the historic data as aquaculture has entered into the world of Big Data for decision making. To handle problems like shrimp disease frame work using Big Data Analytics have been developed that provides many solutions to be recommended based Hadoop and Hive. It helps the aqua farmers to have more yield in the shrimp production.

REFERENCES

Arora, D., & Malik, P. (2015). Analytics: Key to go from generating big data to deriving business value. *Proceedings of the IEEE First International Conference on Big Data Computing Service and Applications*. doi:10.1109/BigDataService.2015.62

Boulon, J., Konwinski, A., Qi, R., Rabkin, A., Yang, E., & Yang, M. (2008). Chukwa, A large-scale monitoring system. *Proceedings of CCA* (Vol. 8, pp. 1–5).

Chen, X.-W., & Lin, X. (2014). Big data deep learning challenges and perspective. *IEEE Access.*, 2, 514–522. doi:10.1109/ACCESS.2014.2325029

Emani, C. K., Cullot, N., & Nicolle, C. (2015). Understandable Big Data: A survey. *Computer Science Review*, *17*, 70–81. doi:10.1016/j.cosrev.2015.05.002

Gandomi, A., & Haider, M. (2015). Beyond the hype: Big data concepts, methods, and analytics. *International Journal of Information Management*, *1*(35), 137–144. doi:10.1016/j.ijinfomgt.2014.10.007

Gartner. (n. d.). IT Glossary. Retrieved from http://www. gartner.com/it-glossary/big-data

Hu, H., Wen, Y., Tat-Seng, C., & Li, X. (2014). Toward Scalable Systems for Big Data Analytics: A Technology Tutorial. *Practical Innovations: Open Solutions.*, *7*(1), 1–36.

Lam, C., & Warren, J. (2010). *Hadoop in action* (1st ed.). Greenwich: Manning Publications.

Laney, D. (2001). 3D data management: Controlling data volume, velocity and variety. Meta Group Inc Research Note.

Marx, V. (2013). Biology: The big challenges of big data. *Nature*, *498*(7453), 255–260. doi:10.1038/498255a PMID:23765498

Nordberg, H., Bhatia, K., Wang, K., & Wang, Z. (2013). Biopic: A hadoop-based analytic toolkit for large-scale sequence data. *Oxford Bioinformatics.*, *29*(33), 3014–3019. doi:10.1093/bioinformatics/btt528 PMID:24021384

Ratner, B. (2011). *Statistical and machine-learning data mining: Techniques for better predictive modeling and analysis of big data* (2nd ed.). CRC Press Taylor and Francis Group. doi:10.1201/b11508

Schumacher, A., Pireddu, L., Niemenmaa, M., Kallio, A., Korpelainen, E., Zanetti, G., & Heljanko, K. (2014). Simple and scalable scripting for large sequencing data sets in hadoop. *Bioinformatics (Oxford, England)*, *30*(1), 119–120. doi:10.1093/bioinformatics/btt601 PMID:24149054

Shvachko, K., Kuang, H., Radia, S., & Chansler, R. (2010). The hadoop distributed file system. *Proceedings of IEEE 26th Symposium on Mass Storage Systems and Technologies*.

Song, Y. (2013). Storage mining: Where it management meets big data analytics. *Proceedings of IEEE International Congress on Big Data*, New York, USA (pp. 421–422). doi:10.1109/BigData.Congress.2013.66

Thusoo, A. (2009). Hive- A warehousing solution over a map-reduce framework. *ACM Digital Library*, *2*(2), 1626–1629.

Wang, C., Rayan, I. A., & Schwan, K. (2012). Faster, larger, easier: reining real-time big data processing in cloud. *Proceedings of the Posters and Demo Track, Middleware '12* (pp. 4:1–4:2). New York: ACM. doi:10.1145/2405153.2405157

Yu, Y., & Wang, X. (2015). World Cup 2014 in the Twitter World: A big data analysis of sentiments in U.S. sports fans tweets. *Computers in Human Behavior*, *48*, 392–400. doi:10.1016/j.chb.2015.01.075

Zhang, H., Chen, G., Ooi, B. C., Kian-Lee, T., & Zhang, M. (2015). In-Memory Big Data Management and Processing: A Survey. *IEEE Transactions on Knowledge and Data Engineering*, *27*(7), 1920–1948. doi:10.1109/TKDE.2015.2427795

Zhang, H., Wei, X., Zou, T., Li, Z., & Yang, G. (2014). Agriculture big data: Research status, challenges and countermeasures. *Proceedings of Computer and Computing Technologies in Agriculture, China* (pp. 137–143).

KEY TERMS AND DEFINITIONS

Aquaculture: Aquaculture refers to the breeding, rearing, and harvesting of plants and animals in all types of water environments. Aquaculture serves a variety of purposes. Most U.S. marine aquaculture is shellfish while a small percentage is marine finfish.

Big Data: It is huge amount of semi structured, structured and unstructured data from where information can be extracted.

Experts: An Expert is person in general with wide knowledge based on research in a particular area of study.

Hadoop: An open source frame based on java that stores and process large data sets in a distributed environment.

Hive: Apache Hive is an infrastructure that is built on top of Hadoop for providing summarization of the data summarization, queries, and analysis.

Shrimp: The term shrimp is used to refer to some decapod crustaceans, although the exact animals covered can vary.

Chapter 3
Big Data Mining:
A Forecast to the Future

V. Sucharita
K. L. University, India

A. Satya Kalyan
K. L. University, India

P. Venkateswara Rao
ASCET, India

P. Rajarajeswari
K. L. University, India

ABSTRACT

At present in Big Data era mining of Big Data can help us find learning which nobody has possessed the capacity to find some time recently. There is a developing interest for tools and techniques which can prepare and investigate Big Data effectively and proficiently. In this chapter, the accessible information mining tools and techniques which can deal with Big Data have been abridged. This paper additionally concentrates on tools and techniques for mining of data and information streams. Through better analysis of the vast volumes of information that are getting to be accessible, there is the potential for making speedier progresses in numerous scientific areas what's more, making strides the productivity what's more, victory of numerous organizations. The challenges incorporate not just the self-evident issues of scale, be that as it may too heterogeneity, need of structure, error handling, protection, opportunities at all stages of the analysis from acquisition of data to obtaining to result.

INTRODUCTION

Big Data is a collection of data that represents huge and complex data which is very hard to manage using traditional DBMS and tools of Processing data(Diebold,2000). Before Big Data emerged, the data was in data warehouses that consisted of structured databases. Slowly the sources of data are diversified and are heterogeneous. The big data analysts analyze the future of the customer data. Though companies are collecting, storing and doing data analysis most of them are struggling with the data of the project which is very big. This chapter explains how the big data tools and techniques gain new insight by doing analysis of various data sets that are very large. The production of the sources of data are associated with various V's like volume, velocity and variety has more contribution to the growth of big data in the present trend. At present the data is in various unstructured formats like text, sensor reading and videos

DOI: 10.4018/978-1-5225-2947-7.ch003

Copyright © 2018, IGI Global. Copying or distributing in print or electronic forms without written permission of IGI Global is prohibited.

and data sets are in petabytes which is very difficult to manage. All the data which is created, duplicated and used per year will reach to Exabyte's. At present, less data is being analyzed with potential to increase to higher range if the data is properly analyzed. There are wide variety of techniques that have been developed and modified to visualize, analyze, operate and aggregate big data to make this kind of data well structured. The various techniques include Time series analysis, A/B testing, Cluster analysis, Network analysis, Ensemble learning, Data fusion Association rule learning, Machine learning, etc. The A/B testing technique is used to compare various options to determine what treatments will progress a given objective; Cluster analysis is used for classifying objects that splits a diverse group into smaller groups of similar objects. Ensemble learning uses multiple predictive models to obtain better predictive performance. Network analysis analyzes connections between nodes in a network and their strength. Lastly, Machine learning helps in learning and training automatically. There is no meaning of Big Data if unable to analyze the information that is valuable. There are mainly four things in analytics they are collection of data, cleaning of data, modeling and reporting of data. Collecting the data is more relevant is very important. Data cleaning is required when data is collected from various sources. After data cleaning is completed it has to be modeled by using various statistical and various machine learning techniques.

TOOLS ON BIG DATA

In the present trend, huge quantities of data are available for decision makers. Big Data will take a reference of data sets that are very large but maintains velocity and variety. So, it is not possible to manage with ordinary tools and techniques. Therefore, solution must be provided to handle and mine knowledge using such large data so that decision makers could take decision rightly with continuous data changing very rapidly like customer interaction and social networking. This can be done using Big Data Analytics. This Chapter analyzes methods to analyze and also that can be applied to Big Data. Also, various opportunities can be analyzed by analytics in different domains for taking the decisions. Big Data is simply not buzzword it is a reality of business value. Tools are mainly used for identifying trends, mine patterns and getting findings that are very much valuable from the huge quantities available to them. Many relational databases. have the capacity to store and manage huge amounts of data may be in petabytes data locally. These relational databases have limited capacity. Semi-structured data is the data stored in a structural form. The data is stored and retrieved using NoSQL. It has not particular scheme, therefore they can handle the data coming from various sources. The distributed storage that is designed for the large databases is BigTable (Chang, 2006). The distributed file system that is designed for providing the access to data using huge clusters of commodity hardware. The programming model for parallel processing is Map-Reduce(Dean,2004). In the Map reduce the input data is split and distributes across different machines so that parallel processing can be done. Also, it collects those results from different machines as a final result. This can be done in Hadoop. The Hadoop and Bigdata terms are used synonymously. The library of the apache hadoop is like a framework that uses simple programming for distributed computing environment. It is mainly used to come out from failures in the application layer for getting better accuracy. Hadoop uses the distributed file system for the storage of data. To make the efficient processing of Big Data so many Hadoop based tools are available like Apache Sqoop and Apache Flume. Apache Hive is a framework built on top of the Hadoop for making the users to store data in tables. All the tools of Bigdata deals only with volume. There is a need for the tools which can also handle data streams. So, Apache storm is used for distributed real time calculations for large streams. All the tools discussed in this section of the chapter are used for streaming and voluminous data. The need of using Bigdata is developing quickly over all businesses. Enterprises like human services, retail, keeping money and so on have TB's of information which is longing to uncover the facts and extracting knowledge to help a business develop. Be that as it may, it additionally offers various obstacles. For example, picking the best machines to store enormous information, doing various computations and calculations to discover the facts is another obstacle. Enormous Data is not accessible on a server, rather it is spread on number of servers which is then to be gathered and accumulated before coming to the phase of calculation. Maybe, it is a surprisingly beneficial turn of events for the database software engineers since that is the place the part of information developer comes. Utilization of NoSQL databases is prevalent to play out this work where it is utilized to concentrate, store and deal with the database. The advantage of utilizing Big Data is that it goes without organizations to take a shot at tests. The measure of advantages that will come using Big Data, there are particular tools which are designated to work on Bigdata.

DATA MINING

The process of finding the patterns in a data in order to predict some data. Mining of data is the extraction of concealed predictive information from extensive databases, is an intense new innovation with incredible potential to help organizations concentrate on the most essential data in their data warehouses. The tools of Data mining foresee future patterns and practices, permitting Business organizations to make proactive, to take better decisions. The analysis done by using data mining move past the examinations of past occasions gave by review for the decision support systems. The tools of the data mining can answer the question related to business generally addresses were excessively tedious, making it impossible to determine. Hidden patterns can be searched from the databases from where predictive information can be found that specialists may miss since it lies outside their expectations. To find the pattern there are so many techniques in data mining they are association-rule mining, classification, clustering, and regression analysis. There are 3 stages in data mining process they are used for Cleaning data, Extracting, Transforming and Loading. There are two types of models in data mining one supervised and the other is unsupervised models. The unsupervised models deal with finding the clusters from the given data where there is no teacher. But the supervised models deal with classification of the data for making predictions. There are so many models in data mining. Some of models are neural networks, Bayes, regression analysis etc. The models that use supervised learning are k-nearest neighbor, decision tree induction, support vector machines, naive Bayesian, regression. There are clustering algorithms: fuzzy c means, k-means, BIRCH, OPTICS, distribution models, neural networks. The techniques that mines frequent patters are Apriori algorithm, FP-growth etc. In supervised learning in order to improve the results the ensemble methods are used. To find the anomalies in the data outlier detection is used. The various mining algorithms discussed in this chapter so far are not able to handle the streams of data. to obtain data from streams new algorithms are required. There are various models for learning data stream. Sliding window model is best suitable for handling concept-drift in data streams. With the advent of Big Data the Data stream algorithms have got more focus to get the desired value from it. The algorithms for clustering of data stream are BIRCH (Zhang, 1997) k-means (Bradley, 1998), ODAC (Rodrigues, 2006), DenStream (Cao, 2006), SWClustering (Zou, 2008), ClusTree (Kranen, 2011), DGClust (Gama, 2011).

The algorithms for classification of data stream can be divided into two categories – incremental learning and ensemble learning algorithms. Ensemble learning combines multiple learning algorithms for prediction and may discard some training data as outdated whereas incremental learning adjusts old results to what has been learned from the new data. The popular algorithms for incremental learning are Incremental Bayesian algorithm (Roure, 1999), Incremental SVM (Syed, 1999). Some ensemble learning algorithms are Streaming Ensemble Algorithm (SEA) (Street, 2001) Accuracy-Weighted Ensemble (AWE), Dynamic Weighted Majority (DWM) (Kolter, 2007). The data streams will come from various sources therefore mining algorithms are required to combining these streams and synchronize so that mining of the data will be efficient. Some of the research works on data stream mining on multiple sources are SPIRIT (Papadimitriou, 2009) which are used for finding patterns from various streams of data.

TOOLS ON BIG DATA MINING

The process of finding the required patterns in the large datasets will use methods like artificial intelligence, statistical analysis, Machine learning for extracting data in the required manner and into an understandable format of the system. The tools used are ARminer, orange, Weka, Rosetta, Tangra etc. ARMiner and Weka are not suitable for distributed systems because they are not scalable. So, Weka was integrated with Hadoop (Wegener, 2009), Also R was integrated with Hadoop (Chu, 2006). use Map reduce technique with the algorithms like SVM, Back Propagation, K-means etc. The data mining tools are classified based on processing type whether it is distributed or not as shown in Figure 1.

Figure 1. Tools of data mining

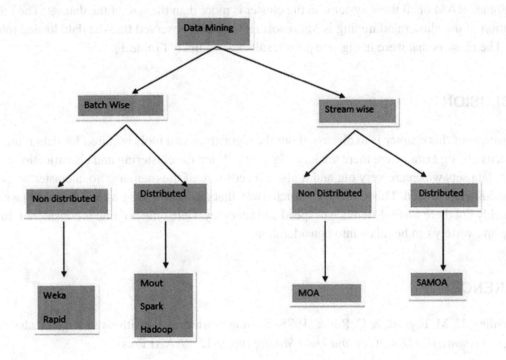

Table 1. Results based on data sets

Data Set	Algorithm	Cluster size		
		2	4	6
Amazon	Distributed K-Means	55 min	55min	6.15 min
Amazon	Deep Learning	-	2hrs	35 min
Flipkart	Distributed Random forest	-	25 min	2.08 min

For large volume s of data tools and techniques are required that give better scalability like apache mahout. It is one of the map reduce implementation. H_2O is another tool for machine learning that gives scalability. Very fast machine learning uses k-means. Deep learning and Random forests are also used. MOA does not support in distributed environment.

EXPERIMENTS AND RESULTS

To provide insight into big data mining, the experiments on large data sets are conducted. The datasets chosen are Amazon datasets for clustering and Flipkart dataset for classification. The Amazon dataset consists of 24 features with 102353496 observations. The Flipkart dataset consists of 28 features with 11000000 observations. The RAM available on the systems was only 2 GB and therefore full datasets could not be loaded in RAM for data mining. To handle the large datasets, a cluster is created such that the combined RAM of all these systems in the cluster is more than the size of the dataset. The tool used for creation of the cluster and mining is Microsoft HPC. It was observed that the data loaded into HPC cluster. The clusters that were in big size gave results very quickly (Table 1).

CONCLUSION

The objective of this chapter is to discuss about the algorithms and tools required for data mining with much focus on Big Data where there are large data sets. When the clustering and classification are done on these data sets which are very big and it also exceeds size of the memory. So, a cluster was created and algorithms were used. The results are in such a way that the clusters that were in big size gave results very quickly but there was a difference in speed and accuracy. Here only volume is considered. In future velocity and variety can be taken into consideration.

REFERENCES

P. S. Bradley, U. M. Fayyad, & C. Reina.(1998) Scaling clustering algorithms to large databases. *Proceedings of Knowledge Discovery and Data Mining* (pp. 9-15). AAAI Press.

Cao, F., Ester, M., Qian, W., & Zhou, A. (2006). Density-based clustering over an evolving data stream with noise., *Proceedings of the Sixth SIAM International Conference on Data Mining* SIAM (pp. 328-339). doi:10.1137/1.9781611972764.29

Chang, F., Dean, J., Ghemawat, S., Hsieh, W. C., Wallach, D. A., Burrows, M., & Gruber, R. E. et al. (2006). *Bigtable: A Distributed Storage System for Structured Data Research.*

Chu, C. T., Kim, S. K., Lin, Y. A., Yu, Y., Bradski, G. R., Ng, A. Y., & Olukotun, K. (2006). Map-Reduce for Machine Learning on Multicore, Proc. 20th Ann. Conf. Neural Information Processing Systems (NIPS'06) (pp. 281-288).

Dean, J., & Ghemawat, S. (2004). MapReduce: Simplified data processing on large clusters, *Proceedings of the 6th OSDI* (pp. 137-150).

Diebold, F. (2000). Big Data: Dynamic Factor Models for Macroeconomic Measurement and Forecasting. *Discussion read to the Eighth World Congress of the Econometric Society.*

Gama, J., Rodrigues, P. P., & Lopes, L. (2011). Clustering distributed sensor data streams using local processing and reduced communication. *Intelligent Data Analysis*, *15*(1), 3–28.

Kolter, J. Z. & Maloof, M. A. (2007). Dynamic Weighted Majority: A New Ensemble Method for Drifting Concepts. *ACM Journal of Machine Learning Research*, (8), 2755-2790.

Kranen, P., Assent, I., Baldauf, C., & Seidl, T. (2011). The clustree: Indexing micro-clusters for anytime stream mining. *Knowledge and Information Systems*, *29*(2), 249–272. doi:10.1007/s10115-010-0342-8

Papadimitriou, S., Sun, J., & Faloutsos, C. (2005). Streaming Pattern Discovery in Multiple TimeSeries. *Proceedings of 31st VLDB Conference.*

Rodrigues, P., Gama, J., & Pedroso, J. (2006).ODAC: Hierarchical clustering of time series data streams. *Proceedings of the Sixth SIAM International Conference on Data Mining* (pp. 499-503). doi:10.1137/1.9781611972764.48

Roure, J., & Sanguesa, R. (1999). Incremental Methods for Bayesian Network Learning.

Street, W. N., & Kim, Y. A. (2001). Streaming Ensemble Algorithm (SEA) for large-scale classification. *Proceedings of the 7th ACM SIGKDD International Conference on Knowledge Discovery and Data Mining* (pp. 377-382).

Syed, N. A., Liu, H., & Sung, K. K. (1999). Handling concept drift in incremental learning with support vector machines. *Proceedings of the 5th ACM SIGKDD International Conference on Knowledge Discovery and Data Mining* (pp. 317-321). doi:10.1145/312129.312267

Wegener, D., Mock, M., Adranale, D., & Wrobel, S. (2009). Toolkit-based High-Performance Data Mining of Large Data on MapReduce Clusters. *Proc. Int'l Conf. Data Mining Workshops (ICDMW'09)* (pp. 296-301). doi:10.1109/ICDMW.2009.34

Zhang, T., Ramakrishnan, R., & Livn, M. (1997). BIRCH: A new data clustering algorithm and its applications. *Data Mining and Knowledge Discovery*, *1*(2), 141–182. doi:10.1023/A:1009783824328

Zhou, F., Cao, F., Qian, W., & Jin, C. (2008). Tracking clusters in evolving data streams over sliding windows. *Knowledge and Information Systems*, *15*(2), 181–214. doi:10.1007/s10115-007-0070-x

KEY TERMS AND DEFINITIONS

Big Data: It is huge amount of semi structured, structured and unstructured data from where information can be extracted.

Data Mining: Extracting the required patterns by examining large pre-existing databases.

Datasets: A collection of related sets of information that is composed of separate elements but can be manipulated as a unit by a computer.

Hadoop: An open source frame work based on java that stores and process large data sets in a distributed environment.

Information: Data which is organized and have relevance with particular meaning.

Machine Learning: It is defined as the ability to learn automatically when new data is given.

Chapter 4
Cloud Computing Education Strategies:
A Review

Syed Hassan Askari
National University of Sciences and Technology
(NUST), Pakistan

Sajid Umair
National University of Sciences and Technology
(NUST), Pakistan

Faizan Ahmad
National University of Sciences and Technology
(NUST), Pakistan

Safdar Abbas Khan
National University of Sciences and Technology
(NUST), Pakistan

ABSTRACT

As due to the predominant money related emergency and the developing needs, Higher Education Institutes establishments are confronting challenges in giving essential information technology backing to instructive, innovative work exercises. The higher education establishment must adventure the open doors managed by cloud computing while minimizing the related security dangers to permit access to cutting edge information technology base, server farms, and applications and ensure touchy data. In this paper, cloud computing building design for higher education organization containing the different sending models, service models and client area is proposed. We at last give the suggestions to a fruitful and effective relocation from customary to cloud based framework. This research also to discover different options for the utilization of IT, while driving colleges to enhance dexterity and get investment funds. The examination system comprised in a thorough investigation of the most recent exploration on cloud computing as a different option for IT procurement, administration and security.

INTRODUCTION

In this technology evolution era, computerized cloud computing has developed as another worldview in the field of system based administrations inside of numerous modern and application space, where applications are run over the cloud network instead of each own work domain (Mircea & Andreescu, 2011). It offers a pool of virtualized processing assets at different levels, covering base of education, research,

DOI: 10.4018/978-1-5225-2947-7.ch004

Copyright © 2018, IGI Global. Copying or distributing in print or electronic forms without written permission of IGI Global is prohibited.

and business and user interactions with other IT resources, especially in the field of Higher Education (HE). For this particular domain, a satisfactory giving structure must be found in the online environment, utilizing the best possible innovations, ensuring the entrance of expansive number of clients, quick and secure administrations, based on cloud environment. Cloud computing presents new components in computation and programming models advancement solutions that are most certainly not present in conventional curricular, which give rise to a new dimension in the field of research & technology. The utilization of the Internet and Information and Communication Technologies (ICTs) to convey instructive assets is considered standard in the 21stcentury, yet in higher education in creating new dynamics for education standard. This has recorded impacts on instructors, students and instructive organizations in developing countries, which regularly incorporate an absence of fundamental ICT foundation and restricted or no backing for the preparation of educators and learners in the utilization of computerized online data sources. In future, most of currently used applications and teaching course content will be accessed through internet referred to as 'Cloud' (Rahul & Shivaji, 2013).

There are three fundamental considerations that hobbies cloud computing: fast decline in equipment cost and structural planning and present day super- computers comprising of a huge number of centers; the exponentially growing IT infrastructure with thousands of computing cores; and the across the board selection of services computing and Web 2.0 applications. The modern trends of clouds are replacing installed applications on campus computers with applications approached via internet, reducing Institutes cost and complexity.

CLOUD COMPUTING

Cloud computing platform is the outcome that has been evolved with many years of diligent efforts in network threads, parallel processing and virtualization. Distributed computing as emerging horizon of information technology shapes computational assets on interest and deliberation of specialized points of interest by the customers. It is a processing model in light of systems, particularly taking into account the Internet, whose errand is to guarantee that clients can basically utilize the registering assets on interest and pay cash as per their use by a metering design like water and power utilization. In this way, it brings another plan of action, where the administrations it gives are getting to be computing assets.

DEMAND OF CLOUD COMPUTING IN EDUCATION SYSTEM

Information technology and education framework, both the terms are definitely not in any kind of connection in the current circumstances of majority education sector. Part of information technology is extremely incomplete in school level instruction framework. Whole works in school are for the most part done in the type of manually written administrative work. Lately, numerous educational foundations are attempting to adjust cloud computing for taking care of issues that are constantly expanding figuring and capacity.

ADVANTAGES OF COMPUTING IN HIGHER EDUCATION PLATFORMS

There are numerous advantages of cloud computing for instructive establishment and underneath are recorded a couple of them. With computing methodologies, Higher Education Institutes (HEI) can open their innovation foundations to organizations and commercial enterprises for research headways. The expanded compass of cloud computing empowers institutes to conduct studies in innovative and diverse ways and offer them some assistance with managing ventures and huge workloads.

Students when approach worldwide gateway, they will compete the estimation of new advancements. Distributed computing permits understudies and instructors to utilize cloud resources without introducing on their Personal Computers (PC) furthermore permits access to spared documents from any PC with an Internet association. (Saidhbi, 2012).

Multi-tenancy: Assets are shared among numerous customers utilizing instruments that shield and detach occupants from one another. Students can access & utilize all cloud resources 365/24 without any hustle with efficiency of time. Decreased execution and support costs expanded accessibility of superior applications to root level educational institutes. (Armbrust, 2009).

RELATED WORK: ADOPTION MODEL

Recently MIT virtually publishes all of its course material online for free. Anyone can take hundreds of courses absolutely free at any time and as per their need. OCW gives free MIT instructive substance you can use to improve or invigorate your insight or educate others. It's best to consider OCW, a free online library, obviously, materials used to show MIT undergrad and graduate courses. As of now, almost 70 percent of advanced education establishments in North America have moved (or are currently moving) their email frameworks to the cloud. Around 50 percent have embraced a cloud based coordinated effort framework to enhance data sharing crosswise over grounds. By using the cloud administrations, North Carolina State University accomplished considerably diminishing costs of programming permitting and in addition decreased the grounds IT staff to 25% representatives. NKN is the state-of the-craftsmanship multi-gigabit skillet India system for giving a brought together fast system spine for all information related organizations in the whole country. It effectively associated 640 foundations and plans integrate India's 572 colleges, more than 25k universities and no less than 2,000 polytechnic institutes for empowering e-Learning and literature distribution crosswise over nation soon. (Wyld, 2010) Oracle cloud keeps on demonstrating solid selection, supporting 70+ million clients and more than 33 billion exchanges every day. It keeps running on 54,000 gadgets and more than 700 petabytes of capacity in 19 server farms the world over. In 2010, the University of Texas moved to a new out of the box $32 million server farm. Generally, double the extent of the college's past server farm and the consequence of two years of esca-lated arranging and design (Rind, 2015).

PROPOSED SOLUTION

We proposed a solution to building up the learning base about cloud computing. The initial step consists in building up the learning base by taking part at theological colleges, meetings, talks with the suppliers and counseling the latest investigates in the field. The achievement of the stage depends on the portion of adequate assets for research, for seeing how cloud registering capacities in various hierarchical structures from colleges furthermore, between establishments, the advantages and hazards, strategies and the best utilization practices of cloud computing. Assessing the present phase of the college from the perspective of the IT needs, structure and use the initial step comprises in comprehension the college IT foundation. The administration situated construction modeling speaks to the base for understanding the information, administrations, forms what's more, applications that might be relocated or should be kept up inside of the college, in order to watch the security arrangement. As for the IT needs, their structure and use, the investigation might begin from the classes of clients who interface with the present IT foundation and their necessities as described in Figure 1.

The cloud computing arrangement will permit to all classes of clients' access to put away documents, email, database and different applications from any place at solicitation, which prompts a more effective utilization of data. This speaks to a move from remote administrations offered to clients in the conventional adaptation to guaranteeing a few "self-service" frame- works, which is gainful in the distributed computing point of view. The goal is to recognize the rising innovations, effective from the perspective of expenses that fulfill the necessities of the understudies and college staff. The equipment and programming needs might then be broken down from the point of view of the three cloud models as described in Figure 2.

Figure 1. IT structure for clients and their necessities
Mircea & Andreescu, 2011.

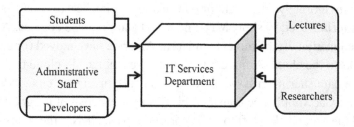

Figure 2. Three Cloud Model
White, 2009.

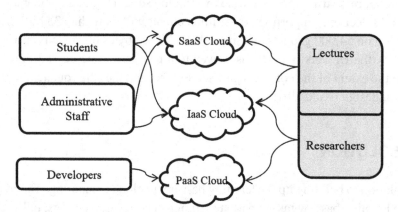

Distributed computing presents new advancement situations and new worries being developed procedure (Rehman & Sakr, 2010) that are not present in conventional nearby or on-reason programming arrangements and advances. A few illustrations are information focus innovation, multitenant innovation, new calculation and programming models that empower dispersed figuring on mists and circulated preparing of vast datasets, for example, Map Reduce (Dean & Ghemawat, 2008) and Apache Hadoop (White, 2009) distributed computing is a complex and quickly advancing idea (Cearley, 2010). There are distinctive apparatuses and cloud administration suppliers included, of which the specialized subtle elements of equipment programming capacities and circumstances change rapidly and contrast among business traders.

Cloud computing are taught through different extra routes too, offering both hypothetical and reasonable trainings to student.

- **Read:** Specific topics are selected and assign the students to prepare at home and discuss in a class. This makes a reasonable association between the perusing and the desires of the students.
- **Class Discussions:** The essential technique to achieve dynamic learning is dialog (Svinicki & Mckeachie, 2011). We discuss the topics in a class that are already assign the students. Usually assignment topics are selected for class discussion.
- **Guest Lectures:** Invite the people from both industry and the scholarly world to give educational upgrade of direct encounters in difficulties and opportunities in industry and additionally look into progress in the examination group of cloud computing.
- **Projects:** Give the projects to the students and ensures that student can comprehend the real ideas and standards, and the most effective method to apply these ideas in operational programming as well as seeing new frameworks and administrations.

COMPARISON

SaaS

Teaching Activities: Need to run institutionalized/known instructive applications. Need to share instructive applications among institute research activities: Need to perform research applications, (for example, logical work processes, superior information representation)

PaaS

Teaching Activities: Need PaaS for students to figure out how to compose applications. This is for the most part for student in software engineering, computational science and designing, and financial matters research activities: Need PaaS for creating research applications and calculations.

IaaS

Teaching Activities: Need to give machines to fundamental courses, for example, working frameworks and essential Information Technology IT abilities. Research Activities: Machines provisioning in light of use necessities.

DaaS

Teaching Activities: Need information administrations for putting away addresses, papers, dataset for testing calculation, presentations, and so forth. Most information is free and open.

Research Activities: Information for examination purposes. Data security concerns are vital the same numbers of information are delicate.

BENEFIT

We can easily access application. Support for teaching and learning. Programming free or pay per use. Increasing functional capabilities. Opening to business environment and pushed research.

LIMITATION

All applications are not running in the cloud. Dangers identified with information assurance and security what's more, records administration, hierarchical backing, and standards adherence. Security and assurance of delicate information.

SECURITY

Nowadays cloud computing is has become the most emerging trend because of big data generated by big users needing more management required but one must be aware of threats related to it. Security is one of the real issues for distributed computing A few dangers to distributed computing are recorded here, i.e. misuse and shameless utilization of distributed computing, unreliable use of programming interface, noxious insiders, vulnerabilities with respect to shared innovations, information spillage, administration, account and activity capturing, obscure danger profile. Creator presents some more transparencies that still should be in presence to deal with these dangers: Firstly, missing virtual and physical server's link amongst secondly; the connections in the middle of virtual and physical server areas. In addition, how documents are built into both physical and additionally virtual memory addresses. This sort of data is without further ado not accessible as a solitary perspective for the clients. Figure 3 describes the layers in cloud computing.

The proposed arrangement of the creator is portrayed as takes after:

Framework layer of the model is the most reduced layer that tracks information compartments through document driven logging. It has three segments operating system OS, record framework and mists interior system. Information layer backings the information reaction furthermore encourages information driven using so as to log provenance lumberjack and consistency lumberjack. The principle center of the work process layer is on review trails and review related information that is found in the product administrations in the cloud. Current research community says that an e-learning cloud system will most probably be the next generation educational institute. Henceforth the present models of e-learning biological systems are inadequate with regards to the backing of hidden distributed computing foundations, which

Figure 3. Abstraction layers of accountability in Cloud Computing

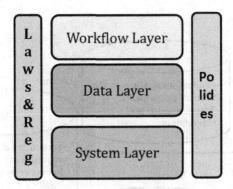

is a promising framework for give calculation and capacity assets as administrations. Thus, this paper brings cloud figuring into an e-learning environment as its base. In this paper, an e-learning environment taking into account cloud processing base is introduced. Distributed computing framework and related instruments take into consideration the security, balance, productive asset use, and supportability of an e-learning biological community.

CLOUD ARCHITECTURE FOR UNIVERSITY

Testing the cloud computing arrangements. The move to cloud might be accomplished step by step, beginning from testing a pilot venture in cloud and after that externalizing the applications decided for cloud. The main step comprises of settling some cloud targets, for example, improvement and environment testing or putting away some information inside the cloud. The following step might comprise of the everyday handling of the inward operations, tending to in the meantime the segments of open and private cloud with a specific end goal to guarantee the security and insurance strategies. The support of low expenses for utilizing the arrangement must be for all time considered. Picking the cloud computing arrangement. The initial step comprises of distinguishing the information and applications, works and fundamental procedures inside of the college. These might be gathered by three substantial classes of exercises from the college: instructing, research and managerial support for the initial two exercises. Figure 4 shows the detail of cloud architecture for university.

Step two is spoken to by the assessment of the components recognized in the initial step by criteria, for example, mission, and significance inside of the college, affectability, secrecy, respectability, accessibility all together to decide the applicant components for cloud.

FUTURE RESEARCH DIRECTIONS

With increasing problems in higher education, cloud computing provides with newer and better solutions in learning process for both students and educators. Technique involves with the introduction of basic course guidelines followed by operational work zone and virtual hands on experience. And lastly to see

Figure 4. Cloud architecture for University
Cearley, 2010.

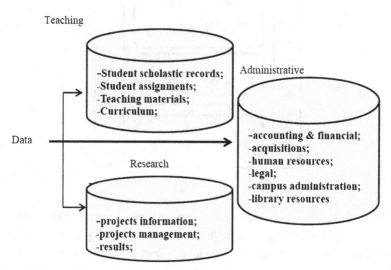

its efficiency for disciplines using cloud computing. As research was attempted to use cloud computing idea in Pakistan and survey was conducted. Responses submitted showed a positive feedback and willingness from wide range of professionals and faculty for implanting cloud computing in higher education for improved learning standards in Pakistan.

CONCLUSION

The thought to utilize cloud computing in advanced higher education is not new in 21st century. The distributed computing is picking up prominence as a cheap method for giving stockpiling and software. This paper examined the reasons why advanced education foundations need to focus on this innovative paradigm. In the first place, set up the understudies to include in distributed introducing so as to compute innovation the fundamental distributed computing courses. Secondly, conduct online classes and virtual research facilities in light of cloud environment. At last, measure the viability of cloud computing innovation for all controls. This is exceptionally financially savvy and productive as contrast with conventional figuring structures of current education system. In the future, with the expansion in the quantity of establishments offering advanced education, cloud computing execution at higher specialized training has gotten to be key fixing to accomplish practical arrangements, to lease computational foundation, to meet infrequent uses for individual, instructive, research works etc. It is all that much important to spare nature. Creative organizations of advanced education look to comprehend why and how to send cloud stages effectively and safely. At last, their decisions with respect to circumstances, approaches, and accomplices have the guarantee to change the part of IT in institutes anywhere in any part of world. HEI should be provided with necessary resources to deploy public and private clouds along with significant decisions when they are settling on choices about cloud computing.

ACKNOWLEDGMENT

The authors would like to thank Dr. Safdar Abbas Khan, Assistant Professor, School of Electrical Engineering and Computer Sciences (SEECS), National University of Sciences and Technology (NUST) Islamabad Pakistan for their complete support, help and guidance.

REFERENCES

ao, J., Gruhn, V., He, J., Roussos, G., & Tsai, W. T. (2013, March 25-28). Mobile Cloud Computing Research - Issues, Challenges and Needs. *Proceedings of the 2013 IEEE 7th International Symposium on Service Oriented System Engineering* (pp. 442, 453).

Armbrust, M., Fox, A., Griffith, R., Joseph, A. D., Katz, R., Konwinski, A., ... & Zaharia, M. (2014). Above the clouds: A Berkeley view of Cloud Computing (Report No. UCB/EECS-2009-28). UC Berkeley EECS. Retrieved July 1, 2016 from http://www.eecs.berkeley.edu/Pubs/TechRpts/2009/EECS-2009-28.html

Cearley, D. W. (2010). Cloud Computing: Key Initiative Overview. *Gartner*. Retrieved July 1, 2016 from http://www.gartner.com/it/initiatives/pdf/KeyInitiativeOverview CloudComputing.pdf

Cisco. (2012). Developing a Cloud-Computing Strategy for Higher Education. Retrieved July 1, 2016 from https://www.cisco.com/web/IN/solutions/strategy/assets/pdf/cloud_101_higher_education_wp.pdf

March, V., Gu, Y., Leonardi, E., Goh, G., Kirchberg, M., & Lee, B. S. (2011). μcloud: Towards a new paradigm of rich mobile applications. *Procedia Computer Science*, 5, 618–624. doi:10.1016/j.procs.2011.07.080

Dean, J., & Ghemawat, S. (2008). Map Reduce: Simplified Data Processing on Large Clusters. *Communications of the ACM*, 51. Retrieved on July 1, 2016 from http://dl.acm.org/citation.cfm?id=1327492

Hinamahgul, R. (2015). Cloud computing on the rise in Pakistan. *Thenews.com*. Retrieved on July 1, 2016 from http://www.thenews.com.pk/print/53809-cloud-computing-on-the-rise-in-pakistan

Marinelli, E. (2009). Cloud Computing on Mobile Devices using MapReduce [Master Thesis Draft]. Computer Science Dept., Carnegie Mellon University (CMU).

Mascolo, C. (2010). The power of mobile computing in a social era. *IEEE Internet Computing*, 14(6), 76–79. doi:10.1109/MIC.2010.150

Mircea, M., & Andreescu, A. (2011). Using Cloud Computing in Higher Education: A Strategy to Improve Agility. *Communications of the IBIMA*. Retrieved July 1, 2016 from http://www.ibimapublishing.com/journals/CIBIMA/cibima.html doi:10.5171/2011.875547

Fernando, N., Loke, S. W., & Rahayu, W. (2013). Mobile cloud computing: A survey. *Future Generation Computer Systems*, 29(1), 84–106. doi:10.1016/j.future.2012.05.023

Prerez, S. (2009). Why cloud computing is the future of mobile. Retrieved from http://www.readwriteweb.com

Rahul, M., & Shivaji, D. M. (2013). Cloud Based Technology In Higher Education: A Need of the Day. *ASM's International E-Journal of Ongoing Research in Management and IT*.

Rehman, M. S., & Sakr, M. F. (2010). Teaching the Cloud, Global Engineering Education. *Paper presented at the Learning Environments and Ecosystems in Engineering Education Conference*. Retrieved July 1, 2016 from https://www.researchgate.net/publication/224238671_Teaching_the_cloud_-_experiences_in_designing_and_teaching_an_undergraduate-level_course_in_cloud_computing_at_the_Carnegie_Mellon_University_in_Qatar

Saidhbi, S. (2012). A Cloud Computing Framework for Ethiopian Higher Education Institutions. *IOSR Journal of Computer Engineering*, *6*(6), 1-9. Retrieved July 1, 2016 from www.iosrjournals.org

Sanaei, S. A. Z., Gani, A., & Khokhar, R. H. (2012). Tripod of requirements in horizontal heterogeneous mobile cloud computing. *Proceedings of the 1st International Conference on Computing, Information Systems, and Communications*.

Svinicki, M. D., & McKeachie, W. (2011). *Teaching Tips: Strategies, Research, and Theory for College and University teachers* (13th ed.). Belmont, CA: Wadsworth.

Umair, S., Muneer, U., Zahoor, M. N., & Malik, A. W. (2015). Mobile computing: issues and challenges. *Paper presented at the 12th International Conference on High-capacity Optical Networks and Enabling/Emerging Technologies*, Islamabad Pakistan. Retrieved July 6, 2016 from http://ieeexplore.ieee.org/xpls/abs_all.jsp?arnumber=7395438

White, T. (2019). Hadoop, the Definitive Guide. O Reilly Media. Retrieved on July 1, 2016 from https://www.iteblog.com/downloads/OReilly.Hadoop.The.Definitive.Guide.4th.Edition.2015.3.pdf

Wyld, D. C. (2009). Moving to the cloud: An Introduction to Cloud Computing in Government. IBM Center for The Business of Government. Retrieved July 1, 2016 from http://faculty.cbpp.uaa.alaska.edu/afgjp/padm601%20fall%202010/Moving%20to%20the%20Cloud.pdf

ADDITIONAL READING

Chun, S. I. B.-G., Maniatis, P., & Naik, M. (2010). Clonecloud: boosting mobile device applications through cloud clone execution. arXiv:1009.3088

Cocking, L. (2012). The Future of Mobile Cloud Infrastructure. Retrieved from http://www.guardtime.com/2012/08/13/the-future-of mobile cloud-infrastructure/

Cuervo, A. B. E., Cho, D.-k., Wolman, A., Saroiu, S., Chandra, R., & Bahl, P. (2010). Maui: making smartphones last longer with code offload. *Proceedings of the 8th international conference on Mobile systems, applications, and services* (pp. 49–62). doi:10.1145/1814433.1814441

Cuervo, A. B. E., Cho, D.-k., Wolman, A., Saroiu, S., Chandra, R., & Bahl, P. (2010).Making smartphones last longer with code offload. *Proceedings of the 8th international conference on Mobile systems, applications, and services* (pp. 49–62).

Kovachev, D., Cao, Y., & Klamma, R. (2009). Mobile Cloud Computing: A Comparison of Application Models. Middleware Springer.

Pocatilu, P., Alecu, F., & Vetrici, M. (2009). Using Cloud Computing for E-Learning Systems. In *Recent Advances on Data Networks, Communications, Computers*. Retrieved July 1, 2016 from http://www.wseas.us/elibrary/conferences/2009/baltimore/DNCOCO/DNCOCO-06.pdf

Samir, T. (2014). The Need for Strategic Planning toward Adopting Cloud Computing in Higher Education. *Paper presented at the International Journal of Information and Communication Technology Research*. Retrieved July 1, 2016 from http://esjournals.org/journaloftechnology/archive/vol4no7/vol4no7_1.pdf

Sheelvant, R. (2009). *10 Things to Know about Cloud Computing Strategy*. IT Strategy.

Spínola, M. (2009). An Essential Guide to Possibilities and Risks of Cloud Computing. Retrieved July 1, 2016 from http://www.mariaspinola.com

Suryawanshi, K., & Narkehde, S. (2012). A Study of Green ICT and Cloud Computing Implementation at Higher Technical Education Institution. *International Journal of Advanced Research in Computer Engineering & Technology*, *1*(8). Retrieved July 1, 2016 from http://ijarcet.org/wp-content/uploads/IJARCET-VOL-1-ISSUE-8-377-382.pdf

Tout, S., & Lawver, G. (2009). Cloud Computing and its Security in Higher Education. *Proc. of ISECON*. Retrieved July 1, 2016 from http://proc.isecon.org/2009/2314/ISECON

Umair, S., Muneer, U., Zahoor, M. N., & Malik, A. W. (2015). Mobile computing: issues and challenges. *Paper presented at the 12th International Conference on High-capacity Optical Networks and Enabling/Emerging Technologies (HONET)*, Islamabad, Pakistan. Retrieved July 6, 2016 from http://ieeexplore.ieee.org/xpls/abs_all.jsp?arnumber=7395438

Umair, S., Muneer, U., Zahoor, M. N., & Malik, A. W. (2016). Mobile Cloud Computing Future Trends and Opportunities. In *Managing and Processing Big Data in Cloud Computing* (pp. 105-120). Hershey, PA: IGI Global.

Wyld, D. C. (2009). Cloud Computing 101: Universities are Migrating to The Cloud for Functionality and Savings. Computer Sight. Retrieved July 1, 2016 from http://computersight.com/programming/cloud-computing-101-universities-aremigrating-to-thecloud- for-functionality-and-savings/

KEY TERMS AND DEFINITIONS

Cloud Computing (CC): Cloud computing is a type of Internet-based computing that provides shared computer processing resources and data to computers and other devices on demand.

Distributed Computing (DC): A field of computer sciences in which components are located on computer in a network form all work together to achieve a common goal.

E-Learning: Learning conducted via electronic media especially internet.

Higher Education (HE): Higher education is an optional final stage of formal learning that occurs after secondary provided by a university. Higher education includes teaching, research, and exacting applied work.

Higher Education Institution (HEI): Higher education institutions include traditional universities and profession-oriented institutions.

Information Technology (IT): The application of computers and internet to store, retrieve, transmit, and manipulate data, or information often in the context of a business or other enterprise.

Infrastructure as a Service (IaaS): Virtualized computing resources available over the internet is the responsibility of infrastructure as a service.

Operating System (OS): Computer software that controls execution of computer programs and may provide various services.

Personal Computer (PC): A small digital computer based on a microprocessor and designed to be used by one person at a time.

Platform as a Service (PaaS): Platform as a service permits the clients to create, run and deal with their applications.

Software as a Service (SaaS): Software as a service is centrally hosted in which software is accredited on subscription basis.

Chapter 5
Computational Linguistic Distances and Big Data:
Optimising the Speech Recognition Systems

Krishnaveer Abhishek Challa
Andhra University, India

Jawahar Annabattula
K. L. University, India

ABSTRACT

Linguistic distance has always been an inter-language issue, but English being a interwoven cluster of rhyming words, homophones, tenses etc., has turned linguistic distance into an intra-language unit to measure the similarity of sounds. In many theoretical and applied areas of computational linguistics i.e., Big Data, researchers operate with a notion of linguistic distance or, conversely, linguistic similarity has become the means to optimise speech recognition systems. The present research paper focuses on the mentioned lines as an attempt to turn the existing systems from delivering good performance to perfect performance, especially in the area of Big Data.

INTRODUCTION

Linguistic distance is how different one language or dialect is from another. Although there is no uniform approach to quantifying linguistic distance between languages, the concept is used in a variety of linguistic situations, such as learning additional languages, historical linguistics, language-based conflicts and the effects of language differences on trade. The proposed measures used for linguistic distance reflect varying understandings of the term itself. One approach is based on mutual intelligibility, i.e. the ability of speakers of one language to understand the other language. With this, the higher the linguistic distance, the lower is the level of mutual intelligibility (Chiswick & Miller, 2005).

DOI: 10.4018/978-1-5225-2947-7.ch005

Copyright © 2018, IGI Global. Copying or distributing in print or electronic forms without written permission of IGI Global is prohibited.

The quest among linguists for a scalar measure of linguistic distance has been in vain. There is no yardstick for measuring distances between or among languages, as there is for the geographic distance between countries (e.g., miles). This arises because of the complexity of languages, which differ by vocabulary, grammar, syntax, written form, etc. The distance between two languages may also depend on whether it is in the written or spoken form. For example, the written form of Chinese does not vary among the regions of China, but the spoken languages differ sharply. Alternatively, two languages that may be close in the spoken form may differ more sharply in the written form (for example, if they use different alphabets, as in the case of German and Yiddish).

Perhaps the way to address the distance between languages is not through language trees which trace the evolution of languages, but by asking a simpler question: How difficult is it for individuals who know language A to learn languages B1 through Bi, where there are 'i' other languages. If it is more difficult to learn language B1, than it is to learn language B2, it can be said that language B1 is more "distant" from A than language B2. Language B3 may be as difficult to learn as is language B1 for a language A speaker, but that does not mean that language B3 is close to language B1. Indeed, it may be further from B1 than it is from A.

Linguistic distance is a concept that seeks to measure the degree of difference between two languages. Since the linguistic distances between languages are as different and variable as the languages themselves, such a concept cannot be accurately applied in a scientifically precise manner. This concept is important due to the increase in globalization, which has led to international trade between business concerns from different countries with different languages and dialects. It is also relevant as a tool to measure the ability of immigrants learning a new language that is different from their mother tongue. This is because the more removed one language is from another; the more difficult it will be for the immigrant to adapt to the new language. This also has big applications in the field of Computational Linguistics (CL).

Linguistic distance can be measured by measuring the mutual intelligibility of the language to the speakers. Mutual intelligibility determines how easy or difficult it will be for the speakers to grasp the fundamentals of the new language. This may be facilitated by the sharing of some common words or the similarity in the arrangement of grammatical and lexical forms. For instance, different territories or countries may speak the same basic language with only some minor or major differences in intonation, meaning of words, and the application of the language in general.

American and British English, for example, are mostly related with only a few easily surmountable variations. The linguistic distance between the methods of speaking the language is very small. On the other hand, Irish brogue and Cockney accent might prove to be a greater challenge for an American listener even though they are still variations of the same language. For these, the linguistic distance is more than that of British English. Even at that, learning to understand and speak these versions of the English language would not be as challenging as learning to speak Russian, since both versions are more related to American English and have a higher measure of mutual intelligibility.

The ability to easily overcome the linguistic distance between two languages is easier for children below the age of seven than it is for adults. This is due to the fact that there is a threshold in which children are still open to absorbing the fundamentals of speech patterns without encumbrance from other learned languages. Children below seven are still able to assimilate the fundamentals of a new language, master it, and speak the language without an accent better than adults. This effect can be observed in new immigrants to a country with a different language. The adults may eventually learn the new language, but the possibility of retaining accents carried over from the mother tongue is very high, especially if the linguistic distance is high. This theory can also be applied in Computation.

In many theoretical and applied areas of computational linguistics researchers operate with a notion of linguistic distance or, conversely, linguistic similarity, which is the focus of the present chapter. While many CL areas make frequent use of such notions, it has received little focused attention.

Word sense disambiguation models often work with a notion of similarity among the contexts within which word (senses) appear and MT identifies candidate lexical translation equivalents via a comparable measure of similarity; Many learning algorithms currently popular in CL, including not only supervised techniques such as memory based learning (k-nn) and support-vector machines, but also unsupervised techniques such as Kohonen maps and clustering, rely essentially on measures of similarity for their processing. Notions of similarity are often invoked in linguistic areas such as dialectology, historical linguistics, stylometry, second-language learning (as a measure of learners' proficiency), psycholinguistics (accounting for lexical "neighbourhood" effects, where neighbourhoods are defined by similarity) and even in theoretical linguistics (novel accounts of the phonological constraints on Semitic roots) (Abe & Li, 1996).

We assume that there is always a "hidden variable" in the similarity relation, so that we should always speak of similarity with respect to some property, and we suspect that there is such a plethora of measures in part because researchers are often inexplicit on this point. It is useful to tease the different notions apart. Finally, it is most intriguing to try to make a start on understanding how some of the different notions might construe as alternative realizations of a single abstract notion.

PRONUNCIATION

Pronunciation John Laver, the author of the most widely used textbook in phonetics, claimed that "one of the most basic concepts in phonetics, and one of the least discussed, is that of phonetic similarity [boldface in original, JN & EH]" (Laver, 1994, p. 391), justifying the attention the workshop pays to it. Laver goes on to sketch the work that has been done on phonetic similarity, or, more exactly, phonetic distance, in particular, the empirical derivation of confusion matrices, which indicate the likelihood with which people or speech recognition systems confusion one sound for another. Miller & Nicely (1955) founded this approach with studies of how humans confused some sounds more readily than others. Although "confusability" is a reasonable reflection of phonetic similarity, it is perhaps worth noting that confusion matrices are often asymmetric, suggesting that something more complex is at play. Clark & Yallop (1995, p. 319ff) discuss this line of work further, suggesting more sophisticated analyses which aggregate confusion matrices based on segments. In addition to the phonetic interest (above), phonologists have likewise shown interest in the question of similarity, especially in recent work. Albright and Hayes (2003) have proposed a model of phonological learning which relies on "minimal generalization". The idea is that children learn e.g. rules of allomorphy on the basis not merely of rules and individual lexical exceptions (the earlier standard wisdom), but rather on the basis of slight but reliable generalizations. An example is the formation of the past tense of verbs ending in [IN], 'ing' (fling, sing, sting, spring, string) that build past tenses as 'ung' [2N]. We omit details but note that the "minimal generalization" is minimally DISTANT in pronunciation. Frisch, Pierrehumbert & Broe (2004) have also kindled an interest in segmental similarity among phonologists with their claim that syllables in Semitic languages are constrained to have unlike consonants in syllable onset and coda. Their work has not gone unchallenged (Bailey and Hahn, 2005; Hahn and Bailey, 2005), but it has certainly created further theoretical interest in phonological similarity.

There has been a great deal of attention in psycholinguistics to the problem of word recognition, and several models appeal explicitly to the "degree of phonetic similarity among the words" (Luce and Pisoni, 1998, p. 1), but most of these models employ relatively simple notions of sequence similarity and/or, e.g., the idea that distance may be operationalized by the number or replacements needed to derive one word from another—ignoring the problem of similarity among words of different lengths (Vitevitch and Luce, 1999). Perhaps more sophisticated computational models of pronunciation distance could play a role in these models in the future. Kessler (1995) showed how to employ edit distance to operationalize pronunciation difference in order to investigate dialectology more precisely, an idea which, particular, Heeringa (2004) pursued at great length. Kondrak (2002) created a variant of the dynamic programming algorithm used to compute edit distance which he used to identify cognates in historical linguistics. McMahon & McMahon (2005) include investigations of pronunciation similarity in their recent book on phylogenetic techniques in historical linguistics. Several of the contributions to this volume build on these earlier efforts or are relevant to them. Kondrak and Sherif (this volume) continue the investigation into techniques for identifying cognates, now comparing several techniques which rely solely on parameters set by the researcher to machine learning techniques which automatically optimize those parameters. They show the the machine learning techniques to be superior, in particular, techniques basic on hidden Markov models and dynamic Bayesian nets. Heeringa et al. (this volume) investigate several extensions of the fundamental edit distance algorithm for use in dialectology, including sensitivity to order and context as well syllabicity constraints, which they argue to be preferable, and length normalization and graded weighting schemes, which they argue against. Dinu & Dinu (this volume) investigate metrics on string distances which attach more importance to the initial parts of the string. They embed this insight into a scheme in which n-grams are ranked (sorted) by frequency, and the difference in the rankings is used to assay language differences. Their paper proves that difference in rankings is a proper mathematical metric. Singh (this volume) investigates the technical question of identifying languages and character encoding systems from limited amounts of text. He collects about 1, 000 or so of the most frequent n-grams of various sizes and then classifies next texts based on the similarity between the frequency distributions of the known texts with those of texts to be classified. His empirical results show "mutual cross entropy" to identify similarity most reliably, but there are several close competitors.

SYNTAX

Although there is less interest in similarity at the syntactic level among linguistic theorists, there is still one important areas of theoretical research in which it could play an important role and several interdisciplinary studies in which similarity and/or distant is absolutely crucial. Syntactic typology is an area of linguistic theory which seeks to identify syntactic features which tend to be associated with one another in all languages (Comrie, 1989; Croft, 2001). The fundamental vision is that some sorts of languages may be more similar to one another—typologically—than would first appear. Further, there are two interdisciplinary linguistic studies in which similarity and/or distance plays a great role, including similarity at the syntactic level (without, however, exclusively focusing on syntax). Language contact studies seek to identify the elements of one language which have been adopted in a second in a situation in which two or more languages are used in the same community (Thomason and Kaufmann, 1988; van Coetsem, 1988). Naturally, these may be non-syntactic, but syntactic contamination is a central concept which is recognized in contaminated varieties which have become more similar to the languages which are the source of contamination. Essentially, the same phenomenon is studied in second-language learning, in which syntactic patterns from a dominant, usually first, language is imposed on a second. Here the focus is on the psychology of the individual language user as opposed to the collective habits of the language community. Nerbonne and Wiersma (this volume) collect frequency distributions of part-of-speech (POS) trigrams and explore simple measures of distance between these. They approach issues of statistical significance using permutation tests, which requires attention to tricky issues of normalization between the frequency distributions. Homola & Kubon (this volume) join Nerbonne ˇ and Wiersma in advocating a surface-oriented measure of syntactic difference, but base their measure on dependency trees rather than POS tags, a more abstract level of analysis. From there they propose an analogue to edit distance to gauge the degree of difference. The difference between two tree is the sum of the costs of the tree-editing operations needed to obtain one tree from another (Noetzel and Selkow, 1999). Emms (this volume) concentrates on applications of the notion 'tree similarity' in particular in order to identify text which is syntactically similar to questions and which may therefore be expected to constitute an answer to the question. He is able to show that the tree-distance measure outperforms sequence distance measures, at least if lexical information is also emphasized. Kubler (this volume) uses the similarity measure in memory-based learning to parse. This is a surprising approach, since memory-based techniques are normally used in classification tasks where the target is one of a small number of potential classifications. In parsing, the targets may be arbitrarily complex, so a key step is select an initial structure in a memory-based way, and then to adapt it further. In this paper Kubler first applies chunking to the sentence to be parsed and selects an initial parse based on chunk similarity.

SEMANTICS

While similarity as such has not been a prominent term in theoretical and computational research on natural language semantics, the study of LEXICAL SEMANTICS, which attempts to identify regularities of and systematic relations among word meanings, is more often than not predicated on an implicit notion of 'semantic similarity'. Research on the lexical semantics of verbs tries to identify verb classes whose members exhibit similar syntactic and semantic behavior. In logic-based theories of word meaning (e.g., Vendler, 1967 and Dowty, 1979), verb classes are identified by similarity patterns of inference, while Levin's (1993) study of English verb classes demonstrates that similarities of word meanings for verbs can be gleaned from their syntactic behavior, in particular from their ability or inability to participate in diatheses, i.e. patterns of argument alternations. With the increasing availability of large electronic corpora, recent computational research on word meaning has focused on capturing the notion of 'context similarity' of words. Such studies follow the empiricist approach to word meaning summarized best in the famous dictum of the British linguist J.R. Firth: "You shall know a word by the company it keeps." (Firth, in Palmer, 1968, p. 11) Context similarity has been used as a means of extracting collocations from corpora, e.g. by Church & Hanks (1990) and by Dunning (1993), of identifying word senses, e.g. by Yarowski (1995) and by Schutze (1998), of clustering verb classes, e.g. by Schulte im Walde (2003), and of inducing selectional restrictions of verbs, e.g. by Resnik (1993), by Abe & Li (1996), by Rooth et al. (1999) and by Wagner (2004). A third approach to lexical semantics, developed by linguists and by cognitive psychologists, primarily relies on the intuition of lexicographers for capturing word meanings, but is also informed by corpus evidence for determining word usage and word senses. This type of approach has led to two highly valued semantic resources: the Princeton WordNet (Fellbaum, 1998) and the Berkeley Framenet (Baker et al., 1998). While originally developed for English, both approaches have been successfully generalized to other languages. The three approaches to word meaning discussed above try to capture different aspects of the notion of semantic similarity, all of which are highly relevant for current and future research in computational linguistics. In fact, the five papers that discuss issues of semantic similarity in the present volume build on insights from these three frameworks or address open research questions posed by these frameworks. Zesch and Gurevych (this volume) discuss how measures of semantic similarity—and more generally: semantic relatedness—can be obtained by similarity judgments of informants who are presented with word pairs and who, for each pair, are asked to rate the degree of semantic relatedness on a predefined scale. Such similarity judgments can provide important empirical evidence for taxonomic models of word meanings such as wordnets, which thus far rely mostly on expert knowledge of lexicographers. To this end, Zesch and Gurevych propose a corpus-based system that supports fast development of relevant data sets for large subject domains. St-Jacques and Barriere (this volume) review ` and contrast different philosophical and psychological models for capturing the notion of semantic similarity and different mathematical models for measuring semantic distance. They draw attention to the fact that, depending on which underlying models are in use, different notions of semantic similarity emerge and conjecture that different similarity metrics may be needed for different NLP tasks. Dagan (this volume) also explores the idea that different notions of semantic similarity are needed when dealing with semantic disambiguation and language modeling tasks on the one hand and with applications such as information extraction, summarization, and information retrieval on the other hand. Dridan and Bond (this volume) and Hachey (this volume) both consider semantic similarity from an application-oriented perspective. Dridan and Bond employ the framework of robust minimal recursion semantics in order to obtain a more adequate measure of sentence similarity than can be obtained by word-overlap metrics for bag-of-words representations of sentences. They show that such a more fine-grained measure, which is based on compact representations of predicate-logic, yields better performance for paraphrase detection as well as for sentence selection in question-answering tasks than simple word-overlap metrics. Hachey considers an automatic content extraction (ACE) task, a particular subtask of information extraction. He demonstrates that representations based on term cooccurrence outperform representations based on term-by-document matrices for the task of identifying relationships between named objects in texts.

REFERENCES

Abe, N., & Li, H. (1996). Learning word association norms using tree cut pair models. *Proceedings of 13th International Conference on Machine Learning*, Bari, Italy.

Albright, A., & Hayes, B. (2003). Rules vs. analogy in English past tenses: A computational/experimental study. *Cognition*, *90*(2), 119–161. doi:10.1016/S0010-0277(03)00146-X PMID:14599751

Bailey, T. M., & Hahn, U. (2005). Phoneme Similarity and Confusability. *Journal of Memory and Language*, *52*(3), 339–362. doi:10.1016/j.jml.2004.12.003

Baker, C. F., Fillmore, C. J., & Lowe, J. B. (1998). The Berkeley FrameNet project. In C. Boitet, & P. Whitelock (Eds.), *Proceedings of the Thirty-Sixth Annual Meeting of the Association for Computational Linguistics and Seventeenth International Conference on Computational Linguistics*, San Francisco, California (pp. 86–90). Morgan Kaufmann Publishers.

Chiswick, B. R., & Miller, P. W. (2005). Linguistic Distance: A Quantitative Measure of the Distance Between English and Other Languages. *Journal of Multilingual and Multicultural Development*, *26*(1), 1–11. doi:10.1080/14790710508668395

Church, K. W., & Hanks, P. (1990). Word association norms, mutual information, and lexicography. *Computational Linguistics*, *16*(1), 22–29.

Clark, J., & Yallop, C. (1995). *An Introduction to Phonetics and Phonology*. Oxford: Blackwell.

Comrie, B. (1989). *Language Universals and Linguistic Typology: Syntax and Morphology*. Oxford: Basil Blackwell.

Croft, W. (2001). *Radical Construction Grammar: Syntactic Theory in Typological Perspective*. Oxford: Oxford University Press. doi:10.1093/acprof:oso/9780198299554.001.0001

Dowty, D. (1979). *Word Meaning and Montague Grammar*. Dordrecht: Reidel. doi:10.1007/978-94-009-9473-7

Dunning, T. (1993). Accurate methods for the statistics of surprise and coincidence. *Computational Linguistics*, *19*(1), 61–74.

F. Palmer (Ed.) (1968). Studies in Linguistic Analysis 1930-1955. Harlow: Longman.

Fellbaum, C. (1998). *WordNet: An Electronic Lexical Database*. MIT Press.

Frisch, S. A., Pierrehumbert, J. B., & Broe, M. B. (2004). Similarity Avoidance and the OCP. *Natural Language and Linguistic Theory*, *22*(1), 179–228. doi:10.1023/B:NALA.0000005557.78535.3c

Hahn, U., & Bailey, T. M. (2005). What Makes Words Sound Similar? *Cognition*, *97*(3), 227–267. doi:10.1016/j.cognition.2004.09.006 PMID:16260261

Heeringa, W. (2004). Measuring Dialect Pronunciation Differences using Levenshtein Distance [Ph.D. thesis]. Rijksuniversiteit Groningen.

Kessler, B. (1995). Computational dialectology in Irish Gaelic. Proc. of the European ACL, Dublin (pp. 60–67). doi:10.3115/976973.976983

Kondrak, G. (2002). Algorithms for Language Reconstruction [Ph.D. thesis]. University of Toronto.

Laver, J. (1994). *Principles of Phonetics*. Cambridge: Cambridge University Press. doi:10.1017/CBO9781139166621

Lebart, L., & Rajman, M. (2000). Computing similarity. In R. Dale, H. Moisl, & H. Somers (Eds.), *Handbook of Natural Language Processing* (pp. 477–505). Basel: Dekker.

Levin, B. (1993). *English Verb Classes and Alternations: a Preliminary Investigation*. Chicago, London: University of Chicago Press.

Luce, P. A., & Pisoni, D. B. (1998). Recognizing spoken words: The neighborhood activation model. *Ear and Hearing*, *19*(1), 1–36. doi:10.1097/00003446-199802000-00001 PMID:9504270

McMahon, A., & McMahon, R. (2005). *Language Classification by the Numbers*. Oxford: Oxford University Press.

Miller, G. A., & Nicely, P. E. (1955). An Analysis of Perceptual Confusions Among Some English Consonants. *The Journal of the Acoustical Society of America*, 27(2), 338–352. doi:10.1121/1.1907526

Noetzel, A. S., & Selkow, S. M. (1999). An analysis of the general tree-editing problem. In D. Sankoff and J. Kruskal (Eds.), Time Warps, String Edits and Macromolecules: The Theory and Practice of Sequence Comparison (pp. 237–252).

Resnik, P. S. (1993). Selection and Information: A Class-Based Approach to Lexical Relationships [Ph.D. thesis]. University of Pennsylvania.

Rooth, M., Riezler, S., Prescher, D., Carroll, G., & Beil, F. (1999). Inducing an semantically annotated lexicon via em-based clustering. *Proceedings of the 37th Annual Meeting of the Association for Computational Linguistics*, Maryland. doi:10.3115/1034678.1034703

Schulte im Walde, S. (2003). Experiments on the Automatic Induction of German Semantic Verb Classes [Ph.D. thesis]. *AIMS Report*, 9(2).

Schutze, H. (1998). Automatic word sense discrimination. *Computational Linguistics*, 24(1), 97–123.

Thomason, S., & Kaufmann, T. (1988). *Language Contact, Creolization, and Genetic Linguistics*. Berkeley: University of California Press.

van Coetsem, F. (1988). *Loan Phonology and the Two Transfer Types in Language Contact*. Dordrech: Foris Publications.

Vendler, Z. (1967). *Linguistics in Philosophy*. Ithaca, NY: Cornell University Press.

Vitevitch, M. S., & Luce, P. A. (1999). Probabilistic Phonotactics and Neighborhood Activation in Spoken Word Recognition. *Journal of Memory and Language*, 40(3), 374–408. doi:10.1006/jmla.1998.2618

Wagner, A. (2004). Learning Thematic Role Relations for Lexical Semantic Nets [Ph.D. thesis]. Universitat Tubingen.

Yarowsky, D. (1995). Unsupervised word sense disambiguation rivaling supervised methods. *Proceedings of 33rd Annual Meeting of the Association for Computational Linguistics*, Cambridge, MA (pp. 189–196). doi:10.3115/981658.981684

Chapter 6
Big Data in Mobile Commerce:
Customer Relationship Management

Muhammad Anshari
Universiti Brunei Darussalam, Brunei

Syamimi Ariff Lim
Universiti Brunei Darussalam, Brunei

ABSTRACT

The purpose of this chapter is to identify the opportunities of big data application that allows Customer Relationship Management (CRM) strategy to gain deeper insights into customer retention and let the businesses make innovation in term of sales, service, and marketing. This chapter is motivated from the concept of big data in CRM by proposing a conceptual model to address mobile commerce in an organization. It examines the progress of big data in creating value for m-commerce. Researchers employed thematic literature analysis and discussed broader issues related to customer behavior in using smartphone and its internet habit activities. Despite the limitation of the study, CRM with big data remains an important area for future research in mobile commerce setting.

INTRODUCTION

Smart mobile devices and smartphone have made mobile commerce (m-commerce) spread very quickly, creating a revolution in e-business. The search costs in e-commerce puts business under increased price competition, resulting in converging prices and ultimately eliminating any extraordinary profits (Bakos, 1997; Benjamin and Wigand, 1995). M-commerce will be a competitive necessity to ensure business survivability and prosperity. Business organizations collect large amount of transactional data, capturing a large amount of information about their customers, suppliers, and operations. Millions of networked sensors are being embedded in the smart mobile devices that generate data in the age of big data (Anshari & Alas, 2015). Organizations activities have been relying on data accuracy and reliability, whether it is census data, climate data, satellite images, transport data, health data, research data, logistic data, energy consumption data, and any data relates to economic transactions that can stimulate innovation on new business opportunities, accelerate business transactions, and produce knowledge sharing across the users.

DOI: 10.4018/978-1-5225-2947-7.ch006

Copyright © 2018, IGI Global. Copying or distributing in print or electronic forms without written permission of IGI Global is prohibited.

In addition, business organizations generate customer relationship management (CRM) data to help them managing their customers. Customers' data have become a critical asset for any organization similar to their other recourses such financial, raw materials, and human capital including massive data from smartphone activities. Big data optimizes capabilities process, high growth, and diversified data that generate value for any organizations. A good customer relationship creates better understanding and trust, which in turn satisfy customers and generate loyalty (Richard and Ronald, 2008; Anshari et al., 2012). In contrast, failure managing a good customer relationship affects customers' distrust and dissatisfaction that may risk the survivability of the organization. CRM aims to create loyalty and awareness of their products or services and organization should realize the expectations of customers in services poses a challenge to fulfil high customers' expectations.

Smart mobile devices have become important big data source and enabled mobile CRM for organization. Customers have become more dependent on a smartphone and they use smartphone due to habitual. They check smartphone repeatedly for a purpose, unconsciously scroll just to recheck text messages or email, have phone in hand all the time, check phone before go to bed are examples of smartphone habit. This can be such as being unaware of their surroundings. People would spend more time conversing on through online instead of having a face to face conversation. Some applications that offers a convenient to order varieties of items. For instance, people are utilizing social media applications also promoting their online business where previously it could actually be done without the smartphone. The study presents how customers' smartphone habit can become important CRM strategies in big data scenario.

Organization seeks to create long lasting values by embracing the opportunities related to the usability of the important resources, which is data and information. This study focuses on service-oriented sustainability through CRM in response to the massive adoption of smartphone among users and how it generates big data for CRM analysis. The study is aimed to format a model on next generation of CRM in supporting m-commerce that can enhance customers' experiences in response to the big data era. Even though, the study is conceptual approach, the discussions may trigger other researchers to expand into different context and scenarios. Big data is used to analyses the next phenomenon of CRM due to the changing of business environment mainly caused by big data deployment. The structure of this report presents on the view of smartphone habit from literatures including the background of theories in Section 2. Section 3 shows methodology followed by discussion in Section 4. Section 5 is conclusion.

BACKGROUND

Mobile Commerce

It is rare nowadays to go to places where only a few people are not looking at their smartphones. Usually, especially in public places such as coffee shops are where almost everyone would be preoccupied with their smartphones (BoHyun, 2013). Smartphones have the capability of downloading applications as such WhatsApp, Instagram, Twitter, applications that could edit photos or videos and so on. However, with these applications that exist in the Smartphones could make the people become addicted to the Social Medias, predominantly the young adults. The number of adolescents owning phones increment.

Messaging has turned into a more agreeable and favored correspondence between today's young adults, permitting teenagers the capacity to control what they compose before sending it. Getting to the Internet has additionally gotten to be well known on smartphones (Soun, 2014). With the growth of new coffee shops has made more people wanting to go out more to these cafes simply because they also have Wi-Fi installed. These cafes usually have a vintage ambiance to it, looking back at current fashion among youngsters and worldwide it is indeed the 'in-thing' at this era. This makes people want to spend on their smartphones longer as they tend to capture the beautiful decorated cafes, spend hours using the café's Wi-Fi and share stories among friends through WhatsApp or Telegram even though they would be actually be sitting next to one another. The average person looks at their phone 150 times a day, or once every six-and-a-half minutes of every waking hour (Spencer, 2013), Especially since now smartphones are equipped with the access to YouTube, Safari, Google Chrome, Instagram and even comes with a dictionary app. A smartphone is everything we need in one device. These are the type of smartphones, we have now, they are 'smart' in a way they are programmed more advanced compared to what it used to be. Almost 90% of the worldwide population spend their time text messaging (Nielsen, 2013).

Smartphones like any other technology have its own pros and cons where these are the most discussed topics among society currently. The usage and ownership of smartphones or mobile phones has a drastic impact, especially among the age group of 16-64 years old (Nielsen, 2013). The negative impacts include less physical interaction among people, whereas we tend to talk over text messages than seeing someone in person. Another impact is, the less communication among family members as each member has their own smartphones and family quality time is decreased especially during the weekends. Smartphones get in the way of our relationships, making it impossible for us to wholeheartedly devote our attention to the present moment (Alingod, 2013).

However, there are also positive impacts for smartphones such as smartphones are considered as a single device, they provide several sources of information. Mainly internet connection which we all need and human interaction has been made easier with the help of applications such as Skype or WhatsApp which are not only accessible by personal computers only but also can be accessed just by using smartphones (Gil, Berlanga, and Molina, 2012). Furthermore, another advantage is how smartphones make it easier for us to organize ourselves as is equipped with daily planner, calendar, reminders and even Microsoft applications can be downloaded into our smartphones and we could easily do our presentations and save important documents in it. In other words, a smartphone has a high level of productivity. With a smartphone, you are able to do so many things faster and more efficiently than you could have without one (Dollard, 2010). In summary, smartphones are now taking over people's life where people are now being dependent on their phones. Therefore, it is important to know how critical it is up to the point where customers deliberately produce big data that is beneficial for private or public sectors.

Customer Relationship Management

The roles of Customer Relationship Management (CRM) in managing customers and improving services to them have been well-recorded in business literatures. Organization uses CRM as a tool to serve customers better (Low & Anshari, 2013). Business takes advantage of the recent development in smart mobile technology embracing mobile commerce (m-commerce). The development of smart mobile devices offer new opportunities for business organizations to create more sophisticated, value added, and convenience services. Convenience means to perform task in an uncomplicated way without having to use so much energy. Customers use smartphones to get information, make transaction and ask services easily just from the access of the Web or Apps. These new mobile services can provide a way to deliver various kinds of information to the customers or to work as an interaction channel between service provider and customer (Alahuhta, Helaakoski, & Smirnov, 2005). Smartphones offer a lot that customers do not need to go to places to make payments. They can just sit on their couch doing it. Rather than queuing in line waiting to make payments, smartphones make it easier and save time.

By using Mobile CRM, CRM team can keep their entire to-do list, all those reminders in their phones. Mobile CRM helps marketing teams to keep on track of what they need to get done. Customer service teams can just gain information in few seconds without having to flip the pages of the books or manuals. CRM teams have been using mobile CRM to have real time access regardless of their location for customer service, marketing orientation, and accelerate sale. Adoption of mobile CRM with customer value at the core of any businesses' strategy will help in developing better relationships with customers (Grandhi & Chugh, 2012). Customers expect sales team coming to them, so access of full set of information in the field will be helpful. CRM teams need immediate access to product information, promotion, customer's history, and contact details to close the sales. These mobile data are considered as the asset and big data source for organization because it provides the key insights to the needs of customers, forecasting trends of customers' behavior, progressively marketing to match with customers varied taste and preferences as well as providing a performance metrics used to evaluate the effectiveness in meeting customers' needs (Economist, 2010). With the data collected can then be used by mobile CRM to take advantage to market the products and services, improve revenue and their brand awareness, but also to do future predictions of customer preferences and behavior.

Big Data and Business Landscape

The massive amount of data is growing quickly, it is expected that by 2020 there will be more than 16 zettabytes of useful data (16 Trillion GB), which implies growth of 236% per year from 2013 to 2020 (Turner et al., 2014). Big data becomes popular terms in business sectors, due to its benefits for high volume, velocity and variety that produce better forecasting, innovative forms of information processing, and enhanced insight and decision-making (Laney, 2012). The growth in big data is not only because a growing number of smartphone users, but also trigger by other smart mobile devices or pervasive computing abilities that is multiplying quickly (Anshari, Alas, Guan, 2015). Big data can be generated either by people or by machines like GPS, digital pictures and videos from CCTV, sensors gathering climate information, satellite images, and transaction records. For instance, smart meters collect and transmit real-time data on energy usage (OECD, 2012a), and smart automobiles are able to transmit real-time data on the state of the car's components and environment (OECD, 2012b). Many of these smart mobile devices are based on sensor or actuators that sense and able to interact with their users over mobile networks namely pervasive computing. Pervasive computing exchanges data and interact with people or computers and other smart devices. More than 30 million interconnected sensors through pervasive computing are now deployed worldwide, in areas such as security, health care, the environment, transport systems or energy control systems, and their numbers are growing by around 30% a year (MGI, 2011).

From the whole data digital universe (more than 13,000 Exabytes), it is predicted there will be one third having big data value if it is analysed. Not all data is useful for big data analytics, however, some data types are important for analysis, such as a surveillance camera, embedded device, pervasive computing, social media, consumer images (IDC, 2012). Organization with CRM needs to consider the emerging big data management, analytics, tools, and technologies in managing strategic plan of customer relations.

The study revealed that 92% of the executives that use big data were satisfied with the results by increasing the customer relationship 63%, the development of the products by 58%, and improving operations by 56% (Jobidon, 2014). Big data lies valuable patterns and information that previously require amount of work and cost to extract them (Dumbill, 2012). Adopting big data can bring about several benefits to e-commerce as it provides a better understanding into customer behaviour and industry trends. It contributes to a more accurate decisions as to improve customer retention, marketing and every aspects of business (Ghandour, 2015). Process of extracting big data is known as big data analytics. Small and larger organizations have adopted big data analytics as it plays a vital role in e-commerce. Big data analytics is able to disclose understandings hidden previously by data too costly to process, such as peer influence among customers revealed by analysing customers' transactions, social and geographical data (Syed et al., 2013; Ghandour, 2015).

Data as Asset

The use of smartphones has increased significantly worldwide which is being driven by more affordable prices, as well as by the large and increasingly tech-savvy youth population. With the recent trends in social networks, mobile technology, and cloud computing technology, customers with smartphone has gained more bargaining power as they can compare prices and services from their suppliers (Strachan, 2012). The study of big data relates to the smartphone habits of customers in m-commerce activities was deemed worthwhile.

It is important for business to consider strategies to survive. Changes may take place in the business because the demands of interested customers must be addressed to make business at the competitive state. Businesses are dependent on the availability for resources. They need to develop strategies that will allow them to acquire these resources, and modern business organization treats data as one of the resource or organization's asset. M-commerce generates real time data that can be used to increase productivity, gains competitive advantage and promptness in decision making based on big data analytics. Based on the literature review, we propose a model that can be used as a strategy for organization to respond customer preference. The model operates in the domains of CRM, big data, and smartphone usage to prevail customers' acceptance. Figure 1 depicts the model as a strategic tool for organization in accommodating big data in m-commerce's context. It offers holistic views in identifying possible mechanisms that might account for ways in which organizations reshape the strategy to prevail the changes.

Firstly, CRM with big data produces big data analytic. Data analytic produces pattern and trends of customers. Patterns and trends are derived from big data sources which is structured and unstructured sources. Unstructured sources can be video, audio, pictures, and RFID data. Structured data sources can be social network analytics, smartphone log activities, and online activities. Those sources lead to create values for m-commerce activities into sales, services, and marketing. For instance, organization needs to understand their asset specificity and factors that create uncertainty in delivering m-commerce. M-commerce strategy needs to overcome uncertainty by maintaining distinct market or unique market segmentations. The idea of niche and market segmentation are supported from the big data analytics, it can come up with a list of loyal customers. Personalization of service will make loyal customers are valued. While loyalty leads to lower transaction cost instead of attracting new customers.

Secondly, adopting new technology like CRM with big data in delivering m-commerce plays a critical role for creating asset specificity which escalates business operations. Indeed, the m-commerce is powerful channels for organizations to develop, enhance interactions and implement relationship practices with customers since m-commerce facilitate creativity, collaboration, sharing among users rather than just for email and retrieving information. The best part from big data analytic can come up with intelligent grouping of customers with the same interest so that the collaboration and sharing are more

Figure 1. CRM with Big Data in generating values of m-commerce
Source: Authors' Compilation, 2016.

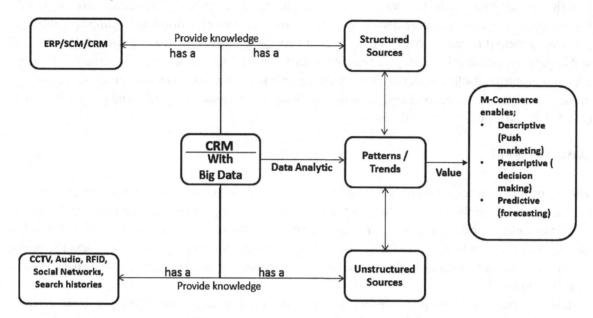

meaningful and relevant for all parties. While, many organizations adjust their marketing strategy since it affects the way customers' control the flow of data and conversation. With smartphone, customers are gaining more control over the flow of information where they have more information which come from various conversations taking place in their social networks. Service provider can utilize big data analytic to accommodate push marketing strategies to each customer the smartphone of interactions based on their conversation and interest.

Finally, CRM with big data can promote continuous innovation in providing customer services. Innovations should be directed to improve the customer experience, satisfaction through understanding the customer's needs, aligning the individual skills on the front line supported by the organization's culture, technology and processes. The model is to respond the changes in customers' preference due to smartphone habit while for the organization is to avoid market's uncertainty or maintain asset specificity. Big data plays critical role in understanding customer habits, identifying niche markets, and providing personalization of products and services. Through personalization, there are groups of customers who prefer service due to specific purposes that cannot be accomplished through a conventional marketing or sales system.

SOLUTIONS AND RECOMMENDATIONS

Value Creation

Big data in business organization offers tools and strategies in order to gain value and control over the benefits. Adopting big data in m-commerce has enabled customers more control in getting information but at the same time customers have been empowered to generate a huge amount of data and those data should be treated as an asset to understand customers' behaviour better than before. Big data can develop m-commerce's strategies in gaining competitive advantage and business values, increase customer retention and loyalty, improve sales and revenues of the companies (Hea et al., 2013). Big data will help creating value in each activity that will be demanded by customers; making those values appreciated by customers who will attract them into becoming loyal customers. Customer loyalty is about attracting the right customers, getting them to buy, buy often, buy in higher quantities, and spread the good news to bring more customers.

In addition, big data paves way in organizing data as an asset for organization just and enabling business to better understand from multitude resources in making decision that can lead to the accomplishment in the organization's performance. For instance, tracking customers' behavior and providing the customers offers and discounts can in turn maximizes their sales and profits. It assists m-commerce in promoting their products and services by catching customers' attention through their smartphone.

Personalization of Service

Personalization through big data in m-commerce aims to facilitate to facilitate personalized shopping experience with the interactive and rich content displays hence improving brand image and loyalty among customers (Valentine, 2015). Personalization in m-commerce enables users to own the data and exercise control over that data so that they can customize what they need and need not. Company supplies subscribers' product subscriptions service to the customers' smartphone regularly according to customers' own preference and thus it helps business to enhance customer loyalty. For instance, many e-commerce sites monitor the cookies and users click stream browser to recognize the patterns of the customers' shopping behavior thus offering good bargain, appropriate advertisements or discount based on their specific interests and preferences (Mosavi & Vaezipour, 2013).

Business must maintain their niche markets in m-commerce by improving their service through personalization to maintain customer loyalty. M-Commerce has become a trend in developing a new business strategies and play a significant role in the CRM transition which revolutionize on managing customers. It facilitates peer-to-peer collaboration and easy access to real time communication (Almunawar & Anshari, 2014). To sum it all in a nutshell, recent m-commerce has allowed virtual interactions, providing tools that emulate human skills and knowledge to cater to customer preferences and to match an individual's requirement.

FUTURE RESEARCH DIRECTIONS

Internet of Things (IoT) will disrupt the way organization conducting commerce. Though, IoT is still in developing stage but it will have impact to the evolution of m-commerce especially in managing relationship with customers. The massive of connected devices to internet will contribute to the complexities of multi channels interaction due to IoT. IoT will form a massive interaction from device to device (D2D), devices to customers (D2C), customer to customer (C2C), customer to organization (C2B), and organization to organization (B2B).

CONCLUSION

As the adoption of smartphone by customers increase, m-commerce have by passed many layers of marketing, services, and sales since it offers direct interaction to customers. Almost all modern business organization have their online promotions available on their smartphone. There are growing customers dependent upon smartphone whereas they are constantly checking for cheaper prices and buying their goods and services online. M-commerce in organization needs to continuously innovate in order to respond the changes of customer habit on smartphone by providing better services aiming to improve customers' satisfaction and experience. CRM with big data can focus on providing niche markets to sustain distinct market in respond to uncertainty.

REFERENCES

Alahuhta, P., Helaakoski, H., & Smirnov, A. (2005, October). Adoption of mobile services in business-case study of mobile CRM. *Proceedings of the IEEE International Conference on e-Business Engineering ICEBE '05* (pp. 531-534). IEEE. doi:10.1109/ICEBE.2005.22

Alingod, J. (2013). How smartphones could be ruining your relationship. *Live Bold and Bloom*. Retrieved from http://liveboldandbloom.com/10/relationships/how-smartphones-couldbe-ruining-your-relationship

Almunawar, M. N., & Anshari, M. (2014). Applying Transaction Cost Economy to Construct a Strategy for Travel Agents in Facing Disintermediation Threats. *Journal of Internet Commerce, Taylor & Francis, 13*(3-4), 211–232. doi:10.1080/15332861.2014.961331

Anshari, M., & Alas, Y. (2015). Smartphones Habits, Necessities, and Big Data Challenges. *The Journal of High Technology Management Research*, 26(2), 177-185. doi:10.1016/j.hitech.2015.09.005

Anshari, M., Alas, Y., & Guan, L. S. (2015). Pervasive Knowledge, Social Networks, and Cloud Computing: E-Learning 2.0. *Eurasia Journal of Mathematics. Science & Technology Education, 11*(5), 909–921. doi:10.12973/eurasia.2015.1360a

Anshari, M., Alas, Y., Yunus, N. M., Sabtu, N. I., & Hamid, M. S. (2016). Online Learning: Trends, Issues, and Challenges in Big Data Era. *Journal of E-Learning and Knowledge Society, 12*(1), 121–134.

Anshari, M., Almunawar, M.N., Low, P.K.C., & Al-Mudimigh A.S. (2012). Empowering Clients Through E-Health in Healthcare Services: Case Brunei. *International Quarterly of Community Health Education, 33*(2), 189-219. doi:10.2190/IQ.33.2.g

Bakos, J. Y. (1997). Reducing Buyer Search Costs: Implications for Electronic Marketplaces. *Management Science, 43*(12), 1676–1692. doi:10.1287/mnsc.43.12.1676

Bakos, J. Y. (1997). Reducing Buyer Search Costs: Implications for Electronic Marketplaces. *Management Science, 43*(12), 1676–1692.

Benjamin, R. I., & Wigand, R. (1995). Electronic Markets and Virtual Value Chains on the Information Superhighway. *Sloan Management Review, 36*(2), 62–72.

BoHyun. K. (2013). Chapter 1: the mobile shift. *Library Technology Reports*, 49(6), 5-8. Retrieved from https://journals.ala.org/ltr/article/view/4509/5291

Caron, A. H., & Caronia, H. (2015). Mobile communication tools as morality building devices. In *Encyclopedia of Mobile Phone Behavior* (pp. 25–45). Hershey, PA: IGI Global.

Chansanchai, A. (2011). 8 in 10 Americans depend on cellphones. *NBC News*. Retrieved from http://www.nbcnews.com/technology/8-10-americans-depend-cellphones-121536

Dumbill, E. (2012). What is big data? An introduction to the big data landscape. *O'Reilly.com*. Retrieved November 9 2015 from http://radar.oreilly.com/2012/01/what-is-big-data.html

Economist. (2010). *Data, data everywhere*. Retrieved 29 October 2015 from the Economist: http://www.economist.com/node/15557443

Ghandour, A. (n. d.). Big data driven e-commerce architecture. *International Journal of Economics, Commerce and Management*, 3(5), 940-947.

Gil, G. B., Berlanga, A., & Molina, J. M. (2012). Incontexto: Multisensor architecture to obtain people context from smartphones. *International Journal of Distributed Sensor Networks*, 15. doi:10.1155/2012/758789

Grandhi, S., & Chugh, R. (2012). Strategic Value of mobile CRM Applications: A Review of Mobile CRM at Dow Corning and DirecTV. *Proceedings of the International Conference on Innovation and Information Management* (*Vol. 36*).

Harny Abu Khair. (2013, September 17). Bru-HIMS records over 50 percent registrations. T*he Borneo Bulletin*. Retrieved from http://www.bt.com.bn/news national/2013/09/17/bru-hims-records-over-50-cent-registrations

Hea, W., Zhab, S., & Li, L. (2013). Social media competitive analysis and text mining: A case study in the Pizza industry. *International Journal of Information Management*, 33(1), 464–472. doi:10.1016/j.ijinfomgt.2013.01.001

Jobidon, P. (2014). *Using big data to enhance e-commerce*. Retrieved 12 November 2015 from http://www.bpostinternational.com/en/content/using-big-data-enhance-e-commerce

Judge, S., Floyd, K., & Jeffs, T. (2014). Using mobile devices and apps to promote young children's learning. In K. L. Heider., & M. R. Jalongo (Eds.), Young children and families in the information age: Application of technology in early childhood (pp. 117-131). Netherland: Springer.

Laney, D. (2012). The Importance of 'Big Data: A Definition. *Gartner*. Retrieved from https://www.gartner.com/doc/2057415/importance-big-data-definition

Low, K. C. P., & Anshari, M. (2013). Incorporating social customer relationship management in negotiation. *International Journal of Electronic Customer Relationship Management*, 7(3/4), 239–252. doi:10.1504/IJECRM.2013.060700

Mosavi, A., & Vaezipour, A. (2013). *Developing Effective Tools for Predictive Analytics and Informed Decisions* (tech. report). University of Tallinn.

Nielsen, A. (2013). What People Watch, Listen To and Buy. *Nielsen*. Retrieved from http://www.nielsen. com/us/en.html

Spencer, B. (2013). Mobile users can't leave their phone alone for six minutes and check it up to 150 times a day. *Daily Mail*. Retrieved from http://www.dailymail.co.uk/news/article-2276752/Mobile-users-leave-phone-minutes-check-150-times-day.html

Strachan, D. (2012). *The best new travel technology*, Retrieved 18 September 2012 from http://www. telegraph.co.uk/travel/columnists/7534231/The-best-new-travel-technology.html

Syed, A., Gillela, K., & Venugopal, C. (2013). The future revolution on Big Data. *Future*, 2(6), 2446–2451.

Turner, V., Gantz, J.F., Reinsel, D., & Minton, S. (2014, April). The Digital Universe of Opportunities: Rich Data and the Increasing Value of the Internet of Things. Report from IDC for EMC.

Zheng, Y. (Ed.), *Encyclopedia of mobile phone behavior*. Hershey, PA: IGI Global.

KEY TERMS AND DEFINITIONS

Big Data: Big data is concept and application that describes the large Volume of data with Variety type of data and Velocity of data processing to gain the Value for decision making.

Customer Relationship Management (CRM): CRM is concept, tools, technology, and strategy to manage customers' relations and interactions for the whole customer life cycles to gain customers' loyalty and satisfaction.

Smartphone: Smartphone is device that serve multiple purposes and equipped with customized software, Internet access, digital cameras, portable music players, GPS functions and many more options.

Chapter 7
Internet of Things:
Concepts, Applications, and Challenges

Varsha Sharma
Rajiv Gandhi Proudyogiki Vishwavidyalaya, India

Vivek Sharma
Rajiv Gandhi Proudyogiki Vishwavidyalaya, India

Nishchol Mishra
Rajiv Gandhi Proudyogiki Vishwavidyalaya, India

ABSTRACT

Recently, Internet of Things (IoT) has aroused great interest among the educational, scientific research, and industrial communities. Researchers affirm that IoT environments will make people's daily life easier and will lead to superior services, great savings as well as a nifty use of resources. Consequently, IoT merchandise and services will grow exponentially in the upcoming years. The basic idea of IoT is to connect physical objects to the Internet and use that connection to provide some kind of useful remote monitoring or control of those objects. The chapter presents the overall IoT vision, the technologies for achieving it, IoT challenges and its applications. This chapter also attempts to describe and analyze threat types for privacy, security and trust in IoT as well as shows how big data is an important factor in IoT. This chapter will expose the readers and researchers who are interested in exploring and implementing the IoT and related technologies to the progress towards the bright future of the Internet of Things

INTRODUCTION

The term Internet of Things was first introduced by K. Ashton (1999). IoT technology itself isn't new. Previously components such as sensors that were expensive are now affordable, which has resulted in the popularity of "smart" products. Mohamed Abomhara and Geir M. Koien (2015) have stated that in the current state of technology, Machine-to-Machine (M2M) is the most popular application form of IoT. IoT enable things to be connected anytime, at anyplace, with anything and anyone ideally using any path/network and any service. In the IoT model, numerous objects that surround us will be on

DOI: 10.4018/978-1-5225-2947-7.ch007

Copyright © 2018, IGI Global. Copying or distributing in print or electronic forms without written permission of IGI Global is prohibited.

the network in one form or another. IoT is a new revolution of the Internet (Vermesan & Friess, 2013). The connectivity between IoT objects can increase reliability and efficiency due to improved access to information which results in better awareness about surrounding objects. Important prerequisites for the IoT are that the things/objects of interest can be uniquely identified and that their environment can be monitored with sensors. IoT objects make them-selves recognizable and can communicate information about them. They can access information that has been aggregated by other things, or they can be components of complex services.

Companies will make use of the IoT in order to efficiently monitor and control their internal business processes which includes the production, distribution, transportation, service, maintenance and recycling of their products. IoT will assist the companies to accurately capture the status of the entire enterprise and processes. To accomplish this goal, physical objects/things of the enterprises have to provide some "smart" functionality. Leonardo W. F. Chaves and Zoltán Nochta (2010) have grouped the smart functionalities provided by smart objects into five classes which are: information storage, information collection, communication, information processing and performance of actions. A given smart object may provide any meaningful subset of the above functionalities depending on specific requirements, available technologies and affordable costs. The things connected to the Internet need to provide value. Similarly, the smart things that are part of IoT need to provide a valuable service at a cost that enables adoption. The creation of value comes from all the components (devices, connectivity, applications) in IoT (Berthelsen, 2016). IoT objects/things are digitally inflated with one of the following:

- Sensors (to sense temperature, light, motion, etc.),
- Actuators (like displays, sound, motors, etc.),
- Computation (to run programs and logic),
- Communication interfaces (wired or wireless).

IoT consists of large scale information systems having application servers, resource planning systems, database management systems etc. The information systems in IoT receive data from the network of devices. IoT results in the generation of tremendous amounts of data which has to be stored processed and presented in a consistent, efficient, and easily understandable form (Gubbi, Buyya, Marusic et al., 2013). IoT requires three different types of software: backend server and database applications, firmware embedded in devices and mobile apps to interact with and control devices (Anders Wallgren, 2016).

According to business enterprises, there are three components of any IoT service: the edge, the platform and the user (Nicole Laskowski 2016):

- **The Edge:** where data originates, or is aggregated and analyzed according to experts. Rather than transmit every signal from a sensor to a centralized data warehouse and overwhelm the network, data is collected at an aggregation point close to the user and only the data points that require immediate attention are transmitted in real time. Aggregation points aren't always necessary, but the more IoT devices a business is gathering information from, the more critical they become. When there are thousands of IoT objects, there is a requirement of some aggregation in the middle or IoT platform will overflow with data.
- **The Platform:** Where data is absorbed-- typically in the cloud, analytics are performed and an internally developed algorithm takes an action. Incoming data is sent to a real-time stream processing engine, which decides if an action needs to be taken immediately or if the data can be

pushed away for future use. The platform also performs analytics by integrating historical data with real-time data to look at trending analysis; it also contains a policies engine and an orchestration engine to manage the platform.

- **The User:** Where data drives a business action. Data that has been analyzed can move from the IoT platform to a user in one of three ways: The user can use an API to "call" or query the data, the IoT platform can call out or signal to the business user when it finds a predetermined set of events or both can be done over an API bus.

The aim of this chapter is to make IoT interesting for a new reader/user to promote research in this area. For this, the upcoming sections in this chapter will first discuss IoT basic concepts like IoT elements, characteristics, technologies, architecture, applications and challenges. IoT data is often very sensitive, and thus brings a number of privacy challenges associated with it. Trust, Security, Privacy, Vulnerabilities and various attacks in IoT are discussed in this chapter. The collection and processing of IoT data gives rise to unprecedented challenges in mining and processing such data. Such data needs real time and highly distributed processing. Even if the data is stored offline, the size of the data is often so large that big data analytical tools are required for its processing. IoT data analytics perspective about mining and managing IoT data is finally discussed in the chapter.

Hence, the contribution of this chapter is to provide a good foundation for researchers and practitioners who are interested to gain insights into the IoT technologies and protocols to understand the overall architecture and role of the different components that constitute the IoT.

BACKGROUND

IoT Building Blocks

Al-Fuqaha, Guizani, Mohammadi et al. (2015) have identified six building blocks/elements of IoT which are as follows:

Identification

Unique identification of 'Things' is crucial in IoT because it allows to uniquely identify a large number of devices and also to control remote devices through the Internet. The essential attributes for creating a unique address are: uniqueness, reliability, persistence and scalability. Two important identification methods available for the IoT are: electronic product codes (EPC) and ubiquitous codes (uCode). Addressing the IoT objects discriminates between object ID and its address. Object ID refers to name such as "T1" for an individual temperature sensor and object's address refers to its address within a communications network. Addressing methods of IoT objects include IPv6 and IPv4. Distinguishing between object's identification and address is compulsory since identification methods are not globally unique, so addressing assists to uniquely identify objects. Additionally, objects within the network might use public IPs and not private ones. Identification methods are used to provide a clear identity for each object within the network. The scalability of the device address of the existing network must be continuous. The addition of more networks and devices must not impede the performance of the network, the functioning of the devices, and the reliability of the data over the network or the effective use of the devices from the user interface. To solve these problems, the URN (Uniform Resource Name) system is considered essential for the development of IoT. WSNs (considering them as building blocks of IoT), run on a different stack compared to the Internet and cannot possess IPv6 stack to address individually. Hence a subnet with a gateway having a URN will be required. There is a need of a layer for addressing sensor devices by the relevant gateway. At the subnet level, the URN for the sensor devices could be the unique IDs rather than human-friendly names as in the www, and a lookup table at the gateway to address these devices (Gubbi, Buyya, Marusic et al., 2013).

Sensing

Sensing means collecting data from related objects within the network and sending it to a data warehouse, database or cloud. The collected data is analyzed to take specific actions based on required services. The IoT sensors can be smart sensors, actuators or wearable sensing devices. Single Board Computers (SBCs) integrated with sensors and built-in TCP/IP and security functionalities are typically used to realize IoT products.

Communication

In IoT, communication technologies connect heterogeneous objects together to provide specialized services. IoT systems can connect to the Internet or gateway in different ways such as: long-range Wi-Fi/Ethernet using IP protocols, short range Bluetooth, short-range Near Field Communication and medium-range radio networks. Point-to-point radio links and serial lines are also used. Some IoT devices connect directly to the Internet via an IP protocol and others connect via specific IoT protocols, such as Message Queue Telemetry Transport (MQTT) or Constrained Application Protocol (CoAP). MQTT is a "subscribe and publish" messaging protocol designed for lightweight machine-to-machine communications. Originally developed by IBM, it is now an open standard. It needs a gateway or receiver (broker) to communicate. However, its main purpose is to allow a device to send a very short message one hop to an MQ broker and to receive commands from that broker. Every message is published to a location, called a topic. Clients (the sensors) subscribe to various topics and when a message is published to the topic, the client/sensor gets it. CoAP is a software protocol that enables simple constrained "things" such as low-power sensors and actuators to communicate interactively via the internet. It runs on devices that support the User Datagram Protocol (UDP), and implements a "lightweight" application layer that features small message sizes, message management and lightweight message overhead ideally suited for low-power, low-memory devices.

Computation

Processing units (e.g., microcontrollers, microprocessors) and software applications express the computational ability of the IoT. Many hardware platforms were developed to run IoT applications such as Arduino, UDOO, FriendlyARM, Intel Galileo, Raspberry PI, Gadgeteer, BeagleBone, Cubieboard, Z1, WiSense, Mulle, and T-Mote Sky. Many software platforms are also utilized to provide IoT functionalities. Among these, Operating Systems are important since they run for the whole activation time of a device. There are several Real-Time Operating Systems (RTOS) that are good candidates for the development of RTOS-based IoT applications. For instance, the Contiki RTOS has been used widely in IoT scenarios.

Contiki has a simulator called Cooja which allows researchers and developers to simulate and emulate IoT and wireless sensor network (WSN) applications. TinyOS, LiteOS and Riot OS also offer light weight OS for IoT environments. Cloud Platforms make up crucial computational part of the IoT since they provide facilities for smart objects to send their data to the cloud, for big data to be processed in real-time, and ultimately for end-users to benefit from the knowledge extracted from the collected big data.

Services

IoT services can be classified into four categories: Identity-related Services, Information Aggregation Services, Collaborative-Aware Services and Ubiquitous Services. Identity-related services are the fundamental services that are used by other types of services. Every application that demands to bring real world objects to the virtual world has to identify those objects. Information Aggregation Services collect and summarize raw sensory measurements that need to be processed and reported to the IoT application. Collaborative-Aware Services act on top of Information Aggregation Services and use the received data to take decision and react accordingly. Ubiquitous Services, however, focus to provide Collaborative-Aware Services anytime they are needed to anyone who needs them anywhere.

Semantics

Semantic in the IoT refers to the ability to extract knowledge smartly by different machines to provide the required services. Knowledge extraction includes discovering and using resources and modeling information. Also, it includes recognizing and analyzing data to make sense of the right decision to provide the exact service. Thus, semantic represents the brain of the IoT by sending demands to the right resource. This requirement is supported by Semantic Web technologies such as the Resource Description Framework (RDF) and the Web Ontology Language (OWL).

IoT Characteristics

The characteristics of IoT can be stated as follows:

Dynamic and Self Adapting

IoT devices and systems have the capability to dynamically adapt to the changing contexts and take actions according to their operating conditions, user's contexts or sensed environment. As an example, consider a system comprising of a number of surveillance cameras. The surveillance cameras can adapt their modes based on whether it is day or night. Cameras could switch from lower resolution to higher resolution modes when any motion is detected and alert nearby cameras to do the same.

Self-Configuring

IoT devices may have self-configuring capability allowing a large number of devices to work together to provide certain functionality. These devices have the ability to configure themselves, setup the network and fetch latest software upgrades with minimal manual or user intervention.

Interoperable Communication Protocols

IoT devices may support a number of interoperable communications protocols and can communicate with other devices and also with the infrastructure.

Unique Identity

Each IoT device has a unique identity like IP address. IoT systems may have intelligent interfaces which adapt based on the context; allow communicating with users and the environment contexts. IoT device interfaces allow the users to query the devices, monitor their status and control them remotely in association with the control, configuration and management infrastructure.

Integrated Into Information Network

This allows them to communicate and exchange data with other devices and systems. IoT devices can be dynamically discovered in the network by other devices and/or the network and have the capability to describe themselves to other devices or user applications. For example, a weather monitoring node can describe its monitoring capability to other connected node so that they can communicate and exchange data. Integration into the information network helps in making IoT systems smarter due to the collective intelligence of the individual devices in collaboration with the infrastructure. Thus, the data from the large number of connected weather monitoring IoT devices can be aggregated and analyzed to predict the weather.

Technologies to Implement the IoT

Leonardo W. F. Chaves and Zoltán Nochta (2010) have discussed that IoT needs technologies that are used to identify and track objects and to sense their environment which are as follows:

Barcode

A barcode can be one- or two-dimensional. It can code an identification number for an item. The barcode can be printed on a label which is later affixed to an item, or it can be directly printed onto the item. It is very cheap, and has negligible costs when it is directly printed onto an item. However, barcode identification faces many problems. Only items which are in line-of-sight can be identified. Items inside boxes or pallets cannot be identified without significant manual intervention. Furthermore, only one item can be identified at once thereby increasing the manual work when identifying items with barcodes.

Passive RFID

By using Radio Frequency Identification (RFID), numerous items can be identified uniquely at once without line-of-sight contact. Passive RFID tags operate without a battery. They use the power of the reader's interrogation signal to communicate the ID to the RFID reader. Passive RFID has applications particularly in retail and supply chain management. The applications can be found in transportation and access control. The passive tags are currently being used in many bank cards and road toll tags. Passive

RFID tags are too expensive for wide-spread market adoption. On average, current RFID tags that are fully converted to a label ready for attaching on to an object cost between 0.09 US$ and 0.15 US$ depending on volume. Traditional RFID tags based on single crystal silicon chips will not hit the ultralow costs needed for applying the technology in many inexpensive product segments. This is because the production of RFID tags or labels requires many expensive steps: first the RFID chip is produced, and then it is attached to a strap. Also, the RFID antenna has to be produced, laminated, and then connected to the RFID chip. After this the resulting "smart label" has to be attached to an item.

Active RFID

Active RFID tags use batteries to power sensors and to support the wireless communication. These tags are large and cannot be applied to every kind of object. They are very expensive, with costs ranging from 10.00 US$ to 30.00 US$. Therefore, active RFID tags are rarely attached to single items. Mostly one active RFID tag is used to monitor one box, pallet or even container.

Printed Electronics

It is a new technology to manufacture ultra-low cost smart labels. Electronic circuits can be printed using conductive inks. The ultra-low cost smart labels produced by this technology can be printed directly on the package of items in their manufacturing process. Standard industrial printers are used to print organic or inorganic materials. This results in ultra-low-cost electronic components. With printed electronics, several layers of different materials are printed onto each other to form electronic components (additive process). This minimizes the total number of steps in manufacturing. This results in reduced material costs and overall tooling costs, i.e., the production become very simple, fast and cheap. But, printed electronics show lower performance. Both inorganic and organic materials can be used in printed electronics. Inorganic materials, like zinc oxide (ZnO), have good environmental stability and performance. However, inorganic particles are not soluble and therefore they are difficult to process. Organic materials like plastics and polymers have good process ability and their physical properties can be easily customized chemically. With Organic Electronics, components like diodes, transistors, memories, batteries and sensors can be printed and easily integrated. This technology allows the production of new "organic" smart labels that are much cheaper than traditional smart labels. These organic smart labels can contain a multitude of sensors, like temperature, light, pressure and strain sensors. Furthermore, because of its ultra-low-costs, several organic smart labels can be printed onto a single object (multitag).

Wireless Sensor Networks (WSNs)

These networks are composed of several small computers equipped with sensors. They are akin to active RFID tags in terms of size and cost. But, as opposed to active RFID tags, they can also communicate with each other. E.g., several wireless sensors in a room can communicate with each other to determine the average temperature in the room. The components of the WSN monitoring network include:

- **WSN Hardware:** A node in WSN contains sensor interfaces, processing units, transceiver units and power supply.

- **WSN Communication Stack:** An appropriate topology, routing and MAC layer are critical for the scalability and longevity of the deployed network. Nodes in a WSN communicate among themselves to transmit data in single or multi-hop to a base station. Node drop outs, and consequent degraded network lifetimes, are frequent. The communication stack at the sink node should be able to interact with the outside world through the Internet to act as a gateway to the WSN subnet and the Internet.
- **WSN Middleware:** A platform-independent middleware for developing sensor applications is required, such as an Open Sensor Web Architecture (OSWA).
- **Secure Data Aggregation:** An efficient and secure data aggregation method is needed for extending the lifetime of the network as well as for ensuring reliable data collection from sensors. Node failures are a common characteristic of WSNs. The network topology should have the capability to restore itself. Ensuring security and protection is important as the system is automatically linked to actuators.

Cloud Computing

Cloud computing has become one of the chief enablers for IoT. For achieving or maintaining continuous IoT application availability service providers must expand their data center options. Having access to cloud resources provides service providers with the flexibility to quickly provision IoT services. Cloud computing provides organizations a way to manage IoT services. Cloud enables IT as a Service, just as IoT is a service, along with the flexibility to scale when needed. By integrating the enterprise data center with external clouds, the cloud becomes a secure extension of the enterprise's IoT network. This enterprise-to-cloud network connection is encrypted and optimized for performance and bandwidth, thereby reducing the risks and lowering the effort involved in migrating IoT workloads to the cloud.

Reference Architecture for IoT

Iván Corredor Pérez and Ana M. Bernardos Barbolla (2014) have discussed the reference architecture for the IoT research domain. The architecture consists of three major layers which are as follows:

Hardware Layer

This layer is classified into two categories of devices: constrained devices and unconstrained devices. Constrained devices have limited features. Thus, they have to redistribute some processes to be executed by external devices which display their functionalities to clients. Unconstrained devices have sufficient resources to run the important processes or middleware components to provide direct functionalities to clients through a platform or third party cloud services.

Software Layer

This layer has to provide a mechanism to set up the functionalities of the underlying hardware as resources and finally, to compose and orchestrate them in order to build simple or complex services.

User Layer

This layer consists of clients who consume the services. Those clients can be humans using devices (e.g. smart phones, tablets, laptops, etc.) or machine users as smart objects that might request services to perform high or low level tasks (e.g. to turn on an ambient light or analyze the capabilities of peer entities to compose services for making complex smart environments).

IoT APPLICATIONS

There are many application domains to be benefited by the emergence of IoT. Jayavardhana Gubbi et.al (2013) have classified the applications into four applications domains:

- Personal and home,
- Enterprise,
- Utilities,
- Mobile.

Ovidiu Vermesan, Peter Friess (2013) and Charu C. Aggarwal et al. (2013) have described some of the IoT applications which are as follows:

Smart Cities

In future, smart cities will be developed with features like, Smart Economy, Smart Buildings, Smart Mobility, Smart Energy, Smart Information Communication and Technology, Smart Planning, Smart Citizen and Smart Governance. Cities and their services serve an almost ideal platform for IoT research. In smart cities, city requirements are considered and transferred into solutions enabled by IoT technology. The aim of smart city project is to deploy an IoT infrastructure comprising thousands of IoT devices spread across several cities. The main focus is on utilities and environment in the cities and addressing the role of IoT in waste and water management, public lighting and transport systems as well as environment monitoring.

Development plans for smart city are divided into three phases: 1) the initial infrastructure construction phase; 2) the data-processing facility construction phase; 3) the end-phase service platform construction phase.

Smart Energy and Smart Grid

In addition to fossil resources and nuclear energy, future energy supply needs will be based largely on various renewable resources. An intelligent and flexible electrical grid is needed which has the capability to react to power fluctuations by controlling electrical energy sources (generation, storage) and sinks (load, storage). Such functions will be based on networked intelligent devices and grid infrastructure elements, largely based on IoT concepts.

Future energy grids are marked by a high number of distributed small and medium sized energy sources and power plants. In the case of energy outages or disasters, some areas may be detached from the grid and supplied from within by internal energy sources such as photovoltaics on the roofs and power plants or energy storages of a residential area.

This leads to the concept of "Internet of Energy" which is defined as a network infrastructure based on standard and interoperable communication transceivers, gateways and protocols that will allow a real-time balance between the local and the global generation and storage capability with the energy demand. This will also allow a high level of consumer awareness and involvement. The Internet of Energy (IoE) provides a new concept for power distribution, energy storage, grid monitoring and communication. It will allow units of energy to be transferred when and where it is needed.

Smart meters can give information to the user about the instantaneous energy consumption which will allow for identification and elimination of energy wasting devices and for providing hints for optimizing individual energy consumption.

Smart Transportation

The connection of vehicles to the Internet will make transport easier and safer. IoT is an inherent part of the vehicle control and management system. Certain technical functions of the vehicles' on-board systems can be monitored on line by the service center to allow for preventative maintenance, remote diagnostics, instantaneous support and timely availability of spare parts. For this purpose, data from on-board sensors are collected by a smart on-board unit and communicated via the Internet to the service center.

Vehicles should be able to organize themselves to avoid traffic jams and to optimize drive energy usage. This may be done in coordination and cooperation with the infrastructure of a smart city's traffic control and management system. Mutual communications between the vehicles and with the infrastructure enable traffic safety thus contributing to the reduction in the number of traffic accidents.

The user will be offered an optimal solution for transportation from source to destination based on all available and suitable means of transport. Based on momentary traffic situation an ideal solution may be a mix of individual vehicles, vehicle sharing, railway etc.

Technological elements of such systems include smart phones and smart vehicle onboard units which acquire position, destination and schedule information from the user and from on board systems (e.g. vehicle status, position, energy usage profile, driving profile). They communicate with external systems (e.g. traffic control systems, parking management, vehicle sharing managements, electric vehicle charging infrastructure). They also need to initiate and perform the related payment procedures.

Smart sensors in the road and traffic control infrastructures need to collect information about road and traffic status, weather conditions, etc. This requires robust sensors (and actuators) which are able to reliably deliver information to the systems mentioned above. Such reliable communication needs to be based on M2M communication protocols which consider the timing, safety, and security constraints. The expected high amount of data will require sophisticated data mining strategies. Overall optimization of traffic flow and energy usage may be achieved by collective organization among the individual vehicles.

Smart Homes

Electronic devices have started becoming part of the home IP network and due to the increasing rate of adoption of Wi-Fi and mobile computing devices. Mobile devices ensure that consumers have access to a portable 'controller' for the electronics connected to the network.

IoT applications using sensors to collect information about operating conditions combined with cloud hosted analytics software that analyze disparate data points will help facility managers become far more proactive about managing buildings at peak efficiency.

Exploitation of wireless sensor networks (WSNs) to facilitate intelligent energy management in buildings increases occupant comfort while reducing energy demand. Intelligent Building Management Systems are used by facilities managers in buildings to manage energy use and energy procurement and to maintain buildings systems. It is based on the infrastructure of the existing Intranets and the Internet, and therefore utilizes the same standards as other IT devices.

Smart Factory and Manufacturing

The IoT has enabled access to devices and machines in manufacturing systems. IoT will enable to connect the factories with the smart grid, sharing the production facility as a service or allowing more agility and flexibility within the production systems. In this sense, the production system could be considered one of the many Internets of Things (IoT), where a new ecosystem for smarter and more efficient production could be defined.

The convergence of microelectronics and micromechanical parts within a sensing device, the ubiquity of communications, the rise of micro-robotics, the customization made possible by software will significantly change the world of manufacturing.

Smart Health

IoT applications will assist to perform routine tasks like health and activity monitoring, enhancing safety and security, getting access to medical and emergency systems and facilitating rapid health support. The main objective is to improve quality of life for people who need permanent support and monitoring. IoT will reduce the barriers for monitoring important health parameters; avoid unnecessary healthcare costs and efforts. IoT will enable to provide the right medical support at the right time.

The hospitals can use sensors for security purposes. Nurses can receive critical alerts about their patients' medical conditions, like heart rate and oxygen changes that sensors have detected, allowing them to reach patients' bedsides more quickly. Wireless sensors can be installed in refrigerators, freezers and laboratories etc. to ensure that blood samples, medicines and other materials are kept at the proper temperatures. The ability to have wireless alerts will be a great time saver for the staff.

System security will be critical as individual patient data is communicated over networks. In addition, validating data acquired from patients using new cyber-physical technologies against existing data acquisition methods will be a challenge. Cyber-physical technologies will also need to be designed to operate with minimal patient training or cooperation.

Smart Environment

Monitoring and transmitting important environmental parameters like temperature, humidity, pressure etc. can be done by embedded sensor technology. RFID technology can be coupled with sophisticated sensors to send back information which is related to specific objects. Such information can be used to control the environment in an energy-efficient way. For example, smart sensors in a building can be used in order to decide when the lights or air-conditioning in a room in the building should be switched off, if the room is not currently being used.

Product Inventory and Tracking

This is a popular application of IoT and RFID technology. Inexpensive RFID tags can track the movements of large amounts of products. For large organizations, the underlying RFID readers may serve as an intermediate layer between the data collection and internet connectivity. This provides opportunities for product tracking in an automated way. Additionally, it is possible to design software which uses the information from the transmitted data in order to trigger alerts in response to specific events (Charu C. Aggarwal et al., 2013).

Food and Water Tracking and Safety

Organic food and fresh water are highly valued. Adequate distribution of such food items and water is very important. This will lead to attempts to forge the origin or the production process. Using IoT in such scenarios for secure tracking of food or water from the production place to the consumer is one of the important topics.

Air and Noise Pollution Monitoring

IoT based pollution monitoring systems use a number of air and noise monitoring systems deployed at different places in a city. The data on pollution levels from the stations is collected on servers or in cloud. The collected data is then aggregated to produce pollution maps. These pollution maps can help the policy makers to control pollution levels near residential areas, schools and hospitals etc.

Electronic Payment Systems

Many electronic payment systems are now being developed with the use of a variety of smart technologies. The connectivity of RFID readers to the internet can be used in order to implement payment systems. An example is the Texas Instruments's Speedpass, a pay-at-pump system which uses RFID technology to detect the identity of the customer buying gas, and this information is used to debit the money from the customer's bank account (Charu C. Aggarwal et al., 2013).

Participatory Sensing using Community Wisdom

Community wisdom is based on conscious input from people and opinions of individuals. The aim of participatory sensing applications is to utilize each person, mobile phone, car and associated sensors as automatic sensory stations taking a multi-sensor snapshot of the immediate environment. By combining these individual snapshots in an intelligent manner, it is possible to create a clear picture of the physical world that can be shared and for example used as an input to the smart city services decision processes.

Defense

Denise E. Zheng and William A. Carter (2015) have discussed the application of IoT in military. Use of IoT technologies in the military has necessarily focused on combat applications. Millions of sensors organized on a diversity of platforms are used for providing situational awareness to war fighters on the land, seas and air in the tasks of Command, Control, Communications, Computers, Intelligence, Surveillance and Reconnaissance. In fire control systems, deployment of networked sensors and digital analytics enable fully automated responses to threats in real time delivering devastating firepower with pinpoint precision. Some IoT technologies are also deployed in noncombat applications, improving the efficiency and effectiveness of back-end processes. The Defense Logistics and Transportation department use RFID tags to track shipments and manage inventories. IoT is also used in training and simulation exercises. IoT technologies can be used for monitoring, sensing, threat identification, target positioning, marking, vehicles, soldiers' status monitoring, environmental monitoring and medical care (battlefield health monitoring, patients monitoring, etc.). There are a number of obstacles in the way of successful deployment of IoT technologies in defense. Security is the most important challenge, with the large number of simple devices and applications raising unique vulnerabilities to electronic and cyber warfare. Broader deployment of IoT technology across the military also requires investment in increased connectivity, digital analytics, and improved interoperability.

IoT applications are not limited to those discussed above. Other applications of IoT are forest fire detection, indoor air quality monitoring etc.

IoT CHALLENGES

IoT differs from traditional wireless sensor networks as well as computer networks and therefore introduces more challenges to solve. On the one hand, billions of smart objects will be engaged in sensing, interacting and cooperating with each other to enable efficient services to bring benefits to the environment, the economy and the society. On the other hand, they will be very diverse and heterogeneous in terms of resource capabilities, lifespan and communication technologies, complicating the scenario. As a consequence, new problems and challenges emerge in areas of: architecture, communication, addressing, discovery, data and network management, power and energy storage, security and privacy etc. Traditional approaches are not sufficient to solve these issues, and need to be revised to address the complex requirements imposed by IoT. This opens the way for the development of intelligent algorithms, novel network paradigms and new services. Al-Fuqaha, Guizani, Mohammadi et al. (2015), Jim Chase (2013) and Chen, Xu, Liu et al. (2014) have discussed IoT challenges which are as follows:

Internet Everywhere

The success of IoT depends on the availability of Internet everywhere. In order to make it available everywhere, there is a need of huge investment.

Architecture and Connectivity

IoT incorporates a large number of smart interconnected devices and sensors (e.g., cameras, biometric, physical, and chemical sensors) that are often noninvasive, transparent, and invisible. These devices can communicate anytime, anywhere for any related services. This communication is in a wireless and ad hoc manner. IoT services will be more mobile, decentralized, and complex. Thus, data integration over different environments is difficult and will be supported by modular interoperable components. Infrastructure solutions will require systems to combine volumes of data from various sources and determine relevant features, to interpret data and show their relationships, to compare data to historical useful information, and support decision-making. Single reference architecture thus cannot be a blueprint for all applications. In IoT, heterogeneous reference architectures have to exist side-by-side because no sole architecture can address the requirements of all the possible IoT device areas. A scalable architecture can equip service providers for IoT that can add or subtract resources to support a wide variety of scenarios. Architectures should be open, and following standards, they should not restrict users to use fixed, end-to-end solutions. IoT architectures should be flexible to cater for cases such as identification (RFID, tags), intelligent devices, and smart objects (hardware and software solutions)

Hardware Cost

Smart devices with enhanced inter-device communication will lead to smart systems with high degrees of intelligence. Its autonomy enables rapid deployment of IoT applications and creation of new services. Therefore, hardware researches are focusing on designing wireless identifiable systems with low size, low cost yet sufficient functionality. Billions of IoT terminals will be used and the cost of an IoT terminal must be ultra-low.

Data Storage and Management

One of the most important outcomes of IoT is the creation of an unprecedented quantity of data. Storage, ownership and expiry of this data become critical issues. The data have to be stored and used intelligently for smart monitoring and actuation. Methods are required to clean, manage, query and analyze the data in the distributed way. Data cleaning in IoT may be required for several reasons which are: (a) Data collected from conventional sensors may be noisy or incomplete (b) RFID data is noisy, incomplete and redundant because a large number of readings are dropped and there are cross-reads from multiple sensor readers (c) The privacy preservation process may require an intentional reduction of data quality.

Capacity Planning/Bandwidth Requirement

IoT data is typically of continuous nature, and the number of files to store can be very large. Consequently, there is a constant demand for capacity growth. In IoT, the increased demand for Internet will escalate business continuity risks. If critical applications are not assigned their required bandwidth, consumers will be unsatisfied, employee productivity will suffer and enterprise profitability could fall. To ensure high availability of their services, enterprises must add bandwidth and facilitate traffic management and monitoring. This will mitigate business continuity risks and also prevent potential losses. From the project planning viewpoint, organizations would need to do capacity planning and observe the growth rate of the network so that the increased demand for the required bandwidth can be met.

Power Management

Most of the things in IoT will be battery powered or use energy harvesting to be more portable and self-sustaining. Line-powered equipment will need to be more energy efficient. The challenge is to make it easy to add power management to these devices and equipment. Wireless charging will incorporate connectivity with charge management.

Complexity

IoT technology can be complex for variety of reasons. First, there are legacy heterogeneous architectures in the existing networking technologies and applications, e.g., different applications and environments need different networking technologies, and the ranges as well as other characteristics of cellular, wireless local area network, and RFID technologies are much different from each other. Manufacturers are looking to add connectivity to devices and equipment that has never been connected before to become part of the IoT. Second, communication technologies, including fixed and mobile communication systems, power line communications, wireless communication, and short-range wireless communication technologies, for both fixed and mobile devices, either simple or complicated, should be low cost and with reliable connectivity Ease of design and development is essential to get more things connected. All the above may block IoT to connect as many "Things" as possible.

Privacy and Security

IoT prompts consideration of two different concepts: data privacy and security. On one hand, data privacy is considered from the user's perspective, whose personal information may be at risk of compromise. User's personal data is always valuable to data or identity thieves and hackers. On the other hand, data security is considered from the perspective of the providers of products and services who gather information to create value for the company and the consumer. Since IoT is about physical things, hackers that gain access can't just perform the usual digital attacks like stealing data or shutting down websites. They can also cause physical damage by interfering with critical infrastructure like electric grids, healthcare devices, aviation systems etc. Hence, IoT security requires combining physical and cyber security components. Security and privacy issues of IoT become more prominent compared to traditional networks. Much information includes privacy of users, so that protection of privacy becomes an important security issue in IoT. Existing security architecture designed from the perspective of human communication may not be suitable and hence cannot be directly applied to IoT systems. Using existed security mechanisms will block logical relationship between things in IoT. IoT needs low-cost- and M2M-oriented technical solutions to guarantee the privacy and the security. Low cost, low latency and energy-efficient cryptography algorithms will be essential for IoT devices. Other ways to minimize security risks in IoT are: taking security issues into account during the design of IoT products; collecting only essential data; implementing multiple defence layers against threats; Built-in hardware security and use of existing connectivity security protocols is also essential to secure the IoT. Another challenge is simply educating consumers to use the security that is integrated into their IoT devices.

Availability, Reliability, and Fault Tolerance

Availability of IoT must be realized to provide anywhere and anytime services for customers. Availability of software refers to the ability of the IoT applications to provide services for everyone at different places simultaneously. Hardware availability refers to the existence of devices all the time that are compatible with the IoT functionalities and protocols. Reliability is referred to as proper working of the system based on its specification. The aim of reliability is to increase the success rate of IoT service delivery. It is closely related to availability. Reliability is even more important in emergency response applications. In these systems, the main part is the communication network which must be resilient to failures for realizing reliable information distribution. Implementation of reliability must be done in software and hardware throughout all the IoT layers. Structuring Internet of Things in a robust and trustworthy manner would require redundancy on several levels and an ability to automatically adapt to changed conditions.

Mobility

Most of the IoT services are expected to be delivered to mobile users. Connecting users with their desired services continuously while moving is an important requirement of the IoT. Service interruption for mobile devices can occur when these devices transfer from one IoT gateway to another.

Performance

Evaluation of the performance of IoT services is a challenge because it depends on the performance of many components as well as the underlying technologies. Like other systems, IoT needs to continuously develop and improve its services to satisfy user's requirements. The IoT components/devices need to be monitored and evaluated to provide the optimal performance at an affordable price for users. Many metrics can be used to determine the performance of IoT devices including the processing speed, communication speed and cost etc.

TRUST, SECURITY, PRIVACY, AND VULNERABILITIES IN IoT

Ovidiu Vermesan and Peter Friess (2013) have discussed that adoption of IoT essentially depends upon trust. A trust framework is needed to enable the users to have confidence that the information and services being exchanged can be relied upon. The trust framework needs to deal with humans and machines as users, i.e. it needs to convey trust to humans and needs to be robust enough to be used by machines without denial of service. The development of trust frameworks requires the following points to be considered:

- Lightweight Public Key Infrastructures (PKI) forms basis for trust management.
- Encryption using minimum communications and processing resources consistent with the resource constrained nature of many IoT devices.
- Quality of Information is important for IoT systems. Here metadata can be used to provide an assessment of the reliability of IoT data.
- Decentralized and self-configuring systems as alternatives to PKI for establishing trust.
- New methods for assessing trust in people, devices and data. One example is Trust Negotiation.

- Assurance methods for trusted platforms including hardware, software, protocols, etc.
- Access Control to prevent data breaches.

Since IoT will be a main element of the Future Internet and a critical national/international infrastructure, there is a need to provide adequate security for the IoT infrastructure. IoT based applications and services are vulnerable to attacks or information theft. Any IoT project must be designed to incorporate security controls. Preparation is the key to IoT security. Focus on several areas is required to make the IoT secure, including:

- IoT is vulnerable to DoS/DDOS attacks and will require specific techniques and mechanisms to ensure that services cannot be disabled or subverted.
- General attack detection and recovery to withstand IoT specific threats like compromised nodes, malicious code attacks etc.
- Tools/techniques will require to be developed to enable IoT-based infrastructures to be monitored.
- A variety of access control and accounting schemes are required in IoT to support the various authorization and usage models. The heterogeneity and diversity of the devices/gateways that require access control will require new schemes to be developed.
- New techniques and approaches e.g. from machine learning, are required to a self-managed IoT.
- It should be expected that attackers will seek to compromise the supply chain of IoT devices, implanting malicious code and other vulnerabilities to exploit only after the devices have been implemented in an enterprise environment.

George Lawton (2016) has discussed some of the security steps that can be followed for IoT security are as follows:

- The IoT gateway is a device responsible for collecting data from sensors and communicating with actuators when something needs to be controlled. A gateway can be installed in a home, an industrial control system or an automobile. It provides developers with secure I/O access to individual devices. A security framework can be created that uses public-key cryptography for authentication of communication between remote devices and gateways. This can prevent hackers from gaining access to data from IoT devices. It can also make it difficult for hackers to send unauthorized control signals to IoT devices or launch denial-of-service attacks on IoT infrastructure.
- IoT software should be implemented to lower the risk of unauthorized software being installed onto a device. One possible approach is to employ a framework that uses public-key cryptography to certify new software updates before installation.
- Exclusive passwords can be generated for each device.
- Cloud service can be used to simplify the update and management of remote devices.

The connected smart things/objects that will densely populate the IoT will have ability to communicate/interact with both humans and the human environment. This communication/interaction is possible by exchanging information or various types of commands. The information exchanged between connected things in IoT will be related to individuals/humans and objects, their state and their surroundings, that can be used remotely. The connectivity of IoT objects/things carries a risk to privacy and information leakage. In IoT, the data privacy issues may arise both during data collection and data transmission/

sharing. In data collection phase, privacy issues typically arise because of the widespread use of RFID technology, in which the tags carried by a person may become a unique identifier for that person. Privacy in the phase of data sharing and management may arise because much of the transmitted information can be sensitive (like GPS location), but it may also be required to enable useful real-time applications such as traffic analysis (Charu C. Aggarwal et al., 2013).

Since there is much of the personal information in an IoT system, there is a requirement to support anonymity i.e. to securely and privately collect, manage, index, query and process large amounts of IoT data. IoT results in a number of privacy implications where research is required, including:

- Preservation of location privacy, where location can be inferred from things associated with people.
- Prevention of personal information inference, that people would wish to keep private.
- Keeping information as local as possible using decentralized computing and key management.

For privacy in IoT, developments are needed in the following areas:

- Cryptographic techniques that enable protected data to be stored processed and shared, without the information content being accessible to other parties. Technologies such as homomorphic and searchable encryption are potential candidates for developing such approaches.
- Techniques to support Privacy by Design concepts, including data minimization, identification, authentication and anonymity.
- Fine-grain and self-configuring access control mechanism emulating the real world.

Connecting things will expose them to attacks and challenges. Hence, IoT magnifies the impact of security vulnerabilities (Prabhakaran, 2016). The Open Web Application Security Project (OWASP) analyzed the vulnerabilities related to IoT which are as follows:

- Insecure Web Interface,
- Inadequate Authentication/Authorization,
- Insecure Network Services,
- Lack of Transport Encryption,
- Privacy Concerns,
- Insecure Cloud Interface,
- Insecure Mobile Interface,
- Inadequate Security Configurability,
- Insecure Software/Firmware,
- Poor Physical Security.

IoT is also vulnerable due to the use of IPv6. IPv6 introduces certain risks that need to be considered. There are two main vulnerabilities linked to IPv6. The first is that a network vulnerable to attack through scamp router advertisement enables attackers to intercept IPv6 traffic, which can affect both confidentiality and availability. Encryption is used to provide confidentiality but it does not cover the metadata, which can provide attackers with useful information about connections into and out of organizations. The second vulnerability is that IPv6 makes it more difficult for security professionals to observe the organization's network. Since there are so many IPv6 IP addresses, it is virtually impossible to do a scan of the network to find scamp devices, which makes securing an IPv6 network more difficult (Warwick Ashford, 2016).

Understanding the complexity of vulnerabilities and how serious of a threat they pose is very important. Devices such as wireless access points or printers come with known administrator IDs and passwords. Devices may provide a built-in Web server to which admins can remotely connect, log in and manage the device. This is a huge vulnerability that can put IoT devices into attackers' hands. It requires creating a development environment where the initial configuration settings of the devices can be tested, scanned to identify any kind of vulnerabilities that are present, validated and issues solved before the device is moved into the production environment (Kumar, n. d.).

IoT THREATS AND ATTACKS

Any device that can be connected to Internet has an embedded operating system deployed in its firmware. Since security is not a primary consideration in the design of embedded operating systems, vulnerabilities are present in virtually all of them. Similar threats will grow rapidly among IoT devices (Kumar, n. d.). IoT infrastructure is exposed to several risks such as attacks on the control infrastructure, contamination of data, and leakage of confidential data. IoT objects/devices will be exposed to the same attacks as other Internet-connected devices. Mohamed Abomhara and Geir M. Koien (2015) have classified the threats and attacks in IoT. The connected devices or machines in IoT are extremely valuable to cyber-attackers for several reasons:

- A large number of IoT devices operate without humans and it is easy for an attacker to physically gain access to them.
- An attacker could obtain confidential information by eavesdropping as most IoT components communicate over wireless networks.
- IoT components cannot support complex security schemes due to low power and computing resource capabilities.

An attacker can simultaneously attack on multiple layers:

- Manipulate the sensor measurements to infiltrate the system with wrong data.
- Attack the sensors and actuators physically to obtain credentials.
- Attack or impersonate network components to act as a man-in-the middle.
- Obtain sensitive data by attacking the sharing platform with forged or malicious requests.

Some of the threats associated with IoT are discussed by V.P Prabhakaran (2016) and Ajay Kumar (n.d.):

Vulnerable IoT Perimeters

When IoT networks are designed, there is lack of planning of good security implementation which can allow an intruder to easily gain access to the network.

Disruption and Denial of Service Attacks

Ensuring continuous availability of IoT-based devices will be important to avoid potential operational failures and interruptions to enterprise services. Disruptive cyberattacks, such as distributed denial-of-service attacks, could lead to customer frustration resulting in revenue loss, customer dissatisfaction and potentially poor reception in the market.

Data Breaches

Data breaches are one of the biggest threats in IoT devices. Cyber attackers can try to spy on the communications between devices in IoT network. Devices accessed through Internet of Things may be used for cyber espionage purposes by an intelligence agency or by some companies for commercial purposes.

Malware and Botnet Attacks

Malicious users design the code for attempting to attack against IoT networks. Cyber criminals can exploit vulnerabilities in firmware running on the devices and run their arbitrary code, turning IoT components to unplanned use.

Standard network security tools such as firewalls or access control will not serve to prevent such attacks due to the distributed nature of IoT. It is essential that security is built into the infrastructure rather than being added as an extra plug-ins. A compelling approach for protection is to have security in depth, where data and services are protected by several independent systems. The challenge will be to design solutions where no single server has considerable power to control the infrastructure or to access significant amounts of data.

IoT ANALYTICS

Big Data is defined as data having greater variety and arriving in increasing volumes with ever higher velocity. In IoT, sensors are placed on everything and the data from these sensors is transmitted via an Internet connection to a central repository for storage. Once there, it becomes part of big data. This data must be gathered on an ongoing basis, analyzed, and then used to provide insights to the business regarding appropriate actions to take, thus providing value.

Charu C. Aggarwal et.al (2013) have presented a data centric perspective of IoT. From a data centric perspective, scalability, distributed processing, and real time analytics will be important for effective enablement of IoT. The number of connected devices in IoT is expected to accelerate at a rapid rate in future. The large number of devices simultaneously producing data in an automated way will greatly dwarf the information which individuals can enter manually. The physical limitations on how much data can be effectively collected from embedded sensor devices have steadily been increasing with advances in hardware technology. Connected things in IoT will create Big Data which includes device states and data collected by sensors. The richness and variety of data sources in IoT will continue to expand, and from highly structured data, enterprises will need to work with semi-structured as well as completely unstructured data to gain the value from data aggregation. IoT data fulfills all the characteristics of Big

Data. Hence, big data is an important factor in IoT. Due to the nature of IoT Big Data, two issues emerge (Jan Holler et.al, 2014). These issues are:

- Storage and management of temporal knowledge created by IoT solutions.
- Life cycle management of knowledge within IoT.

Big data generated by sensor output and machine communication in IoT leads to more traffic into data centers. An IoT infrastructure changes data center capacity planning and operations. With data centers distributed more geographically, they can operate networks at a lower latency with high quality, which is crucial for the automatic collection and transmission of IoT data to and from connected devices. IoT's rapid development increases storage demands, which can throw a data center into chaos. With this data sprawl, data center teams need a disciplined method to catalog, categorize and contain business information to complement their IoT infrastructure.

Data itself does not have a meaning until it is processed into useful information. The information is then organized and structured to infer knowledge about the system, its users, its environment and its progress towards meeting objectives which allows smarter performance. Analytics of IoT Big Data is the key to making investments in IoT technology worthwhile. More and more companies are now starting to collect and store data from sensors. The next step is to analyze the data. Looking for patterns in it could improve business operations, such as doing more preventive maintenance or designing more efficient delivery routes. Hence, apart from focusing on data collection, companies should plan for analyzing IoT data and acting on those analytics results. One example of this is to analyze data from security cameras to help retailers understand how customers are interacting with in-store displays. Focus on IoT data collection and analysis can give organizations visibility into areas of their operations they've never had before.

Swathija Raman (2016) has described that IoT analytics can be broken down into the following main steps:

- **Report:** For reporting, data is typically prioritized. When network latency is high, only the most critical data are uploaded. When latency improves, data with secondary priority is reported. After that, data with tertiary and quaternary priority be uploaded to the servers.
- **Aggregate:** New strategies are needed in the aggregation and processing of IoT data. NoSQL databases that have looser transactional requirements but much better synchronization and storage capabilities are a better choice for data storage and retrieval than traditional relational database management systems. Processing the large blocks of data that IoT applications collect is often a task better suited to a Hadoop cluster.
- **Analyze:** Analytics tools that work with technologies such as Hadoop, cloud data warehouses, Amazon Web Services-based big data tools and various NoSQL databases should be used for analyzing IoT data.
- **Conclude:** Data mining tools that reveal trends or hidden correlations are vital to helping an organization come to conclusions and make decisions about how to update, change, adjust and improve a system.
- **Extrapolate:** Information gathered from one application may inspire the development of a new or unrelated technology.

IoT systems can have varied data analysis requirements. For some IoT systems, the volume of data is very huge and thus analyzing the data on a single machine is not possible. For such systems, distributed batch data analytics frameworks such as Apache Hadoop can be used for data analysis. For IoT systems which have real-time data analysis requirements, tools such as Apache Storm are useful. For IoT systems which require interactive querying of data, Apache Spark can be used. Hadoop is an open source framework for distributed batch processing of massive scale data (Bahga & Madisetti, 2014).

CONCLUSION

The development of IoT has become an inevitable trend in the modern society. This chapter presented an overview of IoT concepts, its enabling technologies, characteristics and applications. Further, some of the challenges related to the design and deployment of IoT implementations have been presented. Moreover, the interplay between IoT and big data analytics has been discussed. It can be concluded that IoT has great potential for the consumer as well as for enterprises, but not without risk. On one hand IoT will bring us great opportunity of economic development to promote the society development. On the other hand, the massive scale and the open nature of IoT brings a number of corresponding challenges in terms of IP-addressability, privacy, security, data management and analytics. The data processing pipeline of IoT includes data collection, storage, and processing. Numerous research choices exist at the different stages of this pipeline. Research is also important in IoT security for the enterprises and businesses to help them begin preparations for transition from securing PCs, servers, mobile devices and traditional IT infrastructure, to managing a much broader set of interconnected items incorporating wearable devices, sensors and technology in IoT. As a result, research in IoT is likely to remain of great interest to researchers over the next few years.

REFERENCES

Abomhara, M., & Køien, G. M. (2015). Cyber Security and the Internet of Things: Vulnerabilities, Threats, Intruders and Attacks. *Journal of Cyber Security*, *4*, 65–88. doi:10.13052/jcsm2245-1439.414

Aggarwal, C. C., Ashish, N., & Sheth, A. (2013). *The internet of things: a survey from the data-centric perspective. In Managing and Mining Sensor Data*. Springer.

Al-Fuqaha, A., Guizani, M., Mohammadi, M., Aledhari, M., & Ayyash, M. (2015). Internet of Things: A Survey on Enabling Technologies, Protocols, and Applications. *IEEE Communication Surveys & Tutorials*, *17*(4), 2347-2376.

Ashford, W. (2016). IPv6 alone will not secure IoT. *ComputerWeekly Magazine*.

Ashton, K. (2009). That "Internet of Things" Thing In the Real World, Things Matter More than Ideas. *RFID Journal*, *22*, 97–114.

Bahga, A., & Madisetti, V. (2014). *Internet of Things: A Hands-On Approach*. Vijay Madisetti.

Berthelsen, E. (2016). The value engine in IoT data and analytics. *TechTarget*.

Chase, J. (2013). The Evolution of the Internet of Things (white paper). Texas Instruments, Dallas, Texas.

Chaves, L. W. F., & Nochta, Z. (2010). *Breakthrough towards the Internet of Things*. Springer-Verlag Berlin Heidelberg.

Chen, S., Xu, H., Liu, D., Hu, B., & Wang, H. (2014). A Vision of IoT: Applications, Challenges, and Opportunities with China Perspective. *IEEE Internet of Things Journal*, *1*(4), 349-359.

Gubbi, J., Buyya, R., Marusic, S., & Palaniswami, M. (2013). Internet of Things (IoT): A vision, architectural elements, and future directions. Elsevier. *Future Generation Computer Systems*, *29*(7), 1645–1660. doi:10.1016/j.future.2013.01.010

Holler, J., Tsiatsis, V., Mulligan, C., Avesand, S., Karnouskos, S., & Boyle, D. (2014). *From Machine-to-Machine to the Internet of Things: Introduction to a New Age of Intelligence*. Academic Press.

Kumar, A. (2015) Internet of Things (IoT): Seven enterprise risks to consider. In *Internet of Things in the Enterprise* (pp. 13-23).

Laskowski, N. (2016). *Delving into an enterprise IoT initiative. Internet of Things in the Enterprise*. TechTarget.

Lawton, G. (2016). IoT Gateways Need Clear Security Framework. In IoT Poses New Problems for Developers (pp. 3-5).

Pérez, I. C., & Barbolla, A. M. B. (2014). *Exploring Major Architectural Aspects of the Web of Things*. Switzerland: Springer International.

Prabhakaran, V.P. (2016). IoT Security, Threats and Challenges. *HAKIN9 Magazine*.

Raman, S. (2016). Analytics Proves Key To IoT. TechTarget.

Vermesan, O., & Friess, P. (2013). *Internet of Things- Converging Technologies for Smart Environments and Integrated Ecosystems*. River Publishers.

Wallgren, A. (2016). *How is IoT changing software development? Cloud Expo conference, Javits Center*. New York: Published by TechTarget IoT Agenda.

Zheng, D.E., & Carter, W.A. (2015). Leveraging the Internet of Things for a More Efficient and Effective Military. CSIS Strategic Technologies Program.

Chapter 8
Internet of Things for Smart Cities

Pallavi Khare
Matrusri Engineering College, India

Akhil Khare
MVSR Engineering College, India

ABSTRACT

The Internet of Things (IoT) is a system of interrelated computing devices, mechanical and digital machines, objects, animals or people that are provided with unique identifiers and the ability to transfer data over a network without requiring human-to-human or human-to-computer interaction. The Internet of Things (IoT) shall be able to incorporate transparently and seamlessly a large number of different and heterogeneous end systems, while providing open access to selected subsets of data for the development of a plethora of digital services. Building a general architecture for the IoT is hence a very complex task, mainly because of the extremely large variety of devices, link layer technologies, and services that may be involved in such a system.

INTRODUCTION

The Internet of Things (IoT) is a recent communication paradigm that envisions a near future, in which the objects of everyday life will be equipped with microcontrollers, transceivers for digital communication, and suitable protocol stacks that will make them able to communicate with one another and with the users, becoming an integral part of the Internet. The IoT concept, hence, aims at making the Internet even more immersive and pervasive. Furthermore, by enabling easy access and interaction with a wide variety of devices such as, for instance, home appliances, surveillance cameras, monitoring sensors, actuators, displays, vehicles, and so on, the IoT will foster the development of a number of applications that make use of the potentially enormous amount and variety of data generated by such objects to provide new services to citizens, companies, and public administrations.

DOI: 10.4018/978-1-5225-2947-7.ch008

Copyright © 2018, IGI Global. Copying or distributing in print or electronic forms without written permission of IGI Global is prohibited.

Outline

This paradigm indeed finds application in many different domains, such as home automation, industrial automation, medical aids, mobile healthcare, elderly assistance, intelligent energy management and smart grids, automotive, traffic management, and many others (Atzori, Iera & Morabito, 2010). However, such a heterogeneous field of application makes the identification of solutions capable of satisfying the requirements of all possible application scenarios a formidable challenge. This difficulty has led to the proliferation of different and, sometimes, incompatible proposals for the practical realization of IoT systems. Therefore, from a system perspective, the realization of an IoT network, together with the required backend network services and devices, still lacks an established best practice because of its novelty and complexity. In addition to the technical difficulties, the adoption of the IoT paradigm is also hindered by the lack of a clear and widely accepted business model that can attract investments to promote the deployment of these technologies.

Scope of the Work

Today the application of the IoT paradigm to an urban context is of particular interest, as it responds to the strong push of many national governments to adopt ICT solutions in the management of public affairs, thus realizing the so-called Smart City concept. Although there is not yet a formal and widely accepted definition of "Smart City," the final aim is to make a better use of the public resources, increasing the quality of the services offered to the citizens, while reducing the operational costs of the public administrations. This objective can be pursued by the deployment of an urban IoT, i.e., a communication infrastructure that provides unified, simple, and economical access to a plethora of public services, thus unleashing potential synergies and increasing transparency to the citizens. An urban IoT, indeed, may bring a number of benefits in the management and optimization of traditional public services, such as transport and parking, lighting, surveillance and maintenance of public areas, preservation of cultural heritage, garbage collection, salubrity of hospitals, and school. Furthermore, the availability of different types of data, collected by a pervasive urban IoT, may also be exploited to increase the transparency and promote the actions of the local government toward the citizens, enhance the awareness of people about the status of their city, stimulate the active participation of the citizens in the management of public administration, and also stimulate the creation of new services upon those provided by the IoT. Therefore, the application of the IoT paradigm to the Smart City is particularly attractive to local and regional administrations that may become the early adopters of such technologies, thus acting as catalyzes for the adoption of the IoT paradigm on a wider scale.

SMART CITY CONCEPT AND SERVICES

According to Pike Research on Smart Cities, the Smart City market is estimated at hundreds of billion dollars by 2020, with an annual spending reaching nearly 16 billion. This market springs from the synergic interconnection of key industry and service sectors, such as Smart Governance, Smart Mobility, Smart Utilities, Smart Buildings, and Smart Environment (Bellavista, Cardone, Corradi et al., 2013). These sectors have also been considered in the European Smart Cities project (European Smart Cities, n. d.) to define a ranking criterion that can be used to assess the level of "smartness" of European cities.

Nonetheless, the Smart City market has not really taken off yet, for a number of political, technical, and financial barriers. Under the political dimension, the primary obstacle is the attribution of decision-making power to the different stake holders. A possible way to remove this roadblock is to institutionalize the entire decision and execution process, concentrating the strategic planning and management of the smart city aspects into a single, dedicated department in the city. On the technical side, the most relevant issue consists in the non-interoperability of the heterogeneous technologies currently used in city and urban developments. In this respect, the IoT vision can become the building block to realize a unified urban scale ICT platform, thus unleashing the potential of the Smart City vision. Finally, concerning the financial dimension, a clear business model is still lacking, although some initiative to fill this gap has been recently undertaken. The situation is worsened by the adverse global economic situation, which has determined a general shrinking of investments on public services. This situation prevents the potentially huge Smart City market from becoming reality. A possible way out of this impasse is to first develop those services that conjugate social utility with very clear return on investment, such as smart parking and smart buildings, and will hence act as catalyzes for the other added value services. In the rest of this section, we overview some of the services that might be enabled by an urban IoT paradigm and that are of potential interest in the Smart City context because they can realize the win–win situation of increasing the quality and enhancing the services offered to the citizens while bringing an economical advantage for the city administration in terms of reduction of the operational costs.

Structural Health of Buildings

Proper maintenance of the historical buildings of a city requires the continuous monitoring of the actual conditions of each building and identification of the areas that are most subject to the impact of external agents. The urban IoT may provide a distributed database of building structural integrity measurements, collected by suitable sensors located in the buildings, such as vibration and deformation sensors to monitor the building stress, atmospheric agent sensors in the surrounding areas to monitor pollution levels, and temperature and humidity sensors to have a complete characterization of the environmental conditions. This database should reduce the need for expensive periodic structural testing by human operators and will allow targeted and proactive maintenance and restoration actions. Finally, it will be possible to combine vibration and seismic readings in order to better study and understand the impact of light earthquakes on city buildings. This database can be made publicly accessible in order to make the citizens aware of the care taken in preserving the city historical heritage. The practical realization of this service, however, requires the installation of sensors in the buildings and surrounding areas and their interconnection to a control system, which may require an initial investment in order to create the needed infrastructure.

Waste Management

Waste management is a primary issue in many modern cities, due to both the cost of the service and the problem of the storage of garbage in landfills. A deeper penetration of ICT solutions in this domain, however, may result in significant savings and economical and ecological advantages. For instance, the use of intelligent waste containers, which detect the level of load and allow for an optimization of the collector trucks route, can reduce the cost of waste collection and improve the quality of recycling. To realize such a smart waste management service, the IoT shall connect the end devices, i.e., intelligent waste containers, to a control center where optimization software processes the data and determines the optimal management of the collector truck fleet.

Air Quality

The European Union officially adopted a 20-20-20 Renewable Energy Directive setting climate change reduction goals for the next decade. The targets call for a 20% reduction in greenhouse gas emissions by 2020 compared with 1990 levels, a 20% cut in energy consumption through improved energy efficiency by 2020, and a 20% increase in the use of renewable energy by 2020. To such an extent, an urban IoT can provide means to monitor the quality of the air in crowded areas, parks, or fitness trails. In addition, communication facilities can be provided to let health applications running on joggers' devices be connected to the infrastructure. In such a way, people can always find the healthiest path for outdoor activities and can be continuously connected to their preferred personal training application. The realization of such a service requires that air quality and pollution sensors be deployed across the city and that the sensor data be made publicly available to citizens.

Noise Monitoring

Noise can be seen as a form of acoustic pollution as much as carbon oxide (CO) is for air. In that sense, the city authorities have already issued specific laws to reduce the amount of noise in the city centre at specific hours. An urban IoT can offer a noise monitoring service to measure the amount of noise produced at any given hour in the places that adopt the service. Besides building a space-time map of the noise pollution in the area, such a service can also be used to enforce public security, by means of sound detection algorithms that can recognize, for instance, the noise of glass crashes or brawls. This service can hence improve both the quiet of the nights in the city and the confidence of public establishment owners, although the installation of sound detectors or environmental microphones is quite controversial, because of the obvious privacy concerns for this type of monitoring.

Traffic Congestion

On the same line of air quality and noise monitoring, a possible Smart City service that can be enabled by urban IoT consists in monitoring the traffic congestion in the city. Even though camera-based traffic monitoring systems are already available and deployed in many cities, low-power widespread communication can provide a denser source of information. Traffic monitoring may be realized by using the sensing capabilities and GPS installed on modern vehicles, and also adopting a combination of air quality and acoustic sensors along a given road. This information is of great importance for city authorities and citizens: for the former to discipline traffic and to send officers where needed and for the latter to plan in advance the route to reach the office or to better schedule a shopping trip to the city centre.

City Energy Consumption

Together with the air quality monitoring service, an urban IoT may provide a service to monitor the energy consumption of the whole city, thus enabling authorities and citizens to get a clear and detailed view of the amount of energy required by the different services (public lighting, transportation, traffic lights, control cameras, heating/ cooling of public buildings, and so on). In turn, this will make it possible to identify the main energy consumption sources and to set priorities in order to optimize their behavior. This goes in the direction indicated by the European directive for energy efficiency improvement in the next years. In order to obtain such a service, power draw monitoring devices must be integrated with the power grid in the city. In addition, it will also be possible to enhance these services with active functionalities to control local power production structures (e.g., photovoltaic panels).

Smart Parking

The smart parking service is based on road sensors and intelligent displays that direct motorists along the best path for parking in the city. The benefits deriving from this service are manifold faster time to locate a parking slot means fewer CO emission from the car, lesser traffic congestion, and happier citizens. The smart parking service can be directly integrated in the urban IoT infrastructure, because many companies in Europe are providing market products for this application. Furthermore, by using short-range communication technologies, such as Radio Frequency Identifiers (RFID) or Near Field Communication (NFC), it is possible to realize an electronic verification system of parking permits in slots reserved for residents or disabled, thus offering a better service to citizens that can legitimately use those slots and an efficient tool to quickly spot violations.

Smart Lighting

In order to support the 20-20-20 directive, the optimization of the street lighting efficiency is an important feature. In particular, this service can optimize the street lamp intensity according to the time of the day, the weather condition, and the presence of people. In order to properly work, such a service needs to include the street lights into the Smart City infrastructure. It is also possible to exploit the increased number of connected spots to provide Wi-Fi connection to citizens. In addition, a fault detection system will be easily realized on top of the street light controllers.

Automation and Salubrity of Public Buildings

Another important application of IoT technologies is the monitoring of the energy consumption and the salubrity of the environment in public buildings (schools, administration offices, and museums) by means of different types of sensors and actuators that control lights, temperature, and humidity. By controlling these parameters, indeed, it is possible to enhance the level of comfort of the persons that live in these environments, which may also have a positive return in terms of productivity, while reducing the costs for heating/cooling (Schaffers, Komninos, Pallot et al., 2011).

URBAN IOT ARCHITECTURE

From the analysis of the services described earlier, it clearly emerges that most Smart City services are based on a centralized architecture, where a dense and heterogeneous set of peripheral devices deployed over the urban area generate different types of data that are then delivered through suitable communication technologies to a control center, where data storage and processing are performed. A primary characteristic of an urban IoT infrastructure, hence, is its capability of integrating different technologies with the existing communication infrastructures in order to support a progressive evolution of the IoT, with the interconnection of other devices and the realization of novel functionalities and services. Another fundamental aspect is the necessity to make (part of) the data collected by the urban IoT easily accessible by authorities and citizens, to increase the responsiveness of authorities to city problems, and to promote the awareness and the participation of citizens in public matters. In the rest of this section, we describe the different components of an urban IoT system, as sketched in Figure 1. Describing the web service approach for the design of IoT services, which requires the deployment of suitable protocol layers in the different elements of the network, as shown in the protocol stacks depicted in Figure 1, besides the key elements of the architecture. Then, we briefly overview the link layer technologies that can be used to interconnect the different parts of the IoT. Finally, we describe the heterogeneous set of devices that concur to the realization of an urban IoT.

Web Service Approach for IoT Service Architecture

Although in the IoT domain many different standards are still struggling to be the reference one and the most adopted, in this section we focus specifically on IETF standards because they are open and royalty-free, are based on Internet best practices, and can count on a wide community.

The IETF standards for IoT embrace a web service architecture for IoT services, which has been widely documented in the literature as a very promising and flexible approach. In fact, web services permit to realize a flexible and interoperable system that can be extended to IoT nodes, through the adoption of

Figure 1. Conceptual representation of an urban IoT network based on the web service approach

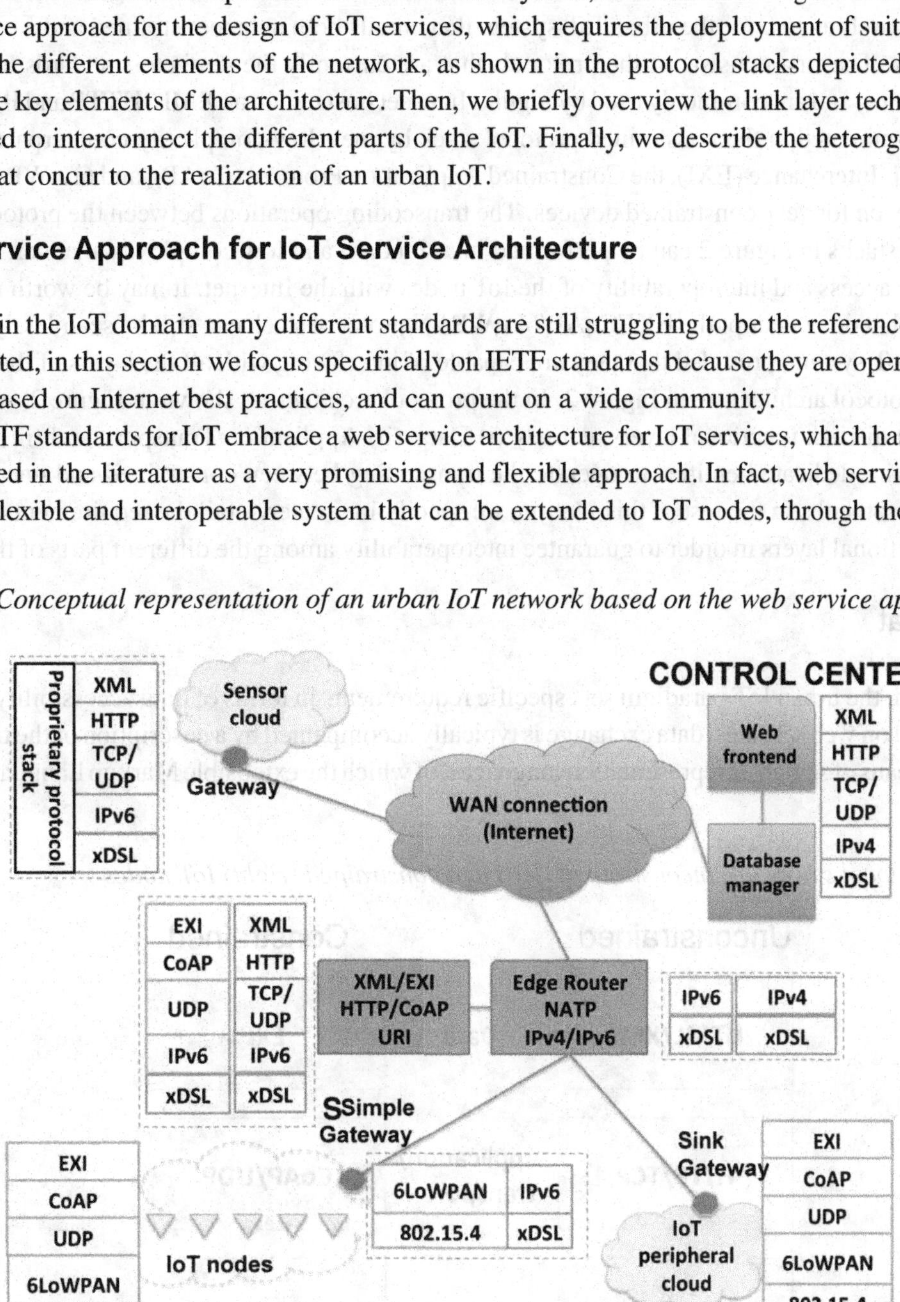

the web based paradigm known as Representational State Transfer (ReST). IoT services designed in accordance with the ReST paradigm exhibit very strong similarity with traditional web services, thus greatly facilitating the adoption and use of IoT by both end users and service developers, which will be able to easily reuse much of the knowledge gained from traditional web technologies in the development of services for networks containing smart objects. The web service approach is also promoted by international standardization bodies such as IETF, ETSI, and W3C, among others, as well as European research projects on the IoT such as SENSEI, 5 IoT-A, 6 and SmartSantander.1 Figure 2 shows a reference protocol architecture for the urban IoT system that entails both an unconstrained and a constrained protocol stack. The first consists of the protocols that are currently the de-facto standards for Internet communications, and are commonly used by regular Internet hosts, such as XML, HTTP and IPv4. These protocols are mirrored in the constrained protocol stack by their low-complexity counterparts, i.e., the Efficient XML Interchange (EXI), the Constrained Application Protocol (CoAP), and 6LoWPAN, which are suitable, even for very constrained devices. The transcoding operations between the protocols in the left and right stacks in Figure 2 can be performed in a standard and low complexity manner, thus guaranteeing easy access and interoperability of the IoT nodes with the Internet. It may be worth remarking that systems that do not adopt the EXI/CoAP/6LoWPAN protocol stack can still be seamlessly included in the urban IoT system, provided that they are capable of interfacing with all the layers of the left-hand side of the protocol architecture in Figure 2. In the protocol architecture shown in Figure 2, we can distinguish three distinct functional layers, namely (i) Data, (ii) Application/Transport, and (iii) Network, that may require dedicated entities to operate the transcoding between constrained and unconstrained formats and protocols. In the rest of this section, we specify in greater detail the requirements at each of the three functional layers in order to guarantee interoperability among the different parts of the system.

Data Format

As mentioned, the urban IoT paradigm sets specific requirements in terms of data accessibility. In architectures based on web services, data exchange is typically accompanied by a description of the transferred content by means of semantic representation languages, of which the extensible Markup Language (XML)

Figure 2. Protocol stacks for unconstrained (left) and constrained (right) IoT nodes

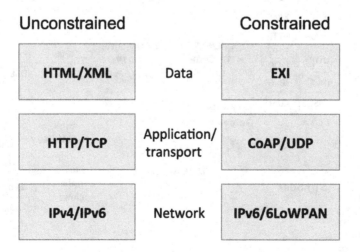

is probably the most common. Nevertheless, the size of XML messages is often too large for the limited capacity of typical devices for the IoT. Furthermore, the text nature of XML representation makes the parsing of messages by CPU-limited devices more complex compared to the binary formats. For these reasons, the working group of the World Wide Web Consortium (W3C)7 has proposed the EXI format, which makes it possible even for very constrained devices to natively support and generate messages using an open data format compatible with XML. EXI defines two types of encoding, namely schema-less and schema-informed. While the schema-less encoding is generated directly from the XML data and can be decoded by any EXI entity without any prior knowledge about the data, the schema informed encoding assumes that the two EXI processors share an XML Schema before actual encoding and decoding can take place. This shared schema makes it possible to assign numeric identifiers to the XML tags in the schema and build the EXI grammars upon such coding. As discussed in, a general-purpose schema-informed EXI processor can be easily integrated even in very constrained devices, enabling them to interpret EXI formats and, hence, making it possible to build multipurpose IoT nodes even out of very constrained devices. Using the schema informed approach, however, requires additional care in the development of higher layer application, since developers need to define an XML Schema for the messages involved in the application and use EXI processors that support this operating mode. Further details about EXI and schema-informed processing can be found in. Integration of multiple XML/EXI data sources into an IoT system can be obtained by using the databases typically created and maintained by high-level applications. In fact, IoT applications generally build a database of the nodes controlled by the application and, often, of the data generated by such nodes. The database makes it possible to integrate the data received by any IoT device to provide the specific service the application is built for. A generic framework for building IoT web applications according to the guidelines described in this section has been proposed in, where the authors also suggest exploiting the Asynchronous JavaScript and XML (AJAX) capabilities of modern web browsers that allow for a direct communication between the browser and the final IoT node, demonstrating the full internetworking of the protocol stack and the open data nature of the proposed approach.

Application and Transport Layers

Most of the traffic that crosses the Internet nowadays is carried at the application layer by HTTP over TCP. However, the verbosity and complexity of native HTTP make it unsuitable for a straight deployment on constrained IoT devices. For such an environment, in fact, the human-readable format of HTTP, which has been one of the reasons of its success in traditional networks, turns out to be a limiting factor due to the large amount of heavily correlated (and, hence, redundant) data. Moreover, HTTP typically relies upon the TCP transport protocol that, however, does not scale well on constrained devices, yielding poor performance for small data flows in loss environments. The CoAP protocol overcomes these difficulties by proposing a binary format transported over UDP, handling only the retransmissions strictly required to provide a reliable service. Moreover, CoAP can easily interoperate with HTTP because: (i) It supports the ReST methods of HTTP (GET, PUT, POST, and DELETE), (ii) there is a one-to-one correspondence between the response codes of the two protocols, and (iii) The CoAP options can support a wide range of HTTP usage scenarios. CoAP to directly talk to IoT devices, the most general and easily interoperable solution requires the deployment of an HTTP-CoAP intermediary, also known as cross proxy that can straightforwardly translate requests/responses between the two protocols, thus enabling transparent interoperation with native HTTP devices and applications.

Network Layer

IPv4 is the leading addressing technology supported by Internet hosts. However, IANA, the international organization that assigns IP addresses at a global level, has recently announced the exhaustion of IPv4 address blocks. IoT networks, in turn, are expected to include billions of nodes, each of which shall be (in principle) uniquely addressable. A solution to this problem is offered by the IPv6 standard, which provides a 128-bit address field, thus making it possible to assign a unique IPv6 address to any possible node in the IoT network. While, on the one hand, the huge address space of IPv6 makes it possible to solve the addressing issues in IoT; on the other hand, it introduces overheads that are not compatible with the scarce capabilities of constrained nodes. This problem can be overcome by adopting 6LoWPAN which is an established compression format for IPv6 and UDP headers over low-power constrained networks. A border router, which is a device directly attached to the 6LoWPANnetwork, transparently performs the conversion between IPv6 and 6LoWPAN, translating any IPv6 packet intended for a node in the 6LoWPAN network into a packet with 6LoWPAN header compression format, and operating the inverse translation in the opposite direction. While the deployment of a 6LoWPAN border router enables transparent interaction between IoT nodes and any IPv6 host in the Internet, the interaction with IPv4-only hosts remains an issue. More specifically, the problem consists in finding a way to address a specific IPv6 host using an IPv4 address and other meta-data available in the packet. In the following, we present different approaches to achieve this goal.

v4/v6 Port Address Translation (v4/v6 PAT)

This method maps arbitrary pairs of IPv4 addresses and TCP/UDP ports into IPv6 addresses and TCP/UDP ports. It resembles the classical Network Address and Port Translation (NAPT) service currently supported in many LANs to provide Internet access to a number of hosts in a private network by sharing a common public IPv4 address, which is used to address the packets over the public Internet. When a packet is returned to the IPv4 common address, the edge router that supports the NATP service will intercept the packet and replace the common IPv4 destination address with the (private) address of the intended receiver, which is determined by looking up in the NATP table the address of the host associated to the specific destination port carried by the packet. The same technique can be used to map multiple IPv6 addresses into a single IPv4 public address, which allows the forwarding of the datagram's in the IPv4 network and its correct management at IPv4-only hosts. The application of this technique requires low complexity and, indeed, port mapping is an established technique for v4/v6 transition. On the other hand, this approach raises a scalability problem, since the number of IPv6 hosts that can be multiplexed into a single IPv4 address is limited by the number of available TCP/UDP ports (65535). Furthermore, this approach requires that the connection be initiated by the IPv6 nodes in order to create the correct entries in the NATP look-up table. Connections starting from the IPv4 cloud can also be realized, but this requires a more complex architecture, with the local DNS placed within the IPv6 network and statically associated to a public IPv4 address in the NATP translation table.

v4/v6 Domain Name Conversion

This method, originally proposed in, is similar to the technique used to provide virtual hosting service in HTTP 1.1, which makes it possible to support multiple websites on the same web server, sharing the same IPv4 address, by exploiting the information contained in the HTTP Host header to identify the specific web site requested by the user. Similarly, it is possible to program the DNS servers in such a way that, upon a DNS request for the domain name of an IoT web service, the DNS returns the IPv4 address of an HTTP CoAP cross proxy to be contacted to access the IoT node. Once addressed by an HTTP request, the proxy requires the resolution of the domain name contained in the HTTP Host header to the IPv6 DNS server, which replies with the IPv6 address that identifies the final IoT node involved in the request. The proxy can then forward the HTTP message to the intended IoT via CoAP.

URI Mapping

The Universal Resource Identifier (URI) mapping technique is also described in. This technique involves a particular type of HTTP-CoAP cross proxy, the reverse cross proxy. This proxy behaves as being the final web server to the HTTP/IPv4 client and as the original client to the CoAP/IPv6 web server. Since this machine needs to be placed in a part of the network where IPv6 connectivity is present to allow direct access to the final IoT nodes, IPv4/IPv6 conversion is internally resolved by the applied URI mapping function.

Link Layer Technologies

An urban IoT system, due to its inherently large deployment area, requires a set of link layer technologies that can easily cover a wide geographical area and, at the same time, support a possibly large amount of traffic resulting from the aggregation of an extremely high number of smaller data flows. For these reasons, link layer technologies enabling the realization of an urban IoT system are classified into unconstrained and constrained technologies. The first group includes all the traditional LAN, MAN, and WAN communication technologies, such as Ethernet, WiFi, fiber optic, broadband Power Line Communication (PLC), and cellular technologies such as UMTS and LTE. They are generally characterized by high reliability, low latency, and high transfer rates (order of Mbit/s or higher), and due to their inherent complexity and energy consumption are generally not suitable for peripheral IoT nodes. The constrained physical and link layer technologies are instead generally characterized by low energy consumption and relatively low transfer rates, typically smaller than 1 Mbit/s. The more prominent solutions in this category are IEEE 802.15.4Bluetooth and Bluetooth Low Energy, IEEE 802.11 Low Power, PLC, NFC and RFID. These links usually exhibit long latencies, mainly due to two factors: 1) the intrinsically low transmission rate at the physical layer and 2) the power saving policies implemented by the nodes to save energy, which usually involve duty cycling with short active periods.

Devices

We finally describe the devices that are essential to realize an urban IoT, classified based on the position they occupy in the communication flow.

Backend Servers

At the root of the system, we find the backend servers, located in the control center, where data are collected, stored, and processed to produce added-value services. In principle, backend servers are not mandatory for an IoT system to properly operate, though they become a fundamental component of an urban IoT where they can facilitate the access to the smart city services and open data through the legacy network infrastructure. Backend systems commonly considered for interfacing with the IoT data feeders include the following.

Database Management Systems

These systems are in charge of storing the large amount of information produced by IoT peripheral nodes, such as sensors. Depending on the particular usage scenario, the load on these systems can be quite large, so that proper dimensioning of the backend system is required. Web sites: The widespread acquaintance of people with web interfaces makes them the first option to enable interoperation between the IoT system and the "data consumers," e.g., public authorities, service operators, utility providers, and common citizens.

Enterprise Resource Planning Systems (ERP)

ERP components support a variety of business functions and are precious tools to manage the flow of information across a complex organization, such as a city administration. Interfacing ERP components with database management systems that collect the data generated by the IoT allows for a simpler management of the potentially massive amount of data gathered by the IoT, making it possible to separate the information flows based on their nature and relevance and easing the creation of new services.

Gateways

Moving toward the "edge" of the IoT, we find the gateways, whose role is to interconnect the end devices to the main communication infrastructure of the system. With reference to the conceptual protocol architecture depicted in Figure 2, the gateway is hence required to provide protocol translation and functional mapping between the unconstrained protocols and their constrained counterparts, that is to say XMLEXI, HTTP-CoAP, and IPv4/v6-6LoWPAN. Note that while all these translations may be required in order to enable interoperability with IoT peripheral devices and control stations, it is not necessary to concentrate all of them in a single gateway. Rather, it is possible, and sometimes convenient, to distribute the translation tasks over different devices in the network. For example, a single HTTP-CoAP proxy can be deployed to support multiple 6LoWPAN border routers. Gateway devices shall also provide the interconnection between unconstrained link layer technologies, mainly used in the core of the IoT network, and constrained technologies that, instead, provide connectivity among the IoT peripheral nodes.

IoT Peripheral Nodes

Finally, at the periphery of the IoT system, we find the devices in charge of producing the data to be delivered to the control center, which are usually called IoT peripheral nodes or, more simply, IoT nodes. Generally speaking, the cost of these devices is very low, starting from 10 USD or even less, depending on the kind and number of sensors/actuators mounted on the board. IoT nodes may be classified based on a wide number of characteristics, such as powering mode, networking role (relay or leaf), sensor/actuator equipment, and supported link layer technologies. The most constrained IoT nodes are likely the Radio

Frequency tags (RFtags) that, despite their very limited capabilities, can still play an important role in IoT systems, mainly because of the extremely low cost and the passive nature of their communication hardware, which does not require any internal energy source. The typical application of RFtags is object identification by proximity reading, which can be used for logistics, maintenance, monitoring, and other services. Mobile devices, such as smart phones, tablet PCs, or laptops, may also be an important part of an urban IoT, providing other ways to interact with it. For instance, the NFC transceiver integrated in last-generation smartphones may be used to identify tagged objects, while the geolocation service provided by most common operating systems for mobile devices can enrich the context information associated to that object. Furthermore, mobile devices can provide access to the IoT in different ways, e.g., 1) through an IP connection provided by the cellular data link service or 2) setting up a direct connection with some objects by using short-range wireless technologies, such as Bluetooth Low Energy, low-power Wi-Fi, or IEEE 802.15.4. Furthermore, it is possible to develop specific applications for mobile devices that can ease the interaction with the IoT objects, and with the system as a whole.

AN EXPERIMENTAL STUDY: PADOVA SMART CITY

The experimental wireless sensor network test bed, with more than 300 nodes, deployed at the University of Padova, has been designed according to these guidelines, and successfully used to realize proof of concept demonstrations of smart grid and health care services. In this section, we describe a practical implementation of an urban IoT, named "Padova Smart City," that has been realized in the city of Padova; thanks to the collaboration between public and private parties, such as the municipality of Padova, which has sponsored the project, the Department of Information Engineering of the University of Padova, which has provided the theoretical background and the feasibility analysis of the project, and Patavina Technologies s.r.l.,9 a spin-off of the University of Padova specialized in the development of innovative IoT solutions, which has developed the IoT nodes and the control software. The primary goal of Padova Smart City is to promote the early adoption of open data and ICT solutions in the public administration. The target application consists of a system for collecting environmental data and monitoring the public street lighting by means of wireless nodes, equipped with different kinds of sensors, placed on street light poles and connected to the Internet through a gateway unit. This system shall make it possible to collect interesting environmental parameters, such as CO level, air temperature and humidity, vibrations, noise, and so on, while providing a simple but accurate mechanism to check the correct operation of the public lighting system by measuring the light intensity at each post. Even if this system is a simple application of the IoT concept, it still involves a number of different devices and link layer technologies, thus being representative of most of the critical issues that need to be taken care of when designing an urban IoT. A high-level overview of the types and roles of the devices involved in the system is given hereafter.

Padova Smart City Components

A conceptual sketch of the Padova Smart City system architecture is given in Figure 3. In the following, we describe in more details the different hardware and software components of the system (Cuff, Hansen & Kang, 2008).

Figure 3. System architecture of "Padova Smart City"

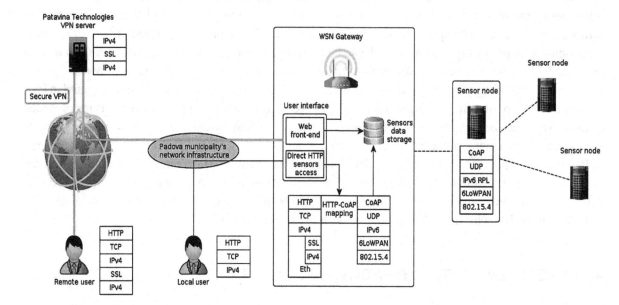

Street Light

It is the leaf part of the system where IoT nodes are placed. Each streetlight is geographically localized on the city map and uniquely associated to the IoT node attached to it, so that IoT data can be enhanced with context information. The monitoring of the correct operation of the bulbs is performed through photometer sensors that directly measure the intensity of the light emitted by the lamps (or, actually, by any source whose light reaches the sensor) at regular time intervals or upon request. The wireless IoT nodes are also equipped with temperature and humidity sensors, which provide data concerning weather conditions, and one node is also equipped with a benzene(C6H6) sensor, which monitors air quality. IoT nodes are generally powered by small batteries, though connection to a low-power grid is required by the benzene sensor. The packaging of the sensor nodes has been designed by considering the specific requirements of this use case. Indeed, sensor nodes have been hosted in a transparent plastic shield that protects the electronic parts from atmospheric phenomena (such as rain or snow), while permitting the circulation of air and light for the correct measurement of humidity, temperature, and light intensity.

Constrained Link Layer Technologies

The IoT nodes mounted on the streetlight poles form a 6LoWPAN multi hop cloud, using IEEE 802.15.4 constrained link layer technology. Routing functionalities are provided by the IPv6 Routing Protocol for Low power and Loss Networks (RPL). IoT nodes are assigned unique IPv6 addresses, suitably compressed according to the 6LoWPAN standard. Each node can be individually accessible from anywhere in the Internet by means of IPv6/6LoWPAN. Nodes collectively deliver their data to a sink node, which represents the single point of contact for the external nodes. Alternatively, each node might publish its own features and data by running a CoAP server, though this feature is not yet implemented in the test bed. In either case, a gateway is required to bridge the 6LoWPAN cloud to the Internet and perform all the transcoding described in the previous section (Vilajosana, Llosa, Martinez et al., 2013).

WSN Gateway

The gateway has the role of interfacing the constrained link layer technology used in the sensors cloud with traditional WAN technologies used to provide connectivity to the central backend servers. The gateway hence plays the role of 6LoWPAN border router and RPL root node. Furthermore, since sensor nodes do not support CoAP services, the gateway also operates as the sink node for the sensor cloud, collecting all the data that need to be exported to the backend services. The connection to the backend services is provided by common unconstrained communication technologies, optical fiber in this specific example.

HTTP-CoAP Proxy

The HTTP-CoAP proxy enables transparent communication with CoAP devices. The proxy logic can be extended to better support monitoring applications and limit the amount of traffic injected into the IoT peripheral network. For instance, it is possible to specify a list of resources that need to be monitored, so that the server can autonomously update the entries in a cache related to those devices. This mechanism can be supported by two different approaches: 1) by polling the selected resource proactively, thus enabling the implementation of traffic shaping techniques at the proxy or at the gateway and 2) by subscribing to the selected resource using the "observe" functionality of CoAP, thus enabling the server on the node to send the updates only when the value measured by the sensor falls outside a certain range. This service is collocated on the switchboard gateway in the Padova Smart City system, though it could also be placed in the backend servers, thus making it possible to control multiple gateways by using a single proxy instance.

Figure 4. Example of data collected by Padova Smart City: (a) temperature and (b) humidity

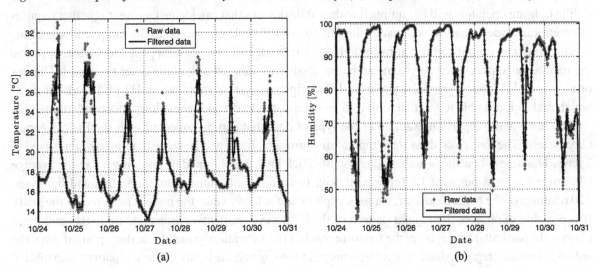

Figure 5. Example of data collected by Padova Smart City: (a) light and (b) benzene

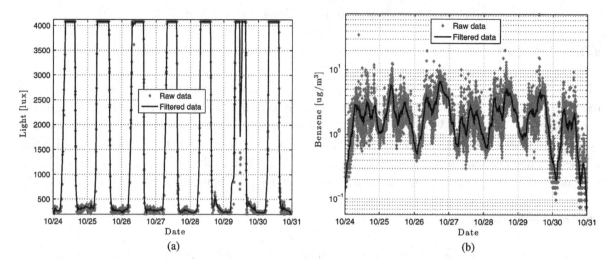

(a) (b)

Database Server

The database server collects the state of the resources that need to be monitored in time by communicating with the HTTP-CoAP proxy server, which in turn takes care of retrieving the required data from the proper source. The data stored in the database are accessible through traditional web programming technologies. The information can either be visualized in the form of a web site, or exported in any open data format using dynamic web programming languages. In the Padova Smart City network, the database server is realized within the WSN Gateway, which hence represents a plug and- play module that provides a transparent interface with the peripheral nodes (Hernández-Muñoz, Vercher, Muñoz et al., 2011).

Operator Mobile Device

Public lighting operators will be equipped with mobile devices that can locate the streetlight that requires intervention, issue actuation commands directly to the IoT node connected to the lamp, and signal the result of the intervention to the central system that can track every single lamppost and, hence, optimize the maintenance plan. Such a system can be successively extended to include other types of IoT nodes or clouds of IoT nodes, provided that each IoT peripheral system supports an HTTP-based interface, which makes it possible to interact with it in an open-, standard-, and technology-independent manner.

Figures 4 and 5 report an example of the type of data that can be collected with the Padova Smart City system. The four plots show the temperature, humidity, light, and benzene readings over a period of 7 days. Thin lines show the actual readings, while thick lines are obtained by applying a moving average filter over a time window of 1 h (approximately, 10 readings of temperature, humidity, and light, and 120 readings of the benzene sensor, whose sampling rate is larger since the node is powered by the grid). It is possible to observe the regular pattern of the light measurements, corresponding to day and night periods. In particular, at daytime, the measure reaches the saturation value, while during night time, the values are more irregular, due to the reflections produced by vehicle lights. A similar pattern is exhibited by the humidity and temperature measurements that, however, are much noisier than those for light. The benzene measurements also reveal a decrease of the benzene levels at nighttime, as expected due to the lighter night traffic, but quite surprisingly there are no evident variations in the daytime benzene levels during the weekend (October 26–27). It is also interesting to note the peak of benzene measured in the early afternoon of October 29. Examining the readings of the other sensors in the same time interval, we can note a sharp decrease of light intensity and temperature, and an increase in humidity. These readings suggest that a quick rainstorm has temporarily obscured the sunlight, while producing congestion in the road traffic and, in turn, a peak of benzene in the air.

CONCLUSION

The analyzed solutions are currently available for the implementation of urban IoTs. The discussed technologies are close to being standardized, and industry players are already active in the production of devices that take advantage of these technologies to enable the applications of interest, such as those described in Section II. In fact, while the range of design options for IoT systems is rather wide, the set of open and standardized protocols is significantly smaller. The enabling technologies, furthermore, have reached a level of maturity that allows for the practical realization of IoT solutions and services, starting from field trials that will hopefully help clear the uncertainty that still prevents a massive adoption of the IoT paradigm. A concrete proof-of-concept implementation, deployed in collaboration with the city of Padova, Italy, has also been described as a relevant example of application of the IoT paradigm to smart cities.

REFERENCES

Atzori, L., Iera, A., & Morabito, G. (2010). The internet of things: A survey. *Computer Networks*, *54*(15), 2787–2805. doi:10.1016/j.comnet.2010.05.010

Bellavista, P., Cardone, G., Corradi, A., & Foschini, L. (2013). Convergence of MANET and WSN in IoT urban scenarios. *IEEE Sensors Journal*, *13*(10), 3558–3567. doi:10.1109/JSEN.2013.2272099

Cuff, D., Hansen, M., & Kang, J. (2008). Urban sensing: Out of the woods. *Communications of the ACM*, *51*(3), 24–33. doi:10.1145/1325555.1325562

European Smart Cities. (n. d.) Retrieved from http://www.smart-cities.eu

Hernández-Muñoz, J. M., Vercher, J. B., Muñoz, L., Galache, J. A., Presser, M., Hernández Gómez, L. A., & Pettersson, J. (2011). Smart Cities at the forefront of the future Internet, The Future Internet. *Lecture Notes in Computer Science*, *6656*, 447–462. doi:10.1007/978-3-642-20898-0_32

Schaffers, H., Komninos, N., Pallot, M., Trousse, B., Nilsson, M., & Oliveira, A. (2011). Smart cities and the future internet: Towards cooperation frameworks for open innovation, The Future Internet. *Lecture Notes in Computer Science*, *6656*, 431–446. doi:10.1007/978-3-642-20898-0_31

Vilajosana, I., Llosa, J., Martinez, B., Domingo-Prieto, M., Angles, A., & Vilajosana, X. (2013, June). A. Angles, and X. Vilajosana, "Bootstrapping smart cities through a self-sustainable model based on big data flows. *IEEE Communications Magazine*, *51*(6), 128–134. doi:10.1109/MCOM.2013.6525605

ADDITIONAL READING

Dohler, M., Vilajosana, I., Vilajosana, X., & Llosa, J. (2011, December). Smart Cities: An action plan. *Proc. Barcelona Smart Cities Congress*, Barcelona, Spain (pp. 1–6).

Laya, A., Bratu, V. I., & Markendahl, J. (2013). Who is investing in machine-to-machine communications? *Proc. 24th Eur. Reg. ITS Conf.*, Florence, Italy (pp. 20–23).

Lynch, J. P., & Kenneth, J. L. (2006). A summary review of wireless sensors and sensor networks for structural health monitoring. *Shock and Vibration Digest, 38*(2), 91–130. doi:10.1177/0583102406061499

Mulligan, C. E. A., & Olsson, M. (2013). Architectural implications of smart city business models: An evolutionary perspective. *IEEE Communications Magazine, 51*(6), 80–85. doi:10.1109/MCOM.2013.6525599

Nuortio, T., Kytöjoki, J., Niska, H., & Bräysy, O. (2006). Improved route planning and scheduling of waste collection and transport. *Expert Systems with Applications, 30*(2), 223–232. doi:10.1016/j.eswa.2005.07.009

Walravens, N., & Ballon, P. (2013). Platform business models for smart cities: From control and value to governance and public value. *IEEE Communications Magazine, 51*(6), 72–79. doi:10.1109/MCOM.2013.6525598

KEY TERMS AND DEFINITIONS

Evolutionary Perspective: Evolutionary psychology is an approach in the social and natural sciences that examines psychological traits such as memory, perception, and language from a modern evolutionary perspective.

Internet of Things (IoT): The Internet of things (IoT) is the inter-networking of physical devices, vehicles (also referred to as "connected devices" and "smart devices"), buildings, and other items—embedded with electronics, software, sensors, actuators, and network connectivity that enable these objects to collect and exchange data.

Open Innovation: Open Innovation is a paradigm that assumes that firms can and should use external ideas as well as internal ideas, and internal and external paths to market, as the firms look to advance their technology.

Smart City: A smart city is an urban development vision to integrate information and communication technology (ICT) and Internet of things (IoT) technology in a secure fashion to manage a city's assets.

Urban Sensing: Urban Sensing is a project area investigating the use of digital environmental sensors in urban environments to promote sustainability.

Chapter 9
PIR–Enabled Security System for Internet of Things Using Raspberry Pi

Mamillapally Nagaraju
Adarsh Degree and PG College, India

Mulukutla Trivikram
Adarsh Degree and PG College, India

ABSTRACT

Internet of Things (IoT) is an evolution of mobile, home and embedded systems that can be connected to internet increasing greater capabilities of data analytics to extract meaningful information, which can further used for decision making. Billions of devices are connected to internet and soon its number may grow higher than number of human beings on this planet. These connected devices integrated together can become a network of intelligent systems that share data over the cloud to analyze. IoT is an emerging technology where several machines are embedded with low power consuming sensors that allow them to rely data from each other with little or no human intervention. Especially, PIR motion sensor plays a key role in security systems for detecting movements, intrusion and occupancy by interacting with other devices simultaneously like alarms, cameras etc. In this paper, researchers studied IoT applications using PIR motion sensor and proposed architecture and algorithms to be implemented for better development of security systems.

INTRODUCTION

IoT has been emerged with an old concept already implemented in cash machines more than 50 years ago. IoT is continuing its success journey till today with an invention of Raspberry Pi, a small credit size computer. Raspberry Pi is a series of single board size computer and can be integrated with many other devices. Raspberry Pi is well suited as an array of sensor hub used to propagate information through remote protocols or via web server. A big contribution of IoT is not about smart devices, but about sensors (Figure 1). Sensors transforms analog data collected from scanning the environment to digital data,

DOI: 10.4018/978-1-5225-2947-7.ch009

Copyright © 2018, IGI Global. Copying or distributing in print or electronic forms without written permission of IGI Global is prohibited.

Figure 1. IoT workflow

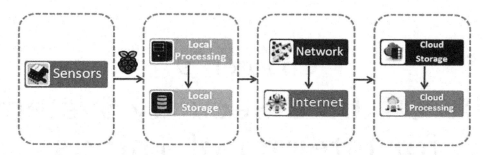

but never do any processing. Advances in sensor fusion for remote computing could also lead to new future applications. These tiny innovative sensors can be attached to everything from solid objects to human organs. They record and send data back to the cloud for analysis to make decisions. In machine to machine learning, sensors are the key to gather information from physical objects to analyze. In recent years, the development of sensor technology, wireless network technology, signal processing technology tracking and recognizing intruders have gradually became the best area for researchers. For better security in most sensitive areas of industries, organizations and homes, the surroundings are equipping with devices embedded with various sensors which further integrated and communicated with other devices to generate some analytical data to overcome the security breaches if any.

Especially in this regard, PIR motion sensor plays a key role in security systems for detecting movements, intrusion and occupancy by interacting with other devices like alarms and cameras simultaneously.

In this area of context, researchers have tried to combine their virtues and proposed to develop a distributed system with various sensor nodes like PIR motion sensor, alarm sensor, camera sensors and facial recognition systems. The proposed distributed sensor network is developed based on the pyroelectric infrared sensor node that can identify the tracking and recognition of human objects in its small area of field. The passive or pyroelectric motion sensor has several advantages like high capability of identifying infrared radiations, low power consumption, high performance with independent of illumination, angular rate of sensitivity range, and responds properly in case of moving objects.

In this paper, researchers studied several IoT applications and identified security based applications are the most serious and sensitive area where IoT can contribute a lot. In this research, authors used a PIR motion sensor and proposed architecture for its better implementation of distributed security systems. Finally authors proposed certain algorithms to be implemented at different levels of security.

This chapter is organized as follows: First, the authors of this chapter reviewed the literature of the research articles and journals to understand clearly about working functionality of the sensors and how they can be implemented in the development of distributed security systems. Second, authors studied opportunities and application of IoT for better understanding of security areas. Third, architecture is proposed by considering PIR motion sensor as a primary device for human/intruder detection. Raspberry pi IoT device is included in the architecture as an interface for data receiving and transferring to other systems and servers for data analysis. Later, authors clearly studied new security system implementation workflow by considering two test cases for human or intruder detection. Authors developed flowcharts to represent the workflow of the system and also developed an algorithm which clearly explains how the system work proceeds. Finally, this chapter identified the limitation and challenges facing by the internet of things during its success race.

RELATED WORK

IoT devices have been more popular in diverse areas like e-commerce, e-health, e-home etc. Due to the vast increase in deployment of IoT devices, in some cases they can be a subject part to malicious attacks making security and privacy of IoT devices compromise. According to Jorge Granjal et al. (2015), Internet of Things brought a new vision of future network technology where users, intelligent systems and many objects possessing sensing capabilities can communicate each other with better convenience and economical benefits. During their context of connectivity, architecture and internet based communication protocols will play a key role. The most fundamental enabling fact of IoT applications are security. There is a need of such mechanisms to be designed and enable a secure communication by such technologies.

Many researchers have also been working on PIR sensors to develop an efficient human identification system. Hao et al. (2006) presented wireless pyroelectric IR sensor tracking system composed of sensor, synchronization and error filtering and data fusion modules The module in this system can detect the angular displacement of human targets moving in the network.

Fang et al. (2006) presented a system to recognize real time human target using a pyroelectric IR sensor array and the hidden Markov chain model. Fang enhanced the system by proposing an algorithm for motion representation feature by using sensor signal system. Zappi et al. (2007) identified that the signal sensor node is used to trigger an alarm and judge the existence of moving human targets while an array of many pyroelectric infrared sensors has the capability to extract few more features of moving targets such as direction and speed. Later Zappi et al. (2010) proposed an algorithm for sensor data fusion and to extract features and to track moving human targets along footpaths and obtained higher tracing precision.

Erickson et al. (2013) based on a camera, PIR sensor and a wireless sensor network implemented a power-efficient occupancy-based energy management system for controlling HVAC system and, thus, increasing energy efficiency and monitoring effectiveness. Gopinathan et al. (2003) developed a pyroelectric tracking system to identify human motion based on coded apertures, which could detect human movements in one of the area using four PIR detectors. Shankar et al. (2006) also developed a human tracking system based on a low-cost PIR sensors cluster consisting of Fresnel lens arrays to implement the required spatial segmentations. Shankar et al. (2006) analyzed the sensor cluster response characteristics and extracted the direction and velocity of the motion over large areas. Hao et al. (2006) presented a human tracking system by using a microcontroller, a radio-frequency transceiver and a radial sensor module with PIR detectors with Fresnel lens arrays arranged in a circle. They showed that the system can be used to track an individual human target by detecting its moving angular displacement. Luo et al. (2009) performed a 3D simulation study for tracking human motion using PIR sensors. Their approach exhibited the visibility modulation of every sensor detector and the sensor modules layout and proposed algorithms for tracking people based on the binary output of the PIR sensors.

Lee (1994) proposed a novel method of detecting the target human motion direction moving in the field of a single PIR sensor view. Zappi et al. (2007) built a wireless network system based on low-cost PIR sensor for detecting the direction of human movement and distinguishing the number of people moving in line, as well as side by side in a hallway. They showed the 100% detection rate of movement direction and 89% accurate detection of the number of people. Zappi (2008, 2010) also built a cluster system with two PIR sensors facing each other in a hallway for detecting the direction of movement and distance intervals when a human is moving. More recently, Yun and Song (2014) presented a generic method of identifying the relative direction of human movement in eight different directions distributed uniformly with two pairs of PIR sensors whose sensing elements are aligned orthogonally. With the raw data sets of the direction of the movement captured they achieved more than a 98% correct detection rate.

Fang et al. (2006) presented a human recognition system using a pyroelectric infrared sensor whose visibility is modulated by an array of Fresnel lens and a method of principal components regression. Fang et al. in (2006) presented a method for identifying areas walking through a dependent and an independent path based on pyroelectric infrared sensors with modulated visibilities and hidden Markov models. They also showed a biometric system embedded with a PIR sensor for human target motion Hao et al. (2009) introduced a wireless PIR distributed system for tracking and identifying multiple human targets based on their body heat radiation and gait. Jaeseok Yun and Sang-Shin Lee presented an empirical study by using a set of PIR sensors to detect human movement and identification. Yun developed a data collection module for monitoring people and performed classification analysis based on machine learning algorithms. Ji Xiong, Fangmin Li proposed an application for empirical mode decomposition and extracted features of moving human target objects both in time and frequency domain.

The PIR motion sensors are widely used in smart surveillance systems for tracking occupants in most sensitive areas in a building for security purposes. Moghavvemi and Seng (2004) recommended the installation of surveillance systems in offices and residents has become a necessity with the increase of break-in cases. The motion sensors also have promising capabilities just as low-power consuming camera enhancers in video monitoring systems. Rajgarhia et al. (2004) uses PIR motion sensors in conjunction with low-cost cameras to address privacy issues. PIR motion sensors are deployed near the entrance door of private rooms while cameras in public areas. Human/Intruder tracking is performed by correlating information from both the two sensor systems. Bai and Teng (2008), proposed a design board for home surveillance by including a PIR motion sensor together with an ARM processor and a Web camera. The motion sensor triggers the Web camera in presence of a human or an intruder in order to capture the snapshot and send to a remote server. Cucchiara et al. (2006) proposed a fusing technique to gather information from a dense network of PIR motion sensors and a set of cameras with the video streaming. The system showed advancement in consistent labeling of people entering within the area of inspection. PIR motion sensors detect human object presence and their direction of movement. Other researchers presented different approaches to perform human tracking using only PIR sensors. Based on coded apertures, Gopinathan et al. (2003) developed a pyroelectric motion tracking system based. The system used a pair of four PIR detectors with a set of apertures shaded using a frame designed to modulate PIR motion visibility over a 1.6 m area. Song et al. (2008) the performance and the applicability of PIR motion sensors were analyzed for security systems and proposed a region-based human tracking algorithm. Hao et al. (2006) have developed a system made up of a number of modules embedded with several pyroelectric detectors and a wireless pyroelectric sensor to track people and as a biometric system. Each module in the system is included with eight PIR sensors to cover 360^0 all together. The module with a set of PIR sensors gathers, filters, and digitalizes the collected data in order to deduce the angular position of the human body with respect to an internal coordinate system. Four similar modules are deployed in a closed environment to track single people movements. An identical approach using modules with different form factor and number of PIR sensors is presented by Shankar et al. (2006).

OPPORTUNITIES AND APPLICATIONS OF IoT

In this section, authors summarize how the IoT technologies and its applications are contributing to the better society. IoT is giving birth to a huge network with trillions of smart devices connected and communicated together. IoT implementation is a mixture of physical world with virtual world by grouping different technical concepts like networking, communication, together. IoT made everything from the virtual or physical world connected for intelligent learning, preserve privacy, fast deployment, interpretation and many more.

IoT is emerged as an extension of existing interaction technologies between the people and the things through a new dimension of applications for communication and integration. According to Shanzhi Chen et al. (2014) IoT is evolving from a domain-specific application development with industry productions and business processes to cross-industry applications. Cross-industry applications can serve both home user needs and production needs. Now-a-days these applications are developing and providing by most of the corporate in large scales. For example, transport and personal vehicles integrated with sensors, communication technologies with GPS enabled for comprehensive detection, entertainment and other information services. This research identified some IoT enabled new technologies like 5G network with IoT, sensor and actuators network, IoT data mining and data analytics, big data and IoT, M2M communication and IoT etc. The world of researchers also identified few IoT enabled applications for:

- **Smart City:** Smart city is a new model using IoT as a primary technology for boosting information sharing and coordinating with the other internal city systems for smart construction and focusing on improving infrastructure and keeping efforts to improve management and utility services.
- **Intelligent Transport:** Using new technologies like IoT, increased traffic congestion in busy areas can be avoided by perception and notifications of traffic state prior.
- **Smart Security:** Smart security is implemented in home and industries by establishing network and controlling various appliances.
- **E-Health Systems:** IoT creates a platform to develop most intelligent hospital management system and there by collecting and analyzing human psychology and medical conditions. IoT develops remote general and emergency medical services for family and community.

ARCHITECTURE FOR DISTRIBUTED SECURITY SYSTEMS

In this section, authors tried to contribute their ideas and proposed architecture for a distributed security system development with PIR motion sensor as a primary sensor and some human recognition application software's.

Internet of Things generally leads to many simulations where network connectivity and computing capabilities are extended to objects. They can transmit data among many connected devices which can transform our lives in countless ways including medical outcomes, creating faster manufacturing, optimizing energy generation and consumption, smart homes, transportation systems.

IoT allows consumer products, cars and trucks, durable goods, utility components, sensors and many more to connect, generate, exchange and transform data and there by applying powerful data analytic capabilities with little human intervention.

Due to low affordability in cost and maintenance, sensors are adapted in organizational automation. These sensors or actuators in wireless mode are handling significant challenges in supporting authorization control systems. Sensors and actuators are two major components while developing loop controlled systems also. A sensor is a device which produces an output signal proportionally when exposed to physical circumstances like temperature and displacement. IoT devices (Raspberry pi) depicted in the architecture (Figure 2) are physical objects which internetwork and embed with sensors and actuators. IoT devices may be non-deterministic interoperable virtual objects and are able to act independently depending on the circumstances or environment. IoT devices and end-user applications are connected through third-party edge services to deliver content through the internet services.

The proposed architecture implementation uses different technical and communication models with their individual characteristics. The Internet Architecture Board (IAB) in March 2015 released some guidelines for networking smart devices. The communication models considered in the paper are as per Karen Rose et al. (2015) differing from device-to-device, device-to-cloud, and device-to-gateway and backend data sharing. IoT local cloud or third-party cloud system provides services to manage data. IoT clouds allow ingesting data generating and transforming continuously by IoT devices.

Security is an every time issue in technology and given higher priority. Organizations that are using IoT devices must trust them and believe that the related data services are secure from vulnerabilities. It is a challenging task to monitor devices which may serve as a potential entry point for cyber attack by allowing malicious code to camouflage into those devices and can cause them to expose to weak data protection environment. The overall resilience of IoT is to function efficiently and how they asses and manage security risks.

Contribution of Raspberry Pi for IoT

Raspberry Pi is a tiny credit-card size computer that can be used to develop real-time applications. It is a single board computer manufactured with several board configurations to connect with various hardware devices. In this research raspberry pi is an IoT device used to implement a distributed security system in the most sensitive areas (entry/exit doors) for enterprises. Raspberry Pi has been used as an intermediate

Figure 2. IoT architecture for smart security

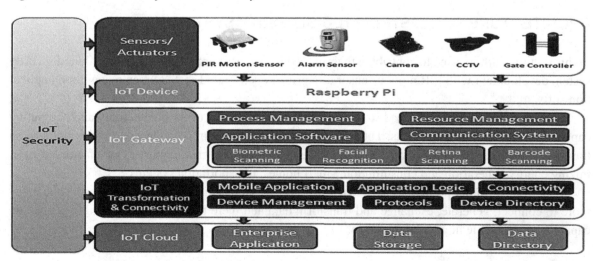

hardware device along with integration of sensors for security system development (Figure 3). It has several processing capabilities through which it become very easy to communicate with other hardware devices so that they can connect, communicate, share, transform and store the data generated by them. Basically, the sensors included in the security system generate analog output signals from its surroundings. Those analog output signals are digitalized using a microcontroller and transferred to raspberry pi computer for further processing like applying data analytics and decision making.

IMPLEMENTATION MECHANISM

The concept of motion sensing has lots of real-time uses in applications like home, office security automation and many more. Researchers in this article used PIR motion sensor as a primary sensor for human detection and applied certain data analytical techniques whether the identified human is an intruder or not. The PIR motion sensor works based on the pyroelectric effect, where some materials generate a voltage when exposed to infrared radiation. This radiation is the part of electromagnetic spectrum. At normal temperature, humans generate infrared at a wavelength of 10μm approximately. This simulation demonstrates how the voltage signal from a PIR motion sensor is measured and detects an infrared (IR) emitting human object movements. The measured sensor signals and the status of motion detection are sent over I2C to a raspberry pi device.

PIR motion sensor is embedded with two or four sensing elements arranged in such a way that voltage generated by one sensor is subtracted by the other. This arrangement generates a voltage only when there is a fluctuation in the incident IR levels on the sensing element.

The sensor is designed with a unique field-of-view to detect IR radiating source when it moved in that field. At a 90⁰ field-of-view, a Fresnel lens is mounted on the sensor to improve sensitivity and the detection rate.

There are certain limitations in the mechanism of PIR motion senor. The sensor by itself cannot determine the number of people in its field of view. But rather it can differentiate if the motion is a walk or just of hand/arm gesture. PIR motion sensor can observe some voltages even when there is no human/ intruder object is out of the viewing range, because the corresponding output signal can be a noise signal.

Figure 3. Raspberry Pi as an intermediate IoT hardware device

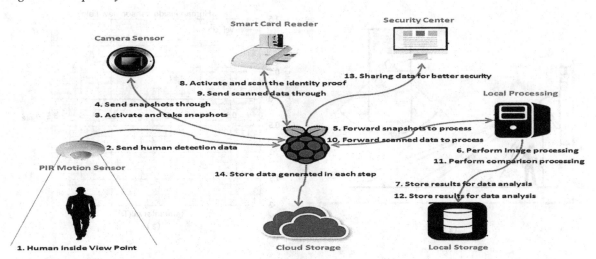

Working of Distributed Security System

A PIR sensor mounted in front of the door detects changes in the amount of infrared radiation strike upon it. The radiations vary depending on the temperature and surface characteristics of the human in front of the sensor. When a human object stand in front of the door, the temperature at that point in the PIR motion sensor's field of view will fluctuate from normal surrounding temperature to identified human body temperature. The sensor immediately converts the input infrared radiation into an output voltage signal, and this triggers the detection. Figure 4 (b) Illustrates that there will be no change in the voltage signal generated by the sensor when the human object is out of its view field in Figure 4 (a).

Figure 5 (b) clearly depicted that when a human object enters into the view field of the senor (a) there will be some fluctuating output voltage signals representing the detection.

Figure 4. (a) Human away from sensor view field; (b) graph representing no changes in the voltage generated by the PIR motion sensor

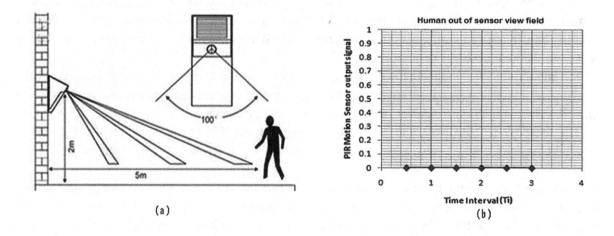

Figure 5. (a) Human inside sensor view field; (b) graph representing voltage fluctuations indicating the human detection

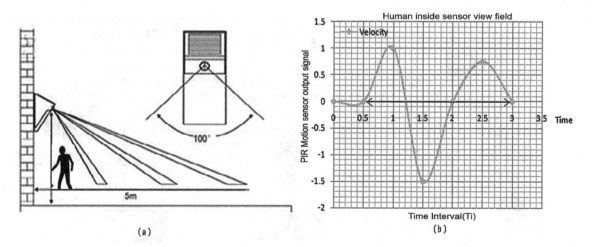

Distributed Security System Workflow

In this section, authors designed Figure 6(a), (b) and (c) which are the flowcharts demonstrating the security system implementation process.

Test Case Scenarios Using Raspberry Pi

In this section, researchers theoretically studied two cases for human detection. The first one in Figure figure 6 depicted an identification of an authorized human personal who granted permission to enter and access the restricted area. Figure 7 depicts intruder detection and denying further access.

Figure 6. (a) (b) (c) Showing the security system implementation workflow

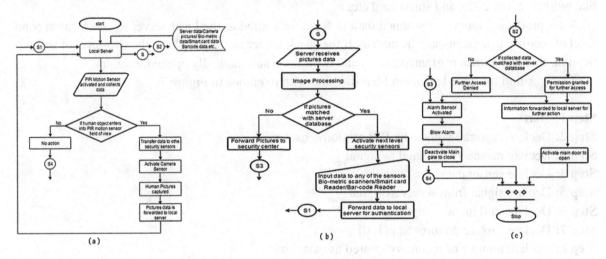

Figure 7. Authorized human identification scenario

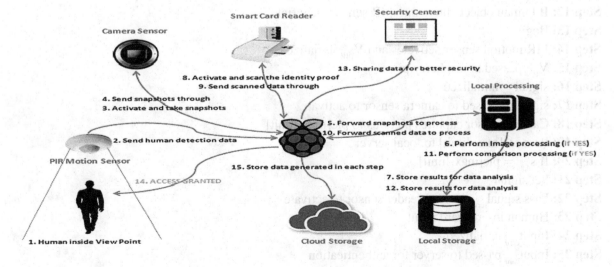

Case 1: Human Identification

In this scenario, a PIR motion sensor is enabled in front of the entrance door which is used to access the most sensitive area is kept active always. The sensor never observes any voltage change when there is no human in its view field and so stays ideal. Otherwise, depends on the voltage fluctuations observed, the motion sensor records the voltage values for further action and the data will be forwarded to the raspberry pi hardware which automatically activates the camera sensor attached very near to motion sensor. Based upon the control forwarded by the raspberry pi, the camera sensor gets activated and the first level of security check is performed. The camera sensor captures the snapshots of the human who stood in the view field of the motion sensor. The same snapshots are forwarded to the local server to determine whether the image captured is matching with the existing humans who are authorized to enter into the sensitive area. If the match is successful, the local server forwards the control to the scanner placed near to the door. The activated scanner waits for the human input to produce some identity object like biometric, bar code, and smart card etc.

After producing input, the scanned data is again forwarded to the local server to check the second level of security to authenticate the human. If the check is successful and clears the two-level of authentication, then the human is granted access and the door is automatically opened for entry.

An algorithm for Case 1: Human Identification with reference to Figure 7.

Step 1: Start
Step 2: Declare captured voltage by PIR motion sensor as V_{PIR}
Step 3: Declare raspberry pi signal as $signal_{rspi}$
Step 4: Declare sensor data as s_{data}
Step 5: Declare signal from server as $signal_{server}$
Step 6: Declare card input as $input_{card}$
Step 7: Declare capture pictures as p[100]
Step 8: Declare number of pictures captured as max-limit
Step 9: PIR motion sensor, camera sensor installed at door
Step 10: PIR sensor will be ideal till human object enters into view field
Step 11: $V_{PIR} \leftarrow 0$
Step 12: If human object enters into PIR sensor view field
Step 13: Begin
Step 14: PIR motion sensor activates and V_{PIR} initialized
Step 15: V_{PIR} passed to raspberry pi
Step 16: $signal_{rspi}$ initialized
Step 17: $signal_{rspi}$ passed to camera sensor to activate
Step 18: Camera sensor captures pictures to pic[max-limit]
Step 19: Pass pic[max-limit] to local server
Step 20: If s_{data} = pic[max-limit]
Step 21: Set $signal_{server} \leftarrow 1$
Step 22: Pass $signal_{server}$ to card reader sensor to activate
Step 23: Human inserts card input
Step 24: $Input_{card}$ initialized
Step 25: $Input_{card}$ passed to server for authentication

Step 26: Begin

Step 27: Authentication successful

Step 28: signal$_{server}$ passed to raspberry pi

Step 29: Door sensor activates and opens the door for access

Step 30: end

Step 31: end

Step 32: Stop.

Case 2: Intruder Detection

The PIR motion sensor activates the camera sensor after observing certain voltage changes when the human enters into its field of view and the same data will be forwarded to the local server. The camera sensor performs the first level of security check by capturing the snapshots of the human pictures and forwards the same to the local server to check whether the identified human is an authorized person for further access or not. If the captured pictures are not matching with any one of the pre-registered humans then the raspberry pi triggers the alarm sensor to blow indicating that the human identified by the sensors is an intruder. The pictures of the intruder and the other relevant data will be forwarded to the security center to make them alert. Meanwhile, raspberry pi activates the door sensors and main gate sensor to shut down automatically until the intruder it traced out.

Due to the similarities in the human faces, there is a chance for an intruder to identify as a registered authorized person. To overcome this issue, a second level of security is performed where the human is asked to scan his identity device with the scanner placed near the door. If the human is an intruder, then he cannot be able to produce the necessary evidence proof of identification. When this security levels conforms that the human is an intruder then the raspberry pi triggers the alarm sensor to blow and makes the doors and main gates to shutdown. At the same time the pictures data and the place of detection data of the intruder are forwarded to the security center for easy identification.

An algorithm for Case 2: Intruder Detection with reference to Figure 8.

Figure 8. Intruder detection scenario

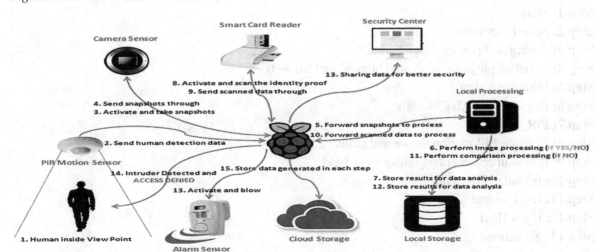

Step 1: Start

Step 2: Assumed variable V_{PIR}, $signal_{rspi}$, $signal_{server}$, s_{data}, $input_{card}$, pic[100], max-limit declared and initialized accordingly

Step 3: On activation of PIR motion sensor, V_{PIR} initialized and passed to raspberry pi

Step 4: Camera captures pictures to pic[max-limit] on receives $signal_{rspi}$

Step 5: pic[max-limit] passes to local server

Step 6: go to step 12

Step 7: Set $signal_{server} \leftarrow 1$

Step 8: Pass $signal_{server}$ to card reader to activate

Step 9: Initialize $input_{card}$ on human card input

Step 10: Pass $input_{card}$ to server

Step 11: If $s_{data} \neq input_{card}$

Step 12: Begin

Step 13: $signal_{rspi} \leftarrow 0$

Step 14: Pass $signal_{rspi}$ to alarm sensor to activate

Step 15: Blow alarm

Step 16: Pass pic [max-limit], $signal_{rspi}$ to security center

Step 17: Gate sensor deactivates and kept shuts down

Step 18: end

Step 19: Stop.

In these test cases, raspberry pi hardware device is considered as an intermediate device for receiving and forwarding the data from and through the sensors.

Implementation Algorithm

In this section, authors derived an algorithm representing an overall implementation of distributed security system. The algorithm continues the system working and contributes to its best in determining whether the identified human object in the view field of PIR motion sensor is an authorized personal or an intruder.

Step 1: Start

Step 2: Server Activation.

Step 3: Authorized personal registration.

Step 4: Initialize pic_max_limit, and human_pic[10] $\leftarrow 0$.

Step 5: Initialize s_data.

Step 6: flag1 $\leftarrow$ false, flag2 $\leftarrow$ false.

Step 7: PIR_data $\leftarrow 0$.

Step 8: Activate PIR motion sensor and collect data.

Step 9: If human object enters sensor view field

Step 10: Initialize PIR_data

Step 11: flag1 $\leftarrow$ true.

Step 12: If not flag1

Step 13: No action.

Step 14: go to step 40.

Else go to step 15

Step 15: Activate Camera sensor.
Step 16: count ← 0.
Step 17: Increment count by 1.
Step 18: Capture pictures to human_pic[count].
Step 19: If count ≠ pic_max_limit

Repeat steps 17 through 19

Step 20: Forward human_pic [count] to local server.
Step 21: Server performs image processing.
Step 22: Set count ← 0.
Step 23: Increment count by 1.
Step 24: If s_data = human_pic[count]

Set flag2 ← true, go to step 31.

Step 25: If count ≠ pic_max_limit and flag ← false.

Repeat steps 23 through 25

Step 26: If flag2 = false.

Go to step 27.

Step 27: Forward information to security system
Step 28: Activate Alarm sensor and blow
Step 29: Deactivate main gate to close
Step 30: Go to step 35.
Step 31: Set smart_card_data ← 0.
Step 32: Activate and capture data from smart card reader
Step 33: Assign collected data to smart_card_data.
Step 34: Forward smart_card_data to local server for authentication
Step 35: If smart_card_data ≠ s_data then

Further ACCESS DENIED

Step 36: Go to step 27

Else

Step 37: Permission granted for further access
Step 38: Forward the same information to local server.

Step 39: Activate door to open.
Step 40: Stop.

LIMITATIONS AND CHALLENGES OF IoT

Internet of things is connecting people with smart devices to lead a better life. But the major challenge of IoT is to handle the huge amount of data generated by the sensors. IoT implementation needs to be deployed with a set of standards which should be unique for all the production and service sectors. IoT has to give the answer by involving in application development which differs widely with different scenarios among industries. IoT development can continue its success only when it can solve various implementation issues like device cost, power consumption, and compatibility, communication, supporting distributed system technologies and distributed intelligence.

IoT provides more opportunities to the industries and end users in many fields of application. Currently, IoT is facing certain challenges in the context of:

1. **Architecture:** There is no specific architecture development for implementation of iot because of the increasing number of devices and sensors involving which are often intrusive, transparent and invisible. there is a need of communication among these devices anytime and anywhere in a wireless or ad hoc mode. the data regularly generated from these smart devices need to be collected, integrated and transformed based on the requirement. data analytics need to be applied to the generated data on which the decision making relies. single reference architecture is not suitable to implement all these aspects. flexible heterogeneous reference architectures should be developed to cater the identification of smart objects and intelligent devices.
2. **Network Technologies:** The existing networks are differing in their technologies and applications. they are categorized into different types based on their characteristics like local area network, cellular, wireless and rfid technologies. communication technologies and their implementation should cost low and reliable connectivity.
3. **Hardware Compatibility:** Designing of hardware for wireless systems with low cost, low size and efficient functionality is a big challenge to iot. the bandwidth of iot terminals differs from device to device and from sensing a single data value to the more complex videos data.
4. **Privacy and Security:** Privacy and security issues of IoT became more particular when compared with traditional networks. The data generated by the sensors and smart devices is user specific, so the protection of privacy leads to security issue in IoT. Security architectures developed before may not be directly suitable to the IoT systems. IoT needs certain M2M oriented technical solutions to assure privacy and security of user data.

CONCLUSION

With the emerging of IoT technology, development and implementation of new distributed security systems became less complicated. IoT made intelligent devices and smart objects to integrate and share data among themselves and keeping it available for applying data analytics. IoT along with big data can be capable for storing and organizing the huge volumes of data generating by integrated objects in the cloud. The proposed architecture and development of distributed security system is opened doors for the industry to manufacture sensors integrated hardware devices to install and utilize the security systems simple.

REFERENCES

Bai, Y. W., & Teng, H. , (2008). Enhancement of the sensing distance of an embedded surveillance system with video streaming recording triggered by an infrared sensor circuit. *Proc. SICE Annual. Conference* (pp. 1657–1662).

Chen, S. C., Xu, H., Liu, D., Hu, B., & Wang, H. (2014). A Vision of IoT: Applications, Challenges, and Opportunities with China Perspective. *IEEE Internet of Things Journal, 1*(4), 350–351.

Chen, Y. C., Han, F., Yang, Y.-H., Ma, H., Han, Y., Jiang, C., & Liu, K. J. R. et al. (2014). Time-reversal wireless paradigm for green Internet of Things: An overview. *IEEE Internet Things Journal, 1*(1), 81–98. doi:10.1109/JIOT.2014.2308838

Chenyang, B. C., Saifullar, A., & Mosha, B. L. (2016). Real-Time Wireless Sensor-Actuator Networks for Industrial Cyber-Physical Systems. *IEEE Proceedings, 104*(5), 1013-1014.

Erickson, V. L., Achleitner, S., & Cerpa, A. E. (2013) POEM: Power-efficient occupancy-based energy management system. *Proceedings of the 12th International Conference on Information Processing in Sensor Networks*, Philadelphia, PA, USA (pp. 203-216).

Fang, J. S., Hao, Q., Brady, D. J., Guenther, B. D., Burchett, J., Shankar, M., & Hsu, K. Y. et al. (2006). Path-Dependent Human Identification using a Pyroelectric Infrared Sensor and Fresnel Lens Arrays. *Opt. Exp, 14*(2), 609–624. doi:10.1364/OPEX.14.000609 PMID:19503378

Fang, J. S., Hao, Q., Brady, D. J., Guenther, B. D., & Hsu, K. Y. (2006). Real-Time Human Identification using a Pyroelectric Infrared Detector Array and Hidden Markov Models. *Optics Express, 14*(15), 6643–6658. doi:10.1364/OE.14.006643 PMID:19516845

Gopinthan, U., & Gopinathan, D. (2003). Brady, and N. Pitsianis. (2003). Coded apertures for efficient pyroelectric motion tracking. *Opt. Exp., 11*(18), 2142–2152. doi:10.1364/OE.11.002142

Granjal, G. J., Monteiro, E., & Sa Silva, J. (2015). Security for the Internet of Things: A Survey of Existing Protocols and Open Research Issues. *IEEE Communications Surveys and Tutorials, 17*(3), 1294–1295. doi:10.1109/COMST.2015.2388550

Han, Z., Gao, R. X., & Fan, Z. (2012). Occupancy and Indoor Environment Quality Sensing for Smart Buildings. *Proceedings of the 5th European DSP Education and Research Conference* (EDERC '12), Graz, Austria (pp. 882-887). doi:10.1109/I2MTC.2012.6229557

Hao, Q., Brady, D. J., Guenther, B. D., Burchett, J. B., Shankar, M., & Feller, S. (2006). Human tracking with wireless distributed pyroelectric sensors. *IEEE Sensors Journal, 6*(6), 1683–1696. doi:10.1109/JSEN.2006.884562

Hao, Q., Hu, F., & Xiao, Y. (2009). Multiple human tracking and identification with wireless distributed pyroelectric sensor systems. *IEEE Sensors Journal, 3*, 428–439.

Shankar, M., Burchett, J. B., Hao, Q., Guenther, B. D., & Brady, D. J. (2006). Human-tracking systems using pyroelectric infrared detectors. *Optical Engineering, 45*(10), 106401–1, 106401–106410. doi:10.1117/1.2360948

Lee, W. (1994). Method and Apparatus for Detecting Direction and Speed using PIR Sensor. U.S. Patent 5291, 020.

Luo, X., Shen, B., Guo, X., Luo, G., & Wang, G. (2009). Human-Tracking using Ceiling Pyroelectric Infrared Sensors. *Proceedings of the IEEE International Conference on Control and Automation,* Christchurch, New Zealand (pp.1716-1721).

Moghavvemi, M., & Seng, L. C. (2004). Pyroelectric Infrared Sensor for Intruder Detection. *Proceedings of the IEEE Region Conference*, Tencon (pp. 656 – 659).

Ning, H. N., Liu, H., & Yang, L. T. (2013). Cyber Entity Security in the Internet of Things. *Computer, 46*(4), 46–53. doi:10.1109/MC.2013.74

Rajgarhia, A., Stann, F., & Heidemann, J. (2004). Privacy-Sensitive Monitoring with a Mix of IR Sensors and Cameras. *Proceedings of 2nd International Workshop Sensor Actor Network Protocol Applications,* Boston, MA (pp. 21-29).

Rose, K. R., Eldridge, S., & Chapin, L. (2015). *The Internet of Things: An Overview understanding the Issues & Challenges of a more connected world. In IoT Society* (pp. 13–22).

Song, B., Choi, H., & Lee, H. S. (2008). Surveillance tracking system using passive infrared motion sensors in wireless sensor network. *Proc. of the International Conference on Information Networking ICOIN '08* (pp. 1–5). doi:10.1109/ICOIN.2008.4472790

Cucchiara, R., Prati, A., Vezzani, R., Benini, L., Farella, E., & Zappi, P. (2006). Using a wireless sensor network to enhance video surveillance. *J. Ubiquitous Comput. Intell., 1(2)*, 187-196.

Yun, J., & Song, M. H. (2014). Detecting Direction of Movement using Pyroelectric Infrared Sensors. *IEEE Sensors Journal, 14*(5), 1482–1489. doi:10.1109/JSEN.2013.2296601

Zappi, P., Farella, E., & Benini, L. (2007). Enhancing the Spatial Resolution of Presence Detection in a PIR based Wireless Surveillance Network. Proceedings of Advanced Video and Signal Based Surveillance, London, UK (pp. 295-300). doi:10.1109/AVSS.2007.4425326

Zappi, P., Farella, E., & Benini, L. (2008). Pyroelectric Infrared Sensors based Distance Estimation. *Proceedings of the 7th IEEE Sensors Conference*, Lecce, Italy (Vol. 8, pp. 716-719).

Zappi, P., Farella, E., & Benini, L. (2010). Tracking motion direction and distance with pyroelectric IR sensors. *IEEE Sensors Journal, 10*(9), 1486–1494. doi:10.1109/JSEN.2009.2039792

Chapter 10
Adaptive Control Strategies for Task Scheduler Using Internet of Things

Adiraju Prashantha Rao
Anurag Group of Institutions, India

ABSTRACT

The Internet of Things comprises billions of devices that can sense, communicate, compute and potentially actuate. The data generated by the Internet of Things are valuable and have the potential to drive innovative and novel applications which are one of the sources of Big Data. IoT connects real world objects to the internet using tiny sensors or embedded devices. One of the biggest advantages of the IoT is the increasing number of low-cost sensors available for many different kinds of functionalities. These sensors include a variety of devices and solutions. The trend is moving towards multi-sensor platforms that incorporate several sensing elements. In such environment, discovering, identifying, connecting and configuring sensor hardware are critical issues. The cloud-based IoT platforms can retrieve data from sensors. Therefore, IoT is a comprehensive inter-disciplinary technology, So, this chapter presents Better scheduling decisions should result in saving the time, utilization of resources and enable to meet the time constraints.

INTRODUCTION

The Internet of Things (IoT) comprises billions of devices that can sense, communicate, compute and potentially actuate presented a paper by authors (Perera, Jayaram & Christwn, 2013). The data generated by the Internet of Things are valuable and have the potential to drive innovative and novel applications. IoT allows people and things to be connected anytime, anyplace, and to anyone, ideally using any path/network and any service presented a paper by authors (Rao, Agarwal, Srinivas et al., 2015) and concepts were discussed in real time systems by authors Liu, Narayanan and Bai (2001). IoT connects real-world objects to the internet using tiny sensors or embedded devices.

DOI: 10.4018/978-1-5225-2947-7.ch010

Copyright © 2018, IGI Global. Copying or distributing in print or electronic forms without written permission of IGI Global is prohibited.

One of the biggest advantages of the IoT is the increasing number of low-cost sensors available for many different kinds of functionalities. A few standard sensors include accelerometer (for movement), linear accelerator, compass, light sensor, camera, microphone, infrared sensor, sound, light, and sensor for temperature, moisture, location, heart rate and heart rate variability. These sensors include a variety of devices and solutions. The trend is moving towards multi-sensor platforms that incorporate several sensing elements are presented by an author Ashton (2009), and Guillemin and Friess (2009). In such environment, discovering, identifying, connecting and configuring sensor hardware are critical issues. The cloud-based IoT platforms can retrieve data from sensors. Therefore, IoT is a comprehensive inter-disciplinary technology, encompassing multiple areas such as RTS, embedded systems, communication, microelectronics, computer science and sensor technology. It creates a multidisciplinary research environment for investigating and experimentally validating highly innovative and revolutionary ideas for new networking and service paradigms. This further improves the research of architectures, protocols, management mechanisms, and service prototypes of future internet.

There are multiple research challenges which will be introduced later in this chapter. This thesis mainly focuses on real time (RT) heterogeneous embedded system that dynamically changes in the environment such as IoT. This thesis does not restrict its scope only to IoT but generalizes present studies to any dynamic heterogeneous RT computing environments.

Real Time System (RTS) bring to attention issues in scheduling, resources, access control and communication between components and sub-systems. The broad aspects of RTS are presented in the overview section.

BACKGROUND

Internet of Things

Zhu Xm, Lu PZ are presented several definitions about the Internet of Things in journal computer science and Technology (2009). One that is in use widely today is provided by U.S National Intelligence Council:

The Internet of Things is the general idea of things, especially everyday objects that are readable, recognizable, locatable, addressable, and controllable via the internet-whether via RFID, wireless LAN, wide-area network, or other means.

The Major Research Challenges of IoT

The first step to make use of the various kinds of embedded devices in the form of a cloud based resource would be to discover and identify configurations of these devices, so that appropriate tasks can be later scheduled. However, this problem is not discussed in the scope of this chapter and the present study assumes some existing framework discussed by authors Melanie Swam (2012), P. Guillemin and P. Friess (2009) and Melanie Swam (2012) for this purpose.

The reasons for the device configuration are important discussed by authors (Guillemin & Friess, 2009).

1. Establish connectivity between device hardware and software systems which allows retrieving data from sensor.
2. It optimizes the sensing and data communication a challenging task in the IoT environment.
3. Designing efficient sampling and scheduling strategies and configuring device under different heterogeneity environments are challenging issue.

Some of these major research challenges of IoT as mentioned by authors Melanie Swam (2012) and P. Guillemin and P. Friess (2009).

Number of Sensors

The popularity of IoT requires a tremendously huge number of devices or sensors to be integrated to the existing IoT. The management of IoT becomes very difficult in a large distributed environment and without a careful management design; it might result in significant performance degradation.

1. **Heterogeneity:** There are different kinds of heterogeneity associated with IoT. They are communication technology, processing capability, functional capabilities, communication sequence and security mechanisms. The communication technologies used by sensors or embedded devices such as ZigBee, GPRS, GSM, Wi-Fi, Bluetooth, etc., and processing capabilities such as microprocessor, sensors, cameras, etc., are heterogeneous in nature. The functional capabilities (e.g. humidity, motion, pressure, temperature) and the types of data (e.g. small size numerical data, audio, large size video data) generated by embedded device or sensors are also heterogeneous. Similarly, communication sequence, as depicted in Figure 1 and security mechanisms used by different sensors are also heterogeneous. This thesis does not the address heterogeneity of communication technology but it addresses the heterogeneity of processing and functional capabilities.
2. **Scheduling, Sampling Rate and Network Communication:** Different sensors or embedded devices generate data at fixed intervals of time. Deciding ideal sampling rate can be a very complex task that has strong relation with the context. The context information plays a key role and its objective is to collect sensor or embedded device data in a better way. The data needed to be collected from those devices should be temporally synchronized and location sensitive to accomplish the task.

Figure 1. Heterogeneity in communication sequences 1

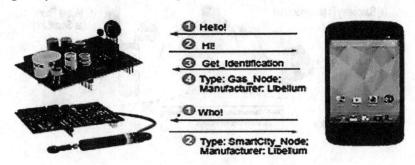

3. **Dynamicity:** Dynamicity refers to the frequency of changing positions /appearing/disappearing of embedded devices at a given location. In order to connect and configure these devices to software platforms to analyze data and understand environment better, these devices need to be searched and dynamically configured in real time. This issue becomes more challenging due to the dynamics of IoT, introduced by its features such as mobility and intermittent connectivity of smart devices. An ideal embedded device or sensor configuration platform should be able to efficiently and continuously discover and re-configure device or sensor in order to cope up with high dynamicity. This chapter assumes that these devices are configured before allocating tasks to them.

Many researchers addressed these challenges and presented articles in referred journals but this chapter does not consider the discovery and configuration of connecting aspects. The present study is to develop adaptive control strategies for task scheduling in RT heterogonous computing environment which will be useful to perform higher level tasks on a cloud of devices that have been configured and made available.

CHAPTER OVERVIEW

An overview of the entire thesis is discussed in the following sections. The proposed system architecture presented by authors (Perera, Jayaraman & Christwn, 2013) about Context-aware dynamic Discovery of Things (CADDOT). The CADDOT model (Figure 2) illustrates two different application strategies. In strategy (a) Raspberry P_i is acting like SmartLink tool and this tool is most suitable for home and office environment where Wi-Fi is available. Raspberry P_i continuously performs the discovery and configuration process and it provides authentication details to the server which is connected to the secured home/office Wi-Fi network. The sensor is expected to send data to the processing server directly over the secured Wi-Fi network.

Another strategy (b) is more suitable for situations where Wi-Fi is not available or is less dynamic. Such strategies are designed to collect data from sensors and to upload to the cloud via 3G. This shows that Figure 2 SmartLink in strategy (a) can be replaced by mobile phones. This thesis presents these architectures to emphasize the fact that result shown by the research has already addressed the communication aspects of such dynamic, heterogeneous cloud based environments.

Figure 2. Existing system application strategies of CADDOT Model

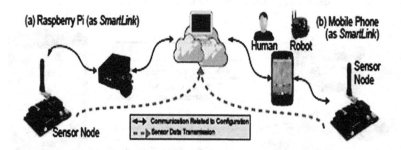

EXISTING CONFIGURATION/CONNECTING ARCHITECTURE

The CADDOT model consists of three main components sensors, a mobile device (i.e. Smart Link) and the cloud middleware. The authors (Guillemin & Friess,2009) & Rajeev Piyare (2013) presented an architecture diagram of CADDOT as shown in Figure 3. All three components need to work collectively in order to perform "sensor discovering" and "configuration" successfully. The core SmartLink applications cannot directly communicate with a given sensor but can communicate through plug-ins. Many researchers have worked in this area or domain and they have published articles in referred journals. The existing architecture (Figure 3) established that such cloud systems of embedded devices is feasible in real world at present and in the near future. Given such feasibility it becomes important to optimally utilize such systems by scheduling larger or distributed tasks. The present study extends their work in scheduling higher level task systems once the configuration is completed. The proposed system architecture is presented in this chapter.

Proposed System Architecture

Better scheduling decisions should result in saving the time, utilization of resources and enable to meet the time constraints. The scheduling decisions primarily depend on machine environment, task characteristics and scheduling environment. The machine environment is known as computing environment and includes 'unrelated heterogeneous' processing elements (PE's). By unrelated heterogeneous computing environments, it is meant that the PE's are non-identical and may have diverse types of system architectures. The scheduling environment decides whether tasks are preemptive or non-preemptive and whether the scheduling is on-line or off-line. The main objective of a scheduling algorithm is to map tasks to the processor dynamically and efficiently.

The present research proposes that is drawn using scheduling parameters as shown in the Figure 4. Here user's applications are envisaged, these applications generate a workload where tasks are essential to be scheduled. A global scheduler picks up one of the schedulers available which in turn identifies the appropriate <task, processor> pairs.

Figure 3. Existing CADDOT architecture model

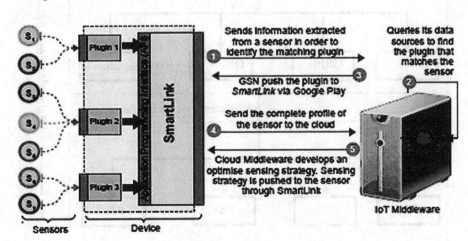

A RT application may contain different types of RT tasks and non-RT tasks. These tasks are scheduled together if required. The scheduler allocates a mixture of tasks to an individual processor in such a way that each processor queue contains both RTT and non-RTT. The scheduler may have queues for all incoming tasks and these tasks are distributed among PE's using a partitioned scheduling algorithm presented by author K.Ashton (2009). Each processor will have a local queue, and this queue will be constantly monitored by means of a feedback controller shown in Figure 4.

The architecture shown in the Figure 4 is divided into three major parts called application layer, scheduler and computing environment.

The Box A is known as application layer. The workload can be computed basing on incoming tasks for a given application and estimate total load required. The workload produced by a RTS must be completed within the specific time frame. In many RTS, the workload is modeled using the concept of 'total execution units' within a certain fixed interval of time. The total load required by the system equals to the total execution units at a particular point of time. This workload consists of different tasks (e.g. HRTS, SRTS, Non-RTT) for proper scheduling under unrelated heterogeneous computing environment. The total workload submitted by the user can be computed at each instance for a given scheduler for further processing. Once a job is initiated, it must successfully complete its execution by a specified deadline.

Figure 4. Proposed scheduler architecture

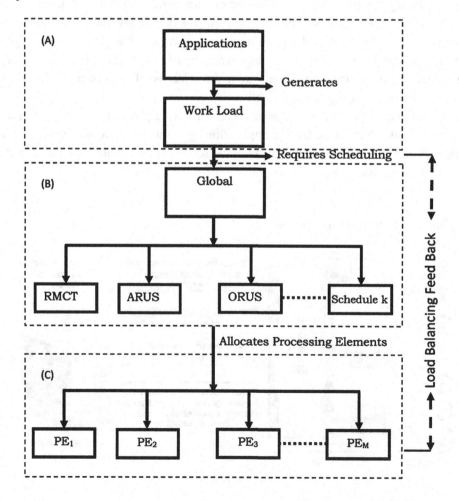

For a HRTS to be temporally correct, each job must be completed within its own deadline. For SRTS deadlines may be harsh but deviations should not exceed 5%.

The Box B is known as scheduler, which takes the input from Box A. The global scheduler takes inputs submitted by the user and analyzes them properly before calling the scheduling algorithm. The Box B identifies type scheduler required for scheduling the incoming tasks based on Expected Time Matrix ETM (i,j) and scheduling policy. There many such algorithms such as self-configurable scheduling (SCS) algorithm, RMCT algorithm which is known to be period oriented scheduling algorithm under identical multiprocessor system. Similarly ARUS, ORUS or any schedule generated from different clusters which are generated from ETM (i,j).

The Box C known as computing environment consist of a number of PE's. The PE's are identical and they have same architecture therefore they are called as homogeneous. If they differ then they are termed heterogeneous. The set of heterogeneous computing resources around us along with dedicated systems present in the system are known as 'Distributed Heterogeneous Multiprocessor System' whose environment changes dynamically. The computing resources around us may have small computing power but increase their computing power by combining them together. The collection of heterogeneous computing resources includes not only dedicated systems but also other devices in the environment. Each computing element will be a set of hardware resources that includes processor(s), memory, cache, and processor/memory interconnect, etc.

Most of the researchers on RT scheduling algorithms have focused predominantly on uniprocessor systems over the past three decades. Earlier research that has addressed multiprocessor RTS has assumed a relatively simple task model for RT workloads, specifically much of the earlier research has assumed that the set of jobs generated by any task are homogenous (i.e., the execution characteristics and deadline constraints of each job are identical) and that the deadline of any job coincides with the arrival of the next job of the same task. Unfortunately, such simple task models preclude the consideration of RT applications that exhibit more complex behavior (e.g., tasks that generate heterogeneous workloads) or dynamically change their computational requirements at run-time.

Further, there is a need to support RTS scheduling algorithms on unrelated heterogeneous computing platforms or multi-core architecture platforms or small scale distributed computing devices like mobile phones or laptops. The emergence of commercial systems such as the next generation embedded and RT hardware platforms will undoubtedly have the capability of parallel execution, increasing the need for multiprocessor RT analysis. Unfortunately, many scheduling algorithms covered in the literature are suitable only for identical multiprocessor systems but evidently there is clearly a need to develop an adaptable scheduling algorithm with advanced computing technologies for example technologies which use soft computing methods.

The main purpose of this study is to develop an abstract framework for adaptable dynamic scheduler that will continuously monitor and update the best suitable processor for a given task, across all available unrelated heterogeneous multiprocessor systems. The achievement of this goal implies that proposed scheduling algorithm is more suitable for any type of RT application and the system adapts to schedule different types of tasks. Both system and task are expected to be more dynamic in nature. The proposed scheduling algorithm will scan the entire feasibility set, find the <task, processor> optimum pairs and will give a global throughput optimization scenario. The scope of analyzable RTS can be broadening by providing learning capability using data mining models. For RTS, analytical techniques are developed for formally verifying the feasibility analysis to check correctness of deadline constraints upon unrelated heterogeneous multiprocessor platforms.

MOTIVATION

The proposed research is to utilize better excess computing power that exists in every utility device such as mobile phones, laptops, PCs, or microwave oven that surround us. These diverse devices may just have a microcontroller and some may have a processor with an operating system. Very soon, it is expected that all these machines have their own operating systems along with a processor due to heightened demand for intelligent and customizable devices in the market place. All these devices which surround us can later be used to solve complex problems in the future.

In the recent past, many manufacturers have formed open handset alliance, and are working to build open systems like android. Most of these devices come with on-board sensors such as rotation vector and gyroscope, GPS, and motion sensors, linear acceleration, compass, light sensor, camera, microphone, infrared sensor, etc. The sequence of activities such as editing, saving, loading and playing scenario from a RT device is recorded. The behaviors of these activities are read from sensors. For example, shopping mall and traffic monitoring system at malls are different customer activities which can be monitored through smartphones. Open systems such as android are designed to support such embedded hardware, of which many perform RTT.

Modern mobile devices are packed with lots of computing power with latest processors and high energy efficient hardware to offer longer battery life. It becomes easy to harness that cumulative processing power to process bigger and highly computing intensive tasks using mobile device cloud. By using mobile server cloud computing technologies, this power can be harnessed in the network.

REAL TIME APPLICATIONS

The different applications in dynamic heterogeneous computing environment discussed by A.P. Rao, A. Govardhan, and P. Prasad Rao are presented in this section.

Example 1: Usage of Excess Computing Capacity

As a case study, I would like to discuss the following scenario. Let's assume that there are 100 smart phones each with single or dual core processors within a small community in a closed geographic region. They have average utilization of 30% and will leave 70% of its resources and computing power to other tasks to solve in the cloud. This would equate to at least 10 multi-core multi G Hz CPUs.

Example 2: Military System

Today's military operations scenario is very different. The warfare may be taking place in a completely foreign location, with personnel who are completely unfamiliar with the territory, the local language, culture and environment. This unfamiliarity poses a challenge to the forces that is very different from that faced by troops a decade earlier. In some cases, the opposition forces may camouflage themselves within a larger (sometimes civilian) population. It is evident that in this scenario, it is not possible to satisfy all communication requirements by using simple radio based voice communication. In order to communicate successfully in this environment, it is necessary to use a network of devices, all sharing situational information simultaneously, so as to enable quick decision making. The solution is to have all these networked devices talk to each other, as well as share information with a central controlling device. This central device then communicates with everybody to ensure that there is no discrepancy in the sharing of information.

As is evident from the requirement, all battlefield communication devices must be mobile-enabled. The devices that are commonly used today include robots, GPS-enabled position markers, computers / phones with internet connection etc. Some of the modern devices have inbuilt sensors that automatically sense and inform the troops about approaching danger as they perform in enemy territory. These sensors sense various entities like temperature or noise and then use well-researched mathematical models to trend the sensed values and create a perceived value of threat. In order to operate in all conditions, these devices additionally need to be compatible to all available military systems.

However, in order to operate with the desired speed and to be able to provide analyzed data in real time, the devices need a tremendous amount of computing power. It may be very cumbersome to build the required amount of computation power within the device itself. In such cases, it will be very useful to be able to use the computing power of other offline devices within an acceptable range so that complex analysis can be carried out within the required timeframe. In order to do this, it is necessary to have a scheduler that can dynamically allocate the tasks to these devices as per available computation bandwidth and changes in environment. Most of the scheduling algorithms that are available currently do not support such a heterogeneous computation environment.

Example 3: Shopping Mall and Traffic Monitoring System

Similarly, we can look at another practical scenario of a customer who goes to a shopping mall with a mobile phone handset. The communication system in the mall immediately senses the presence of the mobile device and sends out a request to this customer for permission to add this device to its network. As soon as the customer accepts this request, his phone gets added to the network and it starts getting used to monitor and regulate the customer's business activities like identification and procurement of times, bill payments etc.

Similar systems can also be used to regulate traffic, identify hot spots and implement effective crowd control mechanisms. All of these items require mobile devices to collaborate to increase computation power in order to perform real-time analysis of sensed data.

These devices are bound to be heterogeneous and amount of processing shared by such device might vary. This gives rise to unpredictability and dynamic nature of the environment. The authors (Rao, Govardhan & Pinagali, 2012) discussed about intelligent scheduler to handle heterogeneity and dynamically changing environment. From the above it is clear that most of the scheduling algorithms which were developed till now are useful for dedicated systems. The most important characteristics of these algorithms are determinism and predictability. These algorithms are not suitable for dynamically changing environment where tasks to be handled are unpredictable. Hence, an attempt has been made in this study to develop algorithms which are suitable for application in heterogeneous computing environment. This motivated the researcher to develop adaptable scheduling algorithm that can work on heterogeneous computing environment.

System Model Assumption

By analyzing above applications, the assumption of system model shown in figure 4 can be presented below;

1. System well appropriate for RT application consists of combination both hard and soft real time tasks are presented by (Gubbi, Buyya, Marusic et al., 2013).
2. A set of tasks $\Gamma = \{\tau_1, \tau_2, \tau_3, \tau_4 \dots \tau_n\}$ are independent and required input data available while it executing.
3. System adapts to centralized scheduler model, from which they are distributed to different PE's in a cluster for further execution. Initially it allocates fixed number of tasks to individual PE's by invoking one of the scheduling algorithms. This centralized scheduler acts as centralized server which collects information or feedback from the computing environment.
4. The computation or the run-time for the requested task varies in different computing devices and also the multiple instances of the same task on identical multiprocessing systems will be different. The computation or the run time is known to be the processing time of a given task without interruption. This assumption leads all the computing elements to form an unrelated heterogeneous system.
5. The PE's in the computing environment will establish communication with the centralized server through wireless channel. Each PE maintains its own local priority queue and also assumes some form of communication channel is established.
6. Assumption about PE's: A PE's can be any device or microprocessor that has computing capability, available memory, and capacity to connect to other devices. In addition to, some PE's which may have optional sensing capabilities such as maximum range, manufacturer, resolution, maximum rate at which sensor acquire data. enough battery power, etc.
7. Periodic task model
   a. The tasks which are generated from different sensors are known to be the periodic tasks. The different instances (jobs) of the periodic tasks are generated at regular interval of time.
   b. All periodic tasks are independent and there is no dependence among these tasks.
   c. These periodic tasks may generate another type of tasks known to be aperiodic and they may be dependent task which executed same PE.

Computing System

M is a set of m computing elements and k proper subsets can be formulated with the help of set M. If the elements of a proper subset M_k are identical with regard to a property, then that proper subset M_k is said to be an improper set. All proper sets have distinct properties and each proper set is identical in terms of execution time. In case identical multiprocessor system set M is improper, then all tasks of set M will have identical execution time. k proper sub sets are formed and each proper set is defined in the following manner.

$$M_k = \{m_j \in C_k, \forall k=1..k, \forall j=1..m\} \tag{1}$$

where C_k is a cluster of PE's. One is bereft of prior knowledge of the nature of the computing elements. Resources can be added or deleted from the system depending on the user needs.

SCHEDULE

Schedule is a plan of action for accomplishing an objective, identifying the order and allotting time frame for each task. The given set of tasks $\Gamma = \{\tau_1, \tau_2, \tau_3, \tau_4, ..., \tau_n\}$ is to be scheduled on set of m unrelated heterogeneous computing elements $M = \{m_1, m_2, m_3, ..., m_m\}$. The Expected Time Matrix ETM (i, j) generated where i is the task index and j is processor index and this matrix is bases for generating different schedules. Each schedule will have its own policy and scheduler try to allocates <task, processor> pair properly.

CONCLUSION

There are many real time embedded applications where task execution time should predicable in advance and allocate to that processor only. Those applications use predicable schedulers but up gradation in the computing environment may changes in scheduling the tasks. There is need to develop adaptive scheduler which gives better performance when computing environment changes due the latest advancement in the processor technology or mobiles

REFERENCES

Ashton, K. (2009, June). That 'internet of things' thing in the real world, things matter more than ideas. *RFID Journal*. Retrieved from http://www.rfidjournal.com/article/print/4986

Uckelmann, D., Harrison, M., & Michahelles, F. (Eds.). (2011). *Architecting the Internet of Things*. Springer.

Gubbi, J., Buyya, R., Marusic, S., & Palaniswami, M. (2013). Internet of Things (IoT): A vision, architectural elements, and future directions. *Future Generation Computer Systems*, 29(7), 1645–1660. doi:10.1016/j.future.2013.01.010

Guillemin, P., & Friess, P. (2009, September). Internet of things strategic research roadmap, Technical report, The Cluster of European Research Projects. Retrieved from http://www.internet-of-things-research

Perera, C., Jayaram, P.P., & Christwn, P. (2013). CSIRO Computational Informatics, Research school on Computer Science. arXiv:1312.6721v1 [cs.NI]

Piyare, R. (2013). Internet of Things: Ubiquitous Home Control and Monitoring System using Android based Smart Phone. *International Journal of Internet of Things*, 2(1), 5–11.

Rao, A. P., Agarwal, S., Srinivas, K., & Rani, B. K. (2015). Learning Mechanism for RT Task Scheduling. *Proceedings of the 2015 IEEE International Conference On Computational Intelligence And Computing Research*.

Rao, A.P., Govardhan, A., & Pinagali, P. (2012, March). Scheduling different customer activities with sensing device. International Journal Advanced Information technology.

Liu, F., Narayanan, A., & Bai, Q. (2001). Real-Time Systems. Pearson education.

Swam, M. (2012). Sensor Mania! The Internet of Things Wearable Computing, Objective Metrics and the Quantified Self 2.0. *Journal of Sensor and Actuator Networks, 1*(3), 217–253. doi:10.3390/jsan1030217

Zhu, X. M., & Lu, P. Z. (2009, May). Multi-dimensional scheduling for real-time tasks on heterogeneous clusters. *Journal of Computer Science and Technology, 24*(3), 434–446. doi:10.1007/s11390-009-9235-2

KEY TERMS AND DEFINITIONS

Dedicated Pair: k clusters are formed from ETM (i, j) such that lowest cluster index has more optimal <task, processor> pair combinations and so on. The lowest cluster index has more dedicated or specialized pair than higher index cluster.

Expected Time: The expected time can be defined as the execution time of the task i on machine j and ETM (i, j) contains execution times of all n tasks among m machines. Where i ε n and j εm.

Feasible Schedule: The feasible schedule for a given processor is defined as the total execution time units (T_{jk}) less than or equal to feasibility check parameter ($Tjk \leq d_{lk}$) where T jk is total time execution units allocated to processor j in cluster k and dlk is maximum deadline of a task on processor j.

Threshold Load: The threshold load (TL) is defined as the load on each processor which can be classified as: 1. T $_{jk}$ < d$_{lk}$ Lightly Loaded; 2. T jk = d$_{lk}$ Load balanced; 3. T jk > dlk Heavily Loaded.

Chapter 11
Centralized Fog Computing Security Platform for IoT and Cloud in Healthcare System

Chandu Thota
Infosys Ltd., India

Gunasekaran Manogaran
VIT University, India

Revathi Sundarasekar
Priyadarshini Engineering College, India

Varatharajan R
Sri Ramanujar Engineering College

Priyan M. K.
VIT University, India

ABSTRACT

This chapter proposes an efficient centralized secure architecture for end to end integration of IoT based healthcare system deployed in Cloud environment. The proposed platform uses Fog Computing environment to run the framework. In this chapter, health data is collected from sensors and collected sensor data are securely sent to the near edge devices. Finally, devices transfer the data to the cloud for seamless access by healthcare professionals. Security and privacy for patients' medical data are crucial for the acceptance and ubiquitous use of IoT in healthcare. The main focus of this work is to secure Authentication and Authorization of all the devices, Identifying and Tracking the devices deployed in the system, Locating and tracking of mobile devices, new things deployment and connection to existing system, Communication among the devices and data transfer between remote healthcare systems. The proposed system uses asynchronous communication between the applications and data servers deployed in the cloud environment.

INTRODUCTION

IoT technology is introduced recently which enables people and objects to interact with each other. IoT is used in the following areas such as smart transport systems, smart cities, smart healthcare, and smart energy. The healthcare world urgently demands the transformation of healthcare from a hospital-centered system to a person-centered environment (Eason et al., 1955). It has been predicted that in the following

DOI: 10.4018/978-1-5225-2947-7.ch011

Copyright © 2018, IGI Global. Copying or distributing in print or electronic forms without written permission of IGI Global is prohibited.

decades, the way healthcare is currently provided will be transformed from hospital-centered, first to hospital-home-balanced in 2020th, and then ultimately to home-centered in 2030th (Rahmani et al., 2015). In home-based health care the following arrangements are included such as human computer interaction, communications, imaging technologies embattled at diagnosis, treatment and monitoring patients without disturbing the quality of lifestyle. It can be possible the development of a low cost medical devices used for real-time monitoring of patient physical conditions. Significant security solutions are identified to current wireless networks. These approaches are not directly applicable for IoT-based healthcare applications due to following challenges such as 1) Medical sensor nodes can be easily lost or abducted as they are tiny in terms of size, 2) Security solutions must be resource-efficient as medical sensor nodes have limited processing power, memory, and communication bandwidth. Thus, conventional cryptography techniques require heavy computations are infeasible. Due to resource constraints of medical sensors, it is infeasible to utilize conventional cryptography in IoT-based healthcare (Manogaran et al., 2016b; Manogaran et al., 2016c; Manogaran et al., 2017a). The following security protocols DTLS and OpenSSL are used in the proposed approach. DTLS handshake protocol is used to provide security solution for the transport layer in IoT. Open SSL is an open source project for implementing SSL, TLS and various cryptography libraries such as symmetric key, public key, and hash algorithms.

BACKGROUND

IoT Enabling Technologies and Protocols Overview

In recent years, more number of IoT applications is developed for different domains, so we need to develop different protocols and platforms. For example, a number of wearable sensors and devices are developed for continuous monitoring of personal fitness, healthcare, and physical activity awareness (Jawbone Inc, 2015; FitBitInc, 2015). Nowadays, researchers are interested to develop wearable clinical devices in remote health monitoring systems for continuous storage, management and clinical access to the patient's physiological information (Pantelopoulos, 2010; Paradiso, 2005). Wearable clinical devices can give physical routine by a two–three-day periods of continuous physiological monitoring of patient. During this period, sensors would continuously store the patient's physiological data to a database linked with your device (Skourletopoulos et al., 2015).

Applications of IoT with different technologies are explained in this section in detail. These are categorized based on the terms used in the IoT such as Location tracking, sensing, communication, security and identification. Presently, the hardware and software for sensing, communication and decision-making activities have become more versatile and affordable.

Identification Technology

IoT system may include a large number of nodes, where each node is capable of generating data, and any authorized node can access data irrespective of where those are located. To achieve this goal, it is essential to locate and identify the nodes effectively by assign a unique identifier (UID) to a corresponding device, so that the information exchange through this node is un-ambiguous. The Open Software Foundation (OSF) developed the universally unique identifier (UUID) as a part of the Distributed Computing Environment (DCE), which can operate without a centralized coordination. OSF also introduced the Globally Unique Identifier (GUID).

Communication and Location Technologies

In most cases, short-distance communication is based on wireless technologies, including Bluetooth, RFID, Wi-Fi, Infrared Data Association (IrDA), Ultra-wideband (UWB), ZigBee, etc. This paper reviews only on short-distance technologies.

Sensing Technologies

Sensing technology is pivotal to the acquisition of numerous physiological parameters about the patients. Hence, doctor can adequately diagnose the illness and recommend the treatments. Furthermore, new progress of sensing technologies allows a continual data acquisition from patients, facilitating the improvement of treatment outcomes and the reduction of healthcare costs.

Fog Computing

Cisco defines Fog Computing as a paradigm that extends Cloud computing and services to the edge of the network. Fog computing will grow in helping the emerging network paradigms that require faster processing with less delay and delay jitter. Cloud computing would serve the business community meeting their high-end computing demands lowering the cost based on a utility pricing model. By doing so, Fog reduces service latency, and improves QoS, resulting in superior user-experience. Fog Computing supports emerging Internet of Everything (IoE) applications that demand real-time/predictable latency (industrial automation, transportation, networks of sensors and actuators). Fog supports densely distributed data collection points, hence adding a fourth axis to the often-mentioned Big Data dimensions (volume, variety, and velocity) (Thota et al., 2017).

Now there are different approaches are identified to connect the devices with cloud. We could make integration happen on the data level, a point-to-point level where two applications are sharing chunks of data, or at a method level allowing them to share functionality apart from just data. Integration strategy plays vital role in its success in the enterprise ventures. Also, the company needs to have a clear understanding of the requirements specifying what is to be achieved after integrating the applications and database from flog to cloud so that finite goals can be set. A very important and often neglected aspect of integration is the relevance of devices in the integration scheme.

SCOPE OF THE CHAPTER

IoT-based healthcare systems deal with human-related health data. IoT and Cloud computing in Healthcare industry is a combination of Things (devices and sensors), communication technologies, interconnected apps, computing services in cloud, storage services in cloud and people like patients, doctors and caregivers that would function together as one smart system to monitor, track, store, analyze and visualize patients' health information. Security is a major concern wherever networks are deployed at large scales (González-Valenzuela, et al., 2014). Due to direct involvement of humans in IoT-based healthcare applications, providing robust and secure data communication among healthcare sensors, actuators, patients, and caregivers are crucial. Although collected from innocuous wearable sensors, such data is vulnerable to top privacy concerns. In IoT-based healthcare applications, security and privacy are among major areas of concern as most devices and their communications are wireless in nature (Koblitz, 1987).

IOT IN CLOUD ENVIRONMENT

Cloud computing facilitates end-users or small companies to use computational resources such as software, storage, and processing capacities belonging to other companies are calling as cloud service providers. Definition of cloud computing is based on five attributes Multitenancy (Shared Resources), Massive Scalability, Elasticity, Pay as You go and Self-Provisioning of resources. Cloud Providers are companies that offers some component of cloud computing – typically Infrastructure as a Service (IaaS), Software as a Service (SaaS) or Platform as a Service (PaaS) – to other businesses or individuals. Organizations use the Cloud in a variety of different deployment models are Private, Public, and Hybrid. In the cloud deployment model, networking, platform, storage, and software infrastructure are provided as services that scale up or down depending on the demand as required (Shen et al., 2011). Web services are client and server applications that communicate over the World Wide Web's (WWW) and Hypertext Transfer Protocol (HTTP). As described by the World Wide Web Consortium (W3C), web services provide a standard means of interoperating between software applications running on a variety of platforms and frameworks. Web services are characterized by their great interoperability and extensibility, as well as their machine-processable descriptions, thanks to the use of XML. Web services can be combined in a loosely coupled way to achieve complex operations. Programs providing simple services can interact with each other to deliver sophisticated added-value services. In Java EE 6, JAX-RS provides the functionality for Representational State Transfer (RESTful) web services. REST is well suited for basic, ad hoc integration scenarios. RESTful web services, often better integrated with HTTP than SOAP-based services are, do not require XML messages or WSDL service–API definitions.

IoT With Cloud Computing and Big Data

Nowadays, big data has been playing a vital role in almost all environments such as healthcare, education, business organizations and scientific research (Manogaran et al., 2017b; Manogaran et al., 2017c; Manogaran et al., 2017d). There is a strong relationship in big data and IoE. In general, IoT applications are used to capture or observe some specific values to find the hidden values and take better decisions. When the device connected to the Internet it always senses the specific metric and stores those metrics into a connected data stores. This would increase the size of the data stored in a data store (Malan et al., 2004). Hence, high end devices and scalable storage systems are needed to store such huge size of data. The amount of data to be stored and processed becomes an important problem in real life. Relational data base management system (RDBMS) is generally used to store the traditional data, but day by day the volume, velocity and variety of sensor data is growing towards the Exabyte (Lopez et al., 2014; Lopez et al., 2015; Lopez et al., 2016a; Lopez et al., 2016b) . This requires advanced tools and techniques to store, process and display such large amount of sensor data to the end users. Thus, storing and querying large amount of data requires database clusters and additional resources (Kambourakis et al., 2007). However, storage and retrieval are not the only problem but also extract useful information from huge data (Manogaran et al., 2017e). In order to overcome this issue, cloud computing is used to provide scalable storage systems and high end devices for computation (Koop et al., 2008).

Wireless Sensor Network (WSN) is composed of distributed spatially connected sensor nodes with limited computing power and storage (Lorincz et al., 2004). This chapter consists of an overview of state-of-the-art work on Wireless Sensor-based Cloud Computing (WSCC). Subsequently, integration of WSN and Cloud Computing is highlighted with some insights on how WSN and Clouds can both get benefits from each other. Applications of Wireless Sensors over the cloud are then described. Afterwards, we explain incorporation of mobile sink between WSN and Cloud.

Cloud computing is a type of computing and it is used for the delivery of hosted services over the Internet. In other words, Cloud computing relies on sharing computing resources and hardware's rather than having personal devices or local servers to manage the real-time applications. Mobile cloud can be considered as a marketplace, where the mobile services of the mobile cloud-based system architectures can be leased off via the cloud. In this context, this paper elaborates on a novel fluctuation-based quantification model, which is based on a cost-benefit appraisal, adopting a non-linear and asymmetric approach. The proposed model aims to predict the incurrence and the risk of entering into a new technical debt (TD) in the future and provide insights to inform effective investment decision making. The lease of a cloud-based mobile service was considered, when developing the formula, and the research approach is investigated with respect to the cost that derives from the unused capacity. In general, cloud providers are called as cloud service providers or CSPs. Amazon Simple Storage Service (Amazon S3) is the first cloud offered by Amazon in 2006. There after other cloud providers are developed number of cloud services such as Microsoft, Rackspace, Apple, IBM, Joyent, Google, Cisco, Citrix, Salesforce. com and Verizon/Terremark. Hence, the IoE devices are interconnected with cloud server to store the device generated data. Once the data is stored efficiently into the cloud then there is a need for scalable algorithms to process those data. In order to fulfill the requirements, Amazon Web services provides Elastic MapReduce to process the device generated data.

Fog Computing to Cloud Computing

In this architecture, we are suggesting to store the data into primarily fog servers, which is near edge technology for IoT devices where deployed in IoT applications. Edge computing plays a crucial role in Internet of Things (IoT) (Jara et al., 2009; Jara et al., 2010a; Jara et al., 2010b). Studies related to security, confidentiality and system reliability in the fog computing platform is absolutely a topic for research and has to be discovered. Less demand for bandwidth, as every bit of data's were aggregated at certain points instead of sending over cloud channels. Rather than presenting and working from a central cloud, fog operate on network edge. So, it takes less time. By putting small servers called edge servers in visibility of users, it is possible for a fog computing platform to avoid response time and scalability issues (Hummen, 2014). cloud computing would serve the business community meeting their high-end computing demands lowering the cost based on a utility pricing model. Processing the data of the applications of IoT in Cloud Data centers, we are using the Cloud big data technologies and secure the data by storing the data into different cloud data centers providing by various cloud providers like Amazon, Google, Cisco and Microsoft. Categorize the data of the application and store the data into different data centers as per their categorization as critical, normal, and sensitive and personnel information of the end-users of the applications.

PROPOSING CENTRALIZED FOG COMPUTING SECURITY PLATFORM FOR IOT CLOUD HEALTH SYSTEM

In the paradigms of healthcare IoT, data is collected from smart devices (medical sensors) and transmitted to end-users (caregivers). IoT also enables end-users can access, control, and manage medical sensors through the Internet. Patient data is involved in healthcare IoT applications. Thus, it is necessary to provide secure end-to-end communication between end-users and medical sensors via centralized secure platform. The proposed system has the following tasks to achieve end to end security integration of IoT enabled healthcare system.

Core Functionality of the Proposed System

Identifying the Devices

- **Identifying the Existing Devices in IoT Health System:** The proposed methodology has different tasks to secure the IoT system. First one is to identify the existence of all the devices which are configured and connected in our system. Devices are categorized as wearable and non-wearable, wired and wireless, mobile and non-mobile devices. Above mentioned devices are used to collect, process, transfer the data using internet. These devices use different protocols and technologies to connect and contact each other with wired and wireless communication. Proposed system assigns unique id for each device to identify, track, and find out the existence of device in the system and its connected devices identification. Once the devices are connected, the proposed healthcare system collects the patient information collected from devices (MSNs) and transferring to central Database/Application server (Karlof, 2004). Data should be collected from only identified and existed devices in the system. When intruders and hackers are trying to enter into our system with different devices, the proposed system identifies the unauthorized devices entered into our system using status and history. The proposed methodology continually stores the status and history of each device trying to enter in the system. During the lifecycle of a product, some components could change its unique ID. Hence, it is necessary to maintain the changes of smart devices even when they are reconfigured. Changes in the configuration are critical for maintaining devices, tracking components, and diagnosing failures. In order to overcome the issue the following techniques are followed in the proposed system such as (1) Locate things efficiently based on a global ID scheme, (2) manage identities with the advanced techniques of encoding / encryption, authentication, and repository management, and (3) provide global directory services and IoT service discovery services under diverse UID schemes.

- **Authenticate and Authorize the Devices, Data Identification and Communication Networks:** The privacy of the patients and key negotiation materials should be protected to prevent unauthorized access from learning the contents of the negotiations. It is also important to prevent from malicious activities at the entrance to MSNs. Hence, mutual authentication and authorization of end-users and devices used in healthcare IoT systems is a crucial task (Hill et al., 2004). Proposed architecture performs the authentication and authorization of remote end-users securely and efficiently in the centralized secure platform on behalf of the medical sensors. With the established connection context to the medical sensor nodes, these devices no longer required to authenticate and authorize a remote healthcare center or a caregiver. Thus, any malicious activity can be blocked before entering into a constrained medical domain. The architecture of our proposed centralized secure platform for healthcare IoT monitoring system in home/hospital domain(s) is shown in Figure 2.

Locating and Tracking Devices

- **Locating, Tracking and Connecting Technologies:** Communication technologies support networking services and it can be divided into short-distance and long-distance technologies. However, long-distance technologies mainly involve regular Internet or mobile phones communications. The proposed system properly maintains the locations and track details to efficiently connect the devices in the system. The Global Positioning System (GPS) is a satellite-based navigation system to locate objects under all weather conditions as long as unobstructed lines of sight can be received by four or more satellites. In the healthcare system, the satellite-based positioning system can be used to locate ambulances/transportation network, patients/home network, doctors/hospital network, etc. Since, GPS is insufficient to build an effective healthcare system, it is necessary to compensate GPS with local positioning systems (LPSs) to enhance location accuracy (Rescorla, 2012). LPS locates an object based on the measurement of radio signals travelling among the objects and an array of the pre-deployed receivers. The short-distance communication technologies are essential to implement LPS. For example, UWB radio has a fine temporal resolution, which enables a receiver to estimate the arrival time accurately. Therefore, UWB is an ideal technology for radio-based high-precision positioning.

Mobility Scenario in Healthcare IoT System

- **Identifying, Tracking, Locating and Monitoring for Mobility Devices:** Proposed Architecture is also focusing on identifying the mobile devices identification, which are configured in healthcare system. Tracking and locating the devices to Monitoring the status of the patients, doctors and transport (Moosavi et al., 2016). Mobility support is one of the most important issues in healthcare IoT systems. Improving patients' quality of life is essential in the healthcare system. Continues monitoring of patients is also important when they are walk around the hospital wards. Thus, the connectivity should be good. In addition, when patient to move from his/her base MSN to other rooms/MSN for medical tests they should not lost the connectivity. Mobility can be categorized into two main topics denoted as macro-mobility and micro-mobility. The movement of medical sensors between various medical network domains distinguishes the macro-mobility. Micro-mobility assumes that medical sensors move between different MSNs within the same domain. In this proposed system, where a patient wearing medical sensors decides to move from its room (base network) to other rooms (visited networks). We assume a mobility scenario which consists of several MSNs for remote patient monitoring in a hospital or nursing/home environment. In the considered scenario, patients may roam through the hospital wards or move to other rooms due to take some medical tests (e.g., Laboratory or X-ray). In order to enable seamless transitions of medical sensors, proposed system uses an efficient and robust data handover mechanism to centralized secure platform database. The mobility scenario is discussed in three phases in the following subsections. a) Message exchange in patients' base MSN, b) Entering to a new medical sub network, c) Returning back to the base MSN.

Proposed System Architecture and Its Functionality

Proposed Security Platform Architecture Diagram for end to end Integration of HealthCare system is shown in Figure 1.

Security Methodologies implementation like Authentication/Authorization, PKI Certificate and DTLS Handshake Protocol is shown in Figure 2.

In our proposed methodology, the Security is the major issue while integrating Fog to Cloud environment. The Cloud systems are located within the network by connecting through Internet, with numerous speeds, technologies, topologies and types with no central control. Because of the non-homogeneous and loosely controlled nature of the Internet, there are many issues especially quality of service related ones remain unresolved. One such issue that affects the quality of service severely is network latency. Real time applications with which users directly interact with are badly affected by delay and delay jitter caused by latency in networks (Manogaran et al., 2016a).

The security architecture here we are providing is uses the existing security terminologies as Public key and private key, encryption and decryption, cryptography Identity Access Management and PKI Certificates Authority. The other major issue confronted with cloud computing is security and privacy. Since the cloud systems have been located with the Internet, user requests, data transmission and system responses need to traverse a large number of intermediate networks depending on the distance between

Figure 1. Proposing methodology to secure healthcare System in IoT

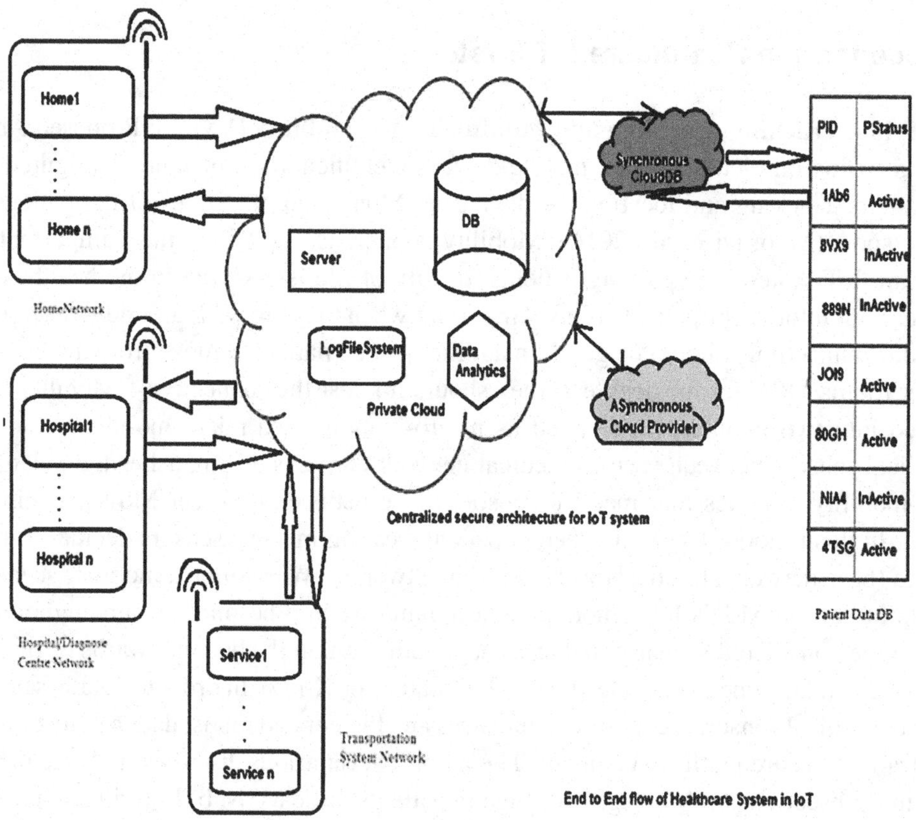

Figure 2. Security architecture for GC architecture for secure integration fog to cloud storage

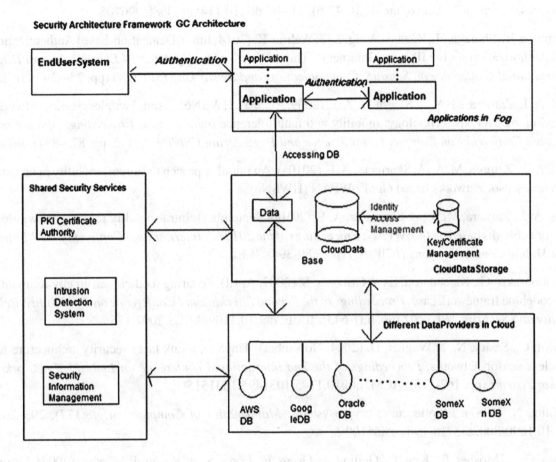

the users and systems. When Patient data is out there in a public cloud, there is a risk of them being compromised of their integrity and confidentiality. Deeper the data inside the Internet, higher the risk as the data has to travel a long distance to and from the user's computer to the cloud system, even if the data is encrypted. Similarly the availability of the cloud systems can also be attacked using various methods. Thus it can be seen that cloud systems at present face various security threats due to very nature of their implementation within the Internet coupled with location independence.

REFERENCES

Eason, G., Noble, B., & Sneddon, I. N. (1955). On certain integrals of Lipschitz-Hankel type involving products of Bessel functions. *Philosophical Transactions of the Royal Society of London A: Mathematical, Physical and Engineering Sciences*, 247(935), 529–551. doi:10.1098/rsta.1955.0005

González-Valenzuela, S., Chen, M., & Leung, V. C. (2011). Mobility support for health monitoring at home using wearable sensors. *IEEE Transactions on Information Technology in Biomedicine*, 15(4), 539–549. doi:10.1109/TITB.2010.2104326 PMID:21216718

Hill, J., Horton, M., Kling, R., & Krishnamurthy, L. (2004). The platforms enabling wireless sensor networks. *Communications of the ACM*, *47*(6), 41–46. doi:10.1145/990680.990705

Hummen, R., Shafagh, H., Raza, S., Voig, T., & Wehrle, K. (2014, June). Delegation-based Authentication and Authorization for the IP-based Internet of Things. *Proceedings of the 2014 Eleventh Annual IEEE International Conference on Sensing, Communication, and Networking (SECON)* (pp. 284-292). IEEE.

Jara, A. J., Zamora, M. A., & Skarmeta, A. F. (2009, August). HWSN6: hospital wireless sensor networks based on 6LoWPAN technology: mobility and fault tolerance management. *Proceedings of the International Conference on Computational Science and Engineering CSE'09* (Vol. 2, pp. 879-884). IEEE.

Jara, A. J., Zamora, M. A., & Skarmeta, A. F. (2010a). An initial approach to support mobility in hospital wireless sensor networks based on 6LoWPAN (HWSN6).

Jara, A. J., Zamora, M. A., & Skarmeta, A. F. (2010b, September). Intra-mobility for hospital wireless sensor networks based on 6LoWPAN. *Proceedings of the 2010 6th International Conference on Wireless and Mobile Communications (ICWMC)* (pp. 389-394). IEEE.

Kambourakis, G., Klaoudatou, E., & Gritzalis, S. (2007, April). Securing medical sensor environments: the codeblue framework case. *Proceedings of the Second International Conference on Availability, Reliability and Security ARES '07* (pp. 637-643). IEEE. doi:10.1109/ARES.2007.135

Karlof, C., Sastry, N., & Wagner, D. (2004, November). TinySec: a link layer security architecture for wireless sensor networks. *Proceedings of the 2nd international conference on Embedded networked sensor systems* (pp. 162-175). ACM. doi:10.1145/1031495.1031515

Koblitz, N. (1987). Elliptic curve cryptosystems. *Mathematics of Computation*, *48*(177), 203–209. doi:10.1090/S0025-5718-1987-0866109-5

Koop, C. E., Mosher, R., Kun, L., Geiling, J., Grigg, E., Long, S., & Rosen, J. M. et al. (2008). Future delivery of health care: Cybercare. *IEEE Engineering in Medicine and Biology Magazine*, *27*(6), 29–38. doi:10.1109/MEMB.2008.929888 PMID:19004693

Li, S., Da Xu, L., & Wang, X. (2013). Compressed sensing signal and data acquisition in wireless sensor networks and internet of things. *IEEE Transactions on Industrial Informatics*, *9*(4), 2177–2186. doi:10.1109/TII.2012.2189222

Lopez, D., Gunasekaran, M., Murugan, B. S., Kaur, H., & Abbas, K. M. (2014, October). Spatial big data analytics of influenza epidemic in Vellore, India. *Proceedings of the 2014 IEEE International Conference on Big Data (Big Data)* (pp. 19-24). IEEE.

Lopez, D., & Manogaran, G. (2016b). Big Data Architecture for Climate Change and Disease Dynamics. In *The Human Element of Big Data: Issues, Analytics, and Performance* (pp. 301-331). CRC Press. 10.1007/978-3-319-49736-5_7

Lopez, D., & Sekaran, G. (2016a). Climate change and disease dynamics-A big data perspective. *International Journal of Infectious Diseases*, *45*, 23–24. doi:10.1016/j.ijid.2016.02.084

Lopez, D., & Gunasekaran, M. (2015). Assessment of Vaccination Strategies Using Fuzzy Multi-criteria Decision Making. *Proceedings of the Fifth International Conference on Fuzzy and Neuro Computing (FANCCO-2015)* (pp. 195-208). Springer International Publishing.

Lorincz, K., Malan, D. J., Fulford-Jones, T. R., Nawoj, A., Clavel, A., Shnayder, V., & Moulton, S. et al. (2004). Sensor networks for emergency response: Challenges and opportunities. *IEEE Pervasive Computing*, *3*(4), 16–23. doi:10.1109/MPRV.2004.18

Malan, D., Fulford-Jones, T., Welsh, M., & Moulton, S. (2004, April). Codeblue: An ad hoc sensor network infrastructure for emergency medical care. *Proceedings of the International workshop on wearable and implantable body sensor networks* (*Vol. 5*).

Manogaran, G., & Lopez, D. (2016b). Health data analytics using scalable logistic regression with stochastic gradient descent. *International Journal of Advanced Intelligence Paradigms*, *9*(1), 1–18.

Manogaran, G., & Lopez, D. (2016c). A survey of big data architectures and machine learning algorithms in healthcare. *International Journal of Biomedical Engineering and Technology*, *23*(4), 1–27.

Manogaran, G., & Lopez, D. (2017b). Disease surveillance system for big climate data processing and dengue transmission. *International Journal of Ambient Computing and Intelligence*, *8*(1), 1–27.

Manogaran, G., & Lopez, D. (2017e). Spatial cumulative sum algorithm with big data analytics for climate change detection. *Computers & Electrical Engineering*, *59*(5), 1–15. doi:10.1016/j.compeleceng.2017.04.006

Manogaran, G., Thota, C., & Kumar, M. V. (2016a). Meta Cloud Data Storage Architecture for Big Data Security in Cloud Computing. *Procedia Computer Science*, *87*, 128–133. doi:10.1016/j.procs.2016.05.138

Manogaran, G., Thota, C., Lopez, D., & Sundarasekar, R. (2017d). Big Data Security Intelligence for Healthcare Industry 4.0. In Cybersecurity for Industry 4.0 (pp. 103-126). Springer International Publishing.

Manogaran, G., Thota, C., Lopez, D., Vijayakumar, V., Abbas, K. M., & Sundarsekar, R. (2017c). Big Data Knowledge System in Healthcare. In *Internet of Things and Big Data Technologies for Next Generation Healthcare* (pp. 133–157). Springer International Publishing.

Manogaran, G., Thota, C., Lopez, D., Vijayakumar, V., Abbas, K. M., & Sundarsekar, R. (2017a). Big data knowledge system in healthcare. In Internet of Things and Big Data Technologies in Next Generation Healthcare. Springer International Publishing.

Moosavi, S. R., Gia, T. N., Nigussie, E., Rahmani, A. M., Virtanen, S., Tenhunen, H., & Isoaho, J. (2016). End-to-end security scheme for mobility enabled healthcare Internet of Things. *Future Generation Computer Systems*, *64*, 108–124. doi:10.1016/j.future.2016.02.020

Rahmani, A. M., Thanigaivelan, N. K., Gia, T. N., Granados, J., Negash, B., Liljeberg, P., & Tenhunen, H. (2015, January). Smart e-health gateway: Bringing intelligence to internet-of-things based ubiquitous healthcare systems. *Proceedings of the 2015 12th Annual IEEE Consumer Communications and Networking Conference (CCNC)* (pp. 826-834). IEEE.

Rescorla, E., & Modadugu, N. (2012). Datagram transport layer security version 1.2.

Shen, W., Xu, Y., Xie, D., Zhang, T., & Johansson, A. (2011, September). Smart border routers for ehealthcare wireless sensor networks. *Proceedings of the 2011 7th International Conference on Wireless Communications, Networking and Mobile Computing (WiCOM)* (pp. 1-4). IEEE. doi:10.1109/wicom.2011.6040606

Skourletopoulos, G., Mavromoustakis, C. X., Mastorakis, G., Rodrigues, J. J., Chatzimisios, P., & Batalla, J. M. (2015, December). A fluctuation-based modelling approach to quantification of the technical debt on mobile cloud-based service level. *Proceedings of the 2015 IEEE Globecom Workshops (GC Wkshps)* (pp. 1-6). IEEE.

Thota, C., Manogaran, G., Lopez, D., & Vijayakumar, V. (2017). Big Data Security Framework for Distributed Cloud Data Centers. Proceedings of the Cybersecurity Breaches and Issues Surrounding Online Threat Protection (pp. 288-310). Hershey, PA: IGI Global. doi:10.4018/978-1-5225-1941-6.ch012

Zheng, K., Yang, Z., Zhang, K., Chatzimisios, P., Yang, K., & Xiang, W. (2016). Big data-driven optimization for mobile networks toward 5G. *IEEE Network*, *30*(1), 44–51. doi:10.1109/MNET.2016.7389830

ADDITIONAL READING

Curran, R. J., & Haskin, R. L. (2010). *U.S. Patent No. 7,840,995*. Washington, DC: U.S. Patent and Trademark Office.

Chandrasekaran, A., & Kapoor, M. (2016). Frost & Sullivan 2011- Market Insight. *Frost.com*. Retrieved 8 January 2016, from http://www.frost.com/prod/servlet/cio/232651119

Gijzen, H. (2013). Development: Big data for a sustainable future. *Nature*, *502*(7469), 38–38. doi:10.1038/502038d PMID:24091969

Hampton, S. E., Strasser, C. A., Tewksbury, J. J., Gram, W. K., Budden, A. E., Batcheller, A. L., & Porter, J. H. et al. (2013). Big data and the future of ecology. *Frontiers in Ecology and the Environment*, *11*(3), 156–162. doi:10.1890/120103

Hashizume, K., Rosado, D. G., Fernández-Medina, E., & Fernandez, E. B. (2013). An analysis of security issues for cloud computing. *Journal of Internet Services and Applications*, *4*(1), 1–13. doi:10.1186/1869-0238-4-5

Hongbing, C., Chunming, R., Kai, H., Weihong, W., & Yanyan, L. (2015). Secure big data storage and sharing scheme for cloud tenants. *Communications, China*, *12*(6), 106–115. doi:10.1109/CC.2015.7122469

Howe, D., Costanzo, M., Fey, P., Gojobori, T., Hannick, L., Hide, W., & Twigger, S. et al. (2008). Big data: The future of biocuration. *Nature*, *455*(7209), 47–50. doi:10.1038/455047a PMID:18769432

Kambatla, K., Kollias, G., Kumar, V., & Grama, A. (2014). Trends in big data analytics. *Journal of Parallel and Distributed Computing*, *74*(7), 2561–2573. doi:10.1016/j.jpdc.2014.01.003

Kayyali, B., Knott, D., & Van Kuiken, S. (2013). *The big-data revolution in US health care: Accelerating value and innovation*. Mc Kinsey & Company.

Kim, G. H., Trimi, S., & Chung, J. H. (2014). Big-data applications in the government sector. *Communications of the ACM, 57*(3), 78–85. doi:10.1145/2500873

Lynch, C. (2008). Big data: How do your data grow? *Nature, 455*(7209), 28–29. doi:10.1038/455028a PMID:18769419

Marchal, S., Jiang, X., State, R., & Engel, T. (2014, June). A Big Data Architecture for Large Scale Security Monitoring. *Proceedings of the 2014 IEEE International Congress on Big Data (Big Data Congress)* (pp. 56-63). IEEE. doi:10.1109/BigData.Congress.2014.18

Mhlanga, F. S., Perry, E. L., & Kirchner, R. (2015). *On Adapting a Military Combat Discrete Event Simulation with Big Data and Geospatial Modeling Toward a Predictive Model Ecosystem for Interpersonal Violence.* Journal Of Information Systems Applied Research.

Pandey, A., & Ramesh, V. (2015). Quantum computing for big data analysis. *History (Historical Association (Great Britain)), 14*(43), 98–104.

Popa, R. A., Stark, E., Valdez, S., Helfer, J., Zeldovich, N., & Balakrishnan, H. (2014). Building web applications on top of encrypted data using Mylar. *Proceedings of the USENIX Symposium of Networked Systems Design and Implementation.*

Reed, D. A., & Dongarra, J. (2015). Exascale computing and big data. *Communications of the ACM, 58*(7), 56–68. doi:10.1145/2699414

Sabahi, F. (2011, May). Virtualization-level security in cloud computing. *Proceedings of the 2011 IEEE 3rd International Conference on Communication Software and Networks (ICCSN)* (pp. 250-254). IEEE. doi:10.1109/ICCSN.2011.6014716

Schmidt, K., & Phillips, C. (2013). *Programming Elastic MapReduce: Using AWS Services to Build an End-to-end Application.* O'Reilly Media, Inc.

Sharma, P. P., & Navdeti, C. P. (2014). Securing big data hadoop: a review of security issues, threats and solution. *Int. J. Comput. Sci. Inf. Technol, 5.*

Shmueli, E., Vaisenberg, R., Elovici, Y., & Glezer, C. (2010). Database encryption: An overview of contemporary challenges and design considerations. *SIGMOD Record, 38*(3), 29–34. doi:10.1145/1815933.1815940

Subashini, S., & Kavitha, V. (2011, October). A metadata based storage model for Securing data in cloud environment. In CyberC (pp. 429-434).

Vayena, E., Salathé, M., Madoff, L. C., & Brownstein, J. S. (2015). Ethical challenges of big data in public health. *PLoS Computational Biology, 11*(2), e1003904. doi:10.1371/journal.pcbi.1003904 PMID:25664461

Wang, W., Chen, L., Thirunarayan, K., & Sheth, A. P. (2012, September). Harnessing twitter" big data" for automatic emotion identification. *Proceedings of the 2012 International Conference on Privacy, Security, Risk and Trust (PASSAT) and 2012 International Conference on Social Computing (SocialCom)* (pp. 587-592). IEEE.

Wang, X., & Sun, Z. (2013). The Design of Water Resources and Hydropower Cloud GIS Platform Based on Big Data. In *Geo-Informatics in Resource Management and Sustainable Ecosystem* (pp. 313–322). Springer Berlin Heidelberg. doi:10.1007/978-3-642-41908-9_32

We Are Social, U. K. (2014). *Global Social Media Users Pass 2 Billion.* Retrieved 8 January 2016, from http://wearesocial.net/blog/2014/08/global-social-media-users-pass-2-billion

KEY TERMS AND DEFINITIONS

Big Data: Big data is high-volume, high-variety and high-velocity information assets that demand cost-effective, innovative forms of information processing that enable enhanced insight, process automation and decision making.

Cloud Computing: Cloud computing is used to connect the computing resources, hardware's and access IT managed services with a previously unknown level of ease.

Hybrid Cloud: Hybrid cloud is a type of cloud computing model which uses a mix of on-premises, private cloud and third-party, public cloud services.

Infrastructure as a Service (IaaS): Infrastructure as a Service (IaaS) is used to deliver the computer infrastructure on an outsourced basis to support enterprise applications.

Platform as a Service (PaaS): Platform as a service (PaaS) is a category of cloud computing model that provides a platform and environment to allow developers to create software applications using tools supplied by the provider.

Private Cloud: A private cloud is a type of cloud computing model that involves a distinct and secure cloud based environment in which only the authorized users can operate.

Public Cloud: A public cloud is a type of cloud computing model, in which a service provider makes resources, such as storage, computing resources and applications available to the all users or the general public over the Internet.

Software as a Service (SaaS): Software as a service (or SaaS) is a software distribution model and it is used to deliver the applications over the Internet as a service.

Chapter 12
An Intelligent Parking System in Smart Cities Using IoT

Amardeep Das
C. V. Raman College of Engineering, India

Prasant Kumar Dash
C. V. Raman College of Engineering, India

Brojo Kishore Mishra
C. V. Raman College of Engineering, India

ABSTRACT

Smart City is the product of accelerated development of the new generation information technology and knowledge-based economy, based on the network combination of the Internet, telecommunications network, broadcast network, wireless broadband network and other sensors networks where Internet of Things technology (IoT) as its core. Traffic congestion caused by vehicle is an alarming problem at a global scale and it has been growing exponentially. Searching for a parking space is a routine (and often frustrating) activity for many people in cities around the world. This search burns about one million barrels of the world's oil every day. A smart Parking system typically obtains information about available parking spaces in a particular geographic area and process is real-time to place vehicles at available positions. In our proposed chapter, we will be discussing the advanced features of IoT in order to development an intelligent parking management system in a smart city i.e. called as Smart Parking system.

INTRODUCTION

Internet of Things (IoT) is the network of devices that are connected together and communicating with each other to perform certain tasks, without requiring human-to-human or human-to-computer interaction. The Internet of Things is about installing sensors (RFID, IR, GPS, laser scanners, etc.) for everything, and connecting them to the internet through specific protocols for information exchange and communications, in order to achieve intelligent recognition, location, tracking, monitoring and management (Introduction to internet of things (n. d.). With the technical support from IoT, smart city need to have three features of

DOI: 10.4018/978-1-5225-2947-7.ch012

Copyright © 2018, IGI Global. Copying or distributing in print or electronic forms without written permission of IGI Global is prohibited.

being instrumented, interconnected and intelligent. Only then a Smart City can be formed by integrating all these intelligent features at its advanced stage of IOT development.

According to the McKinsey report "Disruptive technologies: Advances that will transform life, business, and the global economy, the Internet of things (IoT) is one of the top three technological advancements of the next decade (together with the mobile internet and the automation of knowledge work). The report goes on to say that "The Internet of Things is such a sweeping concept that it is a challenge to even imagine all the possible ways in which it will affect business, economies, and society". Definitions for the Internet of Things vary. According to McKinsey: "Sensors and actuators embedded in physical objects are linked through wired and wireless networks, often using the same Internet Protocol (IP) that connects the Internet" (Uckelmann, Harrison & Michahelles, 2011).

The idea is that not only your computer and your smart phone can talk to each other, but also all the things around you. From connected homes and cities to connected cars and machines to devices that track an individual's behavior and use the data collected for new kind of services. "The Internet of things will involve a massive build-out of connected devices and sensors woven into the fabric of our lives and businesses. Devices deeply embedded in public and private places will recognize us and adapt to our requirements for comfort, safety, streamlined commerce, entertainment, education, resource conservation, operational efficiency and personal well-being.", according to Intel's report "Rise of the Embedded Internet".

PROPERTIES OF INTERNET OF THINGS

The Internet of Things (IoT) is a technological revolution that represents the future of computing and communications (Patrick et. al, 2005). Its development depends on the dynamic technical innovation in a number of important fields, from wireless sensors to nanotechnology. The following are the requirements to fulfill the objective of the IoT. They are:

1. **Connect Both Inanimate and Living Things:** Early trials and deployments of Internet of Things networks began with connecting industrial equipment. Today, the vision of IoT has expanded to connect everything from industrial equipment to everyday objects. The types of items range from gas turbines to automobiles to utility meters. It can also include living organisms such as plants, farm animals and people. For example, the Cow Tracking Project in Essex uses data collected from radio positioning tags to monitor cows for illness and track behavior in the herd. Wearable computing and digital health devices, such as Nike+ Fuel band and Fitbit, are examples of how people are connecting in the Internet of Things landscape. Cisco has expanded the definition of IoT to the Internet of Everything (IoE), which includes people, places, objects and things. Basically, anything you can attach a sensor and connectivity to can participate in the new connected ecosystems.

2. **Use Sensors for Data Collection:** The physical objects that are being connected will possess one or more sensors. Each sensor will monitor a specific condition such as location, vibration, motion and temperature. In IoT, these sensors will connect to each other and to systems that can understand or present information from the sensor's data feeds. These sensors will provide new information to a company's systems and to people.

3. **Change What Types of Item Communicate Over an IP Network:** In the past, people communicated with people and with machines. Imagine if all of your equipment had the ability to communicate. What would it tell you? IoT-enabled objects will share information about their condition and the

surrounding environment with people, software systems and other machines. This information can be shared in real-time or collected and shared at defined intervals. Going forward, everything will have a digital identity and connectivity, which means you can identify, track and communicate with objects. IoT data differs from traditional computing. The data can be small in size and frequent in transmission. The number of devices, or nodes that are connecting to the network are also greater in IoT than in traditional PC computing. Machine-to-Machine communications and intelligence drawn from the devices and the network will allow businesses to automate certain basic tasks without depending on central or cloud based applications and services. These attributes present opportunities to collect a wide range of data but also provide challenges in terms of designing the appropriate data networking and security.

IoT COMPARED TO SIMILAR CONCEPTS

While the Internet of Things is by far the most popular term to describe the phenomenon of a connected world, there are similar concepts that deserve some attention. Most of these concepts are similar in meaning but they all have slightly different definitions.

- **M2M:** The term Machine to Machine (M2M) has been in use for more than a decade, and is well-known in the Telecoms sector. M2M communication had initially been a one-to-one connection, linking one machine to another. But today's explosion of mobile connectivity means that data can now be more easily transmitted, via a system of IP networks, to a much wider range of devices.
- **Industrial Internet (of Things):** The term industrial internet is strongly pushed by GE. It goes beyond M2M since it not only focuses on connections between machines but also includes human interfaces.
- **Internet of Things (IoT):** IoT has yet a wider reach as it also includes connections beyond the industrial context such as wearable devices on people.
- **Web of Things:** The Web of Things is much narrower in scope as the other concepts as it solely focuses on software architecture.
- **Internet of Everything (IoE):** Still a rather vague concept, IoE aims to include all sorts of connections that one can envision. The concept has thus the highest reach.

ARCHITECTURE OF INTERNET OF THINGS

The IoT needs an open architecture to maximise interoperability among heterogeneous systems and distributed resources including providers and consumers of information and services, whether they be human beings, software, smart objects or devices. Architecture standards should consist of well-defined abstract data models, interfaces and protocols, together with concrete bindings to neutral technologies (such as XML, web services etc.) in order to support the widest possible variety of operating systems and programming languages (SRI Consulting Business Intelligence, April 2008). The architecture should have well-defined and granular layers, in order to foster a competitive marketplace of solutions, without locking any users into using a monolithic stack from a single solution provider. Like the Internet, the IoT architecture should be designed to be resilient to disruption of the physical network and should also anticipate that many of the nodes will be mobile, and they may have intermittent connectivity also they may use various communication protocols at different times to connect to the IoT.

IoT nodes may need to form peer networks with other nodes dynamically and autonomously locally or remotely, this should be done through a decentralized, distributed approach to the architecture, with support for semantic search, discovery and peer networking. Anticipating the vast volumes of data which may be generated, it is important that the architecture also includes mechanisms for moving intelligence and capabilities for filtering, pattern recognition, machine learning and decision-making towards the very edges of the network to enable distributed and decentralized processing of the information, either close to where data is generated or remotely located in the cloud. The architectural design will also need to enable the processing, routing, storage and retrieval of events as well as allows for disconnected operations (e.g., where network connectivity might only be intermittent). Effective caching, pre-positioning and synchronization of requests, updates and data flows need to be an integral feature of the architecture. By developing and defining the architecture in terms of opens standards and expects increased participation from solution providers of all sizes and a competitive marketplace that benefits end users. In summary, the following issues have to be addressed:

- Distributed open architecture with end to end characteristics, interoperability of heterogeneous systems, neutral access, clear layering and resilience to physical network disruption.
- Decentralized autonomic architectures based on peering of nodes.
- Architectures moving intelligence at the very edge of the networks, up to users' terminals and things.
- Cloud computing technology, event-driven architectures, disconnected operations and synchronization.
- Use of market mechanisms for increased competition and participation.

Sensor

The IoT is a network of objects connected by things like sensors, RFID tags, and IP addresses. In this respect, sensors have a special role in the IoT paradigm. According to the International Telecommunication Unit (ITU Report 2005), Internet of Things can be defined as a vision "... to connect everyday objects and devices to large databases and networks ... (using) a simple, unobtrusive and cost-effective system of item identification..."

In the IoT, sensors are the edge of the electronics ecosystem (Sensors empower the "Internet of Things", 2010). Sensors allow the physical world to interact with computers, playing an important role in bridging the gap between the physical world and the virtual one. This allows a richer array of data, other than data available from keyboard and mouse inputs. Currently, the internet is full of information that has been input by someone at the keyboard. But the concept of Internet of Things will change where more Internet data originates from sensors rather than keyboard inputs.

A sensor is a device that can measure a physical quality and converts that physical quantity into a signal that can be read by an instrument or an observer. In the idea of the Internet of Things, the ability to detect changes in the physical status of things is also essential for recording changes in the environment (International Telecommunications Union (2005). Sensors collect data from the environment, such as vibrations, temperature, and pressure, among others, and convert them into data that can be processed and analyzed. This allows the Internet of Things to record any changes in the environment or an object.

For example, by having sensors installed on a bridge, the data collected can be used to estimate the number of cars that travel on the bridge, the traffic on the bridge at different times of the day, and the speed of the cars travelling on the bridge. This data can then be used for navigation systems, to allow programs or software to determine the fastest route, depending on the time of day.

Also, the sensors installed on to a bridge can be used to determine the safety of the structure of the bridge. For example, the sensors can be made to detect the vibrations along each part of the bridge, to detect any impending failure or fault. By collecting such information, any problems such as damage to a structure can be detected early on and dealt with, before any problems arise.

Embedded intelligence in things themselves can further enhance the power of the network. This is possible because the information processing capabilities are devolved, or delegated, to the edges of the network. Embedded intelligence will distribute processing power to the edges of the network, and offers greater possibilities for data processing and increasing the resilience of the network. With embedded intelligence, the things or devices connected at the edge of the network can make independent decisions based on the input received at the sensors.

"Smart things" are difficult to define. However, the term implies a certain processing power and reaction to external stimuli. Advances in smart homes, smart vehicles and personal robotics are some of the leading areas. Research on wearable computing is swiftly progressing. Scientists are using their imagination to develop new devices and appliances, such as intelligent ovens that can be controlled through phones or the internet, online refrigerators and networked blinds. The Internet of Things will draw on the functionality offered by all of these technologies to realize the vision of a fully interactive and responsive network environment.

The Internet of Things (IoT) couldn't exist without smart sensors, and the growing use of smart technology is already transforming how manufacturers implement the IoT (Atif, Ding & Jeusfeld, 2016). Smart sensors are also bringing more connectivity and analytics to the supply chain. There are some things to know about how and why this is happening.

First, smart sensors are the indispensable enablers of the IoT and the industrial IoT. Smart sensors, including radio frequency identification (RFID) tags, serve three broad purposes. They identify items, locate them and determine their environmental conditions, all of which have major implications for the supply chain and manufacturing. Smart sensors are particularly useful in plants or warehouses because they can keep track of temperature and humidity, log data for historical records and quality management, or be used as triggers for alarms or process management.

Second, smart sensors impact the supply chain by being embedded in products, which can help improve the manufacturing process or the products themselves. Sensors can live inside products to create "smart products" and new revenue sources from the enhanced features. They can also permeate the manufacturing process to monitor, control, and improve operations, or be added to logistics to streamline how products are delivered. There are a number of specific purposes of sensors, such as measuring temperature, humidity, vibrations, motion, light, pressure and altitude. Companies will need to develop new applications to take advantage of all the big data that the sensors are generating.

Third, the lower costs and more advanced capabilities of RFID tags are starting to enable wider and more effective use. The cost of RFID, which has come down dramatically, is in more than just the tag itself. To determine the true cost per use you have to include the software applications and deployment costs. The combination of lowered costs for tags and improved capabilities means that their value proposition has changed, and represents an opportunity for enterprises to rethink RFID.

Layers of IoT

The internet of things work in different layers and each layer have some responsibility to perform their works towards the goal. The layers shown in figure 1.

Layer 1 - Sense and Identification Layer: A wireless identification and sensing platform (WISP) is an RFID (radio-frequency identification) device that supports sensing an object and computing: a microcontroller powered by radio-frequency energy.

Layer 2 -Network Construction Layer: In this layer, the different types of network like WPAN, WWAN, WLAN and WWAN to communicate the different types of information from one network to another.

Layer 3 - Management Layer: Manage the information how it processes in different areas like Data centre, Search engine, Smart decision, Information security, Data mining in this layer.

Layer 4 - Integrated Application Layer: Integrate and provide the different types of service to different smart technology like Smart logistics, Smart Grid, Green Building, Smart Transport, and Environmental Monitor.

The Internet is a world-wide network of interconnected computer networks, based on a standard communication protocol (TCP/IP). The Internet of Things (IoT) is a world-wide network of interconnected objects which are outfitted with sensors, actuators and RFID devices. These devices are uniquely addressable and use standard communication protocols in a heterogeneous networking environment including objects of totally different functionality, technology and application fields shown in Figure 2.

APPLICATION AREAS FOR IOT

Internet of things examples extend from smart connected homes to wearables to healthcare. It is not wrong to suggest that IoT is now becoming part of every aspect of our lives. Not only is the Internet of Things applications enhancing the comforts of our lives, but also it giving us more control by simplifying routine work life and personal tasks.

With the recent hype about the future prospects of IoT has forced companies to take the initiative of coming up with basic building blocks of internet of things i.e. hardware, software and support to enable developers deploy applications that can connect anything within scope of internet of things. The following are the different application areas where IOT works. They are:

Figure 1. Layers of IOT

Information Application	Integrated Application layer
Information Processing	Management layer
Information Transmission	Network construction layer
Information Generation	Sense and Identification layer

Figure 2. Diagram of IOT

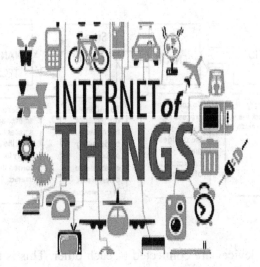

- Smart Home
- Connected Cars
- Wearable
- Industrial Internet
- Smart Cities
- IoT in agriculture
- Smart Retail
- Energy Engagement
- IOT in Healthcare
- IoT in Poultry and Farming

STATE OF THE ART AND CHALLENGES OF IOT

Instead of emerging as a completely new category of systems, the Internet of Things is likely to rise through an incremental development approach. In fact, in order to reach the physical realm, IoT building blocks will be progressively integrated to the existing Internet. In this section, mostly focus on the enabling technologies that are expected to form the IoT building blocks. Each technology is briefly introduced, along with its future impact on IoT.

RFID, Sensor, smart tech and nano technology are combined used in IOT shown in the Figure 3.

Over years the pathway of Internet of things wasn't so smooth, there were many challenges for the Internet of things that it had to face and overcome for purpose of delivering undisruptive technological advancement. Following are the key challenges that Internet of Things (biggest challenges for the internet of things has to face and find solutions to overcome the same in order of delivering effective and efficient servicer are:

Figure 3. State the Art of IOT

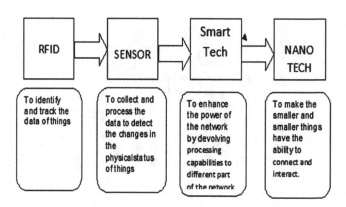

- **Security:** In IOT more devices are connected to each other. This is the biggest threat to IoT security. When TCP/IP-based endpoints are allowed on a LAN without enterprise-level security protocols in place, there is a great deal of risk involved.
- **Trust and Privacy:** The remote sensors and monitoring a core use case for the IoT, there will be heightened sensitivity to controlling access and ownership of data. The third-party vendor can observer the data and stolen credentials to gain access to payment systems.
- **Signalling:** In simple words Signalling refers to the security and reliability of data transfer from one device to another. This transfer can be between device to device, device to server or server to device.
- **Ubiquitous connectivity:** Internet is not still available in many rural Ares of the world. And yet the whole concept of the IoT is predicated on the availability of a constant, reliable network connection.
- **Adaptability:** Trends are changing and so does the need of consumer, with this changing trend there is need for Internet of Things to improve itself and adapt the changing environment. Adaptability is essential for ensuring its survival and growth. Internet of Things should be able to adapt itself and diversify its use with expansion of consumers need and demand.

CHARACTERISTICS OF IOT

The fundamental characteristics of the IoT are as follows (Vermesan & Friess, 2014)

- **Intelligence:** Together algorithms and compute (i.e. software & hardware) provide the "intelligent spark" that makes a product experience smart.
- **Connectivity:** Connectivity in the IoT is more than slapping on a Wi-Fi module and calling it a day. Connectivity enables network accessibility and compatibility. Accessibility is getting on a network while compatibility provides the common ability to consume and produce data. If this sounds familiar, that's because it is Metcalfe's Law and it rings true for IoT.
- **Sensing:** Sensing tend to take for granted our senses and ability to understand the physical world and people around us. Sensing technologies provide us with the means to create experiences that

reflect a true awareness of the physical world and the people in it. This is simply the analog input from the physical world, but it can provide rich understanding of our complex world.

- **Expressing:** Expressing enables interactivity with people and the physical world. Whether it is a smart home or a farm with smart agriculture technology, expressing provides us with a means to create products that interact intelligently with the real world. This means more than just rendering beautiful UIs to a screen. Expressing allows us to output into the real world and directly interact with people and the environment.
- **Energy:** Without energy, life cannot exist. The problem is to create billions of things that all run on batteries. Energy harvesting, power efficiency, and charging infrastructures are necessary part a power intelligent ecosystem that must design. Today, it is woefully inadequate and lacks the focus of many product teams.
- **Safety:** As per the gain efficiencies, novel experiences, and other benefits from the IoT, safety is the major factor. This includes the safety of our personal data and the safety of our physical well-being. Securing the endpoints, the networks, and the data moving across all of it means creating a security paradigm that will scale.

FUTURE OF IOT

There are key challenges and implications today that need to be addressed before mass adoption of IOT can occur. (Uckelmann, Harrison & Michahelles, 2011)

- **Privacy and Security:** As the IoT become a key element of the Future Internet and the usage of the Internet of Things for large-scale, partially mission-critical systems creates the need to address trust and security functions adequately. New challenges identified for privacy, trust and reliability are: providing trust and quality-of-information in shared information models to enable re-use across many applications. Providing secure exchange of data between IoT devices and consumers of their information. Providing protection mechanisms for vulnerable devices.
- **Cost vs. Usability:** IOT uses technology to connect physical objects to the Internet. For IOT adoption to grow, the cost of components that are needed to support capabilities such as sensing, tracking and control mechanisms need to be relatively inexpensive in the coming years.
- **Interoperability:** In the traditional Internet, interoperability is the most basic core value; the first requirement of Internet connectivity is that "connected" systems be able to "talk the same language" of protocols and encodings. Different industries today use different standards to support their applications. With numerous sources of data and heterogeneous devices, the use of standard interfaces between these diverse entities becomes important. This is especially so for applications that supports cross organizational and various system boundaries. Thus, the IOT systems need to handle high degree of interoperability.
- **Data Management:** Data management is a crucial aspect in the Internet of Things. When considering a world of objects interconnected and constantly exchanging all types of information, the volume of the generated data and the processes involved in the handling of those data become critical.

- **Device Level Energy Issues:** One of the essential challenges in IoT is how to interconnect "things" in an interoperable way while taking into account the energy constraints, knowing that the communication is the most energy consuming task on devices.

SMART CITY

The objective of the smart city is to provide an intelligent solution to the environment. Smart city needed three major parameters, like instrumented, intelligent and interconnected.

The core infrastructure elements in a smart city would include:

- Adequate water supply
- Assured electricity supply
- Sanitation, including solid waste management
- Efficient urban mobility and public transport
- Affordable housing, especially for the poor
- Robust IT connectivity and digitalization
- Good governance, especially e-Governance and citizen participation
- Sustainable environment
- Safety and security of citizens, particularly women, children and the elderly
- Health and education.

Smart Parking Systems

Smart Parking systems typically obtain information about available parking spaces in a particular geographic area and process is real-time to place vehicles at available positions. It involves using low-cost sensors, real-time data collection, and mobile phone-enabled automated payment systems that allow people to reserve parking in advance or very accurately predict where they will likely find a spot. When deployed as a system, smart parking thus reduces car emissions in urban centers by reducing the need for people to needlessly circle city blocks searching for parking (Happiest minds, n. d.). It also permits cities to carefully manage their parking supply Smart parking helps one of the biggest problems on driving in urban areas; finding empty parking spaces and controlling illegal parking. This implies M2M technologies aims rightness/safety as well as convenience.

Traffic congestion caused by vehicle is an alarming problem at a global scale and it has been growing exponentially. Car parking problem is a major contributor and has been, still a major problem with increasing vehicle size in the luxurious segment and confined parking spaces in urban cities. Searching for a parking space is a routine (and often frustrating) activity for many people in cities around the world. This search burns about one million barrels of the world's oil every day.

As the global population continues to urbanize, without a well-planned, convenience-driven retreat from the car these problems will worsen. According to a report, Smart Parking could result in 2, 20,000 gallons of fuels saving till 2030 and approx. 3, 00,000 gallons of fuels saved by 2050, if implemented successfully. Smart Parking systems typically obtains information about available parking spaces in a particular geographic area and process is Real-time to place vehicles at available positions. It involves using low-cost sensors, real-time data collection, and mobile-phone-enabled automated payment systems that allow people to reserve parking in advance or very accurately predict where they will likely find a spot. When deployed as a system, smart parking thus reduces car emissions in urban centers by reducing the need for people to needlessly circle city blocks searching for parking. It also permits cities to carefully manage their parking supply Smart parking helps one of the biggest problems on driving in urban areas; finding empty parking spaces and controlling illegal parking. This implies M2M technologies aims rightness/safety as well as convenience.

Smart Parking manages car parks for landholders to ensure that motorists are paying for their use of parking spaces, as renting parking spaces is a business like any other, or that free time limits are being adhered to, which are commonly used by retailers to ensure that there is a regular turnover and availability of parking spaces for their genuine customers. Smart Parking ensures that the car park terms and conditions are adhered to and that the parking spaces are used correctly. Car park abuse is detrimental to landholders, and Smart Parking provides a service that ensures the efficient and regulated use of car parks. The growing population of India has created many problems, one of the challenging ones being car parking which creates congestion almost every day. Besides the problem of space for cars moving on the road, greater is the problem of space for a parked vehicle considering that private vehicles remain parked for most of their time. Roads are being built for cars to ply but are we also giving the vehicles enough space to park? Parking is one of the major problems that is created by the increasing road track. It is an impact of transport development. The availability of less space in urban areas has increased the demand for parking space especially in areas like Central business district. People cannot find parking in popular places. Especially during the holidays (Christmas shopping), traffic is always bad. People cannot locate their car in large parking lots (Theme parks). Difficulty finding parking spots, Parking for cars of different sizes, Maximize utilization space (concerts or other functions).

Literature Review

The following are the need and benefits analysis of smart parking system:

- Accurately predict and sense spot/vehicle occupancy in real-time.
- Guides residents and visitors to available parking.
- Optimize Parking Space Usage.
- Simplifies the parking experience and adds value for parking stakeholders, such as drivers and merchants.
- Help traffic in the city flow more freely leveraging IoT technology.
- Enables intelligent decisions using data, including real–time status applications and historical analytics reports.
- Smart Parking plays a major role in creating better urban environment by reducing the emission of $CO2$ and other pollutants.
- Smart Parking enables better and real time monitoring and managing of available parking space, resulting in significant revenue generation.
- Provides tools to optimize workforce management.

The Internet of Things (IoT) paradigm expands the scope of cloud-based intelligent car parking services in smart cities, with novel applications that better regulate car-parking related traffic (Atif, Ding & Jeusfeld, 2016). Similarly, the authors Sanket Gupte and Mohamed Younis (2015) tell IoT framework that targets one of the biggest challenges in modern cities, namely, Parking Management. Populating parking facilities with sensors imposes unwarranted installation and maintenance costs. And it mainly focuses on reducing the time in finding the parking lots (Mr. Basavaraju S R (December 2015)) and also it avoids the unnecessary travelling through filled parking lots in a parking area. Thus, it reduces the fuel consumption which in turn reduces carbon footprints in an atmosphere.

Types of Smart Parking System

Different types of parking concepts have arisen; out of that some concepts are presented here. They are:

- Park-and-Ride
- Shared Parking
- Bicycle Parking
- "Unbundled" Parking
- Car Sharing

Park-and-Ride

- Parking is located near transit stations for transit riders.
- User fees are sometimes charged.
- Parking usually located on publicly owned land.
- Parking does not need to be immediately adjacent to transit station (Figure 4).

Figure 4. Park-and-Ride

Shared Parking

- Parking is shared among multiple uses.
- It takes advantage of different peak usage hours for parking.
- It can be used in residential and employment environments.
- Figure 5 shows the examples of shared parking.

Bicycle Parking

- Types of Bicycle Parking:
  - Indoor Parking
  - Bicycle Lockers
  - Bicycle Racks
- Approximately 10 bikes can fit in 1 car parking space.

Weather protection and security are critical for use. Bicycle parking example shows in Figure 6.

Unbundled Parking

- Parking is physically or economically separated from its associated use.
- It affects the sizing, design, site and construction of parking.
- It promotes the efficient use of parking resources.

Figure 5. Shared parking

Figure 6. Bicycle parking

Car Sharing

- It gives access to centrally owned and maintained vehicles.
- It is near homes, workplaces or transit hubs.
- It helps lower household auto ownership rates. How to park the cars in parking area shown in Figure 7.

Smart Parking Work Flow

Figure 8 describes the flow of smart parking.

COMPONENTS USED IN SMART MODEL

The following components are required for designing and implementing the smart parking system. They are:

- IR sensor module
- Ultrasonic sensor
- ATmega16 microcontroller
- AVR trainer board
- USB programmer

Figure 7. Car sharing

Figure 8. Work flow

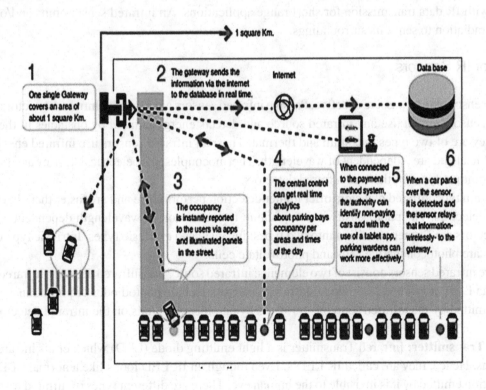

- LED
- Motor(DC-12v,150-200RPM)

Miscellaneous

- Jumper wires
- 12v power adaptor

IR Sensor

Infrared technology addresses a wide variety of wireless applications. The main areas are sensing and remote controls. In the electromagnetic spectrum, the infrared portion is divided into three regions: near infrared region, mid infrared region and far infrared region.

The wavelengths of these regions and their applications are shown below.

- **Near Infrared Region:** 700 nm to 1400 nm — IR sensors, fiber optic.
- **Mid Infrared Region:** 1400 nm to 3000 nm — Heat sensing.
- **Far Infrared Region:** 3000 nm to 1 mm — Thermal imaging.

The frequency range of infrared is higher than microwave and lesser than visible light. For optical sensing and optical communication, photo optics technologies are used in the near infrared region as the light is less complex than RF when implemented as a source of signal. Optical wireless communication is done with IR data transmission for short range applications. An infrared sensor emits and/or detects infrared radiation to sense its surroundings.

Types of IR Sensors

Infrared sensors can be passive or active. Passive infrared sensors are basically Infrared detectors. Passive infrared sensors do not use any infrared source and detects energy emitted by obstacles in the field of view. They are of two types: quantum and thermal. Thermal infrared sensors use infrared energy as the source of heat and are independent of wavelength. Thermocouples, pyroelectric detectors and bolometer are the common types of thermal infrared detectors.

Quantum type infrared detectors offer higher detection performance and are faster than thermal type infrared detectors. The photosensitivity of quantum type detectors is wavelength dependent. Quantum type detectors are further classified into two types: intrinsic and extrinsic types. Intrinsic type quantum detectors are photoconductive cells and photovoltaic cells.

Active infrared sensors consist of two elements: infrared source and infrared detector. Infrared sources include an LED or infrared laser diode. Infrared detectors include photodiodes or phototransistors. The energy emitted by the infrared source is reflected by an object and falls on the infrared detector.

- **IR Transmitter:** Infrared Transmitter is a light emitting diode (LED) which emits infrared radiations. Hence, they are called IR LED's. Even though an IR LED looks like a normal LED, the radiation emitted by it is invisible to the human eye. There are different types of infrared transmitters depending on their wavelengths, output power and response time. A simple infrared transmitter can be constructed using an infrared LED, a current limiting resistor and a power supply. When operated at a supply of 5V, the IR transmitter consumes about 3 to 5 mA of current. Infrared transmitters can be modulated to produce a particular frequency of infrared light. The most commonly used modulation is OOK (ON – OFF – KEYING) modulation.IR transmitters can be found in several applications. Some applications require infrared heat and the best infrared source is infrared transmitter. When infrared emitters are used with Quartz, solar cells can be made.

- **IR Receiver:** Infrared receivers are also called as infrared sensors as they detect the radiation from an IR transmitter. IR receivers come in the form of photodiodes and phototransistors. Infrared Photodiodes are different from normal photo diodes as they detect only infrared radiation. The picture of a typical IR receiver or a photodiode is shown below. Different types of IR receivers exist based on the wavelength, voltage, package, etc. When used in an infrared transmitter – receiver combination, the wavelength of the receiver should match with that of the transmitter. It consists of an IR phototransistor, a diode, a MOSFET, a potentiometer and an LED. When the phototransistor receives any infrared radiation, current flows through it and MOSFET turns on. This in turn lights up the LED which acts as a load. The potentiometer is used to control the sensitivity of the phototransistor.

- **Working Principle:** The principle of an IR sensor working as an Object Detection Sensor can be explained using the following figure (Carnegie Mellon's Robotics Academy. n. d.). An IR sensor consists of an IR LED and an IR Photodiode; together they are called as Photo – Coupler or Opto – Coupler. When the IR transmitter emits radiation, it reaches the object and some of the radiation reflects back to the IR receiver. Based on the intensity of the reception by the IR receiver, the output of the sensor is defined. IR Sensors work by using a specific light sensor to detect a select light wavelength in the Infra-Red (IR) spectrum. By using an LED which produces light at the same wavelength as what the sensor is looking for, you can look at the intensity of the received light. When an object is close to the sensor, the light from the LED bounces off the object and into the light sensor. This results in a large jump in the intensity that can be detected using a threshold. Since the sensor works by looking for reflected light, it is possible to have a sensor that can return the value of the reflected light. This type of sensor can then be used to measure how "bright" the object is. This is useful for tasks like line tracking. IR sensor observed properly from the Figure 9.

This Medium Range Infrared sensor offers simple, user friendly and fast obstacle detection using infrared; it is non-contact detection. The implementations of modulated IR signal immune the sensor to the interferences caused by the normal light of a light bulb or the sunlight. The sensing distance can be adjusted manually. The product features include:

- 5V powered, low current consumption, less than 10mA.
- 3 pin interface which are signal, GND and 5V.
- Small LED as indicator for detection status.
- Obstacle detection up to 8 cm
- Adjustable sensing range (2cm – 8cm).
- Small size makes it easy to assembly.
- Single bit output
- Compatible with all types of microcontrollers and Arduino
- Dimension: 2.6cm x 2cm

Figure 9. IR sensor

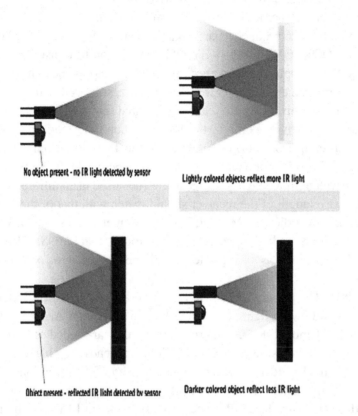

Infrared sensor uses special sensor to modulate IR signal emitted from 2 IR transmitters and detects the modulated IR signal reflected back from a nearby object. This sensor has a built-in IR LED driver to modulate the IR signal at 38KHzto match the built-in detector. The modulated IR signal immunes the sensor from the interferences caused by the normal light of a light bulb or the sunlight. The module will output a HIGH if no object is detected and a LOW if an object is detected.

Table 1 provides further information on the connection made by IR sensors.

Ultrasonic Sensor

Ultrasonic sensor provides an easy method of distance measurement. This sensor is perfect for any number of applications that require you to perform measurements between moving or stationary objects

Table 1. Pins, their names, and their functions in terms of connection

Pin	Name	Function
+	VCC	Connects to Vcc (+4V to + 6V)
-	Ground	Connects to Ground
s	Output signal	Connects to an I/O pin of microcontroller which set to INPUT mode (or transistor/MOSFET).

interfacing to a microcontroller is a snap. Figure 10 shows the ultrasonic sensor. A single I/O pin is used to trigger an ultrasonic burst (well above human hearing) and then "listen" for the echo return pulse. The sensor measures the time required for the echo return, and returns this value to the microcontroller as a variable-width pulse via the same I/O pin.

Due to the following reasons this sensor is used:

- Obstacle Avoidance
- Navigation
- Map Building
- Underwater Exploration!
- Key Features:
  ◦ Provides precise, non-contact distance measurements within a 2cm to 3m range
  ◦ Ultrasonic measurements work in any lighting condition, making this a good choice to supplement infrared object detectors.
  ◦ Simple pulse in/pulse out communication requires just one I/O pin
  ◦ Burst indicator LED shows measurement in progress.
  ◦ 3-pin header makes it easy to connect to a development board, directly or with an extension cable, no soldering required
- Application Ideas:
  ◦ Security systems
  ◦ Interactive animated exhibits
  ◦ Parking assistant systems
  ◦ Robotic navigation

ATmega16 Microcontroller

ATmega16 is an 8-bit high performance microcontroller of Atmel's Mega AVR family with low power consumption Atmega16 is based on enhanced in figure 11. RISC (reduced instruction set computing). Know more about RISC and CISC architecture with 131 powerful instructions (Engineers Garage, n. d.). Most of the instructions execute in one machine cycle. Atmega16 can work on a maximum frequency

Figure 10. Ultrasonic sensor

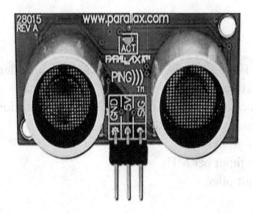

Figure 11. ATmega16 microcontroller

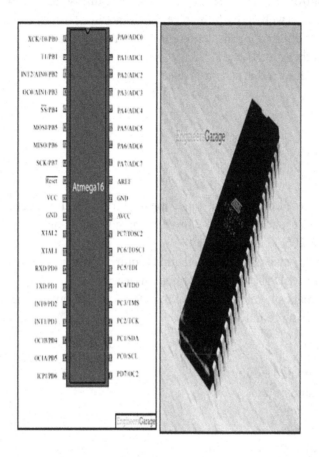

of 16MHz. ATmega16 has 16KB programmable flash memory, static RAM of 1KB and EEPROM of 512 Bytes. The endurance cycle of flash memory and EEPROM is 10000 and 100000 respectively. ATmega16 is a 40-pin microcontroller. There are 32 I/O lines which are divided into four 8-bit ports designated as PORTA, PORTB, PORTC and PORTD.

ATmega16 has various in-built peripherals like USART, ADC, Analog Comparator, SPI, JIAG etc. Each i/o pin has pin has an alternative task related to in-built peripherals.

Pin description of the ATmega16 Microcontroller in Figure 12.

Features

- High Performance, Low Power Atmel®AVR® 8-bit Microcontroller
- Advanced RISC Architecture
  - 131 Powerful Instructions - Most Single Clock Cycle Execution
  - 32 × 8 General Purpose Working Registers
  - Fully Static Operation
  - Up to 1 MIPS throughput per MHz
  - On-chip 2-cycle Multiplier

Figure 12. Pin description of the ATmega16 microcontroller

PIN1 :	I O, T0 (Timer0 External Counter Input) XCK : USART External Clock I O
PIN2 :	I O, T1 (Timer1 External Counter Input)
PIN3 :	I O, AIN0: Analog Comparator Positive Input , INT2: External Interrupt 2 Input
PIN4 :	I O, AIN1: Analog Comparator Negative Input, OC0 : Timer0 Output Compare Match Output
PIN9 :	Reset Pin, Active Low Reset
PIN10 :	VCC=+5V
PIN11 :	GND
PIN12 :	XTAL2
PIN13 :	XTAL1
PIN14 :	(RXD) I O PIN 0,USART Serial Communication Interface
PIN15 :	(TXD) I O Pin 1,USART Serial Communication Interface
PIN16 :	(INT0),I O Pin 2, External Interrupt INT0
PIN17 :	(INT1),I O Pin 3, External Interrupt INT1
PIN18 :	(OC1B),I O Pin 4, PWM Channel Outputs
PIN19 :	(OC1A),I O Pin 5, PWM Channel Outputs
PIN20 :	(ICP), I O Pin 6, Timer Counter1 Input Capture Pin
PIN21 :	(OC2),I O Pin 7,Timer Counter2 Output Compare Match Output
PIN22 :	(SCL),I O Pin 0,TWI Interface
PIN23 :	(SDA),I O Pin 1,TWI Interface
PIN24-PIN27 :	JTAG INTERFACE
PIN28 :	(TOSC1),I O Pin 6,Timer Oscillator Pin 1
PIN29 :	(TOSC2),I O Pin 7,Timer Oscillator Pin 2
PIN30 :	AVCC (for ADC)
PIN31 :	GND (for ADC)
PIN33 – PIN40	PAx: I O,ADCx (Where x is 7 – 0)

- Data and Non-Volatile Program Memory
  - 16/32/64K Bytes Flash of In-System Programmable Program Memory
  - 512B/1K/2K Bytes of In-System Programmable EEPROM
  - 1/2/4K Bytes Internal SRAM
  - Write/Erase Cycles: 10,000 Flash/ 100,000 EEPROM
  - Data Retention: 20 years at 85°C/ 100 years at 25°C (1)
  - Optional Boot Code Section with Independent Lock Bits
- In-System Programming by On-chip Boot Program True Read-While-Write Operation
  - Programming Lock for Flash Program and EEPROM Data Security
- On Chip Debug Interface (debugWIRE)
- CAN 2.0A/B with 6 Message Objects - ISO 16845 Certified
- LIN 2.1 and 1.3 Controller or 8-Bit UART

- One 12-bit High Speed PSC (Power Stage Controller)
  - Non-Overlapping Inverted PWM Output Pins With Flexible Dead-Time
  - Variable PWM duty Cycle and Frequency
  - Synchronous Update of all PWM Registers
  - Auto Stop Function for Emergency Event
- Peripheral Features
  - One 8-bit General purpose Timer/Counter with Separate Prescaler, Compare Mode and Capture Mode
  - One 16-bit General purpose Timer/Counter with Separate Prescaler, Compare Mode and Capture Mode
  - One Master/Slave SPI Serial Interface
  - 10-bit ADCUp To 11 Single Ended Channels and 3 Fully Differential ADC Channel Pairs Programmable Gain (5×, 10×, 20×, 40×) on Differential Channels Internal Reference Voltage Direct Power Supply Voltage Measurement
  - 10-bit DAC for Variable Voltage Reference (Comparators, ADC)
  - Four Analog Comparators with Variable Threshold Detection
  - 100µA ±2% Current Source (LIN Node Identification)
  - Interrupt and Wake-up on Pin Change
  - Programmable Watchdog Timer with Separate On-Chip Oscillator
  - On-chip Temperature Sensor
- Special Microcontroller Features
  - Low Power Idle, Noise Reduction, and Power Down Modes
  - Power On Reset and Programmable Brown Out Detection
  - In-System Programmable via SPI Port
  - High Precision Crystal Oscillator for CAN Operations (16MHz)
  - Internal Calibrated RC Oscillator (8MHz)
  - On-chip PLL for fast PWM (32MHz, 64MHz) and CPU (16MHz)
- Operating Voltage: 2.7V - 5.5V
- Extended Operating Temperature:
  - -40°C to +85°C
- Core Speed Grade:
  - 0 - 8MHz @ 2.7 - 4.5V
  - 0 - 16MHz @ 4.5 - 5.5V

AVR Trainer Board

A AVR Trainer Board (AVR ATmega16 & ATmega32 Trainer Board) is a complete starter kit for the AVR Flash Microcontroller (Indian Hobby Center, n. d.). It is designed to give microcontroller beginners a quick start to develop codes/projects on the AVR Flash Microcontrollers, combined with advanced features for using the starter kit for prototyping and testing of new designs.

- Specifications
  - Input voltage: 7V-24V
  - Maximum input current: 1A

- Features
  - Low cost with high quality.
  - Easy to get used to board with the best silk screen layer.
  - Standard DC jack for power input.
  - In-Built regulated 5V power supply.
  - Power indicator LED.
  - Reset switch.
  - Power ON/OFF switch.
  - On-board 1X8 LED array.
  - On-board 5V buzzer.
  - On-board 12 MHz crystal oscillator.
  - On-board 1X16 header for mounting alphanumeric LCD.
  - 2X5 ISP header for programming the AVR flash microcontrollers.
  - Individual 2X5 headers for each I/O port.
  - 2X5 & 1X3 headers for alphanumeric LCD connection.
  - 1X3 header for buzzer connection.
  - On-board Preset to adjust contrast of alphanumeric LCD.
  - 2X5 header for LED array connection.
  - 12V, 5V and GND headers for external power usage.
  - Easy to interface with other ABLab Solutions products.
- **Microcontrollers Supported:** The AVR Trainer Board-100 currently has support for the following AVR flash microcontrollers in all speed grades:
  - ATmega16
  - ATmega32.

LED

LEDs are used in this project for the detection of the vacant place. When the LEDs are on then the place is occupied by the vehicle and when the LEDs are off the place is vacant and the vehicle is preceded for the parking place. How the LED looks like shown in Figure 13. LEDs are joined in the entry point of the parking place. When the car entry first looks at the LEDs board and then decides where to park their vehicle.

Figure 13. LED

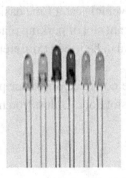

Motor

Motor is used for the power supply to the entire system. The motor should be of DC type and maximum 12volt power supply is applied to the system.

WORKING PRINCIPLE OF SMART PARKING SYSTEM

First this parking system is usually used for the mall/market complex. In this project first take a card board. In the middle of the card board, draw the road for the transportation of the vehicle and build 6 small slots for the parking of the vehicle at the two side of the road. At the entry point of the parking place, deploy 6 LEDs lights for the 6 slots for each slot one LED is deployed. When the LEDs are on then the place is occupied by the vehicle and when the LEDs are off the place is vacant and the vehicle is preceded for the parking place. LEDs are joined in the entry point of the parking place. When the car entry first looks at the LEDs board and then decides where to park their vehicle. At the front of each slot an IR sensor is deployed which is controlled by the microcontroller ATmega16. ATmega16 is an 8-bit high performance microcontroller of Atmel's Mega AVR family with low power consumption Atmega16 is based on enhanced.

When the vehicle enters to the parking place the driver first looks at the LEDs that which place is vacant and then goes forward for parking. The sensor is deployed in front of each garage. When the vehicle enters into the parking place after looking at the LED board then the sensor detects the object. Then the vehicle goes to the free slot and if the slot is free then the shutter is open by the help of a motor and if the slot is not vacant then the shutter remains closed and the vehicle moves to the next slot for parking. The vehicle is parked. At the parking place, there is an ultrasonic sensor is deployed this sensor indicates that how much distance is remains between the wall of the parking slot and the vehicle. When the vehicle is nearer to the wall then an alarm sound is produced. This sound indicates that the vehicle is going to touch the wall and it doesn't go further and remains at that place. When the vehicle is parked then the off LED is become on and it indicates that the place is occupied. Then when the driver needs to take the vehicle from the parking place then he goes to the slot and the LED light is blinking. When the car has left the blinking LED is off and the slot is vacant. Similarly, it applies to all the 6 slots. In this way, this is working.

FUTURE PROSPECTS

- Using PLC microcontroller, 60-70 vehicles at a time easily parked in a parking area.
- Without LED display board, the vacant slot of parking place easily found using mobile application.
- SPS and punch card technique can also be used at different multinational companies and crowded areas as well.
- In this process, parking fees can be collected and after paying fee they give you a card which is used for the opening of the parking slot door. Unless you make your payment, you can't go outside.

CONCLUSION

Finding a parking space in most metropolitan areas, especially during the rush hours, is difficult for drivers. The difficulty arises from not knowing where the available spaces may be at that time or not. So, in this system, design a new Smart Parking System (SPS) to optimize parking management and implement parking policy to balance the benefit of service providers and requirements from the users. Moreover, here present the detailed design, implementation and evaluation of the model for smart parking.

REFERENCES

Atif, Y., Ding, J., & Jeusfeld, M. A. (2016). Internet of Things Approach to Cloud-Based Smart Car Parking. *Proceedings of the 7th International Conference on Emerging Ubiquitous Systems and Pervasive Networks (EUSPN '16)*.

Indian Hobby Center. (n. d.). Avr-trainerboard. Retrieved from http://www.indianhobbycenter.com/product/avr-trainer-board/

Basavaraju, S.R. (2015, December). Automatic Smart Parking System using Internet of Things (IOT). *International Journal of Scientific and Research Publications*, 5(12).

Carnegie Mellon's Robotics Academy. (n. d.). What is an IR sensor? Retrieved from education.rec.ri.cmu.edu/content/electronics/boe/ir_sensor/1.html

Conner, M. (2010, May 27). Sensors empower the "Internet of Things." *EDN Network*. Retrieved from http://www.edn.com/article/509123-sensors_empower_the_Internet_of_Things_.php

Engineers Garage. (n. d.). Atmega16-microcontroller. Retrieved from http://www.engineersgarage.com/electronic-components/atmega16-microcontroller

Gupte, S., & Younis, M. (2015). Participatory-sensing-enabled Efficient Parking Management in Modern Cities. Proceedings of the 40th Annual IEEE Conference on Local Computer Networks (LCN '15), Clearwater Beach, Florida, USA.

Happiest minds. (n. d.). Smart Parking (white paper). Online retrieved from http://www.happiestminds.com/whitepapers/smart-parking.pdf

International Telecommunications Union. (2005). ITU Internet Reports 2005: The Internet of Things Executive Summary.

Iotworm.com. (n. d.). Biggest challenges for the internet of things. Retrieved from http://iotworm.com/biggest-challenges-for-the-internet-of-things/

National Intelligence Council. (2008, April). Disruptive Civil Technologies — Six Technologies with Potential Impacts on US Interests Out to 2025 (Conference Report CR 2008–07). Retrieved from www.dni.gov/nic/NIC_home.html

Saphanatutorial.com. (n. d.). Introduction to internet of things. Retrieved from http://saphanatutorial.com/introduction-to-internet-of-things-part-1/

Sweeney, P. J., & Sweeney, P. J. Ii. (2005). *RFID for dummies*. Wiley Publishing, Inc.

Techquark.com. (n. d.). What is the Internet of things of things. Retrieved from http://www.techquark.com/2014/10/what-is-internet-of-things-iot.html

Uckelmann, D., Harrison, M., & Michahelles, F. (2011). *Architecting the Internet of Things*. Springer. doi:10.1007/978-3-642-19157-2

Vermesan, O., & Friess, P. (2014). Internet of Things– From Research and Innovation to Market Deployment. River Publishers.

Chapter 13
Data Mining for the Internet of Things

Akhil Rajendra Khare
MVSR Engineering College, India

Pallavi Shrivasta
Matrusri Engineering College, India

ABSTRACT

The Internet of Things concept arises from the need to manage, automate, and explore all devices, instruments and sensors in the world. In order to make wise decisions both for people and for the things in IoT, data mining technologies are integrated with IoT technologies for decision making support and system optimization. Data mining involves discovering novel, interesting, and potentially useful patterns from data and applying algorithms to the extraction of hidden information. Data mining is classified into three different views: knowledge view, technique view, and application view. The challenges in the data mining algorithms for IoT are discussed and a suggested big data mining system is proposed.

INTRODUCTION

Outline

The Internet of Things (IoT) and its relevant technologies can seamlessly integrate classical networks with networked instruments and devices. IoT has been playing an essential role ever since it appeared, which covers from traditional equipment to general household objects and has been attracting the attention of researchers from academia, industry, and government in recent years. There is a great vision that all things can be easily controlled and monitored, can be identified automatically by other things, can communicate with each other through internet, and can even make decisions by themselves. In order to make IoT smarter, lots of analysis technologies are introduced into IoT; one of the most valuable technologies is data mining.

DOI: 10.4018/978-1-5225-2947-7.ch013

Copyright © 2018, IGI Global. Copying or distributing in print or electronic forms without written permission of IGI Global is prohibited.

Data mining involves discovering novel, interesting, and potentially useful patterns from large data sets and applying algorithms to the extraction of hidden information. Many other terms are used for data mining, for example, knowledge discovery (mining) in databases (KDD), knowledge extraction, data/pattern analysis, data archaeology, data dredging, and information harvesting. The objective of any data mining process is to build an efficient predictive or descriptive model of a large amount of data that not only best fits or explains it, but is also able to generalize to new data (Figure 1). Based on a broad view of data mining functionality, data mining is the process of discovering interesting knowledge from large amounts of data stored in either databases, data warehouses, or other information repositories (Tsai, Lai & Vasilakos, 2014).

On the basis of the definition of data mining and the definition of data mining functions, a typical data mining process includes the following steps (Jiawei & Kamber, 2011)

Scope

We can view data mining in a multidimensional view.

1. In knowledge view or data mining functions view, it includes characterization, discrimination, classification, clustering, association analysis, time series analysis, and outlier analysis.
2. In utilized techniques view, it includes machine learning, statistics, pattern recognition, big data, support vector machine, rough set, neural networks and evolutionary algorithms.
3. In application view, it includes industry, telecommunication, banking, fraud analysis, bio data mining, stock market analysis, text mining, web mining, social network and e-commerce.

A variety of researches focusing on knowledge view, technique view and application view can be found in the literature. However, no previous effort has been made to review the different views of data mining in a systematic way, especially in nowadays big data; mobile internet and Internet of Things grow rapidly and some data mining researchers shift their attention from data mining to big data. There are lots of data that can be mined, for example, database data (relational database, No SQL database), data warehouse, data stream, spatiotemporal, time series, sequence, text and web, multimedia, graphs, the World Wide Web, Internet of Things data, and legacy system log. Motivated by this, we attempt to make a comprehensive survey of the important recent developments of data mining research. This survey focuses on knowledge view, utilized techniques view, and application view of data mining.

Figure 1. The data mining overview

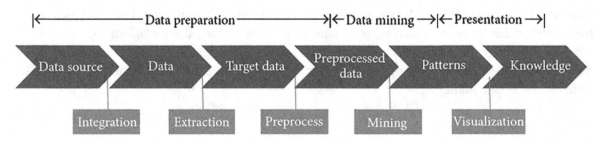

DATA MINING FUNCTIONALITIES

Data mining functionalities include classification, clustering, association analysis, time series analysis, and outlier analysis (Jing, Vasilakos, Wan et al., 2014).

1. Classification is the process of finding a set of models or functions that describe and distinguish data classes or concepts, for the purpose of predicting the class of objects whose class label is unknown.
2. Clustering analyzes data objects without consulting a known class model.
3. Association analysis is the discovery of association rules displaying attribute-value conditions that frequently occur together in a given set of data.
4. (iv)Time series analysis comprises methods and techniques for analyzing time series data in order to extract meaningful statistics and other characteristics of the data.
5. Outlier analysis describes and models regularities or trends for objects whose behaviour changes over time.

Classification

Classification is important for management of decision making (Figure 2). Given an object, assigning it to one of predefined target categories or classes is called classification. The goal of classification is to accurately predict the target class for each case in the data (Mukhopadhyay, Maulik, Bandyopadhyay et

Figure 2. The research structure of classification

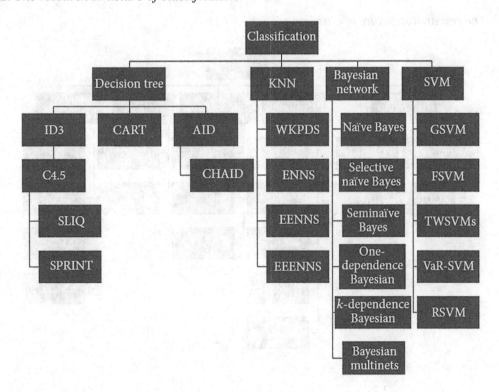

al., 2014). For example, a classification model could be used to identify loan applicants as low, medium, or high credit risks.

Clustering

Clustering algorithms divide data into meaningful groups so that patterns in the same group are similar in some sense and patterns in different group are dissimilar in the same sense (Figure 3). Searching for clusters involves unsupervised learning. In information retrieval, for example, the search engine clusters billions of web pages into different groups, such as news, reviews, videos, and audios. One straightforward example of clustering problem is to divide points into different groups.

Association Analysis

Association rule mining focuses on the market basket analysis or transaction data analysis, and it targets discovery of rules showing attribute value associations that occur frequently and also help in the generation of more general and qualitative knowledge which in turn helps in decision making (Figure 4).

Time Series Analysis

A time series is a collection of temporal data objects; the characteristics of time series data include large data size, high dimensionality, and updating continuously. Commonly, time series task relies on 3 parts of components, including representation, similarity measures, and indexing (Figure 5).

Figure 3. The research structure of clustering

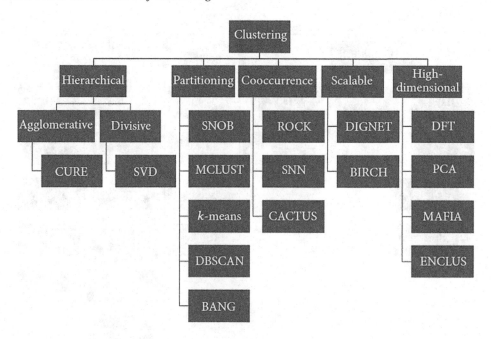

Figure 4. The research structure of association analysis

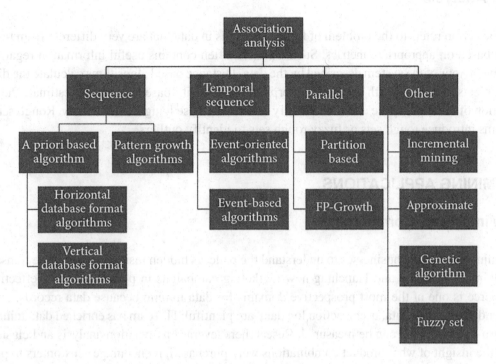

Figure 5. The research structure of time series analysis

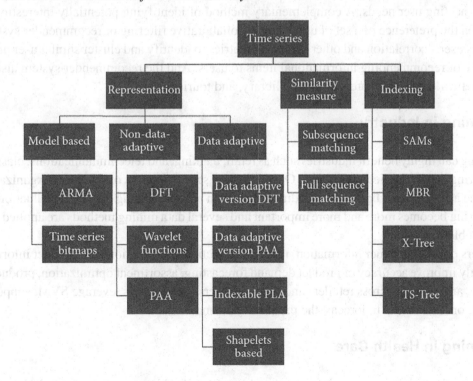

Outlier Analysis

Outlier detection refers to the problem of finding patterns in data that are very different from the rest of the data based on appropriate metrics. Such a pattern often contains useful information regarding abnormal behaviour of the system described by the data. Distance based algorithms calculate the distances among objects in the data with geometric interpretation. Density-based algorithms estimate the density distribution of the input space and then identify outliers as those lying in low density. Rough sets based algorithms introduce rough sets or fuzzy rough sets to identify outliers.

DATA MINING APPLICATIONS

Data Mining in E-Commerce

Data mining enables the businesses to understand the patterns hidden inside past purchase transactions, thus helping in planning and launching new marketing campaigns in prompt and cost-effective way. E-commerce is one of the most prospective domains for data mining because data records, including customer data, product data, users' action log data, are plentiful; IT Team has enriched data mining skill and return on investment can be measured. Researchers leverage association analysis and clustering to provide the insight of what product combinations were purchased; it encourages customers to purchase related products that they may have been missed or overlooked. Users' behaviours are monitored and analyzed to find similarities and patterns in Web surfing behaviour so that the Web can be more successful in meeting user needs. A complementary method of identifying potentially interesting content uses data on the preference of a set of users, called collaborative filtering or recommender systems, and it leverages user's correlation and other similarity metrics to identify and cluster similar user profiles for the purpose of recommending informational items to users. And the recommender system also extends to social network, education area, academic library, and tourism.

Data Mining in Industry

Data mining can highly benefit industries such as retail, banking, and telecommunications; classification and clustering can be applied to this area. One of the key success factors of insurance organizations and banks is the assessment of borrowers' creditworthiness in advance during the credit evaluation process. Credit scoring becomes more and more important and several data mining methods are applied for credit scoring problem.

Retailers collect customer information, related transactions information, and product information to significantly improve accuracy of product demand forecasting, assortment optimization, product recommendation, and ranking across retailers and manufacturers. Researchers leverage SVM, support vector regression, or Bass model to forecast the products' demand.

Data Mining in Health Care

In health care, data mining is becoming increasingly popular, if not increasingly essential. Heterogeneous medical data have been generated in various health care organizations, including payers, medicine providers, pharmaceuticals information, prescription information, doctor's notes, or clinical records produced day by day. These quantitative data can be used to do clinical text mining, predictive modelling, survival analysis, patient similarity analysis, and clustering, to improve care treatment and reduce waste. In health care area, association analysis, clustering, and outlier analysis can be applied.

Treatment record data can be mined to explore ways to cut costs and deliver better medicine. Data mining also can be used to identify and understand high-cost patients and applied to mass of data generated by millions of prescriptions, operations, and treatment courses to identify unusual patterns and uncover fraud.

Data Mining in City Governance

In public service area, data mining can be used to discover public needs and improve service performance, decision making with automated systems to decrease risks, classification, clustering, and time series analysis which can be developed to solve this area problem. E-government improves quality of government service, cost savings, wider political participation, and more effective policies and programs, and it has also been proposed as a solution for increasing citizen communication with government agencies and, ultimately, political trust. City incident information management system can integrate data mining methods to provide a comprehensive assessment of the impact of natural disasters on the agricultural production and rank disaster affected areas objectively and assist governments in disaster preparation and resource allocation. By using data analytics, researchers can predict which residents are likely to move away from the city, and it helps to infer which factors of city life and city services lead to a resident's decision to leave the city.

ROLE OF DATA MINING IN IoT AND BIG DATA ERA

With the rapid development of IoT, big data, and cloud computing, the most fundamental challenge is to explore the large volumes of data and extract useful information or knowledge for future actions (M. Chen, S. Mao, and Y. Liu 2014). The key characteristics of the data in IoT era can be considered as big data; they are as follows.

1. Large volumes of data to read and write: the amount of data can be TB (terabytes), even PB (peta bytes) and ZB (zetta byte), so we need to explore fast and effective mechanisms.
2. Heterogeneous data sources and data types to integrate: in big data era, the data sources are diverse; for example, we need to integrate sensors data, cameras data, social media data, and so on and all these data are different in format, byte, binary, string, number, and so forth. We need to communicate with different types of devices and different systems and also need to extract data from web pages.
3. Complex knowledge to extract: the knowledge is deeply hidden in large volumes of data and the knowledge is not straightforward, so we need to analyze the properties of data and find the association of different data.

Challenges

There are lots of challenges when IoT and big data come; the quantity of data is big but the quality is low and the data are various from different data sources inherently possessing a great many different types and representation forms, and the data is heterogeneous, as-structured, semi-structured, and even entirely unstructured. We analyze the challenges in data extracting, data mining algorithms, and data mining system area. Challenges are summarized below.

1. The first challenge is to access, extracting large scale data from different data storage locations. We need to deal with the variety, heterogeneity, and noise of the data, and it is a big challenge to find the fault and even harder to correct the data. In data mining algorithms area, how to modify traditional algorithms to big data environment is a big challenge.
2. Second challenge is how to mine uncertain and incomplete data for big data applications. In data mining system, an effective and security solution to share data between different applications and systems is one of the most important challenges, since sensitive information, such as banking transactions and medical records, should be a matter of concern.

Open Research Issues

In big data era, there are some open research issues including data checking, parallel programming model, and big data mining framework (Rong, Chen, Deng et al., 2011).

1. There are lots of researches on finding errors hidden in data. Also, the data cleaning, filtering, and reduction mechanisms are introduced.
2. Parallel programming model is introduced to data mining and some algorithms are adopted to be applied in it. Researchers have expanded existing data mining methods in many ways, including the efficiency improvement of single-source knowledge discovery methods, designing a data mining mechanism from a multisource perspective, and the study of dynamic data mining methods and the analysis of stream data. For example, parallel association rule mining and parallel k-means algorithm based on Hadoop platform are good practice. But there are still some algorithms which are not adapted to parallel platform, this constraint on applying data mining technology to big data platform. This would be a challenge for data mining related researchers and also a great direction.
3. The most important work for big data mining system is to develop an efficient framework to support big data mining. In the big data mining framework, we need to consider the security of data, the privacy, the data sharing mechanism, the growth of data size, and so forth. A well-designed data mining framework for big data is a very important direction and a big challenge.

Suggested System Architecture for IoT

According to the survey of big data mining system and IoT system, we suggest the system architecture for IoT and big data mining system (Chen, Rong, Deng et al., 2011). In this system, it includes 5 layers (see Figure 6).

Figure 6. The suggested big data mining system

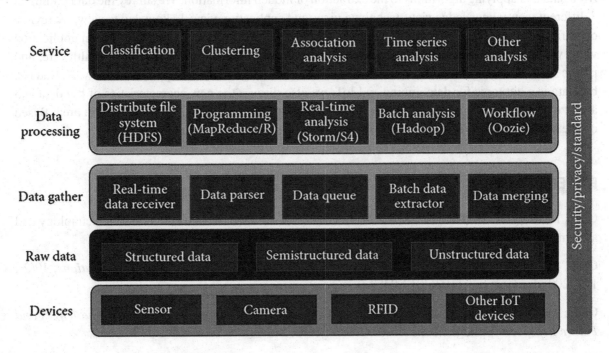

1. **Devices:** Lots of IoT devices, such as sensors, RFID, cameras, and other devices, can be integrated into this system to apperceive the world and generate data continuously.
2. **Raw Data:** In the big data mining system, structured data, semi-structured data, and unstructured data can be integrated.
3. **Data Gather:** Real-time data and batch data can be supported and all data can be parsed, analyzed, and merged.
4. **Data Processing:** Lots of open source solutions are integrated, including Hadoop, HDFS, Storm, and Oozie.
5. **Service:** data mining functions will be provided as service.
6. **Security/Privacy/Standard:** Security, privacy, and standard are very important to big data mining system. Security and privacy protect the data from unauthorized access and privacy disclosure. Big data mining system standard makes data integration, sharing, and mining more open to the third part of developer.

CONCLUSION

The Internet of Things concept arises from the need to manage, automate, and explore all devices, instruments, and sensors in the world. In order to make wise decisions both for people and for the things in IoT, data mining technologies are integrated with IoT technologies for decision making support and system optimization. Data mining involves discovering novel, interesting, and potentially useful patterns from data and applying algorithms to the extraction of hidden information. We survey the data mining in 3 different views: knowledge view, technique view, and application view. In knowledge view, we review classification, clustering, association analysis, time series analysis, and outlier analysis. In application view, we review the typical data mining application, including e-commerce, industry, health care, and public service. The technique view is discussed with knowledge view and application view. Nowadays, big data is a hot topic for data mining and IoT; we also discuss the new characteristics of big data and analyze the challenges in data extracting, data mining algorithms, and data mining system area. Based on the survey of the current research, a suggested big data mining system is proposed.

REFERENCES

Chen, F., Rong, X.-H., Deng, P., & Ma, S.-L. (2011). A survey of device collaboration technology and system software. *Tien Tzu Hsueh Pao*, *39*(2), 440–447.

Chen, M., Mao, S., & Liu, Y. (2014). Big data: A survey. *Mobile Networks and Applications*, *19*(2), 171–209. doi:10.1007/s11036-013-0489-0

Chen, M., Mao, S., Zhang, Y., & Leung, V. (2014). *Big Data: Related Technologies, Challenges and Future Prospects*. Springer. doi:10.1007/978-3-319-06245-7

Jiawei, H., & Kamber, M. (2011). *Data Mining: Concepts and Techniques*. Morgan Kaufmann.

Jing, Q., Vasilakos, A. V., Wan, J., Lu, J., & Qiu, D. (2014). Security of the internet of things: Perspectives and challenges. *Wireless Networks*, *20*(8), 2481–2501. doi:10.1007/s11276-014-0761-7

Mukhopadhyay, A., Maulik, U., Bandyopadhyay, S., & Coello, C. A. C. (2014). A survey of multiobjective evolutionary algorithms for data mining: Part I. *IEEE Transactions on Evolutionary Computation*, *18*(1), 4–19. doi:10.1109/TEVC.2013.2290086

Rong, X. H., Chen, F., Deng, P., & Ma, S. L. (2011). A large-scale device collaboration mechanism. *Journal of Computer Research and Development*, *48*(9), 1589–1596.

Tsai, C.-W., Lai, C.-F., & Vasilakos, A. V. (2014). Future internet of things: Open issues and challenges. *Wireless Networks*, *20*(8), 2201–2217. doi:10.1007/s11276-014-0731-0

KEY TERMS AND DEFINITIONS

Collaboration Technologies: *Collaboration Technologies* a software development, technology and consultancy centre.

Data Mining: The practice of examining large pre-existing databases in order to generate new information.

Evolutionary Algorithm: An evolutionary algorithm (EA) is a subset of evolutionary computation, a generic population-based metaheuristic optimization algorithm. An EA uses mechanisms inspired by biological evolution, such as reproduction, mutation, recombination, and selection.

IoTSF: IoTSF aims to be the home for providers, adopters and beneficiaries of IoT products and services." Other companies are working on setting up platforms that will enable large networks of IoT devices to identify and authenticate each other in order to provide higher security and prevent data breaches.

Chapter 14
A Study on Performance of E–Commerce Web Applications

Sreedhar G
Rashtriya Sanskrit Vidyapeetha (Deemed University), India

ABSTRACT

The growth of World Wide Web and technologies has made business functions to be executed fast and easier. E-commerce has provided a cost efficient and effective way of doing business. In this paper the importance of e-commerce web applications and how Internet of Things is related to e-commerce is well discussed. In the end-user perspective, the performance of e-commerce application is mainly connected to the web application design and services provided in the e-commerce website. A grading system is used to evaluate the performance of each e-commerce website.

INTRODUCTION

In the present-day scenario, the World Wide Web (WWW) is an important and popular information search tool. It provides convenient access to almost all kinds of information from education to entertainment. The World Wide Web is the key source of information and it is growing rapidly. The growth of World Wide Web and technologies has made business functions to be executed fast and easier. E-commerce has provided a cost efficient and effective way of doing business. As a large amount of transactions are performed through ecommerce sites and the huge amount of data is stored, valuable knowledge can be obtained by applying the Web Mining techniques. Using Web Mining, companies can understand customer behaviour, improve design of e-commerce site, improve customer services and relationship, and measure the success of marketing efforts and to provide personalized services. The extension in web mining research will lead to success of e-commerce sites and also it will improve the services for customers. In e-commerce websites, you can sell, advertise, and introduce different kinds of services and products in the web.

DOI: 10.4018/978-1-5225-2947-7.ch014

Copyright © 2018, IGI Global. Copying or distributing in print or electronic forms without written permission of IGI Global is prohibited.

BACKGROUND

E-Commerce Web Applications

E-commerce websites have the advantage of reaching a large number of customers regardless of distance and time limitations. The advantage of e-commerce over traditional businesses is the faster speed and the lower expenses for both e-commerce website owners and customers in completing customer transactions and orders. Because of the above advantages of e-commerce over traditional businesses, a lot of industries in different fields such as retailing, banking, medical services, transportation, communication, and education are establishing their business in the web. But creating a successful online business can be a very difficult and costly task if not taking into account e-commerce website design principles, web engineering techniques, and what e-commerce is supposed to do for the online business. Unfortunately, to most companies, web is nothing more than a place where transactions take place. All the e-commerce sites have high traffic. People surf the sites very often but the income is not always very high. So, the web data mining appeared and also nowadays much attention is paid to it. It is very important to apply web data mining to e-commerce in order to gather knowledge about users and rank data accordingly. It is advance successful technology through which information is filtered easier. So, web data mining became a publicly accessible source that gives promising results. With the use of e-commerce through internet, companies find a new and better way to do business. After developing the web site thought companies get benefits, they have to implement Web mining systems to understand their customers' profiles and to identify their own strength and weakness of their E-marketing efforts on the web through continuous improvements. Internet is a gold mine, but only for those companies who realize the importance of Web mining and adopt a Web mining strategy now. Web mining technology has many important roles that should be mentioned. It can automatically find, extract information from the variety web resources. It also develops, improves and enhances the quality and the efficiency of search engines, determines web pages or files, makes classifications (Purandare, 2008). It can also generate large-scale real-time data. Web data mining discovers useful information from the Web hyperlink and page content. It has already changed the face of many business functions in a modern competitive enterprise. It is obviously easier to make right business decisions or understand the information that came from customers with the help of web data mining. It helps e-commerce to understand how to improve its services for special groups of customers and clients, and what tasks to realize. The e-commerce site can increase the exposure of its product pages and so average order size can be increased. Companies can save percentage of its budget per month owing to knowledge that was received from web mining analysis. Web data mining gathers implicit knowledge about clients and instructs e-commerce in every aspect. Then, it extracts valuable and comprehensible information from huge web resources to instruct e-commerce. It also gathers the information in an automated way and builds models used to predict customer purchasing decisions. Web mining is very precious to the company in the fields of understanding customer behaviour, improving customer services and relationship, launching target marketing campaigns, measuring the success of marketing efforts, and so on. Attractiveness of the site depends on its reasonable design of content and organizational structure. Web Mining can provide details of user behaviour, providing web site designers basis of decision making to improve the design of the site (TIAN Meirong, CHEN Xuedong, 2010). E-Commerce generally refers to a new business model, where consumer makes online shopping, online transactions between merchants and online electronic payments and a variety of business activities, trading activities, financial activities and related integrated services activities, buyers and sellers are not met to conduct various business activities based on browser/server application mode.

Internet of Things (IoT)

Internet of Things (IoT) is a network which is composed with Radio Frequency Identification (RFID), infrared sensors, global positioning systems, laser scanners, gas sensors and other information sensing device, according to the agreed protocol, any goods are connected with the Internet for information exchange, communication, IoT is used to make intelligent identification, positioning, tracking, monitoring and management. The schematic diagram IoT is shown in Figure 1.

With the rapid development of e-commerce, its technology requirements will also increase on all aspects of future e-commerce. Firstly, the e-commerce applications are combined with IoT development and IoT technologies are applied in three important aspects of e-commerce, such as inventory, logistics and payment. An e-commerce system includes inventory, logistics, electronic payment and other important aspects, if IoT technology is used in various aspects of e-commerce, e-commerce will greatly improve the efficiency of the system. The diagram of E-Commerce with combined IoT is shown in Figure 2.

ANALYZING PERFORMANCE OF E-COMMERCE WEB APPLICATIONS

The procedure for analysing performance of e-commerce website initially starts with a web program. The program consists of two parts: extracting components of website with download time and down-

Figure 1. Schematic diagram of internet of things

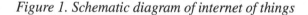
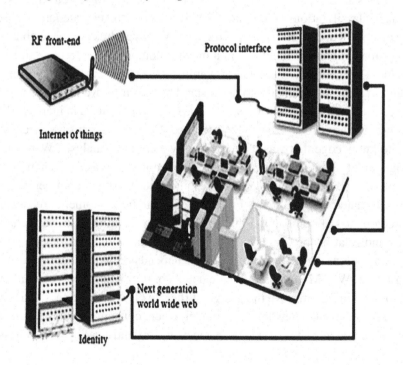

Figure 2. E-commerce web application with Internet of Things
Source: (GTmetrix, n. d.).

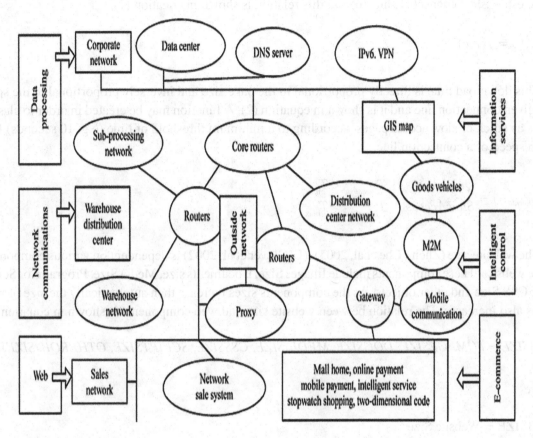

load time performance grades. In the web program, all the components of website with corresponding downloading time are extracted using a web tool namely Web Page Analyser (Figure 1). The Download time performance grade is obtained using the web tool GTMetrix (Figure 2). The GTMetrix web tool analyses the website download time and evaluates the download time performance in A, B, C, D, E and F grades as described in Table 1.

The size of a web page is measured considering all its images, sounds, videos and textual components. For each page, the size in bytes can be obtained. The size of pages is an important issue in order to ap-

Table 1. Description of web application performance grades

Web Application Performance Grade	Description
A	Very Good
B	Good
C	Better than Average
D	Average
E	Poor
F	Very Poor

preciate the site efficiency. The download time (T) is related with the size of a page (τ) and the speed in the established connection line (c) and this relation is shown in equation (1).

$$T_{Download} = f(\tau, c) \tag{1}$$

This download time is directly proportional to the page size and inversely proportional to the speed of a given connection line and it is shown in equation (2). A function may be created in order to classify pages as quick or slow access pages, according to a minimum threshold of time (e.g. 10 seconds) for a given speed of a connection line.

$$g\left(T_{Download}\right) = \begin{matrix} QuickAccess & T_{Download} < T_{\max} \\ SlowAccess & T_{Download} \geq T_{\max} \end{matrix} \tag{2}$$

The website size (Zheng Che et al, 2003), (E. Glover et al, 2002) is dependent on various components of the website. These components include Images Size, Documents size, Media Size, Programs or Scripts Size, CSS Size and other objects. As the components sizes increase then automatically the size of website is also increases. The relation between website size and web components is shown in equation (3).

WEBSIZE = f (IMAGESIZE, DOCSIZE, MEDIASIZE, CSSSIZE, SCRIPTSIZE, OTHEROBJSIZE) ...

$$\tag{3}$$

where

WEBSIZE = Website Size
IMAGESIZE = Images Size
DOCSIZE = Documents Size
MEDIASIZE = Multimedia Size
SCRIPTSIZE = Scripts or Programs Size
CSSSIZE = Cascading Style Sheet Size
OTHEROBJSIZE = Other Objects Size like Active X Control Objects, Applets etc.

A regression analysis is carried out to analyse the relationships among these variables. The analysis is carried out through the estimation of a relationship using equation. The results serve the following two purposes.

- Answer the question of how much web size changes with changes in each of the web component's size
- Forecast or predict the value of web size based on the values of the web component's size

In analyzing the download time performance of the websites, the websites of 10 e-commerce websites are considered in evaluation process. The download time of each e-commerce website is analyzed (Figure 3) using web program and the corresponding download time performance grade is derived using GTMetrix web tool. The performance of e-commerce websites is shown in Figure 4 and Table 2.

Figure 3. Website analysis

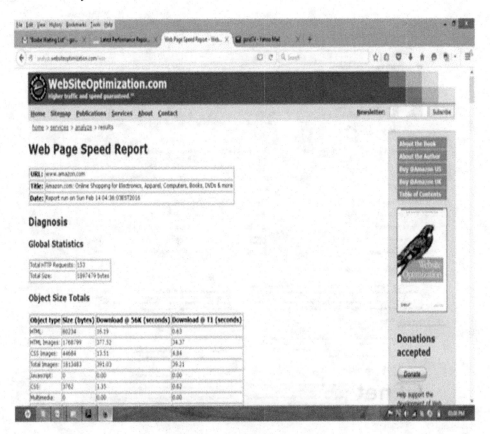

Table 2. Performance of e-commerce web applications

S.No.	E-Commerce Website	Download Time (in secs)	Web Page Size (in M.B)	Performance Grade
1	http://goidirectory.nic.in/ministries_departments_view.php	18.3	1.76	F
2	http://goidirectory.nic.in/state_departments.php?ou=AP	4.3	0.5	F
3	http://www.amazon.com	5.8	4.89	A
4	http://www.flipkart.com	4.7	1	A
5	http://fitness.reebok.com/international	10.4	2.78	A
6	http://www.spyder.com	5	2.31	B
7	http://www.apple.com	1.8	1.25	B
8	http://ebay.com	4.2	2.49	B
9	http://myspace.com	7.3	5.98	C
10	http://www.hp.com	5.2	4.01	C

Figure 4. Performance of e-commerce website

CONCLUSION

The main objective of the chapter is how to understand the performance of the system. In this paper the importance of e-commerce web applications and how Internet of Things is related to e-commerce is well discussed. In the end-user perspective, the performance of e-commerce applications is mainly connected to the web application design and services provided in the e-commerce website. In this paper a focused approach has been made to identify all possible parameters in the web design with specific reference to some of the major e-commerce websites. The performance of each e-commerce web application is measured in terms of web page speed and loading time of the website. Hence performance evaluation of web applications is very much necessary to fulfill the need of online user and web developer can enhance the features based on the performance report of e-commerce website.

REFERENCES

Chen, Z., Liu, S., Wenyin, L., Pu, G., & Ma, W.-Y. (2003). Building a Web Thesaurus form Web Link Structure. *Proceedings of SIGIR* (pp. 48-55).

Glover, E. J., Tsioutsiouliklis, K., Lawrence, S., Pennock, D. M., & Flake, G. W. (2002). Using Web Structure for Classifying and Describing Web Pages. *Proceedings of WWW '02*.

GTmetrix. (n. d.) Analyze your site's speed and make it faster. Retrieved from www.GTMetrix.com

Meirong, T. I. A. N., & Xuedong, C. H. E. N. (2010). Application of Agent-based Web Mining in E-business. *Proceedings of the Second International Conference on Intelligent Human-Machine Systems and Cybernetics*.

Page, L., Brin, S., Motwani, R., & Winograd, T. (1998). *The PageRank Citation Ranking: Bring Order to the Web. Technical Report*. Stanford University.

Websiteoptimization.com. (2017, March 30). Webpage Analyzer (Web Page Speed Analysis). Retrieved from www.websiteoptimization.com

Purandare, P. (2008). Web Mining: A Key to Improve Business On Web. *Proceedings of the IADIS European Conference Data Mining*.

KEY TERMS AND DEFINITIONS

Ecommerce Website: E-commerce websites have the advantage of reaching a large number of customers regardless of distance and time limitations.

GTMetrix: The download time of each e-commerce website is analyzed using web program and the corresponding download time performance grade is derived using GTMetrix web tool.

Internet of Things: Internet of Things (IoT) is a network which is composed with Radio Frequency Identification (RFID), infrared sensors, global positioning systems, laser scanners, gas sensors and other information sensing device, according to the agreed protocol, any goods are connected with the Internet for information exchange, communication, IoT is used to make intelligent identification, positioning, tracking, monitoring and management.

Web Mining: Web mining is very precious to the company in the fields of understanding customer behaviour, improving customer services and relationship, launching target marketing campaigns, measuring the success of marketing efforts, and so on.

Website Download Time: The website download time is related with the size of a page and the speed in the established connection line.

Website Size: The size of a web site is measured considering all its images, sounds, videos and textual components.

Chapter 15
Performance Improvement IoT Applications Through Multimedia Analytics Using Big Data Stream Computing Platforms

Rizwan Patan
VIT University, India

Rajasekhara Babu M
VIT University, India

Suresh Kallam
VIT University, India

ABSTRACT

A Big Data Stream Computing (BDSC) Platform handles real-time data from various applications such as risk management, marketing management and business intelligence. Now a days Internet of Things (IoT) deployment is increasing massively in all the areas. These IoTs engender real-time data for analysis. Existing BDSC is inefficient to handle Real-data stream from IoTs because the data stream from IoTs is unstructured and has inconstant velocity. So, it is challenging to handle such real-time data stream. This work proposes a framework that handles real-time data stream through device control techniques to improve the performance. The frame work includes three layers. First layer deals with Big Data platforms that handles real data streams based on area of importance. Second layer is performance layer which deals with performance issues such as low response time, and energy efficiency. The third layer is meant for Applying developed method on existing BDSC platform. The experimental results have been shown a performance improvement 20%-30% for real time data stream from IoT application.

DOI: 10.4018/978-1-5225-2947-7.ch015

Copyright © 2018, IGI Global. Copying or distributing in print or electronic forms without written permission of IGI Global is prohibited.

INTRODUCTION

Internet of Things

Internet of Things (IoT) is a portion of forthcoming Internet and includes many billions of 'things' or Internet Connected Devices (ICDs) where things can communicate, sense, potentially actuate and compute as well as have multi-modal interfaces, intelligence, virtual/physical attributes and identities. ICDs can include RFIDs, sensors, social media, smart consumer appliances, business transactions, lab instruments, etc. The idea of IoT is to allow 'things' to be connected anyplace, anytime, with anyone and anything, ideally using any network, any service, and any path.

IoT with chips/ sensors getting less expensive, and devices getting smarter, the world is moving toward being always on. This implies increasingly information is always being sent and got between devices. Customarily it was just cellular phones, PCs, and servers conversing with each other, Now dealing multiple features the IoT's is shown in figure 1. the IoT's is associated devices discussing bidirectional with each other progressively. IoT's refers to a technology paradigm wherein ubiquitous sensors numbering in the billions will be able to monitor physical infrastructure and environment, human beings and virtual entities in real-time, process both real-time and historical observations, and take actions that improve the efficiency and reliability of systems, or the comfort and lifestyle of society. The technology building blocks for IoT have been ramping up over a decade, with research into pervasive/ubiquitous computing (Zaslavsky, 2013), and sensor networks (Chandrasekaran, Cooper, Deshpande et al., 2003)

Figure 1. Fusion of IoT's

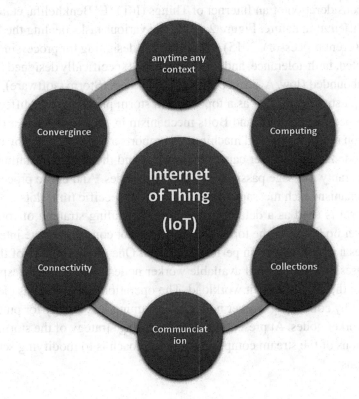

forming precursors. Recent growth in the capabilities of high-speed mobile (e.g., 2G/3G/4G) and ad hoc (e.g., Bluetooth) networks (Cornwall, 2016), smart phones, affordable sensing and crowd-sourced data collection (Data Canvas Dataset, 2016), Cloud data-centers and Big Data analytics platforms have all contributed to the current inflection point for IoT.

This IoT idea has recently give growing to the view of IoT Big Data applications that possibly will produce billions of data streams and Zeta byte of data to deliver the information required to support timely decision making. Some are developing IoT Big Data applications include smart manufacturing, customer sentiment analysis, emergency situations awareness, remote sensing, image processing, credit card fraud detection, and so on. IoT Big Data applications need to manage and process streaming and geographically distributed data sources for multidimensional data. All these data sources are available in the present in different locations, different formats and consistent at various self-assurance levels.

Big Data

Big Data is changing too fast, which is too large, and too discrete is the ability of available software and hardware is beyond the range. Big data (Mohanty, 2015) technology is numerously increasing various fields and dealing various issues. It deals with two different computing areas like (1) stream computing (Sun, Zhang, Yang et al., 2015), and (2) batch computing (Li, Bao & Li, 2015) with three different processing types, (1) real time processing, (Arvind Gopinath, 2014) (2) online and Interactive processing (Interactive or Online Processing 2016), and (3) batch processing (V. Beal, 2015). In Stream, computing focused on dealing with both real time and online or interactive data sets. In Batch computing focusing only the batch related data sets. Using populated platforms to dealing that is Hadoop (J. P. Verma et al. 2015) in there Mapreduce (M. Bhandarkar, 2010) and HDFS (Hadoop Distributed File System, 2016) framework. But in consideration of an Internet of Things (IoT) (E. Benkhelifa, et. al 2014) Application data characteristic different in nature. Figure 2 shows the various tasks dealing the big data technology.

In storm (Storm (event processor), 2015) platform it is a designing for processing a data streams, and it is parallel, distributed, fault-tolerance, and low-latency. It is specifically designed for the real-time data processing for an unbounded flow. A storm programming model (Storm (software), 2016) designing for directed acyclic graph structure called as a topology. In storm platform, two different components are there Spout, Bolt respectively. Spouts and Bolts mechanism in one single cluster of multiple tasks are performing parallel on multiple physical machines. It supports a fault-tolerance by observing all worker nodes any worker node failure the user capable to re-start and the reason for failure it provides, and it is responsible for guaranty message passing for all worker nodes. And entire process maintaining time based operation mechanism each message passing allocating specific time slots.

The storm platform is used as a default and simple scheduling strategy of round robin algorithm for assigning a worker node across the topology. And here not considering the inter-process and inter-node traffic, it makes a major impact on performance, and One more problem of the default scheduler is that it always causes Storm to use all available worker nodes in a cluster, irrespective of workload. It is identified that in the case of a light workload. The operational cost such as electricity cost can be reduced significantly by combining worker nodes it consuming less energy for putting them into sleep for remaining idle worker nodes. At present default scheduling strategy of the storm will not be satisfying in all the conditions of the stream computing. Our approach is to modifying scheduling strategy to fulfil all the conditions.

Figure 2. Fusion of Big Data

Background

One of the most critical challenges in the big data era is, to be able to collect and process massive and heterogeneous data flows. In this context, the IoT's ecosystem generates an enormous amount of data from billions of internet-connected devices. The Cisco Internet Business Solutions Group (IBSG) predicts that, by 2020, the world will count 50 billion connected devices supporting various applications such as healthcare services, air pollution monitoring, transportation, energy, and so on

Real time processing of this massive data flow generated by the IoT's cannot be implemented with a traditional cluster based solution, as it obviously cannot scale to process billions or trillions of tuples

Figure 3. Background flow of the IoT's in BDSC

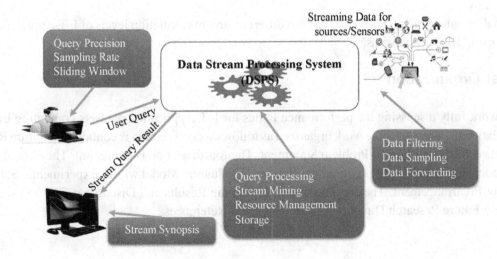

on-the-fly. Therefore, fully decentralized architectures are required. This raises new challenges in terms of data collection, data transportation, and data processing. In Figure 3 shows that basic background flow of an an IoT's and BDSC relation.

Motivation

By our clear study and observation found an issue on IoT's expansion/installing is easy but handling their quires and provide services in real-time is difficult. In the current scenario, less potentiality of big data in real-time while handling IoT application data. In this point of view, many performance related issues are there example fault-tolerance, response time, resource allocation, high energy utilizing, etc. a specific storm platform of the currently dealing with the stream data processing it is an inefficient to solve IoT Application data effectively. The Application aware resource scheduling features. Focused on both terms it is already done by the different researcher termed SVSstream, T-storm, re-Storm, and re-stream, individually are doing modification in scheduling aspect but different factor considers our approach is to combination individual approaches as a single approach achieve Application aware online scheduling. Moreover, improve performance big data stream computing environment for IoT Application.

Contributions

A summarized workflow of the work as following

1. A study of a dataset from a popular IoT applications generated and their nature of data forms generated, the velocity of data arriving rate to computing, query response time required.
2. List out the issues are facing the current BDSC system while handling IoT applications in real time.
3. Classify the list of Existing BDSC platforms/tools are there to dealing real-time IoT stream data.
4. Together are individually modified scheduling strategies, but in different logics, they are considered to overcome this two different issues one is traffic aware online consolidation and second is improving energy efficiency.
5. Moreover, adapt both different techniques in one single modified scheduling approach towards high energy efficiency, low response time with efficient in different circulation levels of IoT data streams.
6. Finally achieved High Performance with different stream circulation levels of IoT Application data by using BDSC Platforms.

Chapter Organization

In This work fully discussing the performance issues for IoT Application datasets computing by using BDSC platforms. The rest of the work organized as follows second section is contains Literature Review. The third section is containing Problem Statement. The fourth section is containing Theoretical Evaluation Model. The fifth section is containing Practical Evaluation Model within Experimental Setup and Parameter Prearrangement. The sixth section is containing Results and Discussion. The last section is containing Future Research Directions, Conclusion and References.

LITERATURE REVIEW

In real time data, IoT data sets are very critical fashion. The real-time data through big data techniques facing difficulty fulfilling. First, it is Not satisfactory factors is listed out for literature to see gap and challenges for the big data stream computing environment. Existing approaches they are used to the full filling their gap and their logics.

Zaharia et al. (2013), developed advanced a Discretized Streams (D-Stream) on top of Spark platform, using streams for a fault tolerances aspect they focused on fastest recovery without the overhead of duplication the needs among this state and older data observable at a fine granularity explicitly for fast, repeatedly sub-second, recovery from stragglers and faults, in superior scales on data stream computing environments. In this only concentrating the fault tolerances.

Chen et al. (2012), in this article, considered the problem of together scheduling all three levels of a MapReduce process. They presented outlined several heuristics and approximation algorithms to resolve the joint scheduling problem.

Taking into Consideration of Performance Issue

Xu et al. (2014), developed a T-Storm on top storm platform, using this trying to controlling the speed of traffic of a high speed streams by using the hot-swapping technique in traffic aware online resource scheduling algorithm designed to assigning a task in an effective manner however reducing a worker node in a storm system. T-Storm achieves more effective to distribute tasks and moreover improved performance.

Aly et al. (2012), in this, introduced a reformed MapReduce architecture model, it allowed data to be pipelined among operators. This covers the MapReduce programming model beyond batch processing and can decrease processing time and expand system utilization for batch jobs with various sizes of data.

Dusi et al. (2012), the author introduced to the Blackmon technique similar to the s4, storm but focusing on web based content sensing data.

In Daoud, and Kharma (2011), a two-stage list-based booking calculation, known as Hybrid Heuristic-Genetic Scheduling (H2GS) calculation, for information stream planning on heterogeneous conveyed processing frameworks, is proposed. The primary stage executes a heuristic list-based calculation, named LDCP, to create a great calendar. In the second stage, the LDCP-produced plan is infused into the underlying populace of a tweaked hereditary calculation, which continues to develop shorter calendars. Errand duplication is a method to diminish the important correspondence between the processors. Some essential undertakings will be copied and executed on more than one processors. In Sinnen et al. (2011), a conflict mindful assignment duplication booking calculation is proposed. It works under the general dispute model, and its algorithmic segments are based on state-of-the-craftsmanship procedures utilized as a part of assignment duplication and mindful dispute calculations.

In Y. Xu et al. (2013), a Double Molecular Structure-based Chemical Reaction Optimization (DMSCRO) calculation, for coordinated non-cyclic bunch information stream planning on heterogeneous processing frameworks, is created. In DMSCRO, one atomic structure is used to encode the execution request of the assignments in a DAG work, while the other sub-atomic structure to encode the errand to-registering hub mapping. DMSCRO additionally outlines the essential basic synthetic response operations and the wellness capacity reasonable for the situation of DAG booking. To compress, current execution situated information stream booking are not restricted in one or another viewpoint. Up to now, the vast majority of the scrutinizes are done in static booking. All the data about booking is assessed, unaltered, and must be ahead of time. However, when the volume of the information stream is changed, the booking may not be a shrewd technique. In the event that static booking is utilized in the new station, tremendous variances will happen. In enormous information stream situations, the volume of the information stream is changed.

Social media connecting with smart devices and sensing huge amount of streaming data increasing double by two to three years, this is also one type of IoT data because connected with GPS temperature, etc. devices. It is only suitable needs of the one type of big data only data forms are changing in different sectors as well as changing the traffic levels.

Taking into Consideration of Energy Issue

Sun, Zhang, Yang et al. (2015), developed a Re-Stream on top storm platform, using this trying to re-allocating their streams directed acyclic graphs and dividing as two segments, one critical vertex and non-critical vertex based strategies throw words reducing energy efficiency to managing their stream graphs. Energy-aware dynamic scheduling of critical vertices algorithm.

In K. Kanoun et al. 2014, in this article evolving a low power many core architecture model for big data stream computing with integrating able to adapt scalable, low-power and reconfigurable cores for reducing energy with different memory levels. This is very expensive to modify hardware equipment and reconfigure with the IcyFlex4 Core for achieving high performance.

In Baskiyar, and Abdel-Kader (2010), an energy mindful DAG booking, EADAGS, on heterogeneous processors is proposed. EADAGS joins Dynamic Voltage Scaling (DVS) with Decisive Path Scheduling (DPS) to accomplish the twin targets of minimizing completion time and energy utilization. In the main stage, after DPS is keeping running on the DAG to give a low complete time, the energy expended is assessed for all processors. In the second stage, voltage scaling is connected amid slack times to decrease energy while keeping up the timetable length.

In Hsu et al. (2014), an Energy-mindful Task Consolidation (ETC) procedure is proposed. And so forth accomplishes energy mindful assignment combination by confining CPU use beneath a predefined crest limit. And so on does energy mindful assignment union by solidifying undertakings amongst virtual groups. Also, the energy cost model considers system inertness when an errand moves to another simulated bunch.

In Kima et al. (2014), a model for assessing the energy utilization of each virtual machine, a virtual machine planning calculation that gives processing assets as per the energy spending plan of each virtual machine, is proposed. Those plans are actualized in the Xen virtualization framework.

In Zong et al. (2011), two energy productive duplication-based planning calculations, Energy-Aware Duplication (EAD) and Performance Energy Balanced Duplication (PEBD), are proposed. Conserving energy is to quickly swing processors to the most minimal voltage once no errand is holding up or no undertaking is prepared for execution. This approach guarantees that undertakings can be executed as quick as could reasonably be expected. In the interim, assignments on the basic way will be copied under the condition that no noteworthy energy overhead is presented by the reproductions. Duplications can stay away from the execution corruption brought about by holding up messages. The method of the reasoning behind this methodology is twofold. In the first place, energy overhead caused by errand copies could be counterbalanced by energy investment funds in also interconnects, by shortening plan length. Second, the general execution is enhanced by the uprightness of copies.

The above all are trying to fulfill their needs using different platforms and computing engines. Fully not considering overall needs of IoT's generated real-time sensing data using big data. Partially fulfill very few techniques, so seeing this literature find a gap on a different type of organization sensing different circulation levels of data with using different types of sensor devices, RFID, and etc.

PROBLEM STATEMENT

To Developing a novel real-time Application level resource allocation and device control methods for an IoT devices handling by using the BDSC platforms. In-stream computing usually handling motion data, it is real-time. Different IoT's are dissimilar circulation levels data Streams. For the device, intelligence is provided making IoT devices as connected real-time effectively. It is improving the living off the devices.

THEORETICAL EVALUATION MODEL FOR IOT STREAM

Proposed System

IoT-Stream technique applied along with existing BDSC platforms like a storm, S4 and spark. Now first in this chapter are applying for storm platform. It is open source platform to dealing streaming data. In this performance, aware issues are not considered like energy, Response-time, resource allocation, etc. Our proposed Model as energy efficiency performance scalable platform. Overview of IoT-Stream process workflow is shown in Figure 4.

To controlling the Stream computing platform in big data while computing IoT application data. It is facing difficulty consequently search for further gap filling to overcome this issue. In-Stream Computing Storm (Storm (event processor), 2016) platform is open sourced with fulfilling the maximum needs of existing streaming data aspect. In this one using scheduling strategy is Round Robin (Round-robin scheduling, 2016) as by default one. It does not satisfy the data circulation is very high in the point processing slow and energy consumption very for that purpose many failures. Devices generated data. The process flows in internally in the storm platform shown in Figure 5.

Figure 4. Overview IoT-stream processing

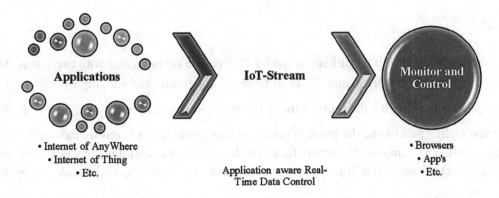

Figure 5. Internal workflow of the storm

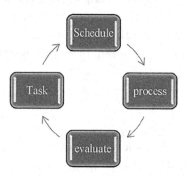

In the time of real-time computing data, three different type of data sensing devices are there in IoT (1) event-driven communication (Meng et al. 2013), (2) periodical communication (E. A. Billard et al. 1993), (3) Communication on request. For processing this kind of data, it wants for more computation power. Modifying scheduling approach passion for meeting the different type of data sets handling very effective way. Modified algorithm mentions below algorithm 1, in this algorithm mention calculating their time complexity using. For the further computation steps mention in the algorithm itself with a double slash.

The below algorithm 1 is working with three strategies. First is optimizing their stream graphs by using DVFS (Dynamic Voltage Frequency Scaling) (E. Le Sueur and G. Heiser, 2010) approaches to reduce energy. Second is Hot-swapping (Hot swapping, 2015) technique for online re-scheduling their worker nodes. The third is assigning both one and two approaches to scaling their performance.

For usage of the mathematical calculation process followed by simplifying the streaming graph. To computing a stream graphs, process is given below

Classification of Stream Computing

A continues sequence of datasets is called stream. An infinite sequence of data sets is called streams, more than one stream processed at the same time is called parallel streams. A program used to process continues data streams is called stream computing. Generally, stream computing processing by the Data stream graph (DSG) is derived by the Directed Acyclic Graph (DAG). Below definitions providing a correct measurable view of DSG.

Definitions

DSG is considered as DAG, is a resultant by the DAG. Every G is continuing with two parameters G=, in this V_G is a vertex of the group and E_G is an Edges of the group. And subgraph $G_s, \forall V_i \in V_{G_s}$ then $\forall V_i \in V_{G_s}$, the path it is going the route of the DAG. It is a direction of an (V_s, V_e) if $S \neq E$ the starting point and ending point same the graph is not a directed graph, and it is mostly indicating null node. Topological Sort (TS) is another characteristic graph the graph not containing any cycle's formations.it must be a DAG. DAG means it is Topology sort order. Partitioning a graph, it is considering by the DAG

Algorithm 1. IoT Application Real-Time Data Management

```
Input: IoT Real-Time data streams as a source.
Output: Computed Data Streams with High performance
Begin
     Get IoT Real-Time Data Streams
Process
     Calculate No. of executors
             E= (No. of Requests DAG+1)
                        // Not more than
     Calculate No. of worker nodes
             = (number of worker nodes in cluster * number cores per worker
node) - (number of hacker tasks)
                                             // Evaluate by
     Calculate Existing Load of each Executer
           = (E/) *100
                                          //Evaluate by
Loop for i=1 to No. of Schedule iteration
// for Application, aware association using factor for estimate X
          Update "Q" permitting to the
          Partition by   of giving to the performance ratio.
          Send data to the worker nodes
          Calculating load by using the formula (1)
          i+;
loop end
 Energy Calculating for each node measured by (5)
 Return Application-aware schedule allocation factor is X
 Total Energy Feasting system measured by (4)
 Performance Calculating by (6)
End
```

based on a TS us splitting the vertices of a graph. Partition graph (G_P) is a partitioning vertex based on the topology sort $G_P = \left\{ G_{P_1}, G_{P_2}, G_{P_3}, ... \right\}$ for each partition will having

$$G_{P_1} = \{V_1, V_2, V_3, ...\} \in G, G_{P_2} = \{V_1, V_2, V_3, ...\} \in G.$$

It is subgroup containing $\forall i \neq j i, j \in (1, n)$ then $G_{P_i} \cup G_{P_j} = \varnothing$, $U_1^n G_{(P_i)} = V_G$ and

$$G = (V_G, E_G)$$

Each Vertex and edge containing some tuples

$$V_G = (id_v, f_v, c_v, i_v, o_v)$$
$$E_G = (id_e, c_e)$$
$$P(V_s, V_e)$$

where

Graph Vertices $= V_G - \{V_1, V_2, V_3, \ldots \ldots V_i\}$,

Graph Edges $= E_G - \{E_1, E_2, E_3, \ldots \ldots E_j\}$,

Start vertex and End vertex$= V_s, V_e$

Vertices identification, function, computation cost, input data stream, the output data stream$= id_v, f_v, c_v, i_v, o_v$

id_e, C_e = identification of directed edge, communication cost of directed edge.

In Figure 6 the graph is a stat's at V_1 and ends V_2 it does not contain circles and it

$$\{V_1, V_2, V_3, V_4, V_5, V_6, V_7, V_8\} \in G$$

and in this one subgraph are assumed for example $\{V_1, V_3, V_5, V_6, V_8\} \in G$, and the path is two paths in this above graph $\{V_1, V_2, V_4, V_7, V_8\}$ and $\{V_1, V_3, V_5, V_6, V_8\} \in G$. The above graph moreover TS. The workflow nature it is telling the order of a storm execution flow. Each task depending upon another task it won't be executing parallel and worker node assigning a particular task it is relative to their task strength in that time achieve more simulative results. For example, DAG is shown in Figure 6.

Figure 6. Paired IoT data stream directed acyclic graph

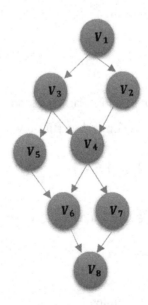

Below are provide appropriate equations to calculate an energy efficiency, response time and traffic aware energy aware scheduling strategies (S. Zhuravlev et al. 2013) and their mathematical relations among the energy efficient (Rizwan et al. 2015) with response time, energy efficient inter-node processing, energy efficient traffic consolidation and worker node assigning with low response time.

The mathematical formulas and their proofs, calculation energy and response time for DAG. Executers assigning a slot computing by using formula (1)

$$s^* = \arg\min_{(q \in Q)} \sum_{i'=1}^{N_e} \left[r_{\pi(i')i} \sum_{w(s) \neq w(q)} \left(X_{i'j} \right) + \left(r_{i'\pi(i)} \right) \right] \tag{1}$$

DSG Scheduling Strategies

In commonly allocation of resources is done by the appropriate scheduling aspects like array format, graph format, tree format, etc. different type of mechanism follows different types scenarios to allocate their resources. In concentrating the various scheduling, strategies are there for solving DSG corresponding DAG. Previously are discoursed by the DAG and their role in the stream and related issues. Applying scheduling schemes example on top Figure 7(a), it modifies shown in Figure 7(b).

Finding energy consumption with response time as factors, and circulation consolidation computed by Equation 2

$$E_{(cn_i)} = \int_{t_0}^{t_{(n-1)}} P_{(cn_i)}(\mu_i(t)) dt \tag{2}$$

where computation node is "cn_i", computation node Energy is "E_{cn_i}", computation node Power is "P_{cn_i}", node indicator is "i", $\left[t_0, t_{n-1} \right]$ time interval is "t".

Figure 7. Example stream DAG splinter structures

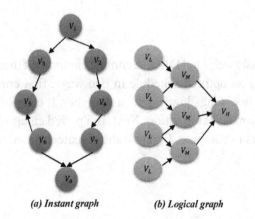

(a) Instant graph   *(b) Logical graph*

The specific component is Power consumption by computer is network, memory, Disk storage, CPU. Applying DVFS approach for power consumption of ith . i^{th} computation node computing by Equation (3) according to the Equation 2

$$P_{cn_i}(\mu_i(t)) \begin{cases} P_{cn_i}^{\ idl} = \alpha P_{cn_i}(MAX), X \in [0,1] \\ P_{cn_i}^{\ spd} = (1-\alpha).P_{cn_i}(MAX).\mu_i(t), \mu_i(t) \in [0,1] \end{cases} \tag{3}$$

Theorem 1: for computing by Equation 4 an E_{sys} . E_{sys} s energy consumption by the system. For big data stream computing environment.

$$E_{sys} = \sum_{(i=0)}^{num-1} E_{(cn_i)} \tag{4}$$

Theorem 2: for computing by Equation 5 an E_{cn_i} . E_{cn_i} energy consumption, $[t_0, t_{n-1}]$ is time intervals, divided into $[t_0, t_1, t_2, ...t_{n-1}]$ by formula proof D. (Sun, Zhang, Yang et al., 2015)

$$E_{(cn_i)} = \left(\alpha.P_{cn_i}(MAX)\right).\left(t_{(n-1)} - t_0\right) + \left((1-\alpha).P_{cn_i}(MAX)\right)\sum_{k-1}^{n-1}\left(\mu_{(i_{(k-1)})}.\left(t_k, t_{(k-1)}\right)\right) \tag{5}$$

where E_{cn_i} . E_{cn_i} according to the Equation 4, measure the energy consumption while the total power consumed (Rajasekhara Babu et al., 2013) by each computing node of the data storage, for directly measured by the fully utilized state.

For Estimating the performance using the formula Equation 6

$$PF_j = w \times \left(\frac{\dfrac{1}{T_j}}{\sum \forall n_{i \in s}\left(\dfrac{1}{T_j}\right)} \right) \tag{6}$$

For example, consider a basic weighted DAG. A complex amount of their node weight ranges is taken. To computing those applying an optimal schedule in two ways. first computing weight of each node and categories by using the three wings lower, mid, and higher. It categorization is done by using their weights. This called logical flow transformation. Next, is a paired categorization is usually categorized by using the tree triangle pairs to compute. Figure 8 shown categorization of the stream workflows.

Figure 8. Illustration optimizing, schedule stream for the DAG

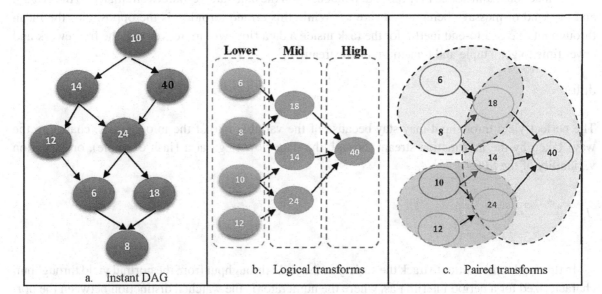

a. Instant DAG   b. Logical transforms   c. Paired transforms

Performance Metrics

Evaluating BDSC for the IoT's workload discussion the factors like latency, jitter, throughput, CPU and Memory Utilization.

Memory and CPU Utilization

Gushing IoT data flows are relied upon to be asset concentrated, and the capacity of the DSPS to utilize the appropriated assets effectively with negligible overhead is vital. This additionally influences the VM assets and ensuing cost to be paid to run the application utilizing the given stream handling stage. Here track the CPU and memory usage for the data flow as the normal of the CPU and memory use over all the VMs that are being utilized by the dataflow's assignments. The per-VM data can likewise distinguish which VMs facilitating which errands are the potential bottlenecks and can profit by information parallel scale-out.

Latency

Each message latency generated by the task. The process time of each task is calculated by took the time in seconds. The message is generated to involve one or more inputs. If $\sigma = N: M$ is the selectivity for an endeavor T, the time λ_M^T it took to eat up N messages to casually make those M yield messages is the dormancy of the M messages, with the typical latency per message given by $\overline{\lambda^T} = \dfrac{\lambda_M^T}{|M|}$. When consideration of the typical dormancy λ of the data flow application, it is the ordinary of the time contrast between each message used at the source assignments and all its causally subordinate messages delivered at the sink endeavors.

The inaction per message may move dependent upon the data rate, resources circulated to the errand, and the kind of message being taken care of. While this errand torpidity is the opposite of the mean throughput, the end-to-end inertia for the task inside a data flow will moreover join the framework and cover time to get a tuple and transmit it downstream.

Jitter

The perfect yield throughput may stay because of the variable rate of the info streams, change in the ways taken by the information stream through the data flow (e.g., at a Hash example), or execution variability of the SPS.

$$J_t = \frac{\omega^o - \sigma \times \omega^i}{\overline{\sigma \omega^i}}$$

In this work utilize jitter to track the variety in the yield throughput from the normal yield throughput, characterized for a period interim t as, where the numerator is the watched distinction between the normal and real yield rate amid interim t, and the denominator is the normal long haul normal yield rate given a long haul normal information rate x^i. In a perfect case, jitter will tend towards zero.

Throughput

The yield throughput is the totaled rate of yield messages discharged out of the sink assignments, measured in messages every second. The throughput of a data flow relies on upon the information throughput and the selectivity of the data flow, gave the asset allotment, and execution of the SPS are sufficient. In a perfect world, the yield throughput $\omega^o = \sigma \times \omega^i$, where ω^i is the information throughput for a data flow with selectivity σ. It is likewise helpful to gauge the pinnacle throughput that can be bolstered by a given application, which is the greatest stable rate that can be handled utilizing a settled quantum of assets. Both throughput and inactivity estimations are applicable just under stable conditions when the SPS can maintain a given data rate, i.e., when the stable per message and line size on the information frame stay stable and don't increment indefensibly.

PRACTICAL EVALUATION MODEL

Experimental Setup

For real-time computing, our model determination is frame a simulation environment. Hardware requirement is used to creating simulation environment. Intel i3 processor, 16 GB RAM, 512 Mbps speed network connectivity, using 4 core machines 10 for testing our model. All the modified scheduling approaches applied on top of the Ischeduler of the storm platform. Software requirement using for the computing the results, storm 0.10.0, Ubuntu server Version 14.01, java 1.8.25, zookeeper 3.4.0, python 3.0. Deploying modified energy efficient self-scheduling algorithm monitoring their results are observing on the StormUI.

The storm is used to estimating results StormUI. For synchronizing the worker nodes using the NTP protocol (Mills, 1985) standards. Average time bound are considering is 10 minutes. And total rest of mechanism as like on default strategy of the storm. Focusing on the two different aspect to getting for accurate results. One is a StormUI for monitoring the values of minutes' pulse, and also worker nodes count. The second one is an NTP protocol is getting there results in second's pulse with very accurate for using to monitor and as well as traffic level scaling.

Parameter

The parameter values setup to be considering different IoT stream generated sources. Arranging all the values as far the experiment requirements. One is a StormUI for monitoring the values of minutes' pulse, and also worker nodes count. The second one is an NTP protocol is getting there results in second's pulse with very accurate for using to monitor and as well as traffic level scaling. Show the tuple range will be 0-100 and are submitting their tuples with different circulation mediums to test case their accuracy $y = 0.0003x2 + 0.0343x + 13$ $R^2 = 0.9923$ for storm platform and IoT-Stream platform $y = 4.8273x0.3222$ $R^2 = 0.6348$.

The values are taken by the particular task is given in Table 1.

For the above values are taken for calculating the performance metric. To getting the accurate results multiple fusion of the IoT's. Basically, we are considering the datasets are taken by the CityPulse Smart city datasets. Getting multi-fashion data are taken by the different real-time sources. Sample are taken by the 6 different application sources like smart traffic system, smart home automation, etc.

RESULTS AND DISCUSSION

The testing source input and applying testing strategies (Rajasekhara Babu et al. 2013) in this article applied different testing strategies. collected data sets in the CityPulse dataset (CityPulse, 2016) collection web forum for source input for our technique analysis. It contains different real-time data sets are having to open source access. And addition to adding the additional real-time tools for creating a regulation environment. To deliver information with irrelevant circulation ranges on storm platform. The results for accuracy are divided into three different categories of streams tuple ranges are considered. One the range it should be the initial stage of tuple range 0-100. In this aspect are considering values variant

Table 1. Producing experimental value

S. No.	Bounds	Values
1	Monitoring load and Estimation period	50 sec.
2	Coefficient estimation (α)	0.5
3		
4		
5	Each Experiment Running Time E_{RT}.	00 sec.

manner but range is taken it is a constant one-tuples. Figure 9(a) Show the tuple range will be 0-100 and are submitting their tuples with different circulation mediums to testing their accuracy $y = 0.0003x^2 + 0.0343x + 13$ $R^2 = 0.9923$ for storm platform and IoT-Stream platform $y = 4.8273x^{0.3222}$ $R^2 = 0.6348$.

The second medium is the range it should be an average of tuple range 100-250. In this aspect are considering values variant manner but range is taken it is a constant one-tuples. Figure 9(b) Show the tuple range will be 100-250 and 0are submitting their tuples with different traffic mediums to testing their accuracy $y = 29.434e^{0.0017x}$ $R^2 = 0.9829$ for storm platform and modified IoT-Stream platform $y = -0.0003x^2 + 0.189x + 15.943$ $R^2 = 0.9189$. The third medium is the range it should be the maximum stage of tuple range 250-above. In this aspect are considering values variant manner but range is taken a constant one-tuples. Figure 9(c) Show the tuple range will be 250-above and are submitting their tuples with different circulation mediums to testing their accuracy $y = 25.407e^{0.0021x}$ $R^2 = 0.9185$ for storm platform with adding modified IoT-Stream platform $y = -0.0004x^2 + 0.3607x - 34.457$ $R^2 = 0.8664$.

Measuring the performance shown based on the Figure 10 multimedia data analytics. Different type of the file type messages arriving for computing. the distinctive measurements assessed shown in figure 10 (a) for the reduced scale standard assignments on Storm when running at their peak input rate upheld on a remote D1 VM with one string. The peak supported throughput per undertaking appears in log-scale.

Figure 9. IoT data stream load will be low, mid, high range of tuples generation

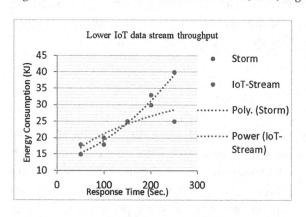 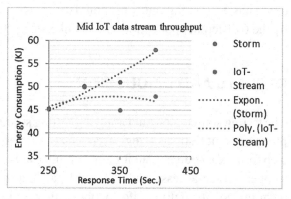

a) *Tuple range 0-100.*   b) *Tuple range 100-250.*

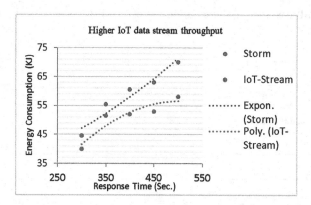

c) *Tuple range 250-above.*

We see that most undertakings can bolster 3, 000 msg/sec or higher rate, going up to 68, 000 msg/sec for BLF, KAL, and DAC. XML parsing is exceedingly CPU bound and has a high point throughput of just 310 msg/sec, and the IoT's operations are I/O bound on the BDSC benefit and significantly slower.

The backward of the peak maintained throughout gives the mean inactivity. Be that as it may, it is intriguing to look at the end-to-end inactivity, computed as the time taken between discharging a message from the source, having it go through the benchmarked assignment, and land at the sink task. This is the positive time contributed to the aggregate tuple inactivity by this assignment running inside Storm, including structure overheads. We see that while the mean latencies shown in figure 10 (e) ought to be in sub milliseconds for the watched throughputs, the container plot for end-to-end dormancy differs broadly up to 2, 600 ms for Q3.

Figure 10. Performance measurement of IoT's application generated input tasks at the top range

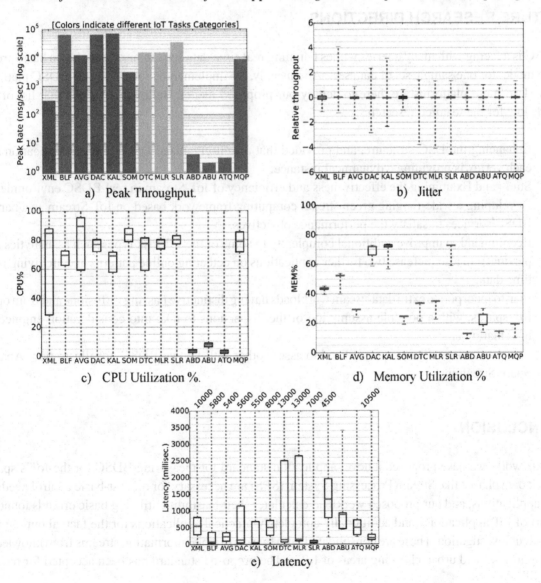

a) Peak Throughput.

b) Jitter

c) CPU Utilization %.

d) Memory Utilization %

e) Latency

$$\text{Runtime of Application} = \frac{7D \times 24H \times 60M \times 60S}{10000 \times Scaling} \text{ secs} = 1.008 \text{ mins}$$

The jitter values show Figure 10 (b) closer values to the zero in all cases. This specifies the long-term constancy of Storm in processing the tasks at the highest frequency, deprived of unmaintainable queuing of input messages. The broader whiskers indicate the irregular disparity between the probable and experimental output rates.

The CPU utilization Figure 10 (c) shows the single-core VM efficiently used at 80% or above in all cases but for the IoT tasks that are I/O bound. The memory utilization shown in figure 10 (d) appears to be difficult for tasks that provision a high throughput, possibly representative the memory spent by messages waiting in queue slightly than spent by the task goal itself.

FUTURE RESEARCH DIRECTIONS

BDSC is a facing with many queries whiles handling real-time data sets. In our work shown basic prototype model for one sample set of data sets. And usually, we implemented for the Single BDSC platform only. Two more platforms are there to deploy our proposed model. Bellow mentioned that list of the workflow for the featured research:

1. Enhancing the DSG structure, and provided that a well-organized DSG for each application and each vertex is providing a dynamical instance.
2. Study and Examining the effectiveness and efficiency of IoT-Stream in real BDSC environments.
3. Developing a wide-ranging green stream computing framework based on IoT-Stream as a part of BDSC services to satisfy the performance objectives.
4. Recommend to improve additional complexity to some of the IoT task types such as analytics and parsing, and also increase two further applications on detecting online patterns and archiving real-time data.
5. Plan to incorporate extra data stream workloads having distinctive passing diffusions and from other IoT spaces, with a possible assumption of the dispersions to take into consideration engineered information era.
6. The standard can likewise be utilized to assess other well-known BDSC, for illustration, Apache Spark Streaming.

CONCLUSION

In this work, we have proposed a novel application standard for measuring BDSC for the IoT's space. Quick data phases like Stream Processing System (SPS) are necessary for the fast-basic control needs of IoT applications, and our proposed workload calculates their feasibility utilizing basic errands found as a part of IoT applications, and additionally completely practical applications for the factual outline and prescient investigation. These are consolidated with two certifiable information streams from knowledge transportation and urban checking areas of IoT's. The proposed standard has been accepted for the exceedingly well known Apache Storm SPS, and the execution measurements introduced. To build execution of the parallel machines, a dynamic task planning calculation for enormous data stream handling in mobile Internet services is proposed, and the stream query graph is worked to establish the weight of each edge. The renovation comes about demonstrate that the correct number of the logic machine will significantly decrease framework response time, and more tuples scheduled at one time will lower framework connection switching. the calculation proposed by this work can enhance the productivity of enormous data stream preparing in portable Internet services. However, the scheduling rate is decreased will lead IoT's Application effectively.

REFERENCES

Aly, M., Sallam, A., Gnanasekaran, B. M., Aref, W. G., Ouzzani, M., & Ghafoor, A. (2012). M3: Stream Processing on Main-Memory MapReduce. *Proceedings of ICDE* (pp. 1253–1256).

Baskiyar, S., & Abdel-Kader, R. (2010). Energy aware DAG scheduling on heterogeneous systems. *Cluster Computing*, *13*(4), 373–383. doi:10.1007/s10586-009-0119-6

Beal, V. (2015). Batch processing. Webopedia. QuinStreet Inc. Retrieved 5 November 2015 from http://www.webopedia.com/TERM/B/batch_processing.html

Benkhelifa, E., Abdel-Maguid, M., Ewenike, S., & Heatley, D. (2014). The Internet of Things: The eco-system for sustainable growth. *Proceedings of the 2014 IEEE/ACS 11th International Conference on Computer Systems and Applications (AICCSA)* (pp. 836–842). doi:10.1109/AICCSA.2014.7073288

Bhandarkar, M. (2010). MapReduce programming with apache Hadoop. *Proceedings of the 2010 IEEE International Symposium on Parallel & Distributed Processing (IPDPS)*. doi:10.1109/IPDPS.2010.5470377

Billard, E. A., & Pasquale, J. C. (1992). Effects of periodic communication on distributed decision-making. Proceedings of the IEEE International Conference on Systems, Man and Cybernetics, Chicago, IL (Vol. 1, pp. 49-54). doi:10.1109/ICSMC.1992.271803

Chandrasekaran, S., Cooper, O., Deshpande, A., Franklin, M. J., Hellerstein, J. M., Hong, W., … Shah, M. A. (2003). Telegraphic: Continuous dataflow processing for an uncertain world. In ACM SIGMOD international conference on Management of data (pp. 668-668). doi:10.1145/872757.872857

Chen, F., Kodialam, M., & Lakshman, T. V. (2012). Joint scheduling of processing and shuffle phases in MapReduce systems. *Proceedings of IEEE INFOCOM '12* (pp. 1143–1151).

CityPuls. (2016). CityPulse Dataset Collection. Retrieved 10 May 2016 from iot.ee.surrey.ac.uk:8080/datasets.html

Cornwall, P. (2016). Ericsson mobility report (tech. report). Ericsson. Retrieved 10 June 2016 from https://www.ericsson.com/res/docs/2016/ericsson-mobility-report-2016.pdf

Daoud, M. I., & Kharma, N. (2011). A hybrid heuristic-genetic algorithm for task scheduling in heterogeneous processor networks. *Journal of Parallel and Distributed Computing*, *71*(11), 1518–1531. doi:10.1016/j.jpdc.2011.05.005

Data Canvas Dataset. (2016). Retrieved 7 February 2016 from http://datacanvas.org/sense-your-city/

Dusi, M., D'Heureuse, N., Huici, F., Di Pietro, A., Bonelli, N., Bianchi, G., & Niccolini, S. et al. (2012). Blockmon: Flexible and high-performance big data stream analytics platform and its use cases. *NEC Tech. J.*, *7*(2), 102–106.

Gopinath, A. (2014) Analytics on Big Fast Data using a real time stream data processing architecture. Retrieved 18 May 2016 from https://fifthelephant.talkfunnel.com/2014/1066-analytics-on-big-fast-data-using-real-time-stream-

Hadoop Distributed File System (HDFS). (2016). Definition from WhatIs.com. Retrieved 7 February 2016 from http://searchbusinessanalytics.techtarget.com/definition/Hadoop-Distributed-File-System-HDFS

Hsu, C. H., Slagter, K. D., Chen, S. C., & Chung, Y. C. (2014). optimizing energy consumption with task consolidation in clouds. *Inform. Sci.*, *258*, 452–462. doi:10.1016/j.ins.2012.10.041

Wikispaces. (2015). Interactive or Online Processing. Retrieved 5 November 2015) from http://dis-dpcs.wikispaces.com/3.3.5+Batch,+Online+%26+real+time+Processing

Kanoun, K., Ruggiero, M., Atienza, D., & Van Der Schaar, M. (2014). Low Power and Scalable Many-Core Architecture for Big-Data Stream Computing. Proceedings of the 2014 IEEE Computer Society Annual Symposium on VLSI (pp. 468–473). doi:10.1109/ISVLSI.2014.77

Kima, N., Chob, J., & Seob, E. (2014). Energy-credit scheduler: An energy-aware virtual machine scheduler for cloud systems. *Future Generation Computer Systems*, *32*(3), 128–137. doi:10.1016/j.future.2012.05.019

Le Sueur, E., & Heiser, G. (2010). Dynamic voltage and frequency scaling: the laws of diminishing returns. *Proc. 2010 Int. Conf. Power-aware Comput. Syst.* (pp. 1–8).

Li, J., Bao, Z., & Li, Z. (2015). Modeling Demand-Response Capability by Internet Data Centers Processing Batch Computing Jobs. *IEEE Transactions on Smart Grid*, *6*(2), 737–774. doi:10.1109/TSG.2014.2363583

Meng, X., & Chen, T. (2013) Event-driven communication for sampled-data control systems. *Proceedings of the Am. Control Conf. (ACC)* (Vol. 1, pp. 3002–3007).

Mills, D. (1985). Network time protocol (NTP). Retrieved 24 May 2016 from https://tools.ietf.org/html/rfc958

Mohanty, H. (2015). Big Data: An Introduction. In H. Mohanty, P. Bhuyan, & D. Chen (Eds.), Big Data (Vol. 11). India: Springer India. doi:10.1007/978-81-322-2494-5_1

Patan, R., & Babu, M.R. (2015). A Study Analysis of Energy Issues in Big Data. *International J. Appl. Eng. Res.*, *10*(6), 15593–15609.

Rajasekhara Babu, M., Alok, A. J. B., & Bhatt, N. (2013). Automation Testing Software that Aid in Efficiency Increase of Regression Process. *Recent Patents Comput. Sci.*, *6*(2), 107–114. doi:10.2174/2 2132759113069990008

Rajasekhara Babu, M, & Krishna, P.V., and Khalid. (2013). A framework for power estimation and reduction in multi-core architectures using basic block approach. *Int. J. Commun. Networks Distrib. Syst.*, *10*(1), 40–51.

Sinnen, O., To, A., & Kaur, M. (2011). Contention-aware scheduling with task duplication. *Journal of Parallel and Distributed Computing*, *71*(1), 77–86. doi:10.1016/j.jpdc.2010.10.004

Sun, D., Zhang, G., Yang, S., Zheng, W., Khan, S. U., & Li, K. (2015). Re-Stream: Real-time and energy-efficient resource scheduling in big data stream computing environments. *Information Science*, *319*, 91-112.

Sun, D., Zhang, G., Zheng, W., & Li, K. (2015). *Key Technologies for Big Data Stream Computing. In Big Data* (pp. 193–214). Chapman and Hall/CRC.

Verma, J. P., Patel, B., & Patel, A. (2015). Big Data Analysis: Recommendation System with Hadoop Framework. *Proceedings of the 2015 IEEE Int. Conf. Comput. Intell. Commun. Technol.* (pp. 92–97). doi:10.1109/CICT.2015.86

Wikipedia. (2015, November 2). Hot swapping. Retrieved 2 November 2015 from https://en.wikipedia.org/wiki/Hot_swapping#References

Wikipedia. (2015, November 20). Round-robin scheduling. Retrieved 20 November 2015 from https://en.wikipedia.org/wiki/Round-robin_scheduling

Wikipedia. (2016, February 25). Storm (event processor). Retrieved 25 February 2016 from https://en.wikipedia.org/w/index.php?title=Storm_(event_processor)&redirect=no

Wikipedia. (2016, February 7). Storm (software). Retrieved 7 February 2016 from https://en.wikipedia.org/wiki/Storm_(software)

Xu, J., Chen, Z., Tang, J., & Su, S. (2014). T-Storm: Traffic-aware Online Scheduling in Storm. *Proceedings of the IEEE Int. Conf. Distrib. Comput. Syst.* (pp. 535-544). doi:10.1109/ICDCS.2014.61

Xu, Y., Li, K., He, L., & Truong, T. K. (2013). A DAG scheduling scheme on heterogeneous computing systems using double molecular structure-based chemical reaction optimization. *Journal of Parallel and Distributed Computing*, *73*(9), 1306–1322. doi:10.1016/j.jpdc.2013.05.005

Zaharia, M., Das, T., Li, H., Hunter, T., Shenker, S., & Stoica, I. (2013). Discretized streams: Fault-tolerant streaming computation at scale. *Proceedings of the Twenty-Fourth ACM Symposium on Operating Systems Principles* (pp. 423–438). doi:10.1145/2517349.2522737

Zaslavsky, A. (2013). Internet of things and ubiquitous sensing. Computing Now. Retrieved from https://www.computer.org/web/computingnow/archive/september2013

Zhuravlev, S., Saez, J. C., Blagodurov, S., Fedorova, A., & Prieto, M. (2013). Survey of Energy-Cognizant Scheduling Techniques. *IEEE Transactions on Parallel and Distributed Systems*, *24*(7), 1447–1464. doi:10.1109/TPDS.2012.20

Zong, Z., Manzanares, A., Ruan, X., & Qin, X. (2011). EAD and PEBD: Two energy-aware duplication scheduling algorithms for parallel tasks on homogeneous clusters. *IEEE Trans. Comput.*, *60*(3), 360–374.

Chapter 16
Predictive Analytics to Support Clinical Trials Get Healthier

Ankit Lodha
University of Redlands, USA

Anvita Karara
Carnegie Mellon University, USA

ABSTRACT

The concept of clinical big data analytics is simply the joining of two or more previously disparate sources of information, structured in such a way that insights are prescribed from examination of the new expanded data set. The combination with Internet of Things (IoT), can provide multivariate data, if healthcare organizations build the infrastructure to accept it. Many providers are able to integrate financial and utilization data to create a portrait of organizational operations, but these sources do not give a clear idea of what patients do on their own time. Embracing the centrality of the IoT would relinquish the idea that provider is the only pillar around which healthcare revolves. This chapter provides deeper insights into the four major challenges: costly protocol amendments, increasing protocol complexity and investigator site burden. It also provides recommendations for streamlining clinical trials by following a two dimension approach-optimization at a program level (clinical development plan) as well as at the individual trial candidate level.

INTRODUCTION

Despite the billions of dollars spent annually discovering and developing new drugs, the global output of innovative new medicines is at its lowest point in several decades. This is not as illogical as it first sounds. As an industry, we have become accustomed to expecting that financial investment will equate to positive outcomes - this in spite of the fact that we have seen more breathtaking failures in drug launches in the past ten years than ever before.

All that money was not necessarily spent in vain. The completion of the Human Genome, the deciphering of more mechanisms of actions of diseases than ever before, the ability to analyze millions of

DOI: 10.4018/978-1-5225-2947-7.ch016

Copyright © 2018, IGI Global. Copying or distributing in print or electronic forms without written permission of IGI Global is prohibited.

samples a day and new sophisticated detection platforms, are all fundamental to how we discover and develop drugs today and will continue into the future.

BACKGROUND

In the last ten years, a "data deluge" has been created, with new and evolving methods of communication and processes of storing information. The increasing amounts of electronic data have been generated and stored daily in multiple forms and locations in almost every market (Tibco, 2011). Switzerland's pharmaceutical giant, Roche, reported in 2010 that the company is producing so much data, that it is doubling every 15 months. These data are not just generated from internal research and development, but also from a networked clinical development model involving in-licensing, out-licensing, outsourcing, and collaborations with various contract research organizations, academia, pharmaceutical and healthcare partners. Their model serves as a prime example of why emerging technology that allows for the consolidation and rapid analysis of clinical and non-clinical data is so critical.

ISSUES

The Rapid Growth in Clinical Development

The number of clinical trials underway each year has been increasing steadily, worldwide. In the last five years alone, over 75,000 federally and privately supported trials have been registered with the National Institute of Health's Clinical Trials registry with a growing trend in trials being conducted in Brazil, Russia, India, and China (Lodha, 2016).

With a broad range of study designs, varying data collection methods and time points, efficient data analysis in clinical development has become more important than ever. The more effectively study data are managed, the faster the data can be extracted and analyzed. The analysis of the data is important for each trial stage as valuable insights can be gained. For example, during the early stages of a clinical trial, access to data is vital not only for patient safety, but for solving problems while they are still manageable and before they become costly (Tibco, 2011).

Controversies of 4 "Vs" in IoT and Clinical Big Data Analytics

Like big data in healthcare, the analytics associated with big data is described by three primary characteristics as per IBM: volume, velocity and variety. Over time, health-related data will be created and accumulated continuously, resulting in an incredible volume of data (Raghupathi, 2014). The already daunting volume of existing healthcare data includes personal medical records, radiology images, clinical trial data, FDA submissions, human genetics and population data genomic sequences, etc. Newer forms of big data such as 3D imaging, genomics and biometric sensor readings, are also fueling this exponential growth.

Fortunately, advances in data management, particularly virtualization and cloud computing, are facilitating the development of platforms for more effective capture, storage and manipulation of large volumes of data. Data is accumulated in real-time and at a rapid pace, or velocity (Raghupathi, 2014).

The constant flow of new data accumulating at unprecedented rates presents new challenges. Just as the volume and variety of data that is collected and stored has changed, so too has the velocity at which it is generated and that is necessary for retrieving, analyzing, comparing and making decisions based on the output.

Most healthcare data have been traditionally static - paper files, x-ray films, and scripts. Velocity of mounting data increases with data that represents regular monitoring, such as multiple daily diabetic glucose measurements (or more continuous control by insulin pumps), blood pressure readings, and ECGs (Raghupathi, 2014). Meanwhile, in many medical situations, constant real-time data (trauma monitoring for blood pressure, operating room monitors for anesthesia, bedside heart monitors, etc.) can mean the difference between life and death.

Future applications of real-time data, such as detecting infections as early as possible, identifying them swiftly and applying the right treatments (not just broad-spectrum antibiotics) could reduce patient morbidity and mortality and even prevent hospital outbreaks (Raghupathi, 2014). Already, real-time streaming data monitors neonates in the ICU, catching life-threatening infections sooner. The ability to perform real-time analytics against such high-volume data in motion and across all specialties would revolutionize healthcare. Therein lays variety.

As the nature of health data has evolved, so too have analytical techniques scaled up to the complex and sophisticated analytics necessary to accommodate volume, velocity and variety. Gone are the days of data collected exclusively in electronic health records and other structured formats. Increasingly, the data is in multimedia format and unstructured. The enormous variety of data—structured, unstructured and semi-structured—is a dimension that makes healthcare data both interesting and challenging.

Structured data is data that can be easily stored, queried, recalled, analyzed and manipulated by machine. Historically, in healthcare, structured and semi-structured data includes instrument readings and data generated by the ongoing conversion of paper records to electronic health and medical records. The point of care generated unstructured data includes: office medical records, handwritten nurse and doctor notes, hospital admission and discharge records, paper prescriptions, radiograph films, MRI, CT and other images.

Already, new data streams—structured and unstructured—are cascading into the healthcare realm from fitness devices, genetics and genomics, social media research and other sources. But relatively little of this data can presently be captured, stored and organized so that it can be manipulated by computers and analyzed for useful information (Raghupathi, 2014). Healthcare applications in particular need more efficient ways to combine and convert varieties of data including automating conversion from structured to unstructured data.

The structured data in EMRs and EHRs include familiar input record fields such as patient name, date of birth, address, physician's name, hospital name and address, treatment reimbursement codes, and other information easily coded into and handled by automated databases. The need to field-code data at the point of care for electronic handling is a major barrier to acceptance of EMRs by physicians and nurses, who lose the natural language ease of entry and understanding that handwritten notes provide (Raghupathi, 2014). On the other hand, most providers agree that an easy way to reduce prescription errors is to use digital entries rather than handwritten scripts.

The potential of big data in healthcare lies in combining traditional data with new forms of data, both individually and on a population level. We are already seeing data sets from a multitude of sources support faster and more reliable research and discovery (Raghupathi, 2014). If, for example, pharmaceutical developers could integrate population clinical data sets with genomics data, this development could facilitate those developers gaining approvals on more and better drug therapies more quickly than in the past and, more importantly, expedite distribution to the right patients. The prospects for all areas of healthcare are infinite.

Some practitioners and researchers have introduced a fourth characteristic, veracity, or 'data assurance'. That is, the big data, analytics and outcomes are error-free and credible. Of course, veracity is the goal, not (yet) the reality. Data quality issues are of acute concern in healthcare for two reasons: life or death decisions depend on having the accurate information, and the quality of healthcare data, especially unstructured data, is highly variable and all too often incorrect. (Inaccurate "translations" of poor handwriting on prescriptions are perhaps the most infamous example).

Veracity assumes the simultaneous scaling up in granularity and performance of the architectures and platforms, algorithms, methodologies and tools to match the demands of big data (Raghupathi, 2014). The analytics architectures and tools for structured and unstructured big data are very different from traditional business intelligence (BI) tools. They are necessarily of industrial strength. For example, big data analytics in healthcare would be executed in distributed processing across several servers ("nodes"), utilizing the paradigm of parallel computing and 'divide and process' approach (Raghupathi, 2014). Likewise, models and techniques—such as data mining and statistical approaches, algorithms, visualization techniques—need to take into account the characteristics of big data analytics. Traditional data management assumes that the warehoused data is certain, clean, and precise.

Veracity in healthcare data faces many of the same issues as in financial data, especially on the payer side:

- Is this the correct patient / hospital / payer / reimbursement code / dollar amount?

Other veracity issues are unique to healthcare:

- Are diagnoses / treatments / prescriptions / procedures / outcomes captured correctly.

Improving coordination of care, avoiding errors and reducing costs depend on high-quality data, as do advances in drug safety and efficacy, diagnostic accuracy and more precise targeting of disease processes by treatments. But increased variety and high velocity hinder the ability to cleanse data before analyzing it and making decisions, magnifying the issue of data "trust" (Raghupathi, 2014).

The '4Vs' are an appropriate starting point for a discussion about big data analytics and IoT in healthcare. But there are other issues to consider, such as the number of architectures and platforms, and the dominance of the open source paradigm in the availability of tools. Consider, too, the challenge of developing methodologies and the need for user-friendly interfaces. While the overall cost of hardware and software is declining, these issues have to be addressed to harness and maximize the potential of big data analytics in healthcare.

CHALLENGES AND CONTROVERSIES FOR BIG DATA ANALYTICS AND IoT IN HEALTHCARE

At minimum, a big data analytics platform in healthcare must support the key functions necessary for processing the data. The criteria for platform evaluation may include availability, continuity, ease of use, scalability, ability to manipulate at different levels of granularity, privacy and security enablement, and quality assurance (Raghupathi, 2014). In addition, while most platforms currently available are open source, the typical advantages and limitations of open source platforms apply. To succeed, big data analytics in healthcare needs to be packaged so it is menu-driven, user-friendly and transparent. Real-time big data analytics is a key requirement in healthcare (Raghupathi, 2014). The lag between data collection and processing has to be addressed. The dynamic availability of numerous analytics algorithms, models and methods in a pull-down type of menu is also necessary for large-scale adoption. The important managerial issues of ownership, governance and standards have to be considered. And woven through these issues are those of continuous data acquisition and data cleansing. Health care data is rarely standardized, often fragmented, or generated in legacy IT systems with incompatible formats. This great challenge needs to be addressed as well (Raghupathi, 2014).

Architectural Framework for IoT and Analytics

The conceptual framework for a big data analytics project in healthcare is similar to that of a traditional health informatics or analytics project. The key difference lies in how processing is executed. In a regular health analytics project, the analysis can be performed with a business intelligence tool installed on a stand-alone system, such as a desktop or laptop. Because big data is by definition large, processing is broken down and executed across multiple nodes. The concept of distributed processing has existed for decades. What is relatively new is its use in analyzing very large data sets as healthcare providers start to tap into their large data repositories to gain insight for making better-informed health-related decisions (Raghupathi, 2014). Furthermore, open source platforms such as Hadoop/MapReduce, available on the cloud, have encouraged the application of big data analytics in healthcare.

While the algorithms and models are similar, the user interfaces of traditional analytics tools and those used for big data are entirely different; traditional health analytics tools have become very user friendly and transparent. Big data analytics tools, on the other hand, are extremely complex, programming intensive, and require the application of a variety of skills. They have emerged in an ad hoc fashion mostly as open-source development tools and platforms, and therefore they lack the support and user-friendliness that vendor-driven proprietary tools possess (Raghupathi, 2014).

Big data in healthcare can come from internal (e.g., electronic health records, clinical decision support systems, Computerized physician order entry (CPOE), etc.) and external sources (government sources, laboratories, pharmacies, insurance companies & HMOs, etc.), often in multiple formats (flat files, .csv, relational tables, ASCII/text, etc.) and residing at multiple locations (geographic as well as in different healthcare providers' sites) in numerous legacy and other applications (transaction processing applications, databases, etc.). Sources and data types include:

- **Web and Social Media Data:** Clickstream and interaction data from Facebook, Twitter, LinkedIn, blogs, and the like. It can also include health plan websites, smartphone apps, etc. (Cottle et al., 2013)
- **Machine to Machine Data:** Readings from remote sensors, meters, and other vital sign devices (Cottle et al., 2013)
- **Big Transaction Data:** Health care claims and other billing records increasingly available in semi-structured and unstructured formats (Cottle et al., 2013)

- **Biometric Data:** Fingerprints, genetics, handwriting, retinal scans, x-ray and other medical images, blood pressure, pulse and pulse-oximetry readings, and other similar types of data (Cottle et al., 2013)
- **Human-Generated Data:** Unstructured and semi-structured data such as EMRs, physician's notes, email, and paper documents (Cottle et al., 2013)

For the purpose of big data analytics, this data has to be pooled. In the second component, the data is in a 'raw' state and needs to be processed or transformed, at which point several options are available (Raghupathi, 2014). A service-oriented architectural approach combined with web services (middleware) is one possibility. The data stays raw and services are used to call, retrieve and process the data. Another approach is data warehousing wherein data from various sources is aggregated and made ready for processing, although the data is not available in real-time. According to Raghupati (2009), via the steps of extract, transform, and load (ETL), data from diverse sources is cleansed and readied. Depending on whether the data is structured or unstructured, several data formats can be input to the big data analytics platform.

In this next component in the conceptual framework, several decisions are made regarding the data input approach, distributed design, tool selection and analytics models. Finally, on the far right, the four typical applications of big data analytics in healthcare are shown. These include queries, reports, Online Analytical Processing (OLAP), and data mining. Visualization is an overarching theme across the four applications. Drawing from such fields as statistics, computer science, applied mathematics and economics, a wide variety of techniques and technologies has been developed and adapted to aggregate, manipulate, analyze, and visualize big data in healthcare.

The most significant platform for big data analytics is the open-source distributed data processing platform Hadoop (Apache platform), initially developed for such routine functions as aggregating web search indexes (Borkar et al., 2012). It belongs to the class "NoSQL" technologies—others include CouchDB and MongoDB—that evolved to aggregate data in unique ways (Ohlhorst, 2012). Hadoop has the potential to process extremely large amounts of data mainly by allocating partitioned data sets to numerous servers (nodes), each of which solves different parts of the larger problem and then integrates them for the final result (Zikopoulos et al., 2012). Hadoop can serve the twin roles of data organizer and analytics tool. It offers a great deal of potential in enabling enterprises to harness the data that has been, until now, difficult to manage and analyze. Specifically, Hadoop makes it possible to process extremely large volumes of data with various structures or no structure at all. But Hadoop can be challenging to install, configure and administer, and individuals with Hadoop skills are not easily found. Furthermore, for these reasons, it appears organizations are not quite ready to embrace Hadoop completely. The surrounding ecosystem of additional platforms and tools supports the Hadoop distributed platform (Zikopoulos et al., 2012).

PROBLEMS IN END TO END CLINICAL TRIAL OPTIMIZATION

Despite the varied complexities and diversity in various trials, the end goal of all clinical trials is to achieve reduced clinical trial cost, less cycle time and increased efficiency. The pharmaceutical industry is struggling since several decades to achieve the above goals. In November 2014 Tufts center for the study of drug development has estimated average pre-tax industry cost per new prescription drug approval (inclusive of failures and capital costs) as $2,558 million. This report also highlights an increase in the total capitalized cost per approved new compound to 8.5% (DiMasi, 2014).

Although the clinical trial costs have increased, the approval success rates have significantly declined. The number of NME (New Molecular Entities) approved has considerably decreased by 21% from 2002 to 2013 (Swann, 2013).

Described below are some of the factors contributing to the long trial cycle time and cost:

Costly Protocol Amendments

The rise in the clinical endpoints, complex study designs and the increase in the frequency of procedures are resulting in several protocol amendments. According to a recent Tufts Impact report on Growing Protocol Design Complexity (2008), 20% of Phase II and 33% of Phase II protocol procedures, collect non-core data, which is not associated with a primary endpoint, key secondary endpoint, or regulatory compliance. Table 1 details the distribution of procedures by end point classification, based on the study conducted by Getz and his team (Clinical Study Management at the Tufts University).

This data complexity is a burden for the clinical researchers and study investigators. Such protocol complexity factors often result in amendments. An amendment is defined as any change to a protocol requiring internal approval followed by approval from the Institutional Review Board (IRB), Ethical Review Board (ERB) or regulatory authority (Getz, 2014).

Nearly all protocols require at least one amendment; each amendment is very costly and time consuming. Each amendment takes approximately 65 days to be implemented and costs around $453,932 (Getz, 2011). With a more streamlined operating model and simple protocols, approximately 33% of these protocol amendments are avoidable. The most common causes of these protocol amendments are complex study design consisting of non-core endpoints, regulatory agency request, and recruitment/ retention of participants or new standard of care. A lot of these amendments are also related to project planning flaws by the clinical management team, which aims at unrealistic tight timelines and budget. Not only are these amendments costly, they also increase the duration of the clinical trials.

Increasing Protocol Complexity

Tufts CSDD has reported that changes in the protocol design may adversely affect clinical trial performance. Clinical data collected per protocol has grown exponentially, but not all the data collected is useful. The increasing number of unique procedures, non-core endpoints and high study eligibility criteria,

Table 1. Distribution of procedures by end point classification

Endpoint	Phase II	Phase III
Core	54.4%	47.7%
Required	8.0%	10.0%
Standard	19.7%	17.6%
Non-core	17.9%	24.7%
Total	100%	100%

Source: *(Getz, K. 2014)*

has contributed towards the data and protocol complexity. In 2008 Getz and his team conducted a study based on 10,000 protocols approved during 1999 to 2005.This study indicated an increase of 6.5% in the number of unique procedures per protocol across all therapeutic areas (Getz, Wenger, Campo et al., 2008). It also demonstrated an increase of 8.7% in the procedural frequency, the number of times a unique procedure is conducted during the duration of the study. Such complex protocols result in capturing lot of unimportant data which results in data deluge. Data deluge signifies, a condition where the volume of new data generated is overwhelming, and thus makes it difficult to derive valuable insights. It also increases the load on the resources to collect, manage, clean and validate this data. Table 2 summarizes research conducted by the Tufts CSDD, on growing protocol complexity of a Phase III over two time periods.

Table 2 clearly demonstrates the increase in safety and efficacy procedures, in the past 10 years. In 2012, to demonstrate safety and efficacy, a typical phase III protocol had 170 procedures on average performed on each study volunteer during the course of 11 visits across an average 230-day time span. Ten years ago, the typical phase III protocol had an average of 106 procedures, nine visits and an average 187-day time span (Getz, 2014).

Apart from the data perspective, such complex protocols are burdensome to the investigator site personnel and clinical study volunteers. The increasing protocol complexity certainly has severe downstream effects, and there is an opportunity to optimize this process. Using big data analytics for protocol optimization can lead to increased clinical trial performance. Trial level enrollment and investigator data can help form predictive models for better optimized protocols.

Investigator Site Burden

The rising protocol complexity has an exponential impact on the execution burden of the clinical investigator site personnel. In 2008, Tufts CSDD devised an approach to calculate the work burden to administer study procedures; based on Medicare's Relative Value Unit (RVU) methodology. Analytics derived on a 10 year study period from 2002-2012, revealed the investigator work burden increase to be highest for Phase II trials- 73%. The increase in the work burden in Phase I, III and IV is 48%, 55% and 56% respectively (Getz, 2014). Parallel, to the increase in the investigator site burden, the industry is also facing challenges with investigators not being adequately compensated. The increase in operational requirements for the trials increases the execution time and effort of the investigator personnel. This in turn requires high financial compensation to keep the investigators motivated. Inadequate financial incentive has been identified as a major barrier for physician participation in clinical studies (Rahman, Majumder, Shaban et al., 2011).

Table 2. Growing protocol complexity of a Phase III clinical trial over two time periods

Study Design Characteristics	2002	2012
Total number of endpoints	7	13
Total number of procedures	106	167
Total number of eligibility criteria	31	50
Total number of countries	11	34
Total number of investigative sites	124	196
Total number of patients randomized	729	597

Source: (Getz, Wenger, Campo et al. 2008).

To gain deeper insights into the investigator site burden, DrugDev developed a survey for 750 clinical trial investigators from its Global network of seven countries (Argentina, Australia, Germany, India, South Africa, the UK, and the US). The top two most burdensome issues identified for physicians include: completing contractual and regulatory documents, and getting paid on time (Cascade, Nixon & Sears, 2014). Overall the investigator site burden accompanied by lack of financial incentives has led to decrease in the number of principal investigators (PI's) globally. The Tufts CSDD has reported a sharp decrease in PI's filing FDA form 1572s. The number of FDA form 1572's have dropped from 27,861 in 2008 to 23,935 in 2009 and had a further reduction to 22,243 in 2010 (Redfearn, 2011). The number of active PI's have reduced by 11% globally and 20% in US alone. The clinical investigator landscape has shifted dramatically; this can have a major impact on the conduct of clinical trials. It is important to improve clinical trial planning, reduce protocol complexity and number of procedures per trial. Streamlined clinical planning and better financial compensation can greatly motivate the clinical investigators and thus have a positive impact on clinical trial conduct.

Low Patient Recruitment and Retention Rate

The protocol and study design complexity also has an impact on the patient recruitment and retention rate of a trial. The low recruitment rate has been a major concern for the clinical trial industry, and there needs to be a shift towards making trials more "patient centric". In 2013, Tufts CSDD conducted analysis on 150 clinical studies consisting of more than 16,000 sites. The insights indicated that even though 9 out of the 10 clinical studies were able to achieve their enrollment targets, the timeline for achieving those targets had been doubled (Peters, 2013). The study also highlighted that most clinical trials relied on traditional channels for patient recruitment, and did not explore non-traditional channels like social media.

Applied Clinical Trials interviewed 16 clinical professionals in the United Kingdom consisting of investigators, pharmaceutical representatives, and contract research organizations representatives (Sullivan, J. (2004, April 1). The study details different types of patient recruitment barriers and a lot of these barriers are related to the impact of bad protocols. The protocol related barriers that were identified in this research include: lengthy study periods, excessive patient visit schedules, excessive product dosage and unrealistic change expectations (Sullivan, 2004). A stringent trial eligibility criterion has been another barrier for many interested patients. The unrealistic protocol design and complexity does not keep the patient motivated. The current situation calls for aggressive methods to make the clinical trials more patients centric, via big data analytics and simple study designs. Identifying the right patient through their attitudinal data can greatly help in increasing the patient recruitment and retention rate. Furthermore, simple study design and protocols, using predictive analytics can help perform a more targeted approach for conducting trials.

RECOMMENDATIONS FOR END TO END CLINICAL TRIAL OPTIMIZATION

The abovementioned issues highlight a need for end to end clinical trial optimization. Improvised project planning with simpler study designs and higher operational feasibility are required. This can be achieved by incorporating clinical data analytics and optimization during the formation of the Clinical Development Plan (CDP).

A CDP is defined as a complex document that entails the entire clinical research strategy of a drug, describing the clinical studies that will be carried out for a pharmaceutical entity, created by a pharmaceutical company (Barra, 2013). It is a strategic planning document and helps in identifying the vision and implementation of the clinical studies. Spending time optimizing the CDP and linking key strategies to the attributes of the Target Product Profile (TPP) would greatly streamline the process. The US FDA defines the TPP as a "strategic development process tool" (Delasko, 2007). In 1977, a Clinical Development Working Group consisting of representatives from the FDA and pharmaceutical sponsors recommended the use of a template called Target Product Profile. This template improves the interactions between the sponsors and FDA representatives during the drug development process. (Delasko, 2007). Creation of clinical strategies based on the TPP symbolizes the concept of-beginning with the end goal in mind. It can provide directional guidance for new product indications, comparison with the competitor product features, informing study design and identification of unique product claims and features.

Increasing clinical trial efficiency is a two dimension approach-optimization at a program level (clinical development plan) as well as at the individual trial candidate level. The sponsor investigator and enrollment data can be combined with the clinical design software solutions, to perform what if scenario modelling. This scenario analysis via the model based drug development technology can help the clinical development teams analyze the cycle time, cost and risk tradeoff decisions in present and future. Another technological advancement, is the in silico clinical trial methodology. This involves using computer simulation and modelling to do exploratory clinical trials. Such virtual trials helps in identifying the correct patients for a trial, analyzing the potential outcomes and adverse events and test experiment scenarios (Viceconti, Henney & Morley-Fletcher, 2016). Using technology and big data at the trial level, enables the clinical development teams to take data driven informed decisions.

The clinical data analytics at the trial level also needs to be aligned with the appropriate trial objective and clinical strategy. In order to gain increased trial efficiency, each endpoint in a clinical trial should be mapped to a trial objective, and each trial objective should be further mapped to a clinical strategy in the Clinical Development Plan, which should then be aligned to a Target Product Profile attribute. Such an end to end mapping finally results in Clinical Trial Optimization. Figure 1 is an example of end to end clinical trial optimization framework, where the endpoints are mapped with the trial objectives, and each trial aligns with the CDP strategy which further aligns with the Target Product Profile attribute.

For adaptive trials, there is a need of feedback loop from the trial objectives to the clinical development plan. This is a hybrid approach which encompasses attributes from the top-down and bottom up operational processes.

SOLUTION FOR IoT AND BIG DATA ANALYTICS

Faster Data Review, Quality Assessment, and Process Improvement

The benefits of exploring crucial data (adverse events, lab values, demographics, drug exposure and response) early in the clinical trial process are numerous. They serve to reduce errors, improve quality, and increase productivity by 20-40%. Some specific benefits include:

- 3-4 days per month per trial saved in medical data review
- Better/faster data quality assessment

Figure 1. End to end clinical trial optimization framework

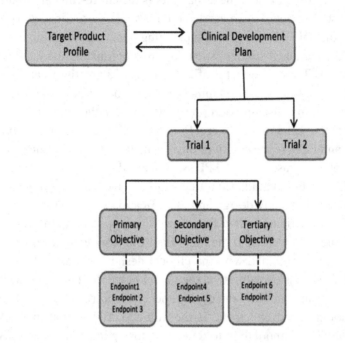

- Reduction of data quality issues – up to 30% reduction in lockdown prep time
- Decreased unfrozen databases by up to 50%
- Fundamental process improvements
- Early identification of protocol violations
- Early identification of drop-outs
- Better site management - can save $20K+ per patient
- Rapid implementation
- Shortest time to value of any system

Survival Analysis

One of the most important outcomes of clinical trials is the "time to event", or the time it takes to reach an endpoint, such as cancer recurrence. These platforms have built-in survival analysis capabilities to perform these tasks, using S+ language. Survival designs provide detailed models for patient accrual, dropout and time-to-event.

Survival Analysis: marking in these platforms drives S+ analysis

- Kaplan-Meier, cumulative incidence plots
- Graphics interact with rest of clinical analysis
- S+ RTF analytics report
- Kaplan-Meier or Cumulative Incidence Plot for inclusion in Clinical Study Report
- Survival library is state-of-art

FUTURE RESEARCH DIRECTIONS

End to end clinical trial optimization will increase the clinical program efficiency by ensuring strategic planning and implementation. Direct mapping of endpoints to the objectives, will reduce the procedures being conducted for non-core endpoints. Rolling up individual trial level objectives to clinical strategies through the clinical development plan, will help in better project planning and execution strategies. These mappings will result in simpler study designs, therefore reducing protocol complexity and amendments. Alignment of the Clinical strategies with the target product profiles will aid in achieving the product attributes for commercial success.

Case Study #1: Life Science Industry

A leading pharmaceutical company was keenly aware that effective management of its worldwide clinical trial programs, with respect to patient safety and clinical data integrity, was among its most important priorities. One route to improved patient safety and better data quality was to target the clinical trial sites that persistently underperformed, but identifying those sites using quantitative methods was a formidable challenge. Clinical trial sites that the company deemed "unhealthy" typically lacked appropriate principal investigator oversight, had high staff turnover, exhibited deviations from study protocols, or had a high number of serious adverse events. No matter which problems a site might demonstrate, the bottom line was that the company wanted to use data driven techniques, aligned to their deep experience base, to make informed and impactful decision to quickly target clinical site issue with enough lead time to remediate.

Clinical data collection, cleaning, analysis and reporting are time-consuming and expensive steps. This effort is compounded as the number of trials increases. Analytical platforms (such as Spotfire, Qlikview, etc.) can streamline clinical trial data analysis with real time access to clinical data during all phases of clinical development, allowing the user to interact with the data as soon as it is collected. What makes these analytics platforms unique and powerful is the ability to produce interactive visualization that allow the user to easily explore the data and ask a multitude of what-if questions. These applications are used by life science companies around the world for critical clinical development analytic tasks such as:

- Clinical data monitoring and review
- Medical / safety review
- Protocol adherence monitoring which is particularly important with complex protocols and therapy areas (i.e. oncology, neuroscience, metabolic, etc.).
- Detailed data cleaning
- Exposure-response analysis and dose-finding in early-phase trials
- Clinical operations 1. KPI analysis 2. Query management - across sites, countries, trials
- Pre-marketing safety analysis
- Post-marketing pharmacovigilance
- Portfolio/project management – risk-adjusted NPV analysis for compound prioritization across portfolio
- Clinical data management operations
- Clinical trial supplies
- Pharmacometrics

Case Study #2: Cost Benefit Analysis

Protocols are the backbones of a clinical trial. Lack of data for informed decision making is one of the major reasons for the several protocol amendments required for each clinical trial. The high cost, cycle time delays and increased trial complexity are just a few downstream impacts of the protocol amendments. A 2008 study at the Tufts Centre for the Study of Drug Development (Tufts CSDD) estimated around 60% of all protocols are amended and the cost for a single protocol amendment is approximately $450K. Upon further investigation, it was found that 34% of these amendments were avoidable. The most common causes for the amendments included changes to the study (18.6%) and study design (18.4%). Incorporating big data analytics into the clinical study design phase can aid in high quality protocols, faster cycle times and reduced cost.

Predictive models incorporating patient, investigator and enrollment analytics will provide the clinical study teams with better insights on study feasibility and efficiency. For example, the historical data for clinical study start up and regulatory time for each country (per therapeutic area) can be combined with the epidemiological patient data, to yield predictive insights for country selection and targeting will reduce trial failure rate and therefore, protocol amendment rates.

Due to the lack of data collection and insights, currently the pharmaceutical industry follows a high cost, high risk model. Since the industry needs are evolving, we as a part of the pharmaceutical industry need to perform a cost-benefit analysis, to prioritize the clinical data analytical needs. One time investments in clinical data collection and management can yield several benefits across the organization. For example, in this case, a one-time investment in predictive analytical tools and capabilities at the study design phase will benefit the all the current and future clinical trials in an organization, with faster cycle times and reduced cost.

Healthcare Initiatives That Need Clinical Analytics

Shift From Fee-for-Service Reimbursements to Value-Based Purchasing

Up until 2010, when the Affordable Care Act established the Hospital Value-Based Purchasing Program, hospitals received payment based on the volume of care they provided (Burton, 2015). This fee-for-service reimbursement program in some cases encouraged the overuse of healthcare services without necessarily improving care outcomes.

Now, health systems are facing the greatest financial challenge in their history as they transition to value-based purchasing — a model that rewards decreased costs and improved quality. It's a challenge health systems can overcome. But to be successful, they need clinical analytics to access to their data to understand how they compare to the many clinical quality measures and the costs related to delivering care. With payments now hinging upon quality, focusing solely on old metrics won't bring financial success, particularly not in a world of accountable care organizations (ACOs), bundled payments, quality measures, and shared savings (Burton, 2015). Instead, health systems must concentrate on lowering the costs of healthcare while also providing higher value and quality.

The challenges of shifting to value-based purchasing may seem overwhelming. But by using clinical analytics to pull from the wealth of data an enterprise data warehouse (EDW) collects, it will be possible for health systems to meet these challenges (Burton, 2015). In specific, clinical analytics make it possible for health systems to do the following:

1. Reduce waste
2. Improve margins
3. Improve performance
4. Streamline operations
5. Automatically track quality measures
6. Succeed in shared savings arrangements
7. Understand the complete picture of the cost structure

Accountable Care Organizations (ACOs)

Accountable care organizations (ACOs) are another healthcare initiative that encourages groups of providers to voluntarily give high-quality, coordinated care to populations of patients (Burton, 2015). The concept of an ACO is still evolving, but typically the groups of providers include doctors, hospitals, health plans, and others.

The coordinated care an ACO offers is designed to give patients the right kind of care without adding extra expenses. ACOs are able to avoid the extra expenses by only ordering care with a proven benefit and by not ordering duplicating services — a significant shift from fee-for-service (Burton, 2015). In addition, ACOs are particularly concerned about making sure the chronically ill receive proper care.

For the providers who work in ACOs, it's critical to focus on preventative healthcare options as well as giving care to the ill or injured because of the new incentive model. With an ACO, there is now a greater financial reward to prevent illness rather than treating those who are already ill (Burton, 2015). Preventative care along with a new focus on using clinically-proven and effective therapies as opposed to choosing expensive, newly developed treatment options should dramatically improve care delivery.

To support ACO goals, health systems need to have several critical information systems: an electronic Medical Record (EMR), a health information exchange (HIE), an activity based costing system (ABC), a patient reported outcomes system (PRO), and an EDW (Burton, 2015). Over the past seven years, the U.S. healthcare industry has experienced an unprecedented $100 billion investment in the first two IT components, EMR and HIE systems. Yet, despite the considerable amount invested in these systems, health systems have yet to realize a decent return on investment (ROI) because they aren't able to measure the quality of care and financial risk for managing their patients.

To unlock the data in their ACO EMR investment, health systems need an EDW. The EDW provides the clinical analytics abilities so desperately needed because the EDW makes it possible for analysts to dig into the data in a single repository that pulls in all of the data from the various source systems (clinical, financial, patient satisfaction, etc.) (Burton, 2015). Yet, less than 25 percent of healthcare organizations have any type of EDW.

Value-Based Insurance Design (VBID)

The sweeping changes occurring in healthcare require innovative models of care from providers and payers. One of these new models is value-based insurance design (VBID).

The basis of VBID is for providers to pay increased costs for specific patient populations early on in their care to reduce the costs of care later on (Burton, 2015). Take, for example, one hospital's goal to target length of stay following an appendectomy as a key opportunity for quality and financial improvement. Their frontline team used clinical data analytics to discover their clinicians were prescribing many types of antibiotics for an appendectomy. When they drilled down into the outcomes data, however, they discovered that one specific, expensive antibiotic significantly decreased length of stay, more than making up for the difference in cost to provide the more expensive antibiotic (Burton, 2015).

When hospitals are trying to cut costs, prescribing a more expensive treatment doesn't seem logical — unless there's evidence-based data that can tell the entire story. By using clinical analytics and easy-to-understand dashboards, clinicians can use real-time data to discover treatments based on best practices and best outcomes. Then, when they have this data, both providers and payers can work together to provide cheaper, more effective, data-driven quality improvements and treatments (Burton, 2015).

CONCLUSION

Big data analytics has the potential to transform the way healthcare providers use sophisticated technologies to gain insight from their clinical and other data repositories and make informed decisions. In the future, we will see the rapid, widespread implementation and use of big data analytics across the healthcare organization and the healthcare industry. To that end, the several challenges highlighted above, must be addressed. As big data analytics becomes more mainstream, issues such as guaranteeing privacy, safeguarding security, establishing standards and governance, and continually improving the tools and technologies will garner attention. Big data analytics and applications in healthcare are at a nascent stage of development, but rapid advances in platforms and tools can accelerate their maturing process.

As the big data analytics industry evolves, life science vendors and developers will initiate the lead in creating products and services to make IoT data meaningful, relevant, and easy to consume through dashboards. Collecting and leveraging patient-generated health data from IoT devices will be key to patient population health management in a changing landscape where reimbursement and outcomes are inexorably intertwined, even as healthcare big data analytics becomes a key competency for organizations seeking a deeper understanding of their responsibilities and opportunities to provide quality patient care.

REFERENCES

Barra, M. (2013, April 27). The Clinical Development Plan. *Pharmupdates*. Retrieved September 24, 2016, from https://pharmupdates.wordpress.com/2013/04/27/the-clinical-development-plan/

Borkar, V. R., Carey, M. J., & Li, C. (2012). *Big data platforms: what's next?* XRDS: Crossroads. *The ACM Magazine for Students, 19*(1), 44–49. doi:10.1145/2331042.2331057

Burton, D. (2015, December). How Clinical Analytics Will Improve the Cost and Quality of Healthcare Delivery. *Health Catalyst Insights*.

Delasko, J. M. (2007, March). U.S. Department of Health and Human Services Food and Drug Administration *(US, Food and Drug Administration, Center for Drug Evaluation and Research (CDER))*. Retrieved from http://www.fda.gov/downloads/drugs/guidancecomplianceregulatoryinformation/guidances/ucm080593.pdf

DiMasi, J. (2014). Clinical Approval Rate. In *Innovation in the Pharmaceutical Industry: New Estimates of R&D Costs*. Tufts. Retrieved September 10, 2016, from http://csdd.tufts.edu/files/uploads/Tufts_CSDD_briefing_on_RD_cost_study_-_Nov_18,_2014.pdf

Getz, K. (2014). Improving Protocol Design Feasibility to Drive Drug Development Economics and Performance. *International Journal of Environmental Research and Public Health IJERPH*, *11*(5), 5069–5080. doi:10.3390/ijerph110505069 PMID:24823665

Getz, K. A., Wenger, J., Campo, R. A., Seguine, E. S., & Kaitin, K. I. (2008). Assessing the Impact of Protocol Design Changes on Clinical Trial Performance. *American Journal of Therapeutics*, *15*(5), 450–457. doi:10.1097/MJT.0b013e31816b9027 PMID:18806521

Lodha, A. (2016). Globalization of Clinical Trials: Ethics and Conduct. *J. Biotechnol. Biomater.*, *6*(2), 229. doi:10.4172/2155-952X.1000229

Lodha A (2016). Clinical Analytics – Transforming Clinical Development through Big Data. *Imperial Journal of Interdisciplinary Research*, *2*(10).

Lodha, A. (2016). Analytics: An Intelligent Approach in Clinical Trail Management. *J. Clin. Trials*, *6*(05), e124. doi:10.4172/2167-0870.1000e124

Lodha, A. (2016). Big data analytics – Clinical integration and visualization.

Ohlhorst, F. J. (2012). *Big data analytics: turning big data into big money*. John Wiley & Sons. doi:10.1002/9781119205005

Peters, S. (2013, January 15). *Tufts Center for the Study of Drug Development*. Retrieved September 24, 2016, from http://csdd.tufts.edu/news/complete_story/pr_ir_jan-feb_2013/

Raghupathi, W., & Raghupathi, V. (2014, February 7). Big data analytics in healthcare: Promise and potential. *Health Inf. Sci. Syst. Health Information Science and Systems*, *2*(1). doi:10.1186/2047-2501-2-3 PMID:25825667

Rahman, S., Majumder, M. A., Shaban, S. F., Rahman, N., Ahmed, M., Abdulrahman, K. B., & D'Souza, U. J. (2011). Physician participation in clinical research and trials: Issues and approaches. *AMEP Advances in Medical Education and Practice*, 85. doi:10.2147/amep.s14103

Redfearn, S. (2011, April 25). New data show number of principal investigators dropping 11% globally, and 20% in U.S. *CenterWatch News Online*. Retrieved September 24, 2016, from http://www.centerwatch.com/news-online/2011/04/25/new-data-show-number-of-principal-investigators-dropping-11-globally-and-20-in-us/#sthash.oLg4K7z5.dpbs

Sullivan, J. (2004, April 1). *Subject Recruitment and Retention: Barriers to Success*. Retrieved September 24, 2016, from http://www.appliedclinicaltrialsonline.com/subject-recruitment-and-retention-barriers-success

Swann, J. (2013, January 18). Summary of NDA Approvals & Receipts, 1938 to the present. Retrieved September 24, 2016, fromhttp://www.fda.gov/aboutfda/whatwedo/history/productregulation/summaryofndaapprovalsreceipts1938tothepresent/default.htm

Tibco. (2011). *Spotfire Analytics – Transforming Clinical Development*. Retrieved from http://spotfire. tibco.com/assets/blt9ebddf0e420042ec/spotfire-clinical-development.pdf

Tufts University. (2008, January/February). Growing protocol design complexity stresses investigators, volunteers (Rep. No. Volume 10 Number 1). Retrieved September 15, 2016, from http://csdd.tufts.edu/ files/uploads/jan-feb_impact_report_summary.pdf

Viceconti, M., Henney, A., & Morley-Fletcher, E. (2016, January). In silico clinical trials: How computer simulation will transform the biomedical industry. *International Journal of Clinical Trials*. doi:10.18203/2349-3259.ijct20161408

Zikopoulos, P., Parasuraman, K., Deutsch, T., Giles, J., & Corrigan, D. (2012). *Harness the power of big data The IBM big data platform*. McGraw Hill Professional.

KEY TERMS AND DEFINITIONS

Clinical Development Plan (CDP): A CDP is defined as a complex document that entails the entire clinical research strategy of a drug, describing the clinical studies that will be carried out for a pharmaceutical entity, created by a pharmaceutical company. It is a strategic planning document and helps in identifying the vision and implementation of the clinical studies. It contains the scientific and commercial rationale as well as the detailed description of the clinical trials that need to be conducted to generate information required to support the label claims.

Clinical Endpoint: An endpoint is the goal or outcome of a clinical study; it is defined at the beginning of the trial and measures the clinical tolerability and efficacy. There are different types of endpoint, amongst which the primary endpoint is the most important. The primary endpoint usually estimates the efficacy of the investigational drug or treatment. A trial can consist of one or more secondary endpoints.

Clinical Study Design: The investigative method used to conduct the clinical study. The study design is based on different parameters like the patient population, methodology, treatments to be investigated and endpoints. Clinical study design can be categorized as a scientific experiment, with different methods of conducting the clinical trials. The most common methodologies include controlled (the investigational drug is compared against a control), randomized (random allocation of cohorts to receive one or the other drug treatment) and non-randomized (using specific categories to allocate each kind of treatment to a specific cohort).

Clinical Trial Protocol: The protocol is a document containing the details of the conduct of a clinical trial including: trial objectives, study design, methodology and statistical concepts. A protocol should is required to be submitted for each clinical trial or study.

Computerized Physician Order Entry (CPOE): It's the process of a medical professional entering medication orders or other physician instructions electronically instead of on paper charts. A primary benefit of CPOE is that it can help reduce errors related to poor handwriting or transcription of medication orders.

Electronic Health Record (EHR): It's an is an electronic version of a patient's medical history, that is maintained by the provider over time, and may include all of the key administrative clinical data relevant to that persons care under a particular provider, including demographics, progress notes, problems, medications, vital signs, past medical history, immunizations, laboratory data and radiology reports.

Electronic Medical Record (EMR): It is a digital version of a paper chart that contains all of a patient's medical history from one practice.

Human Genome: The human genome is the complete set of nucleic acid sequence for humans (Homo sapiens), encoded as DNA within the 23 chromosome pairs in cell nuclei and in a small DNA molecule found within individual mitochondria.

Investigator Site Burden: Operational burden on the investigator site personnel to conduct the clinical trial. The investigator site personnel are responsible for the conduct of a clinical trial as per the clinical protocol and Good Clinical Practice (GCP).

New Molecular Entities: A new molecular entity (NME) is a drug that contains an active moiety that has never been approved by the FDA or marketed in the US.

Online Analytical Processing (OLAP): It performs multidimensional analysis of business data and provides the capability for complex calculations, trend analysis, and sophisticated data modeling.

Chapter 17
Big Data and Internet of Things for Analysing and Designing Systems Based on Hyperspectral Images

Peyakunta Bhargavi
Sri Padmavati Mahila Visvavidyalayam, India

Singaraju Jyothi
Sri Padmavati Mahila Visvavidyalayam, India

ABSTRACT

The recent development of sensors remote sensing is an important source of information for mapping and natural and man-made land covers. The increasing amounts of available hyperspectral data originates from AVIRIS, HyMap, and Hyperion for a wide range of applications in the data volume, velocity, and variety of data contributed to the term big data. Sensing is enabled by Wireless Sensor Network (WSN) technologies to infer and understand environmental indicators, from delicate ecologies and natural resources to urban environments. The communication network creates the Internet of Things (IoT) where sensors and actuators blend with the environment around us, and the information is shared across platforms in order to develop a common operating picture (COP). With RFID tags, embedded sensor and actuator nodes, the next revolutionary technology developed transforming the Internet into a fully integrated Future Internet. This chapter describes the use of Big Data and Internet of the Things for analyzing and designing various systems based on hyperspectral images.

INTRODUCTION

The advances in remote sensor and computer technology are substituting the traditional sources and collection methods of data, by revolutionizing the way remotely sensed data are acquired, managed, and analyzed. The term remote sensing (Nelson, 2012) refers to the science of measuring, analyzing, and interpreting information about a scene acquired by sensors mounted on board the different platforms for

DOI: 10.4018/978-1-5225-2947-7.ch017

Copyright © 2018, IGI Global. Copying or distributing in print or electronic forms without written permission of IGI Global is prohibited.

Earth and planetary observation. Remote sensing instruments measure electromagnetic radiation energy at different wavelengths reflected or emitted by the Earth and its environment (Van Zyll, 2006), which can be influenced by the radiation source, interaction of the energy with surface materials, and the passage of the energy through the atmosphere. The interactions of the energy with surface materials can change the direction, intensity, wavelength content, and polarization of electromagnetic radiation. The nature of these changes is dependent on the chemical make-up and physical structure of the material, exposed to the electromagnetic radiation, and can be used to provide major clues to the characteristics of the investigated objects.

The deployment of latest-generation sensor instruments on board both terrestrial and planetary platforms provides a nearly continual stream of high-dimensional and high-resolution data. More recently, such increases in the data volume, velocity, and variety of data contributed to the term big data that stand for challenges shared with many other scientific disciplines. The importance of incorporating remote sensing into Internet of Things practice has long been recognized by the in real time applications. Recently, Internet technology is integrating more remote sensing techniques into their standard methodologies for managing global world. Furthermore, the integration of geospatial tools and techniques in Internet of Things is a growing research agenda.

HYPERSPECTRAL IMAGES

Recent advances in remote sensing and geographic information has led the way for the development of hyperspectral sensors. Hyperspectral remote sensing, also known as imaging spectroscopy, is a relatively new technology that is currently being investigated by researchers and scientists with regard to the detection and identification of minerals, terrestrial vegetation, and man-made materials and backgrounds.

Hyperspectral imaging is a combination of spectroscopy (visible light dispersed according to its wavelength by a prism) and visible imaging. Instead of just taking a picture and getting a color image, you obtain a spectral measurement for each pixel in the image in the scene. Hyperspectral imaging is used to find objects, identify material and detect processes. Imaging spectroscopy has been used in the laboratory by physicists and chemists for over 100 years for identification of materials and their composition. Spectroscopy can be used to detect individual absorption features due to specific chemical bonds in a solid, liquid, or gas. Recently, with advancing technology, imaging spectroscopy has begun to focus on the Earth. The concept of hyperspectral remote sensing began in the mid-80's and to this point has been used most widely by geologists for the mapping of minerals. Actual detection of materials is dependent on the spectral coverage, spectral resolution, and signal-to-noise of the spectrometer, the abundance of the material and the strength of absorption features for that material in the wavelength region measured.

Hyperspectral remote sensing combines imaging and spectroscopy in a single system which often includes large data sets and requires new processing methods. Hyperspectral data sets are generally composed of about 100 to 200 spectral bands of relatively narrow bandwidths (5-10 nm), whereas, multispectral data sets are usually composed of about 5 to 10 bands of relatively large bandwidths (70-400 nm). Hyperspectral imagery is typically collected (and represented) as a data cube with spatial information collected in the X-Y plane, and spectral information represented in the Z-direction. Different applications of hyperspectral images are shown in Figure 1. For finding real time solutions, developing sensors and other hyperspectral based analysis, remote sensing process is required. Figure 2, Figure 3, and Figure 4 explain the steps of hyperspectral image preprocessing to acquire digital data (Udelhoven, 2013).

Figure 1. Hyperspectral remote sensing

Figure 2. Acquisition of hyperspectral images

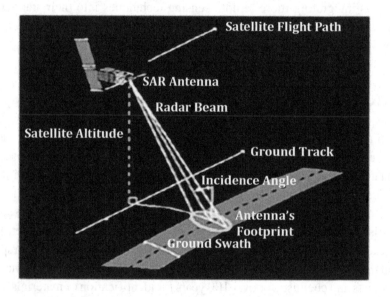

BIG DATA

There is no clear definition for Big Data. It is defined based on some of its characteristics. The big data does not mean the size (Georgakopoulos, 2012). There are three characteristics that can be used to define big data, as also known as 3V's: volume, variety, and velocity (Zikopoulos, 2012). Volume relates to size of the data such as terabytes (TB), petabytes (PB), zettabytes (ZB), etc. Variety means the types of data. In addition, difference sources will produce big data such as sensors, devices, social networks, the web, mobile phones, etc. Velocity means how frequently the data is generated (e.g. every millisecond, second, minute, hour, day, week, month, year).

Big data analytics has found application in several domains and fields. Some of these applications include medical research, solutions for the transportation and logistics sector, global security and prediction and management of issues concerning the socio-economic and environmental sector, to name a few. Apart from standard applications in business and commerce and society administration, scientific

Figure 3. Hyperspectral remote sensing process

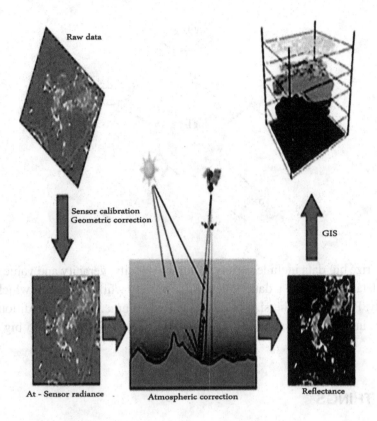

Figure 4. Hyperspectral remote sensing process

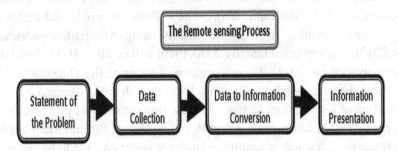

research is one of the most critical applications of big data in the real world (Zhang, 2014). One of the main future applications of big data analytics and cloud computing lies in life sciences (Sleator,2013). Some of the identified high-impact areas include systems biology, structure and protein function prediction, personalized medicine and metagenomics. Besides this, one of the most relevant applications of big data analytics is to improve the existing business models for efficiency and customer satisfaction. Big data, by definition, is a term used to describe a variety of data - structured, semi structured and unstructured, which makes it a complex data infrastructure (Pradeepini,2015). The complexity of this infrastructure requires powerful management and technological solutions. One of the commonly used models for explaining big data is the multi-V model. Figure 5 illustrates the multi-V model. Some of the

Figure 5. The five V's associated with Big Data

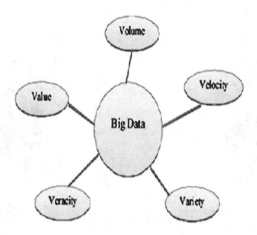

Vs used to characterize big data include variety, volume, velocity, veracity and value (Netto,2015). The different types of data available on a dataset determine variety while the rate at which data is produced determines velocity. Predictably, the size of data is called volume. The two additional characteristics, veracity and value, indicate data reliability and they are worth with respect to big data exploitation, respectively.

INTERNET OF THINGS

The Internet of Things (IoT) is a network of networks, in which, typically, a massive number of objects/things/sensors/devices are connected through the information and communications infrastructure to provide value-added services (Morabito, 2010). The IoT allows people and things to be connected Anytime, Anyplace, with Anything and Anyone, ideally using Any path/network and Any service (Georgakopoulos, 2013). It is predicted that, by 2020, there will be 50 to 100 billion devices connected to the Internet (Georgakopoulos, 2013). These devices will generate Big Data (Georgakopoulos, 2012) that needs to be analysed for knowledge extraction. Even though data collected by individual devices may not provide sufficient information, aggregated data from number of physical devices and virtual sensors(Georgakopoulos,2013) can provide a wealth of knowledge for important application areas including disaster management, customer sentiment analysis, smart cities, and bio-surveillance. Internet of Things has been identified as one of the emerging technologies in IT as noted in Gartner's IT Hype Cycle shown in Figure 6 (Spotless Data, n. d.).

A Hype Cycle is a way to represent the emergence, adoption, maturity, and impact on applications of specific technologies. The popularity of different paradigms varies with time. The web search popularity, as measured by the Google search trends during the last 10 years for the terms Internet of Things, Wireless Sensor Networks and Ubiquitous Computing are shown in Figure 7 (Krishna and Kranthi, 2015). As it can be seen, since IoT has come into existence, search volume is consistently increasing with the falling trend for Wireless Sensor Networks. As per Google's search forecast the dotted line in Figure 7, this trend is likely to continue as other enabling technologies converge to form a genuine Internet of Things.

Figure 6. Gartner hype cycle

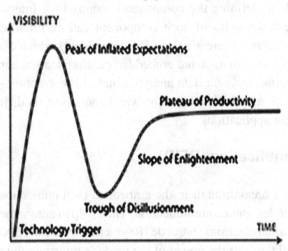

Figure 7. Google search trends since 2004 for terms "Internet of Things, wireless sensor networks and Ubiquitous Computing"

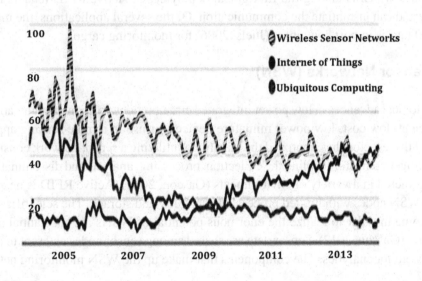

The collection and analysis of data in the IoT applications has many objectives. For example, in case of customer sentiment analysis, such data can be used for improving personalized recommendations hence leading to better customer experiences. On other hand in case of smart cities, governments and city councils can use the knowledge extracted to make strategic decisions for example, placement of traffic lights, construction of new roads/bridges, etc. and future city plans (Georgakopoulos, 2014), (Gascon, 2012). However, the data collected by smart IoT devices may contain very sensitive personal data based on type of application and data sources. Therefore, such data must be managed carefully to avoid any user privacy violations. Consequently, in the subsequent text, we briefly discuss the importance on addressing IoT privacy challenges (Mayer, 2009). Users are the people or the consumers who are using the product or the service.

The taxonomy that aids in defining the components required for Internet of Things from a high-level perspective. Specific taxonomies of each component can be found elsewhere (Brandic, 2009; Heinzelman, 2002; Moller, 2004). There are three IoT components which enable seamless ubicomp: a) Hardware - made up of sensors, actuators and embedded communication hardware b) Middleware - on demand storage and computing tools for data analytics and c) Presentation - novel easy to understand visualization and interpretation tools which can be widely accessed on different platforms and which can be designed for different applications.

Radio Frequency Identification (RFID)

RFID technology is a major breakthrough in the embedded communication paradigm which enables design of microchips for wireless data communication. They help in automatic identification of anything they are attached to acting as an electronic barcode (Raymer, 2009; Juels, 2006). The passive RFID tags are not battery powered and they use the power of the reader's interrogation signal to communicate the ID to the RFID reader. This has resulted in many applications particularly in retail and supply chain management. The applications can be found in transportation (replacement of tickets, registration stickers) and access control applications as well. The passive tags are currently being used in many bank cards and road toll tags which is among the first global deployments. Active RFID readers have their own battery supply and can instantiate the communication. Of the several applications, the main application of active RFID tags is in port containers (Juels, 2006) for monitoring cargo.

Wireless Sensor Networks (WSN)

Recent technological advances in low power integrated circuits and wireless communications have made available efficient, low cost, low power miniature devices for use in remote sensing applications. The combination of these factors has improved the viability of utilizing a sensor network consisting of a large number of intelligent sensors, enabling the collection, processing, analysis and dissemination of valuable information, gathered in a variety of environments (Gascon, 2012). Active RFID is nearly the same as the lower end WSN nodes with limited processing capability and storage. The scientific challenges that must be overcome in order to realize the enormous potential of WSNs are substantial and multidisciplinary in nature (Gascon, 2012). Sensor data are shared among sensor nodes and sent to a distributed or centralized system for analytics. The components that make up the WSN monitoring network include:

- **WSN Hardware:** Typically, a node (WSN core hardware) contains sensor interfaces, processing units, transceiver units and power supply. Almost always, they comprise of multiple A/D converters for sensor interfacing and more modern sensor nodes have the ability to communicate using one frequency band making them more versatile (Gascon, 2012).
- **WSN Communication Stack:** The nodes are expected to be deployed in an adhoc manner for most applications. Designing an appropriate topology, routing and MAC layer is critical for scalability and longevity of the deployed network. Nodes in a WSN need to communicate among themselves to transmit data in single or multi-hop to a base station. Node drop outs, and conse-

quent degraded network lifetimes, are frequent. The communication stack at the sink node should be able to interact with the outside world through the Internet to act as a gateway to the WSN subnet and the Internet (Ghosh, 2008).

- **WSN Middleware:** A mechanism to combine cyber infrastructure with a Service Oriented Architecture (SOA) and sensor networks to provide access to heterogeneous sensor resources in a deployment independent manner (Ghosh, 2008). This is based on the idea of isolating resources that can be used by several applications. A platform independent middleware for developing sensor applications is required, such as an Open Sensor Web Architecture (OSWA) (Xiong, 2006). OSWA is built upon a uniform set of operations and standard data representations as defined in the Sensor Web Enablement Method (SWE) by the Open Geospatial Consortium (OGC).
- **Secure Data Aggregation:** An efficient and secure data aggregation method is required for extending the lifetime of the network as well as ensuring reliable data collected from sensors (Bassi, 2010). As node failures are a common characteristic of WSNs, the network topology should have the capability to heal itself. Ensuring security is critical as the system is automatically linked to actuators and protecting the systems from intruders becomes very important.

Addressing Schemes

The ability to uniquely identify 'Things' is critical for the success of IoT. This will not only allow us to uniquely identify billions of devices but also to control remote devices through the Internet. The few most critical features of creating a unique address are: uniqueness, reliability, persistence and scalability. Every element that is already connected and those that are going to be connected, must be identified by their unique identification, location and functionalities. The current IPv4 may support to an extent where a group of cohabiting sensor devices can be identified geographically, but not individually. The Internet Mobility attributes in the IPV6 may alleviate some of the device identification problems; however, the heterogeneous nature of wireless nodes, variable data types, concurrent operations and confluence of data from devices exacerbates the problem further (Bassi, 2010).

Persistent network functioning to channel the data traffic ubiquitously and relentlessly is another aspect of IoT. Although, the TCP/IP takes care of this mechanism by routing in a more reliable and efficient way, from source to destination, the IoT faces a bottleneck at the interface between the gateway and wireless sensor devices. Furthermore, the scalability of the device address of the existing network must be sustainable. The addition of networks and devices must not hamper the performance of the network, the functioning of the devices, the reliability of the data over the network or the effective use of the devices from the user interface.

To address these issues, the Uniform Resource Name (URN) system is considered fundamental for the development of IoT. URN creates replicas of the resources that can be accessed through the URL. With large amounts of spatial data being gathered, it is often quite important to take advantage of the benefits of metadata for transferring the information from a database to the user via the Internet (Grossmann,2005). IPv6 also gives a very good option to access the resources uniquely and remotely. Another critical development in addressing is the development of a light-weight IPv6 that will enable addressing home appliances uniquely.

Wireless sensor networks (considering them as building blocks of IoT), which run on a different stack compared to the Internet, cannot possess IPv6 stack to address individually and hence a subnet with a gateway having a URN will be required. With this in mind, we then need a layer for addressing sensor devices by the relevant gateway. At the subnet level, the URN for the sensor devices could be the unique IDs rather than human-friendly names as in the www, and a lookup table at the gateway to address this device. Further, at the node level each sensor will have a URN (as numbers) for sensors to be addressed by the gateway. The entire network now forms a web of connectivity from users (high-level) to sensors (low-level) that is addressable (through URN), accessible (through URL) and controllable (through URC).

Data Storage and Analytics

One of the most important outcomes of this emerging field is the creation of an unprecedented amount of data. Storage, ownership and expiry of the data become critical issues. The internet consumes up to 5% of the total energy generated today and with these types of demands, it is sure to go up even further. Hence, data centers that run on harvested energy and are centralized will ensure energy efficiency as well as reliability. The data have to be stored and used intelligently for smart monitoring and actuation. It is important to develop artificial intelligence algorithms which could be centralized or distributed based on the need. Novel fusion algorithms need to be developed to make sense of the data collected. State-of-the-art non-linear, temporal machine learning methods based on evolutionary algorithms, genetic algorithms, neural networks, and other artificial intelligence techniques are necessary to achieve automated decision making. These systems show characteristics such as interoperability, integration and adaptive communications. They also have a modular architecture both in terms of hardware system design as well as software development and are usually very well-suited for IoT applications. More importantly, a centralised infrastructure to support storage and analytics is required. This forms the IoT middleware layer and there are numerous challenges involved which are discussed in future sections. As of 2012, Cloud based storage solutions are becoming increasingly popular and in the years ahead, Cloud based analytics and visualization platforms are foreseen.

Visualization

Visualization is critical for an IoT application as this allows interaction of the user with the environment. With recent advances in touch screen technologies, use of smart tablets and phones has become very intuitive. For a lay person to fully benefit from the IoT revolution, attractive and easy to understand visualization has to be created. As we move from 2D to 3D screens, more information can be provided in meaningful ways for consumers. This will also enable policy makers to convert data into knowledge, which is critical in fast decision making. Extraction of meaningful information from raw data is non-trivial. This encompasses both event detection and visualization of the associated raw and modelled data, with information represented according to the needs of the end-user.

BIG DATA FOR HYPERSPECTRAL IMAGES

Remote sensing is generally defined as the technology of measuring the characteristics of an object or surface from a distance" (Bird, 1991) Big Earth observing data can be defined in terms of – volumes, – degree of diversity and complexity including streaming of data from presently available and upcoming satellite capabilities, and – innovative ground devices -the unpredictable value added derivable from their innovative analyses and fusion (ESA, 2013). NASA's Earth Science Program comprises a series of satellites, a science component and a data system called the Earth Observing System Data and Information System (EOSDIS). The archive currently (2012) exceeds 7.5 petabytes. Figure 8 depicts the earth observation system.

New solutions and practices of big remote sensing data services are:

- Identifying a common ground with respect to regional and global applications and the integration of different data sources.
- Data organisation and provision, and associated costs.
- Development of data intensive and innovative services, with respect to (mass) data processing, integration of additional information from navigation data streams, analytics and correlation of large remote sensing data sets, and integration across heterogeneous resources.
- Identification of challenges, barriers, opportunities for such services, and attempt to define a baseline of activity to make the identified scenarios actionable.
- Physical data aggregation or web processing services approaches; large data holdings associated to commercial hosting, private or public Clouds.

Figure 8. Earth observing system

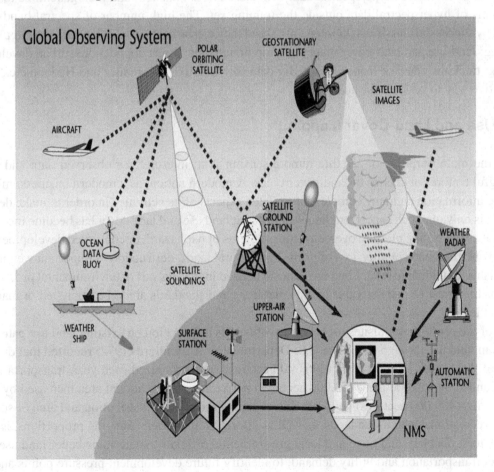

Remote sensing is the practice of deriving information about the earth's land and water surfaces using images acquired from an overhead perspective, using electromagnetic radiation in one or more regions of the electromagnetic spectrum, reflected or emitted from the earth's surface. There are numerous ways of defining remote sensing. Most descriptions have several things in common; remote sensing utilizes the electromagnetic spectrum, it is a process of acquiring information without being in direct contact with the object, and it involves reflected or emitted energy. Remote sensing is highly versatile and can be used in many applications of Big Data. Potential uses for remote sensing in various applications of Big Data include planning, environmental impact assessment, hazard and disaster response, infrastructure management, traffic assessment, and homeland security. The challenges of big data in remote sensing involve not only dealing with high volumes of data. In particular, challenges on data acquisition, storage, management, and analysis are also related to remote sensing problems involving big data.

The needs of a specific remote sensing application that raises the demand for technologies those are scalable with respect to big data. In hyperspectral remote sensing, images are acquired with hundreds of channels over contiguous wavelength bands, providing measurements that we consider as concrete big data. The reasoning includes not only large data volume but also a large number of dimensions. Supervised classification is the essential technique used for extracting quantitative information from remotely sensed data such as the aforementioned hyperspectral images. It consists of learning from a training set of examples (hyperspectral data with class labels attached) and then generalize to find the class labels of hyperspectral data outside the training set. The high number of spectral bands can be handled by successful classifiers (Gascon, 2012) and they can be useful for a wide variety of applications including: land-use and land-cover mapping, crop monitoring, forest applications, urban development, mapping, tracking, and risk management. Big data software like Mapreduce and Hadoop etc., provide an effective way to perform the analysis.

Land-Use and Land-Cover Mapping

One of the main purposes of satellite remote sensing is to interpret the observed data and classify meaningful features or classes of land-cover types. A modern nation, as a modern business, must have adequate information on many complex interrelated aspects of its activities in order to make decisions. Land use is only one such aspect, but knowledge about land use and land cover has become increasingly important as the Nation plans to overcome the problems of haphazard, uncontrolled development, deteriorating environmental quality, loss of prime agricultural lands, destruction of important wetlands, and loss of fish and wildlife habitat. Land use data are needed in the analysis of environmental processes and problems that must be understood if living conditions and standards are to be improved or maintained at current levels.

One of the prime prerequisites for better use of land is information on existing land use patterns and changes in land use through time. The U.S. Department of Agriculture (1972) reported that during the decade of the 1960's 730,000 acres (296,000 hectares) were urbanized each year, transportation land uses expanded by 130,000 acres (53,000 hectares) per year, and recreational area increased by about 1 million acres (409,000 hectares) per year. Knowledge of the present distribution and area of such agricultural, recreational, and urban lands, as well as information on their changing proportions, is needed by legislators, planners, and State and local governmental officials to determine better land use policy, to project transportation and utility demand, to identify future development pressure points and areas, and to implement effective plans for regional development. As Clawson and Stewart (1965) have stated:

In this dynamic situation, accurate, meaningful, current data on land use are essential. If public agencies and private organizations are to know what is happening, and are to make sound plans for their own future action, then reliable information is critical. The variety of land use and land cover data needs is exceedingly broad. Current land use and land cover data are needed for equalization of tax assessments in many States. Land use and land cover data also are needed by Federal, State, and local agencies for water- resource inventory, flood control, water-supply planning, and waste-water treatment (figure 9). Many Federal agencies need current comprehensive inventories of existing activities on public lands

Figure 9. Land use and land cover
Anderson & Witmer, 1976.

EXPLANATION

11	Residential
12	Commercial and services
13	Industrial
14	Transportation, communications, and utilities
15	Industrial and commercial complexes
16	Mixed urban or built-up land
17	Other urban or built-up land
21	Cropland and pasture
22	Orchards, groves, vineyards, nurseries, and ornamental horticultural areas
23	Confined feeding operations
41	Deciduous forest land
51	Streams and canals
53	Reservoirs
75	Strip mines, quarries, and gravel pits
76	Transitional areas

combined with the existing and changing uses of adjacent private lands to improve the management of public lands. Federal agencies also need land use data to assess the environmental impact resulting from the development of energy resources, to manage wildlife resources and minimize man-wildlife ecosystem conflicts, to make national summaries of land use patterns and changes for national policy formulation, and to prepare environmental impact statements and assess future impacts on environmental quality.

Soil Moisture

Big Data techniques can be used for hyperspectral images to predict the soil variations that affect the evolution of weather and climate over continental regions. Initialization of numerical weather prediction and seasonal climate models with accurate soil moisture information enhances their prediction skills and extends their skillful lead times. Information about saturated soils and inundated wetlands can improve estimates of terrestrial methane ($CH4$) emission, which is the 3rd most important greenhouse gas after water vapor and carbon dioxide. Information about freeze and thaw is used to determine the distribution of frozen ground to improve the assessment of land surface conditions in global forecasting systems. Improved seasonal climate predictions will benefit climate-sensitive socioeconomic activities, including water management, agriculture, fire, flood, and drought hazards monitoring. The prediction of soil moisture strongly affects plant growth and hence agricultural productivity, especially during conditions of water shortage and drought. Global estimates of soil moisture and plant water stress must be derived from models. These model predictions can be greatly enhanced through assimilation of space-based soil moisture observations. Improvements in the ability to monitor and forecast agricultural drought will improve famine early warning in the most food-insecure countries in the world. Soil moisture information can be used to predict wildfires, determine prescribed burning conditions, and estimate smoldering combustion potential of organic soils. Improvements in wildfire information with soil moisture products can provide more useful and accurate data on toxic air-quality events and smoke white-outs that increases transportation safety and can inform prescribed fire activities.

Soil prediction is a key variable in water-related natural hazards including floods and landslides. High-resolution observations of soil moisture and landscape freeze/thaw status will lead to improved flood forecasts, especially for intermediate to large watersheds where most flood damage occurs (Figure 10). Surface soil prediction state is also a key to the partitioning of precipitation into infiltration and runoff, and thus is one of the major pieces of information which drives flood prediction modeling. Similarly, soil prediction in mountainous areas is one of the most important determinants of landslides. In cold land regions, the timing of thawing which can be derived from satellite radar measurements is coincident with the onset of seasonal snowmelt, soil thaw, and ice breakup on large rivers and lakes. Hydrologic forecast systems initialized with mapped high-resolution soil moisture and freeze/thaw fields will therefore open up new capabilities in operational flood forecasting and flash flood analysis. In turn, this will improve the response of government agencies and emergency managers to a full range of emergencies and disasters, and potentially provide insurance brokers with an up-to-date indicator of the likelihood of flooding, landslides, droughts, and wildfires in risk models related to business decisions.

Crop Management

Hyperspectral images will enable significant improvements in operational crop productivity and water stress information systems by providing realistic soil moisture and freeze/thaw observations as inputs for

Figure 10. Flow diagram of a Level 4 soil moisture OSSE
Reichle, Crow, Koster, 2008a.

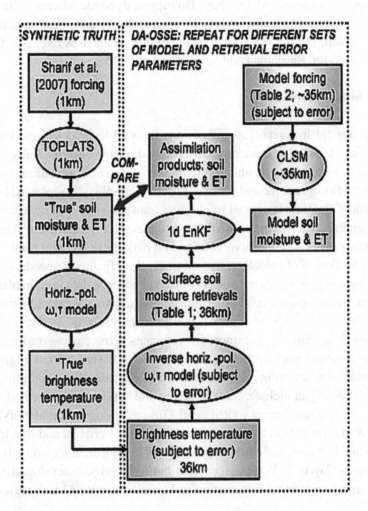

agricultural prediction models. Improved models will provide crucial information for decision-makers managing water and other resources, especially in data-sparse regions. Even without simulation models, farmers can also use soil moisture and freeze/thaw information directly as a proxy for field readiness (i.e., determining when the soil is dry enough for driving heavy machinery). At the global scale, a better grasp of the impact of agricultural drought on crop yield provides better crop supply and demand information for use by producers, commodity markets, traders, and policy makers. Forecasts of the impact of climate fluctuations on crop yields with on-going measurements of soil moisture and freeze-thaw will also improve management of agriculturally-important pests and disease in developing countries.

Crops management using remote sensing and meteorological data requires the storage of huge amount of diverse data each day, and in some cases many times in one day, this fast growth of data size requires horizontal scaling, which is the ability to extend the database over additional servers. Besides, managing rapidly changing data needs greater flexibility in schema definition which is not available in classical databases. Thus, the traditional database management systems have shown their limitations. Several alternatives have been developed in order to meet the needs of the fast-growing data, these products are grouped within the NoSql family. Each product fits a particular area and support horizontal scaling thanks to automatic replication and auto-sharding. They also support dynamic schemas allowing for transparent real-time application changes. The main databases belong to the relational database management system (RDBMS) such as: MySql, PostgreSQL. There are also other databases like: Big Table, Hyper Table, MongoDB, Hbase, Casandra, Rasdaman and so on (Michel, 2015).

Transportation Management

The big data techniques for hyperspectral images can be used to help address the country's critical transportation problems. Generally, these projects involve drainage design, roadway design, mitigation plans, environmental evaluations, and public presentations. Specific applications include using

Transportation is the flow of people and goods between geographically separated locations. Therefore, efficient management of the flow is critical to efficient transportation. Public agencies responsible for providing and maintaining the transportation infrastructure expend significant resources to estimate traffic flow patterns under prevailing conditions and forecast patterns that would result from operational or policy alternatives. Monitoring of vehicle traffic volumes, classifications, speeds, and truck weights are obtained across the state highway network and processed to produce data used in planning and forecasting, pavement design, traffic studies, level of service determination, gas tax redistribution, and accident analysis. However, states find it expensive and difficult to achieve the desired regional coverage. Better quality and more flow data would lead to improved estimates in forecasting traffic flows. Airborne and satellite platforms offer the potential to obtain wide spatial coverage not offered by ground-based sensors and provide a potential for monitoring regional spatial transportation flow conditions.

The objectives of this project include: "Development and application of methodologies demonstrating the use of Remote Sensing Imagery (RSI) and GIS technologies for identifying, characterizing and mapping selected transportation features;" "Development of criteria and metrics for evaluation of benefits over traditional methods, including improvements in information quality, from satellite remote sensing-derived database layers;" "Wide-spread distribution of project-developed data, methods, tools and educational materials supporting information and training needs of local, regional and state transportation planners."

Hyperspectral imagery utilizes large numbers of narrow contiguous spectral bands to gather detailed spectral information, often regarding chemical and mineral properties. Hyper spectroscopic data can provide huge amount of information regarding the properties of asphalt surfaces. Big data analytics offer unique solutions to evaluate road characteristics using hyperspectral data. Figure 11 shows transportation solutions using hyperspectra big data analytics.

INTERNET OF THINGS FOR HYPERSPECTRAL IMAGING

Remote sensing technologies allow farmers and other stakeholders to make management decisions based on datasets at the landscape level, taking into account soil types, water table depth, land coverage, resource use, ecosystems data, pests and diseases and weather. These data can come from sensors positioned across the landscape or from satellites, but there is increasing scope to use Unmanned Aerial Vehicles (UAVs) or drones to monitor local land use in real time and to ground truth satellite information (figure 12). The field of sensors is booming, with the advent of wireless or Bluetooth charging capability,

Figure 11. Transportation solutions using hyperspectra big data analytics

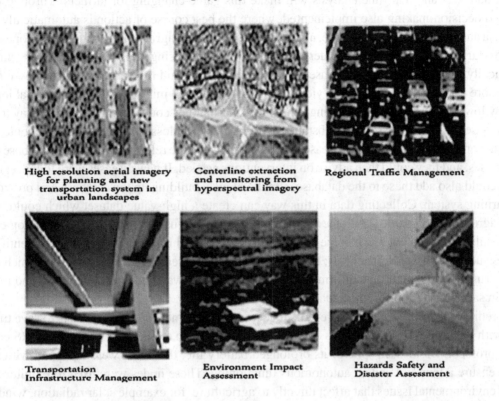

Figure 12. Connections options chart

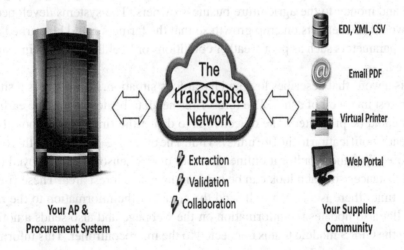

meaning they can be powered remotely. Sensors are an integral part of a new approach called the 'internet of things', where data from different internet connected devices is processed in real time through cloud computing, to determine the best course of action in response to changing conditions. Recommendations could be sent to a farmer's smartphone or tablet through a notification, and this could be as simple as recommending that the farmer irrigates immediately. A straightforward user interface as a front end to complex data sets and real-time analysis will make this game-changing for farmers. Through IoT the automated decision-making also implemented, where the best course of action is automatically implemented via an internet connected device, using the latest precision agriculture technologies; for example, a small on-farm robot, that is able to understand its surroundings using imaging and satellite technology, automatically zapping a weed with a laser. By applying spatial and timely inputs farmers will be able to farm more economically, enhancing yields, reducing waste and minimizing environmental impacts.

A new low cost hyperspectral imaging sensor for smartphones could provide a simple way to detect the early onset of crop diseases and substantially minimize crop losses. The technology would enable extension workers to scan plants for disease signals which would be referenced against a database of possible diseases, and they could then advise on interventions needed. If new diseases were found, extension workers could also add these to the database, simultaneously building up the database and providing an early warning system. Collecting data in this way can create a high-value dataset which could be marketed to agronomy companies, with the revenue generated being used to make these technologies more widely available to those in low income countries. Hyperspectral imaging is also used to identify plant disorders such as nutrient deficiencies; to detect insect disease vectors such as white fly which carries mosaic virus; to obtain real time information on below-ground water and nutrient flows; and to detect sea lice in salmon and trout for the aquaculture industry.

IoT predicts the measurements and events that could help farmers and agronomists to save time and money with its farms. Here the devices communicated directly to the Senseye cloud by GPRS communication protocol. Besides, in spite of its prolonged battery life, the nodes were equipped with a solar panel to ensure a long life and an autonomous functioning. These nodes were used to monitor a wide range of environmental issues that affect directly to agriculture, for example solar radiation, wind speed and direction, rainfall, ambient temperature, humidity, gases, VOCs, soil moisture and temperature. The predictions and warnings about agriculture events can be useful for optimizing crop yields and therefore saving time and money to the agriculture business owners. The systems developed are to predict parameters that would have effects on crop growth so that the farmers could be warned about threats to their yield. Some parameters such as poor weather conditions or likelihood of pest infestation or disease could be prevented.

Fire in itself is a word that describes loss and hazardous situation. Forest fire is a situation in forest that can leave a forest into a bit of ashes. The forest fires need, to be detected at the earliest so that high damage and loss could be prevented. The objective is to detect the fire as fast as possible and its exact localization and early notification to the fire units is vital. The objective of designing this telemetry project is to detect the forest fire and monitor it online. Number of fire sensors are employed that needs to be placed at certain distances so that a look can be kept on the entire forest area. These fire sensors detect the area and if at times there is a fire, it will send the signal or the information to the microcontroller. The microcontroller also updates the information on the webpage and also sends a notification on the webpage through the GPRS module that is connected to the microcontroller. This information is sent to the internet by the network of IoT.

There are a large number of heterogonous devices within the traffic monitoring system using IoT. Among challenges of full deployment IoT is making complete interoperability of these heterogeneous interconnected devices which require adaptation and autonomous behavior. The major issue in IoT is the interoperability between different standards, data formats, heterogeneous hardware, protocols, resources types, software and database systems (Kaykova 2008, Meirong, 2013). Another issue is necessity of an intelligent interface and access to various services and applications. It seems that mobile agents are a convenient tool to handle these issues, provide means for communication among such devices and handle the IoT interoperability. Adding to that mobile agent is a perfect choice in cases of disconnection or low bandwidth, passing messages across networks to undefined destination and to handle the interoperability of IoT. All messaging exchanges among agents are established via the TCP/IP Protocol. A software agent is an autonomous executable entity that observes and acts upon an environment and acts to achieve predefined goals. Agents can travel among networked devices carrying their data and execution states, and must be able to communicate with other agents or human users. A multi-agent system is a collection of such entities, collaborating among themselves with some degree of independence or autonomy. Applying agent technology in the process of monitoring and control traffic is new approach. Such technology perfectly fits for distributed and dislocated systems like traffic monitoring and controlling due to its autonomy, flexibility, configurability and scalability thus reducing the network load and overcoming network latency. Agents can also be used to pass messages across networks where the address of destination traffic device is unidentified. Each traffic object is represented as a software agent (an intelligent object agent). In this infrastructure, the extremely large variety of devices will get interconnected, and will be represented by its own intelligent agent that collects information and responds to others requests. Agents will provide their functionality as a service.

Landslide identification requires a careful knowledge of the slope process and of its relationship with geology, geomorphology, hydrogeology features of the soil. Further influence factors are the climate and the vegetation. The most common monitoring systems are based on topographical and geological data or satellite images, (Lee, 2000; Yongjin, 2010). Segmentation algorithms are used to detect the soil characteristics. In such applications, JSEG algorithm shows the best results, (Vacca, 2013). Models of diagnostic image are based on the analysis of topographic features (slope, soil shape curvature, distance from inhabited areas) and geologic features (geology, distance from lineament), (Ming-Chih, 2011). Further information on type of soil, precipitation, vegetation index is considered for optimizing the recognition of landslide triggering events, (Peijun, 2013). At the moment, assessment or prediction of landslide hazards are based on hydrogeological models. Typically, these models are used to estimate the probability of a landslide occurrence by means of historical or statistical analysis of previous events in the monitored area, (Sheng-guo, 2013). Landslide hazard maps are consequently drawn, (Guzzetti, 2012). Such statistical models often are cause of possible false alarms. Differently, the availability of real-time data based on measurements of soil movements or triggering events could improve the reliability of such hazard assessment models. Consequently, damages and death can be predicted and reduced by means of suitable emergency plans.

CONCLUSION

This chapter aims in increasing amounts of available hyperspectral data originating from airborne and satellite sensors such as AVIRIS, HyMap, and Hyperion with very high spectral resolution containing rich information for a wide range of applications. Remote sensing is highly versatile and can be used in many applications of Big Data. Potential uses for remote sensing in various applications of Big Data include planning, environmental impact assessment, hazard and disaster response, infrastructure management, traffic assessment, and homeland security. The challenges of big data in remote sensing involve not only dealing with high volumes of data. In particular, challenges on data acquisition, storage, management, and analysis are also related to remote sensing problems involving big data. The Wireless Sensor Network (WSN) technologies cuts across many areas of modern day living. This offers the ability to measure, infer and understand environmental indicators, from delicate ecologies and natural resources to urban environments. The use of these devices in a communicating creates the Internet of Things (IoT), wherein, sensors and actuators blend seamlessly with the environment around us, and the information is shared across platforms in order to develop a common operating picture (COP). This chapter described the use of Big Data and Internet of the Things for analyzing and designing various systems based on hyperspectral images with the recent adaptation of a variety of enabling wireless technologies such as RFID tags and embedded sensor and actuator nodes.

REFERENCES

Asin, A., & Gascon, D. (2012). *50 Sensor Applications for a Smarter World.*

Assuncao, M. D., Calheiros, R. N., Bianchi, S., Netto, M. A. S., & Buyya, R. (2015). *Big Data Computing and Clouds*: Trends and Future Directions. *J. Parallel Distrib. Computing, 79-80*, 3–15. doi:10.1016/j.jpdc.2014.08.003

Atzori, L., Iera, A., & Morabito, G. (2010). The Internet of Things: A survey. *Computer Networks, 54*(15), 2787–2805. doi:10.1016/j.comnet.2010.05.010

Buyya, R., Yeo, C. S., Venugopal, S., Broberg, J., & Brandic, I. (2009). Cloud computing and emerging IT platforms: Vision, hype, and reality for delivering computing as the 5th utility. *Future Generation Computer Systems, 25*(6), 599–616. doi:10.1016/j.future.2008.12.001

Chen, C. L. P., & Zhang, C. Y. (2014). *Data-intensive applications, challenges, techniques and technologies*: A survey on Big Data. *Information Sciences, 275*, 314–347. doi:10.1016/j.ins.2014.01.015

Data, S. (n. d.) Amara's Law. Retrieved from https://spotlessdata.com/amaras-law

Eaton, C., Deroos, D., Deutsch, T., Lapis, G., & Zikopoulos, P. (2012). *Understanding Big Data.* McGraw-Hill Companies.

Elachi, C., & Van Zyll, J. (2006). *Introduction to the Physics and Techniques of Remote Sensing.* Hoboken, NJ, USA: Wiley. doi:10.1002/0471783390

Ghosh, A., & Das, S. K. (2008). *Coverage and connectivity issues in wireless sensor networks*: A survey. *Pervasive and Mobile Computing, 4*(3), 303–334. doi:10.1016/j.pmcj.2008.02.001

Guzzetti, F., Mondini, A.C., Cardinali, M., Fiorucci, F., Santangelo, M., & Chang, K. (2012). Landslide inventory maps: New tools for an old problem. *Earth-Science Reviews, 112*(1– 2), 42-66.

Honle, N., Kappeler, U. P., Nicklas, D., Schwarz, T., & Grossmann, M. (2005). *Benefits of Integrating Meta Data into a Context Model.* doi:10.1109/PERCOMW.2005.20

Anderson, J.R., Hardy, E.E., Roach, J.T., & Witmer, R.E. (1976). *A Land Use and Land Cover Classification System For Use With Remote Sensor Data.*

Juels, A. (2006). RFID security and privacy: A research survey. *IEEE Journal on Selected Areas in Communications, 24*(2), 381–394. doi:10.1109/JSAC.2005.861395

Katasonov, A., Kaykova, O., Khriyenko, O., Nikitin, S., & Terziyan, V. Y. (2008). Smart Semantic Middleware for the Internet of Things. Proceedings of the 5th International Conference on Informatics in Control, Automation and Robotics, Intelligent Control Systems and Optimization (pp. 169-178).

Khorram, S., Koch, F. H., Van der Wiele, C. F., & Nelson, S. A. C. (2012). *Remote Sensing* (1st ed.). New York, NY, USA: Springer-Verlag; doi:10.1007/978-1-4614-3103-9

Lee, S., Ryu, J., Min, K., Choi, W., & Won, J. (2000) Development and application of landslide susceptibility analysis techniques using geographic information system (GIS). *Proceedings of the IEEE International Geoscience and Remote Sensing Symposium* (*Vol. 1*, pp. 319-321).

Leppanen, T., Liu, M., Harjula, E., Ramalingam, A., Ylioja, J., Narhi, P., ... & Ojala, T. (2013). Mobile Agents for Integration of Internet of Things and Wireless Sensor Networks. *Proceedings of the IEEE International Conference on Systems, Man, and Cybernetics (SMC)* (pp. 14-21).

Lu, M. C., Tang, T. Y., Tsai, C. P., Wang, W. Y., & Li, I. H. (2011). Image-based landslide monitoring system. *Proceedings of the IEEE International Conference on System Science and Engineering (ICSSE)* (pp. 638-643).

Manekar, A., & Pradeepini, G. (2015). A Review on Cloud-based Big Data Analytics. ICSES Journal on Computer Networks and Communication, 1(1). doi:10.1109/CICN.2015.160

Mayer C.P. (2009). Security and Privacy Challenges in the Internet of Things. *Proceedings of the Workshops der Wissenschaftlichen Konferenz Kommunikation in Verteilten Systemen '09.*

Morello, R., De Capua, C., Fabbiano, L., & Vacca, G. (2013, May 4-5). Image-Based Detection of Kayser-Fleischer Ring in Patient with Wilson Disease. *Proceedings of the IEEE 8th International Symposium on Medical Measurement and Applications*, Gatineau, Canada. doi:10.1109/MeMeA.2013.6549715

ODriscoll, A., Daugelaite, J., & Sleator, R. D. (2013, October). Big Data, *Hadoop and Cloud Computing in Genomics. Journal of Biomedical Informatics, 46*(5), 774–781. doi:10.1016/j.jbi.2013.07.001 PMID:23872175

Pan, F., & Sheng-guo, C. (2013). The Profiles and the Analysis of the Features on the Typical Landslides in the History of the Three Gorges Reservoir Area. *Proceedings of the IEEE International Conference on Intelligent System Design and Engineering Applications (ISDEA)* (pp. 1494-1497). doi:10.1109/ISDEA.2012.358

Perera, C., Zaslavsky, A., Christen, P., & Georgakopoulos, D. (2013). Context Aware Computing for The Internet of Things: A Survey. *IEEE Communications Surveys and Tutorials, 16*(1), 414–454. doi:10.1109/SURV.2013.042313.00197

Perera, C., Zaslavsky, A., Christen, P., & Georgakopoulos, D. (2014). Sensing as a Service Model for Smart Cities Supported by Internet of Things. *Transactions on Emerging Telecommunications Technologies, 25*(1), 81–93. doi:10.1002/ett.2704

Reichle, R. H., Crow, W. T., Koster, R. D., Sharif, H., & Mahanama, S. P. P. (2008a). Contribution of soil moisture retrievals to land data assimilation products. *Geophysical Research Letters*, *35*(1), L01404. doi:10.1029/2007GL031986

Sang, Y., Shen, H., Inoguchi, Y., Tan, Y., & Xiong, N. (2006). Secure Data Aggregation in Wireless Sensor Networks: A Survey. Proceedings of the Seventh International Conference on Parallel and Distributed Computing, Applications and Technologies PDCAT '06 (pp. 315–320). doi:10.1109/PDCAT.2006.96

Sayad, Y. O., Mousannif, H., & Le Page, M. (2015). *Crop Management Using BIG DATA*. IEEE.

Tilak, S., Abu-Ghazaleh, N., & Heinzelman, W. (2002). A taxonomy of wireless micro-sensor network models. *ACM Mobile Computing and Communications Review*, *6*(2), 28–36. doi:10.1145/565702.565708

Tiwari, K.P., & Dewangan, K.K. (2015). Introduction to Internet and its Challenges. *International Journal of Research in Engineering, Science and Technologies- Circuit Branches*, *1*(2), 26-34.

Tory, M., & Moller, T. (2004). Rethinking Visualization: A High-Level Taxonomy. *Proceedings of the IEEE Symposium on Information Visualization* INFOVIS '04 (pp. 151–158). doi:10.1109/INFVIS.2004.59

Udelhoven, T. (2013). Big data in Environmental Remote Sensing Challenges and Chances. *Proceedings of the UniGR Workshop on Big Data Challenges and Opportunities*.

Welbourne, E., Battle, L., Cole, G., Gould, K., Rector, K., Raymer, S., & Borriello, G. et al. (2009). Building the Internet of Things Using RFID The RFID Ecosystem Experience. *IEEE Internet Computing*, *13*(3), 48–55. doi:10.1109/MIC.2009.52

Weng, Q. (2011). *Advances in Environmental Remote Sensing: Sensors, Algorithms, and Applications*. Boca Raton, FL, USA: CRC Press. doi:10.1201/b10599

Xu, Y., Yang, S., Tang, Y., Gao, Y., & Du Q. (2010). Study and application of landslide disaster refinement forecast system in district level based on GIS. *Proceedings of the IEEE International Conference on Geoinformatics* (pp. 1-4). doi:10.1109/GEOINFORMATICS.2010.5567657

Yang, W., Wang, M., & Shi, P. (2013). Using MODIS NDVI Time Series to Identify Geographic Patterns of Landslides in Vegetated Regions. *IEEE Geoscience and Remote Sensing Letters*, *10*(4), 707–710. doi:10.1109/LGRS.2012.2219576

Zaslavsky, A., Perera, C., & Georgakopoulos, D. (2012). Sensing as a Service and Big Data. *Proceedings of the International Conference on Advances in Cloud Computing (ACC '12)*, Bangalore, India.

Zorzi, M., Gluhak, A., Lange, S., & Bassi, A. (2010). *From Todays Intranet of Things to a Future Internet of Things: A Wireless- and Mobility-Related View. IEEE Wireless Communication*, *17*(6), 43–51. doi:10.1109/MWC.2010.5675777

Chapter 18
Can LTE–A Support Real–Time Smart Meter Traffic in the Smart Grid?

Elias Yaacoub
Arab Open University (AOU), Lebanon

ABSTRACT

The chapter investigates the scheduling load added on a long-term evolution (LTE) and/or LTE-Advanced (LTEA) network when automatic meter reading (AMR) in advanced metering infrastructures (AMI) is performed using internet of things (IoT) deployments of smart meters in the smart grid. First, radio resource management algorithms to perform dynamic scheduling of the meter transmissions are proposed and shown to allow the accommodation of a large number of smart meters within a limited coverage area. Then, potential techniques for reducing the signaling load between the meters and base stations are proposed and analyzed. Afterwards, advanced concepts from LTE-A, namely carrier aggregation (CA) and relay stations (RSs) are investigated in conjunction with the proposed algorithms in order to accommodate a larger number of smart meters without disturbing cellular communications.

INTRODUCTION

Current power grids are having a hard time coping with the increasing power consumption and thus are becoming unsustainable. This motivates the ongoing activities and research related to developing a "Smart Grid" (Bannister & Beckett, 2009).

The main purposes of the smart grid are to add intelligence to the grid in order to perform self-coordination, self-awareness, self-healing, and self-reconfiguration, to boost the deployment of renewable energy sources, to augment the efficiency of power generation, transmission, and usage, in addition to shifting and customizing consumers' energy demands by managing peak loads via demand response (DR) techniques. This necessitates advanced distribution automation and dynamic pricing models relying on automatic meter reading (AMR) and advanced metering infrastructure (AMI) (Lo & Ansari, 2012).

DOI: 10.4018/978-1-5225-2947-7.ch018

Copyright © 2018, IGI Global. Copying or distributing in print or electronic forms without written permission of IGI Global is prohibited.

An AMI is one of the main features in smart power grids. It depends on AMR for measuring, collecting, and analyzing energy usage data (Fatemieh et al., 2010), which would represent an essential component of the Big Data era. The deployment of smart meters has several important benefits. For example, it allows real-time information feedback, thus leading to more accurate billing. Furthermore, it allows reducing the peak power demand through the implementation of demand response programs (SUPERGEN, 2012). To perform this interaction with smart meters, a communication media is needed. AMI communications consist mainly of two networks (Purva et al., 2011):

- **A Home Area Network (HAN):** In this network, power consuming devices inside the home communicate with the power supplier. In most common forms, this takes place via a gateway integrated into the smart power meter. Low power wireless transceivers or in home power line communications (PLC) can be used to carry these communications.
- **A Neighborhood Area Network (NAN):** This network mainly serves to connect energy meters to data aggregators/collectors. Different means can be used to establish this link. This connection can be performed wirelessly, by a data wired connection to the smart meter, or over the power lines via PLC technology. Once the data reaches the aggregation stations, these can then communicate with the power utility's central servers using leased access lines, wireless microwave links, or PLC.

This chapter presents an AMR/AMI communication approach that can be applied either to directly transmit the data from the smart meters to the utility servers, or to transmit data collected by aggregators to these servers. The proposed approach implements radio resource management (RRM) in an orthogonal frequency division multiple access (OFDMA) system, using the channel state information (CSI) to optimize performance.

An overview of the most relevant works in the literature is presented next, and the differences with the proposed approach are outlined, before proceeding with the rest of the chapter.

In (ON Semiconductor, 2011), PLC is suggested for communications between smart meters and a concentrator that relays the data using GPRS to a central information system. However, PLC faces the challenge of the lack of capacity at higher frequencies (SUPERGEN, 2012). Furthermore, measurements have shown that the characteristics of the PLC channel vary significantly between different countries or regions, due to different wiring practices and loads connected to the system (Bannister & Beckett, 2009). Hence, a solution suitable for one country might not be suitable for another. OFDMA was proposed in (Bannister & Beckett, 2009) to enhance the throughput and reliability of PLC. Although significant enhancements were reached, it was noted in (Bannister & Beckett, 2009) that more sophisticated channel estimation and adaptive feedback techniques are needed in order to further enhance throughput and reliability.

Wireless communications could be thought of as the most cost-efficient solution for smart meter deployments, especially when compared to laying additional cables or to using PLC data communications, which would require an upgrade to the power distribution hardware (Purva et al., 2011). Thus, thousands of meters can form a mesh network and communicate using protocols in the public industrial scientific and medical (ISM) frequency bands. The role of the mesh network would be to route the meter data to an aggregator, which in turn relays this data to the power utility, generally using cellular data services such as GPRS (Fatemieh et al., 2010). However, mesh networks face significant challenges related to security and signal privacy. These challenges need to be addressed before promoting the use of mesh networks for AMI (SUPERGEN, 2012).

A two-tier approach was proposed in (Fatemieh et al., 2010) in order to allow the use of TV white spaces for AMI communication: In the first tier, WhiteFi, a system providing connectivity similar to Wi-Fi using the white spaces (Bahl et al., 2009), is used for allowing aggregators to collect the smart meters data. In the second tier, this data is relayed by the aggregators to the utility provider using IEEE 802.22.

One can notice that the majority of the cited previous works above focus on the NAN wireless communication part. This is due to the fact that NAN communications constitute the most challenging part since, within the HAN, devices could communicate with a smart power meter using known short-range communication protocols such as Bluetooth, ZigBee, and WiFi.

In (Le & Le-Ngoc, 2011), a queuing-based resource allocation framework for OFDMA-based wireless networks was proposed. The model can be useful as the last-mile or high speed backhaul part of the power grid communications infrastructure.

In (Khan & Khan, 2012a), WiMAX communications are used to transmit the data of phasor measurement units (PMUs) in the smart grid. The unsolicited grant service (UGS), real-time polling service (rtPS) and best-effort (BE) WiMAX scheduling services are compared and analyzed. PMU measurements are strictly delay-sensitive and they can trigger protection and control systems. The results of (Khan & Khan, 2012a) show that UGS performs best while consuming a significant amount of radio resources. Although periodic frequent AMR readings are important in the smart grid, they can be performed at intervals of few minutes, and are not as critical as critical messages from PMUs that could be due to an alarming situation in the grid.

The performance of a heterogeneous (HetNet) WiFi/WiMAX network was shown to lead to a better delay performance in transmitting the meter readings than a pure WiMAX network in (Khan & Khan, 2012b). In fact, it is expected that this two-tier network, with the presence of WiFi access points closer to the smart meters, and ready to relay the aggregated meter data (using significantly less wireless channels) to the WiMAX network, would lead to better results. However, it should be noted that the proposed approach can be implemented in a HetNet framework, either by implementing the method itself on the two hops (between the meters and aggregator, then between the aggregators and BS), or on the first hop (between the meters and aggregator, then using LTE between the aggregators and BS), or on the last hop (using WiFi between the meters and neighboring aggregators, then using the proposed approach between the aggregators and the BS).

With AMI, most of the traffic is expected to be in the uplink direction. Hence, LTE Time Division Duplex (TDD) was investigated in (Brown & Khan, 2012b) as a possible solution for AMR/AMI using LTE TDD configurations 0, 1, or 6, that are uplink biased. In (Brown & Khan, 2012a), it was compared with LTE Frequency Division Duplex (FDD). Interestingly, although TDD can provide greater flexibility when the split between uplink and downlink data is asymmetrical, FDD leads to better uplink performance in terms of latency. The reasons are mainly due to the delays caused by the alternation of the uplink and downlink slots in LTE TDD. Detailed analysis can be found in (Brown & Khan, 2012a; Brown & Khan, 2012b).

In (Li et al., 2011), it was found that contention based schemes (Aloha) outperform schemes with dedicated channels (TDMA and OFDMA) in terms of delay and packet loss rate. The measurements performed in (Li et al., 2011) led to the conclusion that power consumption changes can be approximated using a Poisson process with small arrival rate, and hence it would be better to send the AMR report only when there is a significant change in the power consumption.

This Chapter investigates the big data challenge imposed by the expected ubiquitous deployment of smart meters along with their real-time transmission of AMR data through machine-to-machine (M2M) communications in the IoT paradigm. AMR/AMI communications in dense deployments of smart meters could have severe impacts on LTE, due to frequent and simultaneous transmission of low data rate information by a very large number of devices. The use of efficient LTE radio resource management (RRM) is studied and analyzed in order to assess if LTE/LTE-A networks can raise this challenge. Thus, this chapter investigates the number of simultaneous smart meter transmissions that can be supported in LTE while using low complexity RRM methods. The investigated approach can be applied either to direct data transmission from the smart meters to the LTE base stations (BSs), or to transmit data collected by aggregators/relay stations (RSs) to the BSs. A high level comparison with the other techniques is presented in Table 1.

This chapter is organized as follows. After presenting the system model in Section 2, the proposed LTE resource allocation algorithms are presented in Section 3. Simulation results are described and analyzed in Section 4. Practical limitations and implementations are discussed in Section 5. The use of advanced techniques such as carrier aggregation and relays to enhance performance is analyzed in Section 6. Finally, Section 7 presents the conclusions.

System Model

The scenario investigated in this chapter consists of smart meters sending real-time measurements to an LTE BS. The system model studied includes two approaches that can be used for AMR in the smart grid. The first approach is depicted in Figure 1 and consists of smart meters communicating directly with the cellular BS. Although this scenario can be implemented in both urban and rural environments, it is mostly beneficial in rural areas where the sparse habitations and the large distances do not justify the

Table 1. Comparison of the various AMR/AMI techniques

Technology	Advantages	Limitations
PLC	Use existing infrastructure, low cost	Location dependent, throughput and reliability problems
Wireless Mesh network	Resiliency and robustness to errors	Privacy of consumers compromised (data of a consumer might go through the device of another)
WiFi	Free spectrum, high data rates	High collisions, assumes presence of aggregators that will use other techniques for long distance transmission (GPRS, LTE, WiMAX, etc.)
LTE	High data rates, long range communications, user privacy protected	High signaling overhead (for relatively frequent but small amounts of data transmitted), possibility of network congestion
Contention-based	Reduces signaling with BS/AP (random access), can be used for long range or short range (as in the Hetnet model)	Possibility of high collisions at very high network loads
Proposed	Same as LTE method, but can be applied to short-range and long-range communications, can be adapted to reduce the signaling overhead, and can use relays and carrier aggregation to increase the number of accommodated meters without disrupting cellular communications	Relatively increased complexity in designing and planning the network

Figure 1. Scenario with direct communications between smart meters and the BS

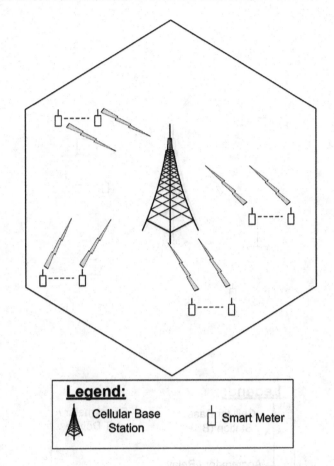

Legend:

Cellular Base Station   Smart Meter

aggregation of data. The second approach is displayed in Figure 2, and consists of smart meters sending their data to local aggregators. The aggregators collect data from meters in each building or street, and then forward the aggregated data to the LTE BS. ZigBee, Wi-Fi, Bluetooth, PLC, or wired communications can be used on the first short range link between the meters and aggregators. LTE communications can then be used on the second long-range link to send the collected data from the aggregators to the BS. The RRM methods and techniques presented in this chapter are applicable to both scenarios. Therefore, the term "devices" is used in the sequel to refer to either smart meters or aggregators communicating with the BS. The term "node" is used to refer to any node in the network, be it a "device" (smart meter or aggregator), or the cellular BS.

Orthogonal frequency division multiple access (OFDMA) is used as the accessing scheme in LTE downlink (DL). On the other hand, in the LTE uplink (UL), single carrier frequency division multiple access (SCFDMA), which is a modified form of OFDMA, is used (Myung & Goodman, 2008). The LTE spectrum is divided into resource blocks (RBs), such that each RB consists of 12 adjacent subcarriers. The smallest RB allocation time unit is $T_{TTI} = 1$ ms, which is the duration of one transmission time interval (TTI), or, equivalently, the duration of two 0.5 ms slots (3GPP, 2016a; 2016b). Bandwidth scalability is an important feature of LTE. In fact, a bandwidth of 1.4, 3, 5, 10, 15, and 20 MHz can be used, corresponding, respectively, to 6, 15, 25, 50, 75, and 100 RBs (Myung & Goodman, 2008; 3GPP, 2016b).

Figure 2. Scenario showing the use of aggregators to relay smart meter data to the LTE BS

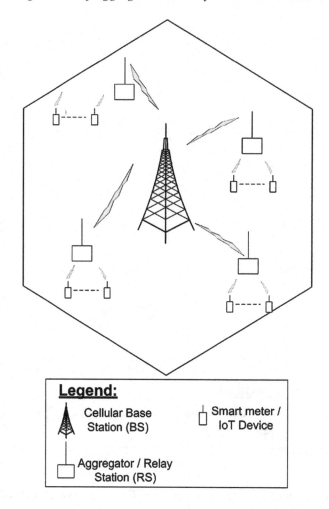

In this chapter, scenarios with 6, 15, 25, or 50 RBs available for resource allocation at the LTE BS are investigated. Actually, this is not the total LTE bandwidth. Instead, this is the bandwidth assumed available for AMR transmissions, out of a total bandwidth of 20 MHz (corresponding to 100RBs). Additional bandwidth can even be available if carrier aggregation is assumed implemented in an LTE-Advanced (LTE-A) setup. This extra bandwidth could be used for other services and/or traditional (i.e. not M2M or AMR) cellular communications. Since in AMI/AMR the most important challenge is to ensure reliable transmissions from the smart meters to the BS, the UL direction is studied in this chapter. Each device is assumed to transmit at a maximum power of 125 mW. This power is equally subdivided among the subcarriers allocated to that device.

Channel Model

The expression of the channel gain on the wireless link between nodes k and j over subcarrier i can be expressed as:

$$H_{k,j,i,dB} = \left(-\kappa - \lambda \log_{10} d_{k,j}\right) - \xi_{k,j,i} + 10 \log_{10} F_{k,j,i} \tag{1}$$

In (1), the first factor corresponds to propagation loss, with κ denoting the pathloss constant, $d_{k,j}$ denoting the distance in km between nodes k and j, and λ denoting the path loss exponent. The second factor, $\xi_{k,j,i}$, represents log-normal shadowing assumed to have zero-mean and a standard deviation σ_{ξ}. Finally, the third factor, $F_{k,j,i}$, is used to capture the effect of fast Rayleigh fading with a Rayleigh parameter a such that $E[a^2] = 1$, with $E[]$ being the expectation operator.

Data Rate Calculations

Assuming there are K devices transmitting to a destination j having N subcarriers to be allocated, and denoting by $P_{k,j,i}$, $H_{k,j,i}$, and $\sigma^2_{k,j,i}$, the transmit power, channel gain, and total noise power, respectively, of a transmitting device k, the signal-to-noise ratio (SNR) between nodes k and j over subcarrier i is expressed as:

$$\gamma_{k,j,i} = \frac{P_{k,j,i} H_{k,j,i}}{\sigma^2_{k,j,i}}, k = 1,...,K; i = 1,...,N; \tag{2}$$

The peak power constraint of device k is given by:

$$\sum_{i=1}^{N} P_{k,j,i} \leq P_{k,\max}, k = 1,...,K; \tag{3}$$

The inequality in (3) means that the power spent by a device to transmit on all its allocated subcarriers cannot exceed the device's maximum transmission power $P_{k,\max}$.

The total data rate achieved by node k transmitting to node j is given by:

$$R_{k,j} = \sum_{i=1}^{N} R^d_{k,j,i}\left(\gamma_{k,j,i}\right) \tag{4}$$

In (4), $R^d_{k,j,i}$ corresponds to the discrete data rate that can be achieved on the link between nodes k and j over subcarrier i. Discrete rates represent the quantized bit rates achievable in a practical system, as opposed to continuous rates that can take any non-negative real value according to the Shannon capacity formula $\log_2(1 + \gamma_{k,j,i})$. Discrete rates are expressed as follows:

$$R^d_{k,j,i}\left(\gamma_{k,j,i}\right) = \begin{cases} r_0, & \eta_0 \leq \gamma_{k,j,i} < \eta_1 \\ r_1, & \eta_1 \leq \gamma_{k,j,i} < \eta_2 \\ r_2, & \eta_2 \leq \gamma_{k,j,i} < \eta_3 \\ \vdots \\ r_{L-1}, & \eta_{L-1} \leq \gamma_{k,j,i} < \eta_L \end{cases} \tag{5}$$

In (5), η_l is the SNR target needed to achieve the rate r_l with a predefined bit error rate (BER). Note that in the limit, the following equalities hold: $r_0 = 0$, $\eta_0 = 0$, and $\eta_L = \infty$.

In the LTE standard, UL RBs allocated to a single device must be consecutive. Furthermore, the same modulation and coding scheme (MCS) is used and equal power should be allocated for transmission over the subcarriers forming these RBs (3GPP, 2016b). Hence, the rate $R_{k,j}$ of a node k communicating with a node j using an MCS with rate r_n bits/symbol over its allocated subcarriers, is given by:

$$R_{k,j} = \frac{r_n \cdot N_{RB}^{(k,j)} \cdot N_{SC}^{RB} \cdot N_{Symb}^{SC} \cdot N_{Slot}^{TTI}}{T_{TTI}} \qquad (6)$$

In (6), $N_{RB}^{(k,j)}$ is the number of RBs allocated by node j to node k, N_{SC}^{RB} is the number of subcarriers per RB (equal to 12 in LTE), N_{Symb}^{SC} corresponds to the number of symbols per subcarrier during one time slot (equal to six or seven in LTE, depending whether an extended cyclic prefix is used or not), N_{Slot}^{TTI} represents the number of time slots per TTI (two 0.5 ms time slots per TTI in LTE), and T_{TTI} is the duration of one TTI (1 ms in LTE) (3GPP TS 36.211, 2016). The adaptive modulation and coding schemes used in LTE are shown in Table 2 (3GPP TS 36.211, 2016; 3GPP TS 36.213, 2016).

Table 2. Discrete rates and SNR thresholds with LTE MCSs

Modulation	Coding Rate	r_l (bits)	η_l (dB)
No Transmission	0	0	-∞
QPSK	78/1024	0.1523	-7.2
QPSK	120/1024	0.2344	-5.8
QPSK	193/1024	0.3770	-3.7
QPSK	308/1024	0.6016	-1.5
QPSK	449/1024	0.8770	0.1
QPSK	602/1024	1.1758	1.8
16-QAM	378/1024	1.4766	4.1
16-QAM	490/1024	1.9141	6.8
16-QAM	616/1024	2.4063	8.9
64-QAM	466/1024	2.7305	10.7
64-QAM	567/1024	3.3223	11.6
64-QAM	666/1024	3.9023	13.9
64-QAM	772/1024	4.5234	16.2
64-QAM	873/1024	5.1152	18.1
64-QAM	948/1024	5.5547	22.4
64-QAM	1 (uncoded)	6.0	26.8

LTE Resource Allocation Algorithms

According to the study of (Purva et al., 2011), in order for a smart meter to send real-time readings about energy consumption, it should transmit an amount of information in bits D_{th} during a time period of duration T_{th}, thus achieving a target data rate R_{th}. Therefore, in this section, two LTE RRM algorithms are presented in order to transmit the required number of bits within the specified duration. One algorithm is a simple channel state information (CSI)-unaware algorithm, whereas the other is more advanced since it uses channel state information and is thus a CSI-aware algorithm.

Denoting by $I_{RB,k,j}$ the set of RBs allocated to device k communicating with a device j (could be the BS or an RS), N_{RB} the total number of RBs, and K the number of devices, $U(R_{k,j} | I_{RB,k,j})$ is defined as the utility of user k as a function of the data rate $R_{k,j}$ on the link between nodes k and j, given the allocation $I_{RB,k,j}$.

Channel State Information (CSI) Unaware Resource Allocation Algorithm

Algorithm 1 is a simple CSI-unaware algorithm that systematically allocates one RB per device without considering channel quality in the allocation. Hence, under this approach, each device receives an LTE RB every TTI when the number of devices is less than the number of RBs (Lines 6-15). Otherwise, the devices take turns on the available RBs every TTI, until all the devices are served (Lines 17-29). Algorithm 1 can be considered as a modified version of the well-known round robin (RR) algorithm. The main enhancement is in taking into account a dense deployment of devices ($K > N_{RB}$) and considering the cumulative performance over T_{th} rather than per TTI scheduling over a duration T_{TTI}.

CSI-Aware Resource Allocation Algorithm

Algorithm 2 is a utility maximization CSI-aware algorithm. Line 1 determines the number of TTIs available to transmit, by each device, the number of data bits D_{th} calculated at Line 2 (where $\lceil \cdot \rceil$ corresponds to the ceiling operation). The method presented at Lines 7-28 is implemented at each TTI. It consists of allocating to device k the RB n that maximizes the difference $\Lambda_{k,j,n}$ (Line 14), with $\Lambda_{k,j,n}$ representing the marginal utility. This metric corresponds to the gain in the utility function U when RB n is allocated to device k communicating with device j, compared to the utility of device k before RB n was allocated to it. The condition at Lines 19-21 ensures RB continuity in LTE uplink, by forcing the RBs allocated to a given device at a certain TTI to be contiguous. If a device succeeds in transmitting its information before T_{th} has elapsed (e.g. due to high data rates achievable when the channel conditions are favorable), the device is excluded from the resource allocation process (Lines 26-28), in order to allow the devices that did not complete their transmissions to use the remaining resources.

The utility function depends on the data rate, and different functions can be selected depending on the desired quality of service (QoS) requirements. For example, with $U=R_{k,j}$, the algorithm leads to a maximization of the sum-rate of the cell. In this case, devices closer to the BS and/or RS will be favored, whereas other devices will suffer from being in outage. Utility functions providing more fairness can be used to address this problem. When $U=\ln(R_{k,j})$ is used (with ln denoting the natural logarithm), this leads to proportional fair resource allocation (Yaacoub & Dawy, 2012; Song & Li, 2005). Using, in the logarithm, the achievable data rate at the current scheduling instant achieves proportional fairness in frequency (PFF), whereas including the previous scheduling instants by using the cumulative rate (since

Algorithm 1. CSI-Unaware RRM Algorithm

1:   $N_{\text{TTI}} = \left\lceil T_{\text{th}} / T_{\text{TTI}} \right\rceil$

2:   $D_{\text{th}} = R_{\text{th}} \cdot T_{\text{th}}$

3:   **For all** k **do**

4:      $D_{k,j} = 0$

5:   **End For**

6:   **If** $K \leq N_{\text{RB}}$ **Then**

7:      **For** $t=1$ to N_{TTI} **do**

8:         **For** $k=1$ to K **do**

9:            **For** $n=1$ to K **do**

10:               Allocate RB n to device k: $I_{RB,\,k,j} = I_{RB,\,k,j} \cup \{n\}$

11:               Set $R_{k,j} = R_{k,j,n}$

12:               $D_{k,j} = D_{k,j} + R_{k,j} \cdot T_{\text{TTI}}$

13:            **End For**

14:         **End For**

15:      **End For**

16:   **Else**

17:         **If** $K > N_{\text{RB}}$ **Then**

18:         Divide devices into N_{G} groups: $N_{\text{G}} = \left\lceil K / N_{\text{RB}} \right\rceil$

19:         $i=0$

20:         **For** $t=1$ to N_{TTI} **do**

21:            **For** $n=1$ to N_{RB} **do**

22:               Allocate RB n to device $k = i \cdot N_{\text{RB}} + n$. Hence: $I_{RB,\,k,j} = I_{RB,\,k,j} \cup \{n\}$

23:               Set $R_{k,j} = R_{k,j,n}$

24:               $D_{k,j} = D_{k,j} + R_{k,j} \cdot T_{\text{TTI}}$

25:            **End For**

26:            $i = \mathrm{mod}(i+1, N_{\text{G}})$

27:         **End For**

28:      **End If**

29:   **End If**

the start of the data transmission by the device in the current T_{th} time interval), leads to proportional fairness in time and frequency (PFTF) (Yaacoub & Dawy, 2012).

PFTF is actually equivalent to using $U = \ln(D_{k,j})$, with $D_{k,j}$ denoting the number of bits transmitted by device k to device j since the start of the current time interval of duration T_{th}. In this chapter, a PFTF utility is used in Algorithm 2, which is a modified version of the algorithm presented in (Yaacoub & Dawy, 2012). It is customized to AMR by considering the overall performance at a time interval of T_{th} rather than T_{TTI}, and by excluding the devices that complete their data transmissions from additional RB allocations within the current T_{th} interval.

Algorithm 2. CSI-Aware RRM Algorithm

```
1:      N_TTI = ⌈T_th / T_TTI⌉
2:      D_th = R_th · T_th
3:      For all k do
4:          D_{k,j} = 0
5:      End For
6:      For t=1 to N_TTI do
7:          Consider the set of RBs available for scheduling I_{avail_RB} = {1,2,···,N_RB}
8:          Consider the set of devices available for scheduling I_{avail_dev} = {1,2,···,K}
9:          For all k do
10:             R_{k,j} = 0
11:         End for
12:         For n=1 to N_RB do
13:             For All k such that D_{k,j} < D_th do
14:                 Λ_{k,j,n} = U(R_{k,j} | I_{RB,k,j} ∪ {n}) - U(R_{k,j} | I_{RB,k,j})
15:             End for
16:             Find k* = arg max_{k;k∈I_{avail_dev}} Λ_{k,j,n}
17:             Allocate RB n to device k*: I_{RB,k*,j} = I_{RB,k*,j} ∪ {n}
18:             Delete the RB from the set of available RBs: I_{avail_RB} = I_{avail_RB} - {n}
19:             If arg max_k Λ_{k,j,n} ≠ arg max_k Λ_{k,j,n-1} then
20:                 I_{avail_dev} = I_{avail_dev} - {arg max_k Λ_{k,j,n-1}}
21:             End If
22:             Calculate the rate of device k* over RB n: R_{k*,j,n}
23:             Set R_{k*,j} = R_{k*,j} + R_{k*,j,n}
24:         End For
25:         D_{k*,j} = D_{k*,j} + R_{k*,j} · T_TTI
26:         If D_{k*,j} ≥ D_th then
27:             I_{avail_dev} = I_{avail_dev} - {k*}
28:         End If
29:     End For
```

Simulation Results: Analysis and Comparison of the Results of the Two Algorithms

In this section, the simulation results using Algorithms 1 and 2 are presented and analyzed. According to the study of (Purva et al., 2011), to model real-time data transmission by a smart meter, it is assumed that a transaction is performed every two minutes. It consists of accessing the channel for a duration of 430 ms, in order to transmit the meter's data at a rate of 60 kbps. Extending these constraints to an LTE network deployment scenario, a group of devices are considered to be simultaneously scheduled for transmission in an interval $T_{th} = 500$ ms, consisting of 500 TTIs, with their turn coming periodically every two minutes. The devices that fail to achieve an average target rate $R_{th} = 60$ kbps within this time period are assumed to be in outage.

Simulation Results

This section presents the MATLAB simulation results obtained by implementing the methods described in " LTE Resource Allocation Algorithms" under the system model of Section 2. A single LTE cell of radius 500 m is considered, with the BS equipped with an omnidirectional antenna and placed at the cell center. Algorithm 1 is referred to by "RR" and Algorithm 2 by "PFTF". The fraction of users in outage is displayed in Figure 3 for both RR and PFTF scheduling, with different numbers of RBs available. PFTF

Figure 3. Fraction of devices in outage

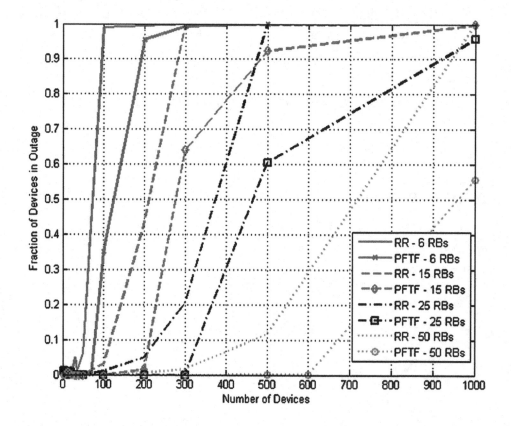

outperforms RR as expected, due to intelligently using CSI in the RRM process. Consequently, more devices are served with PFTF scheduling due to using CSI awareness in the RRM process. However, the price to pay in this case is increased signaling, due to regular CSI feedback to the BS in order to perform CSI-aware scheduling. More details on this problem are discussed and analyzed in "Analysis of Signaling and Feedback Load for AMR in LTE".

In addition, the outage rate is reduced with both methods when the number of RBs increases. Actually, in this case, more resources become available for RRM, thus allowing to serve more devices. Although this is an expected result, it is described in this chapter in order to outline less investigated challenges specific to AMR in the smart grid, or M2M communications in general. Actually, under the IoT paradigm, billions of devices using M2M communications need to coexist with the more "traditional" human-to-human (H2H) cellular traffic, already causing by itself significant load increase on the networks in order to meet the increasing demands. Consequently, the wireless resources should be carefully and judiciously subdivided between H2H and M2M traffic, so that the QoS requirements of both scenarios are successfully met. Table 3 presents the number of smart meters that can be supported for each available bandwidth and RRM method. In other words, Table 3 shows the number of smart meters that can send successfully their data in real-time to the LTE BS with a negligible outage rate. A "negligible" outage rate is considered to be below 0.2% in this chapter.

Using the previously described guidelines for real-time transmission of smart meter data, it can be concluded that when K meters are scheduled simultaneously for transmission slots at any given time instant, each BS can accommodate $240K$ smart meters without having any of them in outage. In fact, there are 240 time windows of $T_{th} = 500$ ms each within a two-minute duration. One of the 240 time windows can be assigned to each smart meter by the BS scheduler in order to transmit periodically the meter readings to the utility company. An example is shown in Figure 4(a). With K different smart meters accessing the network successfully at each time window (K can be determined from Figure 3), a total of $240K$ smart meters can be installed per 500 m cell, according to the scenario depicted in Figure 1. For example, $K = 500$ in the case of PFTF with 50 RBs, and $K = 50$ in the case of PFTF with six RBs, corresponding to 144000 and 16800 meters in the cell, respectively.

In the scenario of Figure 2, smart meters send their data to an aggregator first, using PLC, a wired connection, or a short range wireless transmission on the ISM band. Afterwards, a number K of aggregators can be determined from Figure 3. These K aggregators can simultaneously transmit to the BS the data that they have previously aggregated, without having any of them in outage. In this scenario, the same number of meters ($240K$) can still be accommodated. In fact, each aggregator can collect the data of 240 smart meters, by receiving the data from each meter in a separate 500 ms time window (in a sort of TDMA fashion for a total duration of two minutes). Then, it can relay this data to the BS over the LTE network without interruption over the two-minute periodic interval, as shown in the example of Figure 4(b). Thus, instead of having K smart meters scheduled to transmit simultaneously in time windows of

Table 3. Number of smart meters that can be served successfully for different numbers of available RBs using the two RRM algorithms

	6 RBs	15 RBs	25 RBs	50 RBs
Round Robin (RR)	9500	19000	24000	60000
Proportional Fair (PFTF)	16800	43200	72000	144000

Figure 4. Transmission over slots of T_{th} = 500 ms within two-minute periodic intervals: (a) Direct transmission from smart meters to the BS; (b) Transmission by the aggregator to the BS after receiving the data from the smart meters.

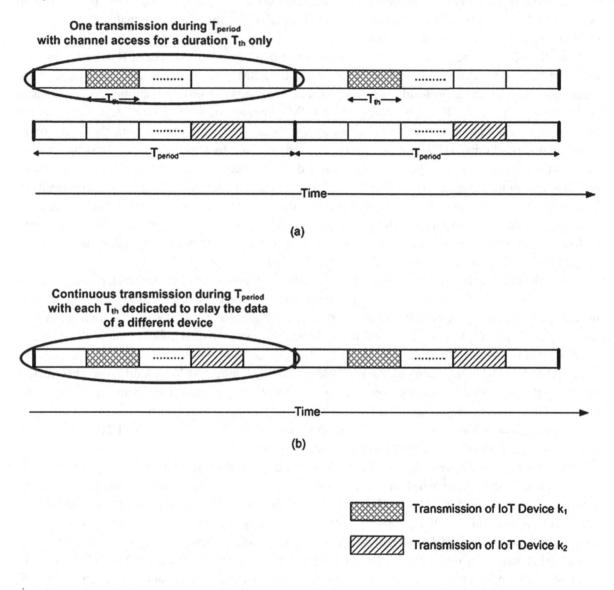

(a)

(b)

500 ms, there will be *K* aggregators, each sending the data of 240 meters, and transmitting continuously at a rate of 60 kbps. Additional details on using relays and carrier aggregation are discussed in "Using LTE-A Concepts to Accommodate Large Numbers of Smart Meters".

Analysis of Signaling and Feedback Load for AMR in LTE

In the LTE standard, whenever a device has data to transmit, it sends a scheduling request to the BS. The BS responds by sending to the device an initial uplink grant (3GPP, 2014b). After transmitting on the allocated resources, if the device still has data to transmit, it sends to the BS a buffer status report containing the amount of remaining data. The BS then sends subsequent uplink grants as appropriate in order to allow the device to transmit all its data (3GPP, 2014a). The delays incurred during this process are analyzed in detail in (Brown & Khan, 2012a).

In this section, some ideas that can reduce the overhead of RRM in LTE uplink in the specific case of AMR/AMI are discussed. In the AMR/AMI scenario, devices are fixed and hence the channel is not expected to change too fast. Consequently, the frequency of CSI feedback or estimation can be reduced. Scheduling is performed at the scale of 1 ms in order to give turns for all devices to transmit, not because the channel conditions change at this speed. CSI estimation on uplink frequencies can be done at a much slower timescale, e.g. hundreds of milliseconds. In addition, since the transmissions are periodic and the amount of data at each transmission is known, the BS can assign the scheduling grant for that device in advance without having to wait for the device to ask for a grant. The device can then transmit periodically using this grant in its specified time. The BS can always change the grant, e.g. after CSI feedback/estimation, or to make sure the device is synchronized to the time interval allotted to it by the BS. This process can be done periodically at fixed (relatively long) time intervals, at a much slower time scale than the current procedure in the standard. Moreover, whenever meter data is not received, or received in error, there is no need for frequent retransmissions, except when critical information is being sent by the meter. Retransmissions can be reduced or canceled in the case of "routine" readings. For example, if the role of AMR is to perform simple readings in real-time, then in case of outage due to packet losses, the updated information can be transmitted at the next transmission period, e.g., after two minutes in the approach of (Purva et al., 2011) adopted in the simulation model of this chapter. These enhancements are in-line with planned enhancement in LTE release 14 (LTE-Advanced Pro) in terms of latency reduction, especially for small data packets, and enhancements for machine type communications (standard term referring to M2M) (Astely et al., 2016).

Using LTE-A Concepts to Accommodate Large Numbers of Smart Meters

OFDMA-based relays are part of the state-of-the-art and next generation LTE-based wireless communications systems (Akyildiz et al., 2010; Osseiran et al., 2011). RRM in the presence of relays faces an additional challenge, since resource allocation should be performed on the links between the BS and RS, in addition to the links between the BS/RS and the mobile users (Salem et al., 2010) or M2M devices. Carrier Aggregation (CA) is an added enhancement in the LTE-Advanced (LTE-A) system that could help address this challenge, by allowing multiple carriers or bands to be aggregated together. Users can thus be scheduled on continuous or non-continuous component carriers (Ratasuk et al., 2010). Another enhancement is the use of re-farmed GSM carriers for IoT/M2M transmissions (Astely et al., 2016). Actually, since a single RB is being allocated for each device at a given TTI, this RB could consist of a re-farmed GSM channel in an "unused" GSM spectrum (or actually used for LTE transmissions). The 200 kHz bandwidth of a GSM channel coincides perfectly with that of an LTE RB (12 subcarriers of 15kHz each, in addition to guard bands). This feature is denoted by "narrowband IoT" in Release 13 of the standard and is expected to be refined in Release 14 (Astely et al., 2016). Thus, the proposed methods can be implemented with classic CA or by using OFDMA transmission over a re-farmed GSM spectrum.

Hence, this section studies the joint use of CA and RSs in OFDMA-based 5G networks to address the problem of M2M communications with a large number of devices using IoT.

In fact, the problems of dimensioning and planning cellular networks should be addressed in order to cope with the increased number of connected devices. Using the RRM techniques described in the previous sections on the long range (LR) BS-RS and the short range (SR) RS-device links, the frequency and network planning process would consist of determining the number of relays to be deployed, their positions, and the resources allocated to each relay, such that the network can simultaneously satisfy the QoS requirements of both the M2M and the traditional human-to-human (H2H) traffic.

Hence, LTE bandwidth can be allocated to IoT traffic in three ways:

- Using bandwidth scalability in LTE, a fraction of the total 20 MHz bandwidth can be made available for SR transmissions from devices to RSs, another orthogonal fraction can be used for LR RS-BS transmissions, while a third fraction can be used for H2H traffic.
- Using CA, up to 100 MHz, corresponding to 500 RBs, can be used, if available, to provide resources for LR and SR M2M links, in addition to the H2H links.
- Re-farmed GSM spectrum (with 200kHz allocations) could also be aggregated with LTE bandwidth for the purpose of IoT transmissions (Astely et al., 2016).

The following discussion presents some network planning and dimensioning guidelines, whereas "Simulation Results for Various RS and CA Scenarios" presents numerical examples.

RS and Resource Planning for IoT Traffic

The following notation is used:

- N_{Sim-D}^{RB}: Number of devices that can be scheduled simultaneously over a single RB using RRM with PFTF scheduling.
- $N_{Cons-D}^{TDMA} = T_{period} / T_{th}$: Number of T_{th} time slots or windows within a transmission period T_{period}.

The BS scheduler allocates one of the N_{Cons-D}^{TDMA} time windows to each device for periodically transmitting its readings, as shown in Figure 4(a). Consequently, the number $N_{Sim-D}^{RB} \cdot N_{Cons-D}^{TDMA}$ of devices can be served by a single RB in a given LTE cell, due to the possibility of allowing N_{Sim-D}^{RB} different devices to access the network at each time window.

Similarly, in a scenario with RS deployment, a number N_{Sim-D}^{RB} of RSs can successfully relay their aggregated data to the BS without being in outage. In such a scenario, the same number of IoT/M2M devices $N_{Sim-D}^{RB} \cdot N_{Cons-D}^{TDMA}$ can be served. In fact, each RS can collect the data of N_{Cons-D}^{TDMA} devices, by receiving the data of each device in a separate T_{th} time window, in a sort of TDMA fashion for a total duration T_{period}. Afterwards, the RS sends the received data to the BS over the LTE network over the whole T_{period} interval without interruption, as shown in the example of Figure 4(b). Thus, instead of scheduling N_{Sim-D}^{RB} devices to transmit simultaneously in time windows of duration T_{th}, a number N_{Sim-D}^{RB} of RSs will be scheduled, with each RS transmitting continuously the aggregated data of N_{Cons-D}^{TDMA} devices at a rate of R_{th} kbps. In this scenario, orthogonal LR and SR RBs would be used due to simultaneous LR and SR transmissions. In addition, the RSs would be operating in duplex mode.

A broad range of practical intermediate scenarios can occur between the two extreme scenarios shown in Figure 4, thus corresponding to different combinations of RSs and IoT devices connected to each RS. Let $N_{RB, LR}$ be the number of RBs allocated by the BS for LR communications between the BS and

RSs, and $N_{RB,RS}$ the number of RBs available per relay for allocation on SR links. As mentioned previously, these RBs should be orthogonal. Furthermore, the required number of RSs can be determined by the density of M2M devices in different hotspots of a given cell. Consequently, the network planning process will involve a tradeoff between the number of RSs, the availability of orthogonal RBs (with or without CA, with or without re-farmed GSM spectrum, etc.), and the frequency reuse factor over the SR relay-controlled areas within the same cell. These tradeoffs are clarified by the following analysis.

Let x and y be two variables that satisfy the following:

$$x \cdot y = N_{Sim-D}^{RB} \cdot N_{Cons-D}^{TDMA} \tag{7}$$

The number of RSs that are required for supporting the IoT/M2M traffic in the considered area is expressed as:

$$N_{RS} = x \cdot \frac{N_{RB,LR}}{N_{RB,RS}} \tag{8}$$

The number of IoT/M2M devices that are sending data to a single relay is expressed as:

$$N_{D,RS} = y \cdot N_{RB,RS} \tag{9}$$

The following discussion presents some numerical results obtained by using equations (7)-(9).

Simulation Results for Various RS and CA Scenarios

Revisiting the simulation results, and considering only those of the CSI-aware Algorithm 2 (using PFTF scheduling), the number of nodes that can be successfully served by a single BS for a given available bandwidth is shown in Table 4. By "successfully served", it is meant that the percentage of nodes in outage does not exceed 0.2%. This represents the number of nodes that can send successfully their data in real-time to the LTE BS while keeping the outage rate negligible. In this case, the term "node" can refer either to an RS or an M2M device (sensor, smart meter, etc.) transmitting its data directly to the BS. To obtain the results shown in Table 4, Algorithm 2 was simulated with a single BS while increasing the number of devices, until the percentage of devices in outage reached 0.2%.

From Table 4, guidelines can be reached for planning an LTE network with relay deployment in order to serve IoT/M2M traffic. In this chapter, the network is planned by using the results of Table 4 after considering a reduction by a safety margin of 15% and then rounding off the numbers. The purpose of this approach is to make sure that the network is not under-dimensioned in terms of the number of needed RSs. Interestingly, it can be seen that using Algorithm 2, almost a fixed number of devices can be served simultaneously over a single RB. By "simultaneously" it is not assumed that the nodes use the RB at the same TTI (which would certainly lead to collisions and interference), but rather that they are simultaneously scheduled to transmit over the same interval $T_{th} = 500$ ms, that consists of 500 LTE TTIs. Through intelligent RRM using PFTF scheduling, each of the nodes receives a subset of these 500

Table 4. Number of smart meters that can be served successfully and simultaneously for different numbers of available RBs using Algorithm 2

	6 RBs	15 RBs	25 RBs	50 RBs
Number of served nodes	70	180	300	600
Number of served nodes after 15% reduction	60	150	250	500
Number of nodes served by RB	10	10	10	10

TTIs to transmit its data, with only one node transmitting at a given TTI over a given subcarrier. Then they wait for $T_{period} = 120$ s in order to be scheduled on another T_{th} slot. Hence, the results of the PFTF algorithm in Table 3 correspond to those of the first row in Table 4, multiplied by $N_{Cons-D}^{TDMA} = 240$.

These results correspond to the LR links. The approach presented in " RS and Resource Planning for IoT Traffic" allows using these simulation results for dimensioning the cellular network depending on the expected locations of the IoT devices, and for determining the required number of relays in order to cover the hotspot areas.

Different configuration examples are shown in Table 5. For example, the first case in Table 5 (500 relays each serving 240 devices) corresponds to a relatively sparse deployment compared to the second case (50 relays each serving 2400 devices), which represents a scenario with dense hotspots of M2M devices. Consequently, a mobile operator can plan his network according to the expected deployment of M2M devices. The operator would determine the number of needed RSs and then allocate a suitable number of RBs for each. For example, the deployment of smart meters in a dense residential area has different network planning requirements than the deployment of environment monitoring sensors in a rural area.

In the scenario of 50 RSs each serving 2400 devices, a possible solution is to have 50 orthogonal RBs, corresponding to a bandwidth of 10 MHz, dedicated for SR links, with each RS scheduling the devices over one RB. Another orthogonal set of 50 RBs would be dedicated for LR links between RSs and the BS. The total bandwidth would be 20 MHz, or 100 RBs, dedicated to M2M communications. With carrier aggregation, H2H traffic can be accommodated over another 20 MHz. This allows the separation the service of the two traffic categories and hence maintaining their QoS separately. This corresponds to serving 120000 M2M devices in a single cell of radius 500 m. If, for example, 500 relays are used, with each relay using one of the 50 orthogonal RBs, then frequency reuse should be implemented in order to minimize interference. In that case, orthogonal RBs can be allocated for groups of 50 RSs, and then reused over other groups, and so on.

Table 5. Examples of capacity planning of the network using different configurations with $N_{Sim-D}^{RB} = 10$ and $N_{Cons-D}^{TDMA} = 240$

Configuration Example	**Configuration Example with $N_{RB,LR} = 50$ and $N_{RB,RS} = 1$**
$N_{RS} = 10N_{RB,LR}/N_{RB,RS}$ relays each serving $N_{D,RS} = 240N_{RB,RS}$ devices	$N_{RS} = 500$ relays each serving $N_{D,RS} = 240$ devices
$N_{RS} = N_{RB,LR}/N_{RB,RS}$ relays each serving $N_{D,RS} = 2400N_{RB,RS}$ devices	$N_{RS} = 50$ relays each serving $N_{D,RS} = 2400$ devices
$N_{RS} = 2N_{RB,LR}/N_{RB,RS}$ relays each serving $N_{D,RS} = 1200N_{RB,RS}$ devices	$N_{RS} = 100$ relays each serving $N_{D,RS} = 1200$ devices
$N_{RS} = 5N_{RB,LR}/N_{RB,RS}$ relays each serving $N_{D,RS} = 480N_{RB,RS}$ devices	$N_{RS} = 250$ relays each serving $N_{D,RS} = 480$ devices

The simulation results of Tables 3-5 are obtained by assuming that devices transmit a their maximum power of 125 mW in the LR. However, in practice, RSs would be placed at much shorter distances from the devices, thus allowing significantly less power to be used for SR transmissions to the RSs. With a reuse factor as large as 50, this leads to a significant interference reduction while at the same time preserving the power of M2M devices (Astely et al., 2016).

CONCLUSION

This chapter investigated the scheduling load added on a long-term evolution (LTE) and/or LTE-Advanced (LTE-A) network when automatic meter reading (AMR) in advanced metering infrastructures (AMI) is performed using internet of things (IoT) deployments of smart meters in the smart grid.

Radio resource management algorithms were proposed in order to perform dynamic scheduling of the meter transmissions, and the simulation results showed that LTE can accommodate a significantly large number of smart meters with real-time readings in a limited coverage area. Methods for reducing the signaling load between the meters and base stations were discussed to allow the practical implementation of the proposed methods.

Furthermore, advanced concepts from LTE-A, such as carrier aggregation and relay stations, were investigated in conjunction with the proposed algorithms in order to support the IoT traffic emanating from a larger number smart meters. Finally, a detailed analysis was presented in order to plan an AMI/AMR network by determining the number of RSs required depending on the density of smart meters, the use of carrier aggregation, and frequency reuse.

It should be noted that current and future LTE standardization releases are moving in the direction presented in this work, namely the support of massive machine type communications (mMTC), MTC being the 3GPP standard term for M2M, in Releases 13 and 14, as mentioned in (Astely et al., 2016) and discussed in this chapter (e.g. in " Using LTE-A Concepts to Accommodate Large Numbers of Smart Meters"). Specifically, the concept of Narrowband IoT is being investigated as a potential solution to frequent low data rate communications from IoT devices, as in smart meter applications. LTE-A mMTC applications span a breadth of industry sectors, including medical and mHealth, building automation, environment monitoring, industrial processes, and vehicular networks, in addition to energy and smart metering/smart grids investigated in this chapter. Products supporting the new standards will gradually emerge in the market, and power retailers are expected to incorporate the new enhancements in future smart meters. Deployments of these smart meters would be performed more efficiently if a collaboration agreement is made between power retailers and the mobile network operators, in order to make sure the cellular networks are adequately planned and dimensioned to support the expected smart meter traffic. Furthermore, such an agreement should cover pricing and billing aspects, since frequent periodic data transmissions over the network should not entail excessive billing, neither for the end-user (having the smart meter installed in his/her apartment for example), nor on the power retailer (responsible for deploying, managing, and maintaining the smart meters). Another aspect that should be taken into consideration is standardization in smart grids, and the presence of various communication systems that can contribute to smart grid deployments. In fact, the National Institute of Standards and Technology (NIST) Framework and Roadmap for Smart Grid Interoperability Standards, Release 1.0, named over 20 IEEE standards among many other IEEE standards that are related to smart grid development, and identified aspects where additional standardization efforts are required. Interoperability between these smart grid standards with the 3GPP standards governing cellular networks should be put in place in order to take full advantage of smart grids and future cellular networks, by carefully planning the HAN/NAN parts of the network and the most suitable technologies used in each part, thus leading to a fruitful synergy between LTE-A and smart grids.

REFERENCES

3rd Generation Partnership Project (3GPP). (2014a). 3GPP TS 36.321 LTE Evolved Universal Terrestrial Radio Access (E-UTRA); Medium Access Control (MAC) Protocol Specification, version 12.2.0, Release 12.

3rd Generation Partnership Project (3GPP). (2014b). 3GPP TS 36.331 LTE Evolved Universal Terrestrial Radio Access (E-UTRA); Radio Resource Control (RRC); Protocol Specification, version 12.2.0, Release 12.

3rd Generation Partnership Project (3GPP). (2016a). 3GPP TS 36.211 3GPP TSG RAN Evolved Universal Terrestrial Radio Access (E-UTRA) Physical Channels and Modulation, version 13.1.0, Release 13.

3rd Generation Partnership Project (3GPP). (2016b). 3GPP TS 36.213 3GPP TSG RAN Evolved Universal Terrestrial Radio Access (E-UTRA) Physical layer procedures, version 13.1.1, Release 13.

Akyildiz, I., Gutierrez-Estevez, D., & Reyes, E. (2010). The Evolution to 4G Cellular Systems: LTE-Advanced. *Physical Communication*, *3*(4), 217–244. doi:10.1016/j.phycom.2010.08.001

Astely, D., Stattin, M., Wikstrom, G., Cheng, J.-F., Hoglund, A., Frenne, M., & Gunnarsson, F. et al. (2016). LTE Release 14 Outlook. *IEEE Communications Magazine*, *54*(6), 44–49. doi:10.1109/MCOM.2016.7497765

Bahl, P., Chandra, R., Moscibroda, T., Murty, R., & Welsh, M. (2009). White Space Networking with Wi-Fi Like Connectivity. *SIGCOMM Comput. Commun. Rev.*, *39*(4), 27–38. doi:10.1145/1594977.1592573

Bannister, S., & Beckett, P. (2009). Enhancing powerline communications in the "Smart Grid" using OFDMA. *Proceedings of the Australasian Universities Power Engineering Conference (AUPEC)*, Adelaide, Australia.

Brown, J., & Khan, J. Y. (2012a). Performance comparison of LTE FDD and TDD based Smart Grid communications networks for uplink biased traffic. *Proceedings of the IEEE International Conference on Smart Grid Communications (SmartGridComm)*, Tainan, Taiwan (pp. 276-281). doi:10.1109/SmartGridComm.2012.6485996

Brown, J., & Khan, J. Y. (2012b). Performance analysis of an LTE TDD based smart grid communications network for uplink biased traffic. Proceedings of the IEEE Globecom Workshops, Anaheim, California, USA (pp. 1502-1507).

Fatemieh, O., Chandra, R., & Gunter, C. A. (2010). Low Cost and Secure Smart Meter Communications using the TV White Spaces. *Proceedings of the 3rd International Symposium on Resilient Control Systems (ISRCS)*, Idaho Falls, ID, USA (pp. 37-42). doi:10.1109/ISRCS.2010.5602162

Khan, R. H., & Khan, J. Y. (2012a). Wide area PMU communication over a WiMAX network in the smart grid. *Proceedings of the IEEE International Conference on Smart Grid Communications (SmartGridComm)*, Tainan, Taiwan (pp. 187-192). doi:10.1109/SmartGridComm.2012.6485981

Khan, R. H., & Khan, J. Y. (2012b). A heterogeneous WiMAX-WLAN network for AMI communications in the smart grid. *Proceedings of the IEEE International Conference on Smart Grid Communications (SmartGridComm)*, Tainan, Taiwan (pp. 710-715). doi:10.1109/SmartGridComm.2012.6486070

Le, L. B., & Le-Ngoc, T. (2011). QoS provisioning for OFDMA-based wireless network infrastructure in smart grids. *Proceedings of the 24th Canadian Conference on Electrical and Computer Engineering (CCECE)*, Niagara Falls, Ontario, Canada (pp. 813-816). doi:10.1109/CCECE.2011.6030568

Li, H., Han, Z., Lai, L., Qiu, R. C., & Yang, D. (2011). Efficient and reliable multiple access for advanced metering in future smart grid. *Proceedings of the IEEE International Conference on Smart Grid Communications (SmartGridComm)*, Brussels, Belgium (pp. 440-444). doi:10.1109/SmartGridComm.2011.6102363

Lo, C.-H., & Ansari, N. (2012). The Progressive Smart Grid System from Both Power and Communications Aspects. *IEEE Communications Surveys and Tutorials*, *14*(3), 799–821.

Myung, H. G., & Goodman, D. J. (2008). *Single Carrier FDMA: A New Air Interface for Long Term Evolution*. Chichester, UK: John Wiley and Sons. doi:10.1002/9780470758717

Osseiran, A., Monserrat, J., & Mohr, W. (2011). *Mobile and Wireless Communications for IMT-Advanced and Beyond*. Chichester, UK: John Wiley and Sons. doi:10.1002/9781119976431

Purva, A., Bumanlag, J., Edelman, B., & Doetsch, U. (2011). *Spectrum Needs for Wireless Smart Meter Communications. Tech. Report*. Boulder: University of Colorado.

Ratasuk, R., Tolli, D., & Ghosh, A. (2010). Carrier Aggregation in LTE-Advanced. *Proceedings of the IEEE VTC Spring 2010* (pp. 1–5).

Salem, M., Adinoyi, A., Rahman, M., Yanikomeroglu, H., Falconer, D., Kim, Y.-D., & Cheong, Y.-C. et al. (2010). An Overview of Radio Resource Management in Relay-Enhanced OFDMA-Based Networks. *IEEE Communications Surveys and Tutorials*, *12*(3), 422–438. doi:10.1109/SURV.2010.032210.00071

Semiconductor, O. N. (2011). Speeding up the Smart Grid: Technique for Delivering More Robust, Higher Data Rate Communications for Automatic Meter Reading (Tech. Report TND6018/D).

Song, G., & Li, Y. (2005). Cross-Layer Optimization for OFDM Wireless Networks-Part I: Theoretical Framework. *IEEE Transactions on Wireless Communications*, *4*(2), 614–624. doi:10.1109/TWC.2004.843065

SUPERGEN. (2012). *HiDEF (Highly Distributed Energy Futures)*. Smart Meters for Smart Grids. Briefing Paper.

Yaacoub, E.E., & Dawy, Z. (2012). Resource Allocation in Uplink OFDMA Wireless Systems: Optimal Solutions and Practical Implementations. IEEE press.

Chapter 19
Mobile Cloud Gaming and Today's World

Hallah Shahid Butt
National University of Sciences and Technology (NUST), Pakistan

Sajid Umair
National University of Sciences and Technology (NUST), Pakistan

Sadaf Jalil
National University of Sciences and Technology (NUST), Pakistan

Safdar Abbas Khan
National University of Sciences and Technology (NUST), Pakistan

ABSTRACT

Mobile cloud computing is the emerging field. Along-with different services being provided by the cloud like Platform as a Service, Infrastructure as a Service, Software as a Service; Game as a Service is new terminology for the cloud services. In this paper, we generally discussed the concept of mobile cloud gaming, the companies that provide the services as GaaS, the generic architecture, and the research work that has been done in this field. Furthermore, we highlighted the research areas in this field.

INTRODUCTION

In past few decades, people like to work on desktop computers. But with the evolution in technology, people are most interested to use mobile devices since it is handy and portable. Moreover, mobile is satisfying the needs of user by providing them facility to play games and providing them online video streaming etc. Mobile devices are now the major source of entertainment for the users Cai and Leung (2013).

According to the survey (Netimperative, 2015), in China, 8% of the total mobile subscribers were increased within one year till January 2015 and 15% of growth was observed in number of active mobile social users. Moreover, the web traffic requested by mobiles till August 2015 was 136% increased. Figure 1 presents the stats of mobile gaming in China by August, 2015.

This signifies that the use of internet resources via mobile in increased. This leads to the need to fulfill or meet the needs of users accordingly. According to Cai and Leung (2013), along with the social activities, mobile devices are also used to play different games. These games can be browser based (Mo-

DOI: 10.4018/978-1-5225-2947-7.ch019

Copyright © 2018, IGI Global. Copying or distributing in print or electronic forms without written permission of IGI Global is prohibited.

Figure 1. Increasing trends of mobile users in China
Netimperative, 2015.

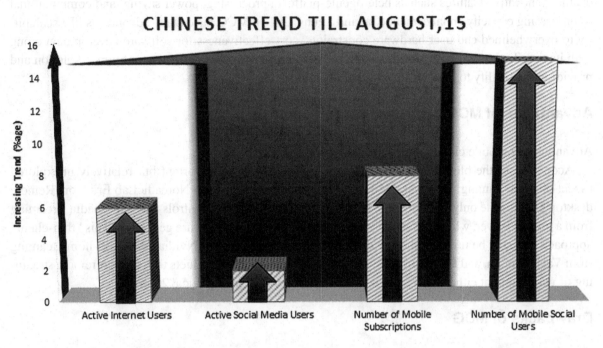

bile Browser Game- MBG) or it can be video based (Mobile Video Gaming). Mobile cloud computing (MCC) - an emerging field- is there to help out such users. Since clouds provide different services based on their infrastructure like Infrastructure as a Service (IaaS), Platform as a Service (PaaS); similarly, Game as a Service (GaaS) is new service being provided by the clouds environment. One interesting advantage of cloud gaming is that it updates games instantly with the web without downloading a new version of the game. By having the ability to push patches to a game, it can be personalized much easier. One of the examples is "The Walking Dead" game, which releases new episodes after two weeks. As each episode is released the data is analyzed and their teams make real-time decisions on how to improve the user experience. The next episode that comes out will be better than the last. (Decker, 2016) The chapter describes the MCG definition, cloud gaming companies, frameworks or models used for it and research areas in this domain.

In this chapter first we will discuss the introduction of mobile cloud gaming which is followed by the identification of cloud gaming companies. General architecture of mobile cloud environment is discussed. Related literature work is also described in this chapter.

MOBILE CLOUD GAMING

Definition

Cloud services are on-demand services. Similarly, gaming on clouds is games on demand service. It is new and emerging trend. Mobile Cloud Gaming is known as collective gaming exhausting mobile devices that connects with the cloud as an outsider system for dealing with game interactions and scenarios. It enables innovative features such as heterogenic-platform processing, power saving, and computational or processing capacity enhancement (Cai and Leung, 2013). MCG have many advantages like scalability to overwhelmed end user hardware constraints, cost-effectiveness for software development along with its distribution, flexible business model to earn profit, providing effective antipiracy solution and providing the facility to click and play games (Cai et al., 2014).

Advantages of MCG

Advantages of mobile cloud gaming are shown in Table 1.

According to the blog (Miica 2016), energy efficiency is an important but relatively unexplored aspect of cloud gaming. However, (Miica 2016) have done research in NomadicLab Ericsson. Remote desktop client is the only software is to be installed that handles the controls and multimedia streaming from a remote server, where the actual video and audio for the desktop are generated. This "thin-client" approach can also be utilized in other contexts, like remote gaming. Nvidia Shield, In-home teaming from Valve Stream, and PlayStation Now are examples of existing products that support remote streaming of game content either from local home PCs or from the cloud (Miica, 2016).

Drawbacks of MCG

Disadvantages of MCG are also shown in Table 2.

Table 1. Advantages of MCG

Advantages	Description
Thin Client	There is no need to install games on mobile devices. Users can access gaming facility using mobile.
Potential Battery Conservation	Since the cloud deals with the rendering and computing of games, power consumption for processing is greatly reduced.
Unlimited Resources	The cloud server hosting the gaming engines, which means that the game has unlimited storage and other computing resources.
Less Chance of Loss	Game data resides in the cloud. This means that, when and where gamers connected to the game, the game content and status, it is still the same. Thus, the player may have seamless game across multiple networks.

Tayade, 2014.

Table 2. Drawbacks of MCG

Drawbacks	Description
Bandwidth Consumption	Clients connect to the cloud via network (internet). Rendering frames of video consume more bandwidth.
Network Dependency	Users are totally dependent on network availability. They are unable to play games if there is no internet connection. Their games may burden the network and cause congestion.
Resource Limitation	Browser games have limitations. Sometimes resources are required for video rendering which might not be visible on mobile browsers.

Tayade, 2014.

Cloud Gaming Companies

The following companies are the providers of cloud gaming.

- **OnLive:** It was one of the commercialized companies to provide cloud games (Cai and Leung 2013). On April 30, 2015, all services provided by OnLive was come to an end since Sony acquired important parts of OnLive (OnLive, 2016).
- **OTOY:** Cai and Leung (2013) and OTOY (2015) mentioned that OTOY is US based company that delivers media and entertainment organizations around the world. They provide GPU-based software solutions that aid in the creation and delivery of digital content. From capture to render to stream, they provide an integrated pipeline for making and distributing 3D content.
- **Gaikai:** According to Cai and Leung (2013) and Gaikai (2013), they provide solutions to stream video games at high quality with low latency. They built the world's fastest interactive entertainment network and won a Guinness World Record for it.
- **G-Cluster:** G-cluster offered operators of the gaming platform in the cloud deployed whiter label that allows users to play through television and various mobile devices. G -cluster instantly becomes corresponding television top box with portable multi-platform cloud gaming on television, PC and tablet. They develop AAA games (Cai and Leung, 2013). Now company is dissolved (G-Cluster, 2016).
- **Playcast Media System:** Cai and Leung (2013) and GTC (2010) mentioned that They developed the first system for providing online on-demand gaming services on live cable network.
- **StreamMyGame:** In Cai and Leung (2013) and StreamMyGame (2012) is declared as only solution that allows applications and games to play remotely. It is free to join online community, by making two sets of current games and video recording. It is the fundamental revolutionary computer game industry, because users can play high-end games low-end equipment.

GENERAL ARCHITECTURE OF MOBILE CLOUD ENVIRONMENT

While discussing mobile cloud architecture, we can say that it is four tier architecture generally. More tiers can be added in this architecture for instance, to ensure security. First tier can be named as client tier in which clients connected with mobile devices can access the network. The improved features in interfaces can help the players to play with ease. This interface is important especially for MBG where web browser is acting as interface. Cai and Leung (2013) Network tier consists of access points and the mobile network service providers. Different networks have their own bandwidths. With different Internet speeds provided by different technologies like 3G and latest 4G, multi-gaming sessions' players are increasing day-by-day (Bose and Saddar, 2015). Clients connect with the Internet tier via access points or mobile network service providers, which in turn connects with the cloud tier. Pictorially, it is represented in the Figure 2.

Figure 2. General architecture of mobile cloud computing
Source: (Cai and Leung, 2013).

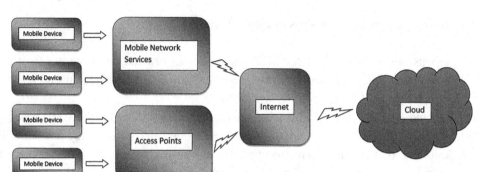

RELATED WORK

In this section, we tried to cover the proposed solutions to the problems in MCG domain. Innovative framework of cloud-based e-learning games can be a source to enhance students learning in any time space. Mobile quiz game is developed on the idea of game rooms with real- time synchronization and the client-server model, by members of University of Hong Kong, whose design is illustrated as: Suggested system, i.e. iGame@Cloud, is designed including the components; Interactive E-Learning Game Server running on the Cloud platform, Administration Console Portal, E-Learning Game Portal and Mobile Devices. After registration, each user logs in our cloud-based ELearning Game Server via the wireless network through the user interaction screen already loaded and displayed onto their mobile devices. During the time of scheduling, the E-Learning Game Server will push some questions for the answer. Each user will be given with 3 options. In each round, those users who had given the wrong answers for three times would be required to quit the current game session. The server will only show the right answer for each round only when all the answers are received from the registered mobile phone. Thus, our cloud based e-learning game platform is a round-based game that requires synchronization of data on the server side (Tam et al., 2013).

Zamith et al. (2011) describe that mobile games are applications that run on mobile devices as smartphones and tablets. The characteristics of current mobile devices make it reality to design extensive game experiences. By using an approach based on distributed processing or computing, games would have lighter requirements regarding hardware. With the idea of cloud computing, games could depend on other terminals to help in processing their assigned tasks. This presents game-loop architecture for 1-player or more than 1-player games, using automatic load balancing and distributing game logic computation among several computers. This focuses at having low-powered devices taking part into complex and difficult games as well as allowing many players to play together through their mobile devices and let the game quality be improved. The current implementation uses HTML 5 for the mobile client (user interface, prompt input and connect to the server cluster) and C plus plus (C++) with Message Protocol Interface (MPI) for processing tasks. The web server is Apache. The component responsible for cluster computing has two parts: the master process, who is assigned to answer client requests, and the slave process, who runs the distributed game loop. For each and every game loop step, the master process gets the current game state from a client, and updates it in each slave process, dividing the problem with all slave processes. Then, the master process amalgamates the solution of each slave process, creating a new game state. In the end, the master process sends to client this new game state. Proposed architecture is illustrated in the Figure 3.

This strategy includes four main components: load balancing; applies the scripting approach and thus analyzes the hardware performance dynamically and adjusts the number of tasks to be processed by the resources, mobile architecture; the input task classes handle user input that comes from several sources. The presentation task and subclasses are responsible for presenting information to the user. The update task classes are assigned to update the game loop state, the network update task; it is responsible for communicating with distributed architecture and updating the game state according to the data received from it, the distributed architecture; the core of the proposed architecture relates to the task manager and the hardware check class, that schedules tasks and changes which processor handles them whenever it is needed.

Kim (2013) says, Client-server architectures are less flexible and scalable, because the bandwidth requirements have grown with the increase in number of gaming user increases. The proposed architecture ensures that a game cloud can provide scalability that enables to host hundreds of mobile games users to have the advantages of cloud computing and local resources for the high quality of games. Following is the architecture proposed, i.e. Efficient Scaling Scheme in the Cloud. Unlike general approach where mobile devices connect to the access network, there presents a mobile network service layer between the wireless access network and mobile cloud computing. Game servers act as proxies for managing the set of their gaming users. Gaming users have no information about interest sets, and are exposed only to enough game state as provided by their server. Using updates published in the low frequency topic, each server periodically determines the interest set of each of its gaming users. The cloud provides an idea of infinite processing power with a highly reliable service, thus removing the need for costly provisioning required resources for mobile games. Although the game state is distributed amongst multiple hosts or nodes, all information resides in the same data center. The size of the set of the gaming users

Figure 3. Proposed architecture
Zamith et al., 2011.

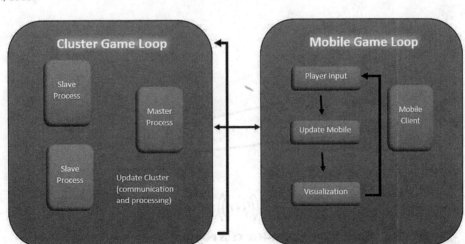

affects game quality and performance. As the interest set size reduces, workload on the cloud is reduced; similarly, large interest sets will result in give an idea of game quality due to frequent updates, but may cause update latencies due to a more workload.

User satisfaction is also important in gaming. Users play games in order to get relax and enjoy. Huang et al. 2014 did experiment in order to quantify the user satisfaction in mobile cloud systems using real game GamingAnywhere which is an open source game. They setup their experiment by connecting desktop client and mobile client with GamingAnywhere server. Desktop client is connected with LAN and mobile client with wi-fi access point. They set up their own GamingAnywhere server on a Windows 7 desktop, Intel Core i7-870 (8 MB cache and 2.93 GHz) and 8 GB of main memory. The desktop client has Windows 7 installed with Intel Core 2 Quad processor Q9400 (6 MB cache and 2.66 GHz) and 4 GB of memory while the mobile client Samsung Galaxy Nexus has 1.2 GHz Dual CPU, 1 GB RAM, 4.65 -inch AMOLED screen, 720P) and Android 4.2.1 features. Desktop Client and Mobile clients connected to the server via the Gigaset Ethernet LAN and Wireless LAN 802.11, respectively. They believed that the two LANs are used in accordance with fair comparison experiments. Figure 4 show the setup of experiment.

They performed their experiment on selected games. Those were:

1. Limbo.
2. Super Smash Bros.
3. Mario Kart 64
4. Super Mario 64
5. To study Customer Satisfaction, they considered four parameters:
    a. Video resolution
    b. Encoding bitrate
    c. Network latency
    d. Frame rate.

They conducted their studies on mobile and desktop clients. Graphics, control and smoothness were rated in their studies. Moreover, impact of selected parameters on above mentioned rated parameters. The results showed that

Figure 4. Experiment setup
Kim, 2013.

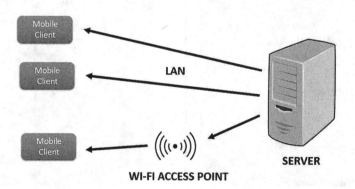

- The players are more satisfied with sound and graphics quality in mobile devices and quality control on the desktop.
- The network latency, bit rate and frame rate affect graphic quality and smoothness.
- Control quality depends upon the devices being used.

Hossain et al. 2015 proposed an architecture for cloud gaming with emotions- awareness. They tackled the issue of tradeoff between player emotion or feeling with resource consumption, which is affected by game screen. The proposed architecture for emotion-aware cloud gaming framework uses emotion technology and remote display technology to give players good experience. For cloud-based video games, game-screens are rendered on servers and streamed to client's devices whereas emotions of users are sent back to the cloud servers to show-off better display screens. The architecture is shown in Figure 5. The player responses, interactions and commands are recorded and sent to emotion -detection engine (server).

Emotion detection function identify the emotions and send a message to remote display server to change the screens. Components of proposed architecture can be summarized as follows:

- **Cloud Manager:** That manages the overall system by web services. Responsibilities of cloud manager includes maintaining player's profile, game and client's device information, user identification and registration and managing the game sessions.
- **Resource Allocation Manager:** Responsible for assigning virtual machines (VM) required for running the game sessions. The VM is responsible for emotion detection, game state updates, streaming and rendering, audio-video playback and screen-effect control. Their system worked in two phases, first is the learning phase, in which the system learns the emotions and classify them. In the second phase, i.e. the operating stage, a linear programming (LP) model is applied to change the screens based on detected emotions.

Figure 5. Player's emotion detecting architecture
Hossain et al., 2015.

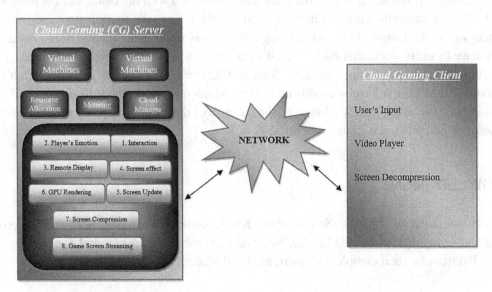

They claimed that bearable amount of workload has been transferred to the cloud server, which may not harm or disturb the processing of server.

Chen 2015 proposed a game theoretic technology for achieving effective and efficient processing offloading for MCC. They adopted the decentralized computation offloading decision making problem among mobile device users as a decentralized computation offloading game. The main contributions of this research are summarized as follows:

- Decentralized processing or computing offloading game formulation.
- Analysis of game structure.
- Decentralized mechanism for achieving Nash equilibrium.

The results showed that the proposed mechanism can achieve the valuable computation offloading work and is scalable as system size increase

FUTURE RESEARCH DIRECTIONS

MCG is new and emerging field. We can have different research directions specifically considering the security and privacy in clouds. Many researchers have proposed different architectures to solve the issue but the work is still insufficient to cope up with the problem. Moreover, supply of user friendly gaming environment over network is also a problem. Change in architectures that can handle network issues should be implemented.

CONCLUSION

We studied the new emerging paradigm of MCG. In this chapter, we defined the term MCG, its types i.e. MCVG and MBG, the companies that provide cloud based games solutions to users. We described the general cloud environment that how the clients are connected with the cloud and get the services of the clouds. We also described the architecture of StreamMyGame. We tried to describe the proposed frameworks for MCG. Despite of research being done in this field, there are still some research areas where we have to focus. As discussed in related work, the emotion-aware screens are displayed which requires constant message passing between client and server. Client's game information along- with their emotions' information have to send time-to-time which may cause the load on server if there are hundreds of players playing games. Moreover, the security of the cloud is a strong research area. Maintaining security and privacy in clouds is a difficult task.

ACKNOWLEDGMENT

The authors would like to thank Dr. Safdar Abbas Khan, Assistant Professor, School of Electrical Engineering and Computer Sciences (SEECS), National University of Sciences and Technology (NUST) Islamabad Pakistan for their complete support, help and guidance.

REFERENCES

Cai, W., Chen, M., & Leung, V. C. M. (2014). Toward Gaming as a Service. *IEEE Internet Computing, 18*(3), 12–18. Retrieved August 08 2016 from http://ieeexplore.ieee.org/xpls/abs_all.jsp?arnumber=6818918 doi:10.1109/MIC.2014.22

Cai, W., & Leung, V. C. M. (2013). Next Generation Mobile Cloud Gaming. *Proceedings of the IEEE Seventh International Symposium on Service-Oriented System Engineering*, 550-559. Retrieved August 04, 2016 from http://www-users.cselabs.umn.edu/classes/Spring-2015/csci8980/papers/Applications/gaming.pdf

Chen, X. (2015). Decentralized Computation Offloading Game For Mobile Cloud Computing. *IEEE Transactions on Parallel and Distributed Systems, 26*(4), 974–983. Retrieved July 28 2016 from http://ieeexplore.ieee.org/xpl/articleDetails.jsp?tp=&arnumber=6787113 doi:10.1109/TPDS.2014.2316834

G- Cluster. (2016). Retrieved July 30, 2016 from http://www.gcluster.com/eng

Gaikai (2013). Retrieved on July 30, 2016 from http://www.gaikai.com

GTC. (2010). Retrieved July 30, 2016 from http://www.nvidia.com/content/GTC-2010/pdfs/4004B GTC2010.pdf

Hossain, M. S., Muhammad, G., Song, B., Hassan, M. M., Alelaiwi, A., & Alamri, A. (2015). Audio-Visual Emotion-Aware Cloud Gaming Framework. *Proceedings of the IEEE Transactions on Circuits and Systems for Video Technology* (pp. 2105-2118). Retrieved July 20, 2016 from http://ieeexplore.ieee.org/xpls/abs_all.jsp?arnumber=7122897

Huang, C., Hsu, C., Chen, D., & Cheni, K. (2014). Quantifying User Satisfaction in Mobile Cloud Games. *Proceeding of Workshop on Mobile Video* Delivery. Retrieved August 01, 2016 from http://ieeexplore.ieee.org/xpls/abs_all.jsp?arnumber=7122897

Huang, C., Hsu, C., Chen, D., & Cheni, K. (2014). Quantifying User Satisfaction in Mobile Cloud Games. *Proceedings of Workshop on Mobile Video Delivery*. Retrieved August 01, 2016 from http://ieeexplore.ieee.org/xpls/abs_all.jsp?arnumber=7122897

Kim, H. (2013). Mobile Games with an Efficient Scaling Scheme in the Cloud. *Proceedings of the 2013 International Conference on Information Science and Applications (ICISA)*. Retrieved August 09, 2016 from http://ieeexplore.ieee.org/xpls/abs_all.jsp?arnumber=6579356

Kim, H. (2013). Mobile Games with an Efficient Scaling Scheme in the Cloud. *2013 International Conference on Information Science and Applications (ICISA)*, 1-3. Retrieved on August 09, 2016 from http://ieeexplore.ieee.org/xpls/abs_all.jsp?arnumber=6579356

Netimperative (2015). China digital trends in 2015: Huge shift to mobile as growth slows. Retrieved August 01, 2016 from http://www.netimperative.com/2015/09/china-digital-trends-in-2015-huge-shift-to-mobile-as-growth-slows/

OnLive. (2016). Retrieved July 30, 2016 from http://onlive.com/

OTOY. (2015). Retrieved on July 30, 2016 from http://www.home.otoy.com

StreamMyGame. (2012). Retrieved August 01, 2016 from http://streammygame.com/smg/index.php

Tam, V., Yi, A., Lam, E. Y., Chan, C., & Yuen, A. H. K. (2013). Using Cloud Computing and Mobile Devices to Facilitate Students Learning Through E-Learning Games. *Proceedings of the IEEE 13th International Conference on Advanced Learning Technologies* (pp. 471 – 472). Retrieved August 03, 2016 from http://ieeexplore.ieee.org/xpls/abs_all.jsp?arnumber=6601990

Tayade, D. (2014). Mobile Cloud Computing: Issues, Security, Advantages, Trends. *International Journal of Computer Science and Information Technologies, 5*(5), 6635-6639. Retrieved August 11, 2016 from http://citeseerx.ist.psu.edu/viewdoc/download?doi=10.1.1.660.8874&rep=rep1&type=pdf

Zamith, M., Joselli, M., Esteban, W. G. C., Montenegro, A., & Regina, C. P. Leal-Toledo; Luis Valente; Bruno Feijó (2011). A Distributed Architecture for Mobile Digital Games Based on Cloud Computing. *Proceedings of the 2011 Brazilian Symposium on Games and Digital Entertainment (SBGAMES)* (pp. 79-88). Retrieved August 02, 2016 from http://ieeexplore.ieee.org/xpls/abs_all.jsp?arnumber=6363221

Zamith, M., Joselli, M., Clua, E. W. G., Montenegro, A., Leal-Toledo, R. C. P., Valente, L., & Feijo, B. (2011). A Distributed Architecture for Mobile Digital Games Based on Cloud Computing. *Proceedings of the 2011 Brazilian Symposium on Games and Digital Entertainment (SBGAMES)* (pp. 79-88). Retrieved August 02, 2016 from http://ieeexplore.ieee.org/xpls/abs_all.jsp?arnumber=6363221

ADDITIONAL READING

Bose, R. & Sarddar, D. (2015). A new approach in mobile gaming on cloud-based architecture using Citrix and VMware technologies. *Brazilian Journal of Science and Technology*. Retrieved November 23, 2016 from http://link.springer.com/article/10.1186/s40552-015-0012-1

Chen, D. Z. H. (2012, March 23). Data security and privacy protection issues in cloud computing. *Paper presented at the International Conference on Computer Science and Electronics Engineering*, Hangzhou, China. Retrieved July 7, 2016 from http://ieeexplore.ieee.org/xpls/abs_all.jsp?arnumber=6187862

Chuah, S. P., & Cheung, N. M. (2014). Layered Coding for Mobile Cloud Gaming. *Proceedings of International Workshop on Massively Multiuser Virtual Environments MoViD'14*. Retrieved August 10, 2016 from http://dl.acm.org/citation.cfm?id=2577395

Cocking, L. (2012). *The future of mobile cloud infrastructure*. Retrieved July 9, 2016 from http://www.guardtime.com/2012/08/13/the-future-of mobile cloud- infrastructure/

Decker, B. (2016). Cloud gaming – what is it and what's the impact of it? *Digitalriver.com*. Retrieved November 21, 2016 from https://www.digitalriver.com/cloud-gaming-what-is-it-and-whats-the-impact-of-it/

Fernando, N., Loke, S. W., & Rahayu, W. (2013). Mobile cloud computing: A survey. *Future Generation Computer Systems, 29*(1), 84–106. Retrieved July 11, 2016 from http://www.sciencedirect.com/science/article/pii/S0167739X12001318

Galli, H., & Padmanabham, P. (2013). Data security in cloud using hybrid encryption and decryption. *International journal of advanced research in computer science and software engineering*. Retrieved July 10, 2016 from http://www.ijarcce.com/upload/2013/august/23-o-Moni%20Tamil%20-data%20security%20and%20privacy%20in%20cloud.pdf

Grobauer, B., Walloschek, T., & Stocker, E. (2011). Understanding cloud computing vulnerabilities. *IEEE Security and Privacy*, 8(2), 50–57. Retrieved July 8 2016 from http://ieeexplore.ieee.org/xpls/abs_all.jsp?arnumber=5487489 doi:10.1109/MSP.2010.115

Huang, C., Hsu, C., Chen, D., & Cheni, K. (2014). Quantifying User Satisfaction in Mobile Cloud Games. *Proceedings of Workshop on Mobile Video Delivery MoViD'14*. Retrieved August 01, 2016 from http://ieeexplore.ieee.org/xpls/abs_all.jsp?arnumber=7122897

Jamil, D. H. Z. (2011). Cloud computing security. *International Journal of Engineering Science and Technology*, 3(4). Retrieved July 8, 2016 from http://link.springer.com/article/10.1007/s00170-012-4163-7

Kevin, H., Khan, L., Kantarcioglu, M., & Thuraisingham, B. (2012). Security issues for cloud computing. In *Optimizing Information Security and Advancing Privacy Assurance: New Technologies*. Retrieved July 8, 2016 from https://books.google.com.pk/books?hl=en&lr=&id=r1-wsl9LbX4C&oi=fnd&pg=PR1&dq=Kevin,+H.,+Khan,+L.,+Kantarcioglu,+M.,+Thuraisingham,+B.+(2012).+Security+issues+for+cloud+computing+Optimizing+Information+Security+and+Advancing+Privacy+Assurance:+New+Technologies.(&ots=Wcf4wgEAKc&sig=CQlX8ctEGhWCtT5NS_Fk8QrZhho#v=onepage&q&f=false

Kim, H. (2013). Mobile Games with an Efficient Scaling Scheme in the Cloud. *Proceedings of the 2013 International Conference on Information Science and Applications (ICISA)*. Retrieved August 09, 2016 from http://ieeexplore.ieee.org/xpls/abs_all.jsp?arnumber=6579356

Kshetri, N. (2013). Privacy and security issues in cloud computing: The role of institutions and institutional evolution. *Telecommunications Policy*, 37(4-5), 372–386. http://www.sciencedirect.com/science/article/pii/S0308596112000717 Retrieved July 9, 2016

Leavitt, N. (2009). Is cloud computing really ready for prime time? *Computer*, 42(1), 15–20. Retrieved July 9 2016 from http://www.hh.se/download/18.70cf2e49129168da0158000123279/1341267677241/8+Is+Cloud+Computing+Ready.pdf doi:10.1109/MC.2009.20

Lee, K., Chu, D., Cuervo, E., Kopf, J., Degtyarev, Y., Grizan, S., . . . Flinn, J. (2015). Outatime: Using Speculation to Enable Low-Latency Continuous Interaction for Mobile Cloud Gaming. Retrieved August 10, 2016 from http://research.microsoft.com/en-us/um/people/alecw/mobisys-2015-outatime.pdf

Marinelli, E. (2009, September). Cloud Computing on Mobile Devices using Map Reduce/ Master Thesis Draft, Computer Science Dept., Carnegie Mellon University (CMU) 2009. Retrieved July 8, 2016 from http://oai.dtic.mil/oai/oai?verb=getRecord&metadataPrefix=html&identifier=ADA512601

Miica (2016). Retrieved November 22, 2016 from https://www.ericsson.com/research-blog/cloud/low-energy-mobile-cloud-gaming/

Popovic, K., & Hocenski, Z. (2010). Cloud Computing Security issues and challenges. *Proceedings of the 33rd International convention MIPRO*. USA: IEEE Computer Society Washington DC. Retrieved July 9, 2016 from http://jisajournal.springeropen.com/articles/10.1186/1869-0238-4-5

Ramgovind, S., Eloff, M. M., & Smith, E. (2010). The management of security in cloud computing. *Paper presented at the 2010 Information Security for South Africa, Sandton, and Johannesburg*. Retrieved July 10, 2016 from http://ieeexplore.ieee.org/xpls/abs_all.jsp?arnumber=5588290

Rohit, B., & Sanyal, S. (2012). Survey on security issues in cloud computing and associated mitigation techniques. *International Journal of Computers and Applications, 47*. Retrieved July 10, 2016 from http://www.ijcaonline.org/archives/volume47/number18/7292-0578

Ruay-Shiung Chang, J. G., & Gao, V. Jingsha He; Roussos, G.; Wei-Tek Tsai. (2013, March 25-28). Mobile cloud computing research - issues, challenges and needs. *Proceedings of the 2013 IEEE 7th International Symposium on Service Oriented System Engineering (SOSE)* (p. 442). Retrieved July 8, 2016 from http://ieeexplore.ieee.org/xpls/abs_all.jsp?arnumber=6525561

Umair, S., Muneer, U., Zahoor, M. N., & Malik, A. W. (2015). Mobile computing: issues and challenges. *Paper presented at the 12th International Conference on High-capacity Optical Networks and Enabling/Emerging Technologies (HONET)*, Islamabad, Pakistan. Retrieved July 6, 2016 from http://ieeexplore.ieee.org/xpls/abs_all.jsp?arnumber=7395438

Umair, S., Muneer, U., Zahoor, M. N., & Malik, A. W. (2016). Mobile Cloud Computing Future Trends and Opportunities. Managing and Processing Big Data in Cloud Computing, 105. Retrieved August 19, 2016 from books.google.com.pk/books?hl=en&lr=&id=9NFYCwAAQBAJ&oi=fnd&pg=PA105&dq=Mobile+Cloud+Computing+Future+Trends+and+Opportunities&ots=fz6JQWOmR5&sig=qPDbyG7woLbqn6-IogYgpNeKlZo#v=onepage&q=Mobile%20Cloud%20Computing%20Future%20Trends%20and%20Opportunities&f=false

Vanhatupa, J. M. (2010). Browser Games for Online Communities. *International Journal of Wireless & Mobile Networks, 2*(3), 39-47. Retrieved August 18, 2016 from http://airccse.org/journal/jwmn/0203ijwmn03.pdf

Vanhatupa, J. M. (2013). On the Development of Browser Games – Current Technologies and the Future. *International Journal of Computer Information Systems and Industrial Management Applications*. Retrieved on August 18, 2016 from http://www.mirlabs.org/ijcisim/regular_papers_2013/Paper81.pdf

Zamith, M., Joselli, M., Clua, E. W. G., Montenegro, A., Leal-Toledo, R. C. P., Valente, L., & Feijo, B. (2011). A Distributed Architecture for Mobile Digital Games Based on Cloud Computing. *Proceedings of the 2011 Brazilian Symposium on Games and Digital Entertainment (SBGAMES)* (pp. 79 – 88). Retrieved August 02, 2016 from http://ieeexplore.ieee.org/xpls/abs_all.jsp?arnumber=6363221

KEY TERMS AND DEFINITIONS

Cloud Computing: The process of providing shared resources and other services to user on demand, that can be accessed from anywhere provided the internet connection.

Cloud Service: Resources that are delivered over the internet are known as cloud service.

Gaming-as-a-Service (GaaS): Cloud services provided for gaming. Other name for Cloud Gaming.

Infrastructure as a Service (IaaS): Virtualized computing resources available over the internet is the responsibility of infrastructure as a service.

MCG: MCG stands for Mobile Cloud Gaming. It is about that user plays game on his mobile device with all processing done on servers. High quality images are sent to user via wireless network (Chuah and Cheung, 2014).

Mobile Browser Gaming (MBG): Mobile Browser Gaming Playing games on mobile without installing games on mobile device is known as MBG. They provide distinct features like multi-user playing, played on web browser, playing with single account and long duration games (Vanhatupa, 2010).

Mobile Cloud Computing (MCC): Mobile Cloud Computing is the combination of cloud computing, mobile computing and wireless networks to bring rich computational resources to mobile users, network operators, as well as cloud computing providers.

Mobile Video Gaming (MVG): Playing video games on mobile without installing games on mobile device is known as MVG.

Platform as a Service (PaaS): Platform as a service allows the customers to develop, run and manage their applications.

Software as a Service (SaaS): Software as a service is centrally hosted in which software is accredited on subscription basis.

Compilation of References

3rd Generation Partnership Project (3GPP). (2014a). 3GPP TS 36.321 LTE Evolved Universal Terrestrial Radio Access (E-UTRA); Medium Access Control (MAC) Protocol Specification, version 12.2.0, Release 12.

3rd Generation Partnership Project (3GPP). (2014b). 3GPP TS 36.331 LTE Evolved Universal Terrestrial Radio Access (E-UTRA); Radio Resource Control (RRC); Protocol Specification, version 12.2.0, Release 12.

3rd Generation Partnership Project (3GPP). (2016a). 3GPP TS 36.211 3GPP TSG RAN Evolved Universal Terrestrial Radio Access (E-UTRA) Physical Channels and Modulation, version 13.1.0, Release 13.

3rd Generation Partnership Project (3GPP). (2016b). 3GPP TS 36.213 3GPP TSG RAN Evolved Universal Terrestrial Radio Access (E-UTRA) Physical layer procedures, version 13.1.1, Release 13.

Abe, N., & Li, H. (1996). Learning word association norms using tree cut pair models. *Proceedings of 13th International Conference on Machine Learning*, Bari, Italy.

Abomhara, M., & Køien, G. M. (2015). Cyber Security and the Internet of Things: Vulnerabilities, Threats, Intruders and Attacks. *Journal of Cyber Security*, *4*, 65–88. doi:10.13052/jcsm2245-1439.414

Aggarwal, C. C., Ashish, N., & Sheth, A. (2013). *The internet of things: a survey from the data-centric perspective. In Managing and Mining Sensor Data*. Springer.

Agrawal, D., Das, S., & Abbadji, A. (2011). Big Data and Computing: Current State and Future Opportunities. Retrieved from https://www.researchgate.net/publication/221103048_Big_Data_and_Cloud_Computing_Current_State_and_Future_Opportunities

Akyildiz, I., Gutierrez-Estevez, D., & Reyes, E. (2010). The Evolution to 4G Cellular Systems: LTE-Advanced. *Physical Communication*, *3*(4), 217–244. doi:10.1016/j.phycom.2010.08.001

Alahuhta, P., Helaakoski, H., & Smirnov, A. (2005, October). Adoption of mobile services in business-case study of mobile CRM. *Proceedings of the IEEE International Conference on e-Business Engineering ICEBE '05* (pp. 531-534). IEEE. doi:10.1109/ICEBE.2005.22

Albright, A., & Hayes, B. (2003). Rules vs. analogy in English past tenses: A computational/experimental study. *Cognition*, *90*(2), 119–161. doi:10.1016/S0010-0277(03)00146-X PMID:14599751

Al-Fuqaha, A., Guizani, M., Mohammadi, M., Aledhari, M., & Ayyash, M. (2015). Internet of Things: A Survey on Enabling Technologies, Protocols, and Applications. *IEEE Communication Surveys & Tutorials*, *17*(4), 2347-2376.

Alingod, J. (2013). How smartphones could be ruining your relationship. *Live Bold and Bloom*. Retrieved from http://liveboldandbloom.com/10/relationships/how-smartphones-couldbe-ruining-your-relationship

Alliance for Telecommunications Industry Solutions. (2017) Retrieved from http://www.atis.org

Almunawar, M. N., & Anshari, M. (2014). Applying Transaction Cost Economy to Construct a Strategy for Travel Agents in Facing Disintermediation Threats. *Journal of Internet Commerce, Taylor & Francis, 13*(3-4), 211–232. doi: 10.1080/15332861.2014.961331

Aly, M., Sallam, A., Gnanasekaran, B. M., Aref, W. G., Ouzzani, M., & Ghafoor, A. (2012). M3: Stream Processing on Main-Memory MapReduce. *Proceedings of ICDE* (pp. 1253–1256).

Amazon S3 Availability Event. (2008). Retrieved November 29, 2012 from http://status.aws.amazon.com/s3-20080720.html

Anderson, J.R., Hardy, E.E., Roach, J.T., & Witmer, R.E. (1976). *A Land Use and Land Cover Classification System For Use With Remote Sensor Data.*

Anshari, M., & Alas, Y. (2015). Smartphones Habits, Necessities, and Big Data Challenges. *The Journal of High Technology Management Research*, 26(2), 177-185. doi:10.1016/j.hitech.2015.09.005

Anshari, M., Almunawar, M.N., Low, P.K.C., & Al-Mudimigh A.S. (2012). Empowering Clients Through E-Health in Healthcare Services: Case Brunei. *International Quarterly of Community Health Education, 33*(2), 189-219. doi:10.2190/IQ.33.2.g

Anshari, M., Alas, Y., & Guan, L. S. (2015). Pervasive Knowledge, Social Networks, and Cloud Computing: E-Learning 2.0. *Eurasia Journal of Mathematics. Science & Technology Education, 11*(5), 909–921. doi:10.12973/eurasia.2015.1360a

Anshari, M., Alas, Y., Yunus, N. M., Sabtu, N. I., & Hamid, M. S. (2016). Online Learning: Trends, Issues, and Challenges in Big Data Era. *Journal of E-Learning and Knowledge Society, 12*(1), 121–134.

ao, J., Gruhn, V., He, J., Roussos, G., & Tsai, W. T. (2013, March 25-28). Mobile Cloud Computing Research - Issues, Challenges and Needs. *Proceedings of the 2013 IEEE 7th International Symposium on Service Oriented System Engineering* (pp. 442, 453).

AOL Apologizes for Release of User Search Data. (2006). Retrieved August 7, 2006 from news.cnet.com/2010-1030_3-6102793.html

Armbrust, M., Fox, A., Griffith, R., Joseph, A. D., Katz, R. H., Konwinsky, A., . . . Zaharia, M. (2009). Above the Clouds: A Berkley View of Cloud Computing. Technical Report No. UCB/EECS-2009-28, Department of Electrical Engineering and Computer Sciences, University of California at Berkley. February 10, 2009. Retrieved from: http://www.eecs.berkeley.edu/Pubs/TechRpts/2009/EECS-2009-28.pdf

Armbrust, M., Fox, A., Griffith, R., Joseph, A. D., Katz, R., Konwinski, A., ... & Zaharia, M. (2014). Above the clouds: A Berkeley view of Cloud Computing (Report No. UCB/EECS-2009-28). UC Berkeley EECS. Retrieved July 1, 2016 from http://www.eecs.berkeley.edu/Pubs/TechRpts/2009/EECS-2009-28.html

Arora, D., & Malik, P. (2015). Analytics: Key to go from generating big data to deriving business value. *Proceedings of the IEEE First International Conference on Big Data Computing Service and Applications.* doi:10.1109/BigDataService.2015.62

Ashford, W. (2016). IPv6 alone will not secure IoT. *ComputerWeekly Magazine.*

Ashton, K. (2009, June). That 'internet of things' thing in the real world, things matter more than ideas. *RFID Journal.* Retrieved from http://www.rfidjournal.com/article/print/4986

Ashton, K. (2009). That "Internet of Things" Thing In the Real World, Things Matter More than Ideas. *RFID Journal, 22*, 97–114.

Asin, A., & Gascon, D. (2012). *50 Sensor Applications for a Smarter World.*

Association for Retail Technology Standards (ARTS). (1997-2017). Retrieved from http://www.nrf-arts.org

Assuncao, M. D., Calheiros, R. N., Bianchi, S., Netto, M. A. S., & Buyya, R. (2015). *Big Data Computing and Clouds*: Trends and Future Directions. *J. Parallel Distrib. Computing*, *79-80*, 3–15. doi:10.1016/j.jpdc.2014.08.003

Astely, D., Stattin, M., Wikstrom, G., Cheng, J.-F., Hoglund, A., Frenne, M., & Gunnarsson, F. et al. (2016). LTE Release 14 Outlook. *IEEE Communications Magazine*, *54*(6), 44–49. doi:10.1109/MCOM.2016.7497765

Atif, Y., Ding, J., & Jeusfeld, M. A. (2016). Internet of Things Approach to Cloud-Based Smart Car Parking. *Proceedings of the 7th International Conference on Emerging Ubiquitous Systems and Pervasive Networks (EUSPN '16)*.

Atzori, L., Iera, A., & Morabito, G. (2010). The internet of things: A survey. *Computer Networks*, *54*(15), 2787–2805. doi:10.1016/j.comnet.2010.05.010

Badger, L., Grance, T., Patt-Corner, R., & Voas, J. (2011, May). Draft Cloud Computing Synopsis and Recommendations. National Institute of Standards and Technology (NIST) Special Publication 800-146. US Department of Commerce. Retrieved November 20, 2012 from http://csrc.nist.gov/publications/drafts/800-146/Draft-NIST-SP800-146.pdf

Baharadwaj, A. (2000). A resource-based perspective on information technology capability and firm performance: An empirical investigation. *Management Information Systems Quarterly*, *24*(1), 169–196. doi:10.2307/3250983

Bahga, A., & Madisetti, V. (2014). *Internet of Things: A Hands-On Approach*. Vijay Madisetti.

Bahl, P., Chandra, R., Moscibroda, T., Murty, R., & Welsh, M. (2009). White Space Networking with Wi-Fi Like Connectivity. *SIGCOMM Comput. Commun. Rev.*, *39*(4), 27–38. doi:10.1145/1594977.1592573

Bai, Y. W., & Teng, H. , (2008). Enhancement of the sensing distance of an embedded surveillance system with video streaming recording triggered by an infrared sensor circuit. *Proc. SICE Annual. Conference* (pp. 1657–1662).

Bailey, T. M., & Hahn, U. (2005). Phoneme Similarity and Confusability. *Journal of Memory and Language*, *52*(3), 339–362. doi:10.1016/j.jml.2004.12.003

Baker, C. F., Fillmore, C. J., & Lowe, J. B. (1998). The Berkeley FrameNet project. In C. Boitet, & P. Whitelock (Eds.), *Proceedings of the Thirty-Sixth Annual Meeting of the Association for Computational Linguistics and Seventeenth International Conference on Computational Linguistics*, San Francisco, California (pp. 86–90). Morgan Kaufmann Publishers.

Bakos, J. Y. (1997). Reducing Buyer Search Costs: Implications for Electronic Marketplaces. *Management Science*, *43*(12), 1676–1692.

Bakos, J. Y. (1997). Reducing Buyer Search Costs: Implications for Electronic Marketplaces. *Management Science*, *43*(12), 1676–1692. doi:10.1287/mnsc.43.12.1676

Bannister, S., & Beckett, P. (2009). Enhancing powerline communications in the "Smart Grid" using OFDMA. *Proceedings of the Australasian Universities Power Engineering Conference (AUPEC)*, Adelaide, Australia.

Barra, M. (2013, April 27). The Clinical Development Plan. *Pharmupdates*. Retrieved September 24, 2016, from https://pharmupdates.wordpress.com/2013/04/27/the-clinical-development-plan/

Basavaraju, S.R. (2015, December). Automatic Smart Parking System using Internet of Things (IOT). *International Journal of Scientific and Research Publications*, *5*(12).

Baskiyar, S., & Abdel-Kader, R. (2010). Energy aware DAG scheduling on heterogeneous systems. *Cluster Computing*, *13*(4), 373–383. doi:10.1007/s10586-009-0119-6

Beal, V. (2015). Batch processing. Webopedia. QuinStreet Inc. Retrieved 5 November 2015 from http://www.webopedia. com/TERM/B/batch_processing.html

Bellavista, P., Cardone, G., Corradi, A., & Foschini, L. (2013). Convergence of MANET and WSN in IoT urban scenarios. *IEEE Sensors Journal*, *13*(10), 3558–3567. doi:10.1109/JSEN.2013.2272099

Benjamin, R. I., & Wigand, R. (1995). Electronic Markets and Virtual Value Chains on the Information Superhighway. *Sloan Management Review*, *36*(2), 62–72.

Benkhelifa, E., Abdel-Maguid, M., Ewenike, S., & Heatley, D. (2014). The Internet of Things: The eco-system for sustainable growth. *Proceedings of the 2014 IEEE/ACS 11th International Conference on Computer Systems and Applications (AICCSA)* (pp. 836–842). doi:10.1109/AICCSA.2014.7073288

Berthelsen, E. (2016). The value engine in IoT data and analytics. *TechTarget*.

Bertion, E., Paci, F., & Ferrini, R. (2009, March). Privacy-Preserving Digital Identity Management for Cloud Computing. IEEE Computer Society Data Engineering Bulletin.

Bhandarkar, M. (2010). MapReduce programming with apache Hadoop. *Proceedings of the 2010 IEEE International Symposium on Parallel & Distributed Processing (IPDPS)*. doi:10.1109/IPDPS.2010.5470377

Biggs & Vidalis. (2009, November). Cloud Computing: The Impact on Digital Forensic Investigations. *Proceedings of the 7th International Conference for Internet Technology and Secured Transactions (ICITST'09)*, London, UK.

Billard, E. A., & Pasquale, J. C. (1992). Effects of periodic communication on distributed decision-making. Proceedings of the IEEE International Conference on Systems, Man and Cybernetics, Chicago, IL (Vol. 1, pp. 49-54). doi:10.1109/ICSMC.1992.271803

Blaze, M., Kannan, S., Lee, I., Sokolsky, O., Smith, J. M., Keromytis, A. D., & Lee, W. (2009). Dynamic Trust Management. *IEEE Computer*, *42*(2), 44–52. doi:10.1109/MC.2009.51

BoHyun. K. (2013). Chapter 1: the mobile shift. *Library Technology Reports*, 49(6), 5-8. Retrieved from https://journals. ala.org/ltr/article/view/4509/5291

Borkar, V. R., Carey, M. J., & Li, C. (2012). *Big data platforms: what's next?* XRDS: Crossroads. *The ACM Magazine for Students*, *19*(1), 44–49. doi:10.1145/2331042.2331057

Boulon, J., Konwinski, A., Qi, R., Rabkin, A., Yang, E., & Yang, M. (2008). Chukwa, A large-scale monitoring system. *Proceedings of CCA* (Vol. 8, pp. 1–5).

Brown, J., & Khan, J. Y. (2012a). Performance comparison of LTE FDD and TDD based Smart Grid communications networks for uplink biased traffic. *Proceedings of the IEEE International Conference on Smart Grid Communications (SmartGridComm)*, Tainan, Taiwan (pp. 276-281). doi:10.1109/SmartGridComm.2012.6485996

Brown, J., & Khan, J. Y. (2012b). Performance analysis of an LTE TDD based smart grid communications network for uplink biased traffic. Proceedings of the IEEE Globecom Workshops, Anaheim, California, USA (pp. 1502-1507).

Bruening, P. J., & Treacy, B. C. (2009). Cloud Computing: Privacy, Security Challenges. Bureau of National Affairs.

Burton, D. (2015, December). How Clinical Analytics Will Improve the Cost and Quality of Healthcare Delivery. *Health Catalyst Insights*.

Buyya, R., Ramamohanarao, K., Leckie, C., Calhieros, N., Dastjerdi, A., & Versteeg, S. (2015). Big Data Analytics-Enhanced Cloud Computing: Challenges, Architectural Elements, and Future Directions. Retrieved from http://arxiv. org/abs/1510.06486

Buyya, R., Yeo, C. S., Venugopal, S., Broberg, J., & Brandic, I. (2009). Cloud computing and emerging IT platforms: Vision, hype, and reality for delivering computing as the 5th utility. *Future Generation Computer Systems*, *25*(6), 599–616. doi:10.1016/j.future.2008.12.001

Cai, W., & Leung, V. C. M. (2013). Next Generation Mobile Cloud Gaming. *Proceedings of the IEEE Seventh International Symposium on Service-Oriented System Engineering*, 550-559. Retrieved August 04, 2016 from http://www-users.cselabs.umn.edu/classes/Spring-2015/csci8980/papers/Applications/gaming.pdf

Cai, W., Chen, M., & Leung, V. C. M. (2014). Toward Gaming as a Service. *IEEE Internet Computing*, *18*(3), 12–18. Retrieved August 08 2016 from http://ieeexplore.ieee.org/xpls/abs_all.jsp?arnumber=6818918 doi:10.1109/MIC.2014.22

Cao, F., Ester, M., Qian, W., & Zhou, A. (2006). Density-based clustering over an evolving data stream with noise., *Proceedings of the Sixth SIAM International Conference on Data Mining* SIAM (pp. 328-339). doi:10.1137/1.9781611972764.29

Carnegie Mellon's Robotics Academy. (n. d.). What is an IR sensor? Retrieved from education.rec.ri.cmu.edu/content/electronics/boe/ir_sensor/1.html

Caron, A. H., & Caronia, H. (2015). Mobile communication tools as morality building devices. In *Encyclopedia of Mobile Phone Behavior* (pp. 25–45). Hershey, PA: IGI Global.

Cearley, D. W. (2010). Cloud Computing: Key Initiative Overview. *Gartner*. Retrieved July 1, 2016 from http://www.gartner.com/it/initiatives/pdf/KeyInitiativeOverview CloudComputing.pdf

Center for the Protection of Natural Infrastructure (CPNI). (2010, March). Information Security Briefing on Cloud Computing. Retrieved November 29, 2012 from http://www.cpni.gov.uk/Documents/Publications/2010/2010007-ISB_cloud_computing.pdf

Chandrasekaran, S., Cooper, O., Deshpande, A., Franklin, M. J., Hellerstein, J. M., Hong, W., ... Shah, M. A. (2003). Telegraphic: Continuous dataflow processing for an uncertain world. In ACM SIGMOD international conference on Management of data (pp. 668-668). doi:10.1145/872757.872857

Chang, F., Dean, J., Ghemawat, S., Wilson, H. C., Wallach, D. A., Burrows, M., . . . Robert, G. E. (2006). Bigtable: a distributed storage system for structured data. Proceedings of the 7th USENIX Symposium on Operating Systems Design and Implementation (OSDI '06) (*Vol. 7*). USENIX Association, Berkeley, CA, USA.

Chang, F., Dean, J., Ghemawat, S., Hsieh, W. C., Wallach, D. A., Burrows, M., & Gruber, R. E. et al. (2006). *Bigtable: A Distributed Storage System for Structured Data Research.*

Chansanchai, A. (2011). 8 in 10 Americans depend on cellphones. *NBC News*. Retrieved from http://www.nbcnews.com/technology/8-10-americans-depend-cellphones-121536

Chase, J. (2013). The Evolution of the Internet of Things (white paper). Texas Instruments, Dallas, Texas.

Chaves, L. W. F., & Nochta, Z. (2010). *Breakthrough towards the Internet of Things*. Springer-Verlag Berlin Heidelberg.

Chen, F., Kodialam, M., & Lakshman, T. V. (2012). Joint scheduling of processing and shuffle phases in MapReduce systems. *Proceedings of IEEE INFOCOM '12* (pp. 1143–1151).

Chen, S., Xu, H., Liu, D., Hu, B., & Wang, H. (2014). A Vision of IoT: Applications, Challenges, and Opportunities with China Perspective. *IEEE Internet of Things Journal*, *1*(4), 349-359.

Chen, Y., Paxson, V., & Katz, R. H. (2010). What's New About Cloud Computing Security? (Technical Report UCB/EECS-2010-5). EECS Department, University of California, Berkeley. Retrieved from http://www.eecs.berkeley.edu/Pubs/TechRpts/2010/EECS-2010-5.html

Chen, C. L. P., & Zhang, C. Y. (2014). *Data-intensive applications, challenges, techniques and technologies*: A survey on Big Data. *Information Sciences*, *275*, 314–347. doi:10.1016/j.ins.2014.01.015

Chen, F., Rong, X.-H., Deng, P., & Ma, S.-L. (2011). A survey of device collaboration technology and system software. *Tien Tzu Hsueh Pao*, *39*(2), 440–447.

Chen, M., Mao, S., & Liu, Y. (2014). Big data: A survey. *Mobile Networks and Applications*, *19*(2), 171–209. doi:10.1007/s11036-013-0489-0

Chen, M., Mao, S., Zhang, Y., & Leung, V. (2014). *Big Data: Related Technologies, Challenges and Future Prospects*. Springer. doi:10.1007/978-3-319-06245-7

Chen, S. C., Xu, H., Liu, D., Hu, B., & Wang, H. (2014). A Vision of IoT: Applications, Challenges, and Opportunities with China Perspective. *IEEE Internet of Things Journal*, *1*(4), 350–351.

Chen, X. (2015). Decentralized Computation Offloading Game For Mobile Cloud Computing. *IEEE Transactions on Parallel and Distributed Systems*, *26*(4), 974–983. Retrieved July 28 2016 from http://ieeexplore.ieee.org/xpl/articleDetails.jsp?tp=&arnumber=6787113 doi:10.1109/TPDS.2014.2316834

Chen, X.-W., & Lin, X. (2014). Big data deep learning challenges and perspective. *IEEE Access.*, *2*, 514–522. doi:10.1109/ACCESS.2014.2325029

Chen, Y. C., Han, F., Yang, Y.-H., Ma, H., Han, Y., Jiang, C., & Liu, K. J. R. et al. (2014). Time-reversal wireless paradigm for green Internet of Things: An overview. *IEEE Internet Things Journal*, *1*(1), 81–98. doi:10.1109/JIOT.2014.2308838

Chenyang, B. C., Saifullar, A., & Mosha, B. L. (2016). Real-Time Wireless Sensor-Actuator Networks for Industrial Cyber-Physical Systems. *IEEE Proceedings*, *104*(5), 1013-1014.

Chen, Z., Liu, S., Wenyin, L., Pu, G., & Ma, W.-Y. (2003). Building a Web Thesaurus form Web Link Structure. *Proceedings of SIGIR* (pp. 48-55).

Chiswick, B. R., & Miller, P. W. (2005). Linguistic Distance: A Quantitative Measure of the Distance Between English and Other Languages. *Journal of Multilingual and Multicultural Development*, *26*(1), 1–11. doi:10.1080/14790710508668395

Chow, R., Golle, P., Jakobsson, M., Shi, E., Staddon, J., Masuoka, R., & Molina, J. (2009, November). Controlling Data in the Cloud: Outsourcing Computation without Outsourcing Control. *Proceedings of the ACM Workshop on Cloud Computing Security (CCSW'09)*, Chicago, Illinois, USA (pp. 85-90). New York, USA: ACM Press. doi:10.1145/1655008.1655020

Chu, C. T., Kim, S. K., Lin, Y. A., Yu, Y., Bradski, G. R., Ng, A. Y., & Olukotun, K. (2006). Map-Reduce for Machine Learning on Multicore, Proc. 20th Ann. Conf. Neural Information Processing Systems (NIPS'06) (pp. 281-288).

Church, K. W., & Hanks, P. (1990). Word association norms, mutual information, and lexicography. *Computational Linguistics*, *16*(1), 22–29.

Cisco. (2012). Developing a Cloud-Computing Strategy for Higher Education. Retrieved July 1, 2016 from https://www.cisco.com/web/IN/solutions/strategy/assets/pdf/cloud_101_higher_education_wp.pdf

CityPuls. (2016). CityPulse Dataset Collection. Retrieved 10 May 2016 from iot.ee.surrey.ac.uk:8080/datasets.html

Clark, J., & Yallop, C. (1995). *An Introduction to Phonetics and Phonology*. Oxford: Blackwell.

Clemons, E., Reddi, S., & Row, M. (1993). The impact of information technology on the organization of economic activity: The move to the middle hypothesis. *Journal of Management Information Systems*, *10*(2), 9–35. doi:10.1080/07421222.1993.11517998

Comrie, B. (1989). *Language Universals and Linguistic Typology: Syntax and Morphology*. Oxford: Basil Blackwell.

Conner, M. (2010, May 27). Sensors empower the "Internet of Things." *EDN Network*. Retrieved from http://www.edn.com/article/509123-sensors_empower_the_Internet_of_Things_.php

Cooper, M., & Mell, P. (2012). Tackling Big Data. Retrieved from: http://csrc.nist.gov/groups/SMA/forum/documents/june2012presentations/f%csm_june2012_cooper_mell.pdf

Cornwall, P. (2016). Ericsson mobility report (tech. report). Ericsson. Retrieved 10 June 2016 from https://www.ericsson.com/res/docs/2016/ericsson-mobility-report-2016.pdf

Croft, W. (2001). *Radical Construction Grammar: Syntactic Theory in Typological Perspective*. Oxford: Oxford University Press. doi:10.1093/acprof:oso/9780198299554.001.0001

Cucchiara, R., Prati, A., Vezzani, R., Benini, L., Farella, E., & Zappi, P. (2006). Using a wireless sensor network to enhance video surveillance. *J. Ubiquitous Comput. Intell., 1(2)*, 187-196.

Cuff, D., Hansen, M., & Kang, J. (2008). Urban sensing: Out of the woods. *Communications of the ACM, 51*(3), 24–33. doi:10.1145/1325555.1325562

Daoud, M. I., & Kharma, N. (2011). A hybrid heuristic-genetic algorithm for task scheduling in heterogeneous processor networks. *Journal of Parallel and Distributed Computing, 71*(11), 1518–1531. doi:10.1016/j.jpdc.2011.05.005

Data Canvas Dataset. (2016). Retrieved 7 February 2016 from http://datacanvas.org/sense-your-city/

Data, S. (n. d.) Amara's Law. Retrieved from https://spotlessdata.com/amaras-law

Dean, J., & Ghemawat, S. (2004). MapReduce: Simplified data processing on large clusters, *Proceedings of the 6th OSDI* (pp. 137-150).

Dean, J., & Ghemawat, S. (2008). Map Reduce: Simplified Data Processing on Large Clusters. *Communications of the ACM, 51*. Retrieved on July 1, 2016 from http://dl.acm.org/citation.cfm?id=1327492

Delasko, J. M. (2007, March). U.S. Department of Health and Human Services Food and Drug Administration *(US, Food and Drug Administration, Center for Drug Evaluation and Research (CDER))*. Retrieved from http://www.fda.gov/downloads/drugs/guidancecomplianceregulatoryinformation/guidances/ucm080593.pdf

Diebold, F. (2000). Big Data: Dynamic Factor Models for Macroeconomic Measurement and Forecasting. *Discussion read to the Eighth World Congress of the Econometric Society.*

DiMasi, J. (2014). Clinical Approval Rate. In *Innovation in the Pharmaceutical Industry: New Estimates of R&D Costs*. Tufts. Retrieved September 10, 2016, from http://csdd.tufts.edu/files/uploads/Tufts_CSDD_briefing_on_RD_cost_study_-_Nov_18,_2014.pdf

Distributed Management Task Force. (2017). Retrieved from http://www.dmtf.org

Dowty, D. (1979). *Word Meaning and Montague Grammar*. Dordrecht: Reidel. doi:10.1007/978-94-009-9473-7

Dumbill, E. (2012). What is big data? An introduction to the big data landscape. *O'Reilly.com*. Retrieved November 9 2015 from http://radar.oreilly.com/2012/01/what-is-big-data.html

Dunning, T. (1993). Accurate methods for the statistics of surprise and coincidence. *Computational Linguistics, 19*(1), 61–74.

Dusi, M., D'Heureuse, N., Huici, F., Di Pietro, A., Bonelli, N., Bianchi, G., & Niccolini, S. et al. (2012). Blockmon: Flexible and high-performance big data stream analytics platform and its use cases. *NEC Tech. J., 7*(2), 102–106.

Eason, G., Noble, B., & Sneddon, I. N. (1955). On certain integrals of Lipschitz-Hankel type involving products of Bessel functions. *Philosophical Transactions of the Royal Society of London A: Mathematical, Physical and Engineering Sciences*, *247*(935), 529–551. doi:10.1098/rsta.1955.0005

Eaton, C., Deroos, D., Deutsch, T., Lapis, G., & Zikopoulos, P. (2012). *Understanding Big Data*. McGraw-Hill Companies.

Economist. (2010). *Data, data everywhere*. Retrieved 29 October 2015 from the Economist: http://www.economist.com/node/15557443

Elachi, C., & Van Zyll, J. (2006). *Introduction to the Physics and Techniques of Remote Sensing*. Hoboken, NJ, USA: Wiley. doi:10.1002/0471783390

Emani, C. K., Cullot, N., & Nicolle, C. (2015). Understandable Big Data: A survey. *Computer Science Review*, *17*, 70–81. doi:10.1016/j.cosrev.2015.05.002

Engineers Garage. (n. d.). Atmega16-microcontroller. Retrieved from http://www.engineersgarage.com/electronic-components/atmega16-microcontroller

Erickson, V. L., Achleitner, S., & Cerpa, A. E. (2013) POEM: Power-efficient occupancy-based energy management system. *Proceedings of the 12th International Conference on Information Processing in Sensor Networks*, Philadelphia, PA, USA (pp. 203-216).

European Network and Information Security Agency (ENISA). (2009). Cloud Computing: Cloud Computing: Benefits, Risks and recommendations for Information Security (report no: 2009).

European Smart Cities. (n. d.) Retrieved from http://www.smart-cities.eu

F. Palmer (Ed.) (1968). Studies in Linguistic Analysis 1930-1955. Harlow: Longman.

Fang, J. S., Hao, Q., Brady, D. J., Guenther, B. D., Burchett, J., Shankar, M., & Hsu, K. Y. et al. (2006). Path-Dependent Human Identification using a Pyroelectric Infrared Sensor and Fresnel Lens Arrays. *Opt. Exp*, *14*(2), 609–624. doi:10.1364/OPEX.14.000609 PMID:19503378

Fang, J. S., Hao, Q., Brady, D. J., Guenther, B. D., & Hsu, K. Y. (2006). Real-Time Human Identification using a Pyroelectric Infrared Detector Array and Hidden Markov Models. *Optics Express*, *14*(15), 6643–6658. doi:10.1364/OE.14.006643 PMID:19516845

Fatemieh, O., Chandra, R., & Gunter, C. A. (2010). Low Cost and Secure Smart Meter Communications using the TV White Spaces. *Proceedings of the 3rd International Symposium on Resilient Control Systems (ISRCS)*, Idaho Falls, ID, USA (pp. 37-42). doi:10.1109/ISRCS.2010.5602162

Fawcett, S. E., Wallin, C., Allred, C., Fawcett, A. M., & Magnan, G. M. (2011). Information technology as an enabler of supply chain collaboration: A dynamic-capabilities perspective. *J. Supply Chain Manag.*, *47*(1), 38–59. doi:10.1111/j.1745-493X.2010.03213.x

Fellbaum, C. (1998). *WordNet: An Electronic Lexical Database*. MIT Press.

Fernando, N., Loke, S. W., & Rahayu, W. (2013). Mobile cloud computing: A survey. *Future Generation Computer Systems*, *29*(1), 84–106. doi:10.1016/j.future.2012.05.023

Foster, I., Kesselman, C., Nick, J.M., Tuecke, S. (2008). Grid services for distributed system integration. *The New Net*, June, 37-46.

Frisch, S. A., Pierrehumbert, J. B., & Broe, M. B. (2004). Similarity Avoidance and the OCP. *Natural Language and Linguistic Theory*, *22*(1), 179–228. doi:10.1023/B:NALA.0000005557.78535.3c

Ft.com. (n. d.). Don't Cloud Your Vision. Retrieved from http://www.ft.com/cms/s/0/303680a6-bf51-11dd-ae63000779fd18c.html?nclick_check=1

G- Cluster. (2016). Retrieved July 30, 2016 from http://www.gcluster.com/eng

Gaikai (2013). Retrieved on July 30, 2016 from http://www.gaikai.com

Gama, J., Rodrigues, P. P., & Lopes, L. (2011). Clustering distributed sensor data streams using local processing and reduced communication. *Intelligent Data Analysis*, *15*(1), 3–28.

Gandomi, A., & Haider, M. (2015). Beyond the hype: Big data concepts, methods, and analytics. *International Journal of Information Management*, *1*(35), 137–144. doi:10.1016/j.ijinfomgt.2014.10.007

Gartner (2012). Hype-Cycle 2012 – Cloud Computing and Big Data. Retrieved from http://www.gartner.com/technology/research/hype-cycles/

Gartner. (2009). Gartner Says Cloud Customers Need Brokerages to Unlock the Potential of Cloud Services. Retrieved from http://www.gartner.com/it/page.jsp?id=1064712

Gartner. (n. d.). IT Glossary. Retrieved from http://www. gartner.com/it-glossary/big-data

Getz, K. (2014). Improving Protocol Design Feasibility to Drive Drug Development Economics and Performance. *International Journal of Environmental Research and Public Health IJERPH*, *11*(5), 5069–5080. doi:10.3390/ijerph110505069 PMID:24823665

Getz, K. A., Wenger, J., Campo, R. A., Seguine, E. S., & Kaitin, K. I. (2008). Assessing the Impact of Protocol Design Changes on Clinical Trial Performance. *American Journal of Therapeutics*, *15*(5), 450–457. doi:10.1097/MJT.0b013e31816b9027 PMID:18806521

Ghandour, A. (n. d.). Big data driven e-commerce architecture. *International Journal of Economics, Commerce and Management*, *3*(5), 940-947.

Ghosh, A., & Das, S. K. (2008). *Coverage and connectivity issues in wireless sensor networks*: A survey. *Pervasive and Mobile Computing*, *4*(3), 303–334. doi:10.1016/j.pmcj.2008.02.001

Gil, G. B., Berlanga, A., & Molina, J. M. (2012). Incontexto: Multisensor architecture to obtain people context from smartphones. *International Journal of Distributed Sensor Networks*, *15*. doi:10.1155/2012/758789

Glover, E. J., Tsioutsiouliklis, K., Lawrence, S., Pennock, D. M., & Flake, G. W. (2002). Using Web Structure for Classifying and Describing Web Pages. *Proceedings of WWW '02*.

González-Valenzuela, S., Chen, M., & Leung, V. C. (2011). Mobility support for health monitoring at home using wearable sensors. *IEEE Transactions on Information Technology in Biomedicine*, *15*(4), 539–549. doi:10.1109/TITB.2010.2104326 PMID:21216718

Gopinath, A. (2014) Analytics on Big Fast Data using a real time stream data processing architecture. Retrieved 18 May 2016 from https://fifthelephant.talkfunnel.com/2014/1066-analytics-on-big-fast-data-using-real-time-stream-

Gopinthan, U., & Gopinathan, D. (2003). Brady, and N. Pitsianis. (2003). Coded apertures for efficient pyroelectric motion tracking. *Opt. Exp.*, *11*(18), 2142–2152. doi:10.1364/OE.11.002142

Gorelik, E. (2013, January). Cloud Computing Models. Retrieved from http://web.mit.edu/smadnick/www/wp/2013-01.pdf

Grance & Mell. (2011). The NIST definition of cloud computing. (NIST Publication No. NIST SP- 800-145). Washington DC: US Department of Commerce. Retrieved from http://csrc.nist.gov/publications/drafts/800-146/Draft-NIST-SP800-146.pdf

Grandhi, S., & Chugh, R. (2012). Strategic Value of mobile CRM Applications: A Review of Mobile CRM at Dow Corning and DirecTV. *Proceedings of the International Conference on Innovation and Information Management (Vol. 36).*

Granjal, G. J., Monteiro, E., & Sa Silva, J. (2015). Security for the Internet of Things: A Survey of Existing Protocols and Open Research Issues. *IEEE Communications Surveys and Tutorials, 17*(3), 1294–1295. doi:10.1109/COMST.2015.2388550

GTC. (2010). Retrieved July 30, 2016 from http://www.nvidia.com/content/GTC-2010/pdfs/4004B GTC2010.pdf

GTmetrix. (n. d.) Analyze your site's speed and make it faster. Retrieved from www.GTMetrix.com

Gubbi, J., Buyya, R., Marusic, S., & Palaniswami, M. (2013). Internet of Things (IoT): A vision, architectural elements, and future directions. Elsevier. *Future Generation Computer Systems, 29*(7), 1645–1660. doi:10.1016/j.future.2013.01.010

Guillemin, P., & Friess, P. (2009, September). Internet of things strategic research roadmap, Technical report, The Cluster of European Research Projects. Retrieved from http://www.internet-of-things-research

Gupte, S., & Younis, M. (2015). Participatory-sensing-enabled Efficient Parking Management in Modern Cities. Proceedings of the 40th Annual IEEE Conference on Local Computer Networks (LCN '15), Clearwater Beach, Florida, USA.

Guzzetti, F., Mondini, A.C., Cardinali, M., Fiorucci, F., Santangelo, M., & Chang, K. (2012). Landslide inventory maps: New tools for an old problem. *Earth-Science Reviews, 112*(1– 2), 42-66.

Hadoop Distributed File System (HDFS). (2016). Definition from WhatIs.com. Retrieved 7 February 2016 from http://searchbusinessanalytics.techtarget.com/definition/Hadoop-Distributed-File-System-HDFS

Hahn, U., & Bailey, T. M. (2005). What Makes Words Sound Similar? *Cognition, 97*(3), 227–267. doi:10.1016/j.cognition.2004.09.006 PMID:16260261

Han, Z., Gao, R. X., & Fan, Z. (2012). Occupancy and Indoor Environment Quality Sensing for Smart Buildings. *Proceedings of the 5th European DSP Education and Research Conference* (EDERC '12), Graz, Austria (pp. 882-887). doi:10.1109/I2MTC.2012.6229557

Hao, Q., Brady, D. J., Guenther, B. D., Burchett, J. B., Shankar, M., & Feller, S. (2006). Human tracking with wireless distributed pyroelectric sensors. *IEEE Sensors Journal, 6*(6), 1683–1696. doi:10.1109/JSEN.2006.884562

Hao, Q., Hu, F., & Xiao, Y. (2009). Multiple human tracking and identification with wireless distributed pyroelectric sensor systems. *IEEE Sensors Journal, 3*, 428–439.

Happiest minds. (n. d.). Smart Parking (white paper). Online retrieved from http://www.happiestminds.com/whitepapers/smart-parking.pdf

Harny Abu Khair. (2013, September 17). Bru-HIMS records over 50 percent registrations. T*he Borneo Bulletin.* Retrieved from http://www.bt.com.bn/news national/2013/09/17/bru-hims-records-over-50-cent-registrations

Hea, W., Zhab, S., & Li, L. (2013). Social media competitive analysis and text mining: A case study in the Pizza industry. *International Journal of Information Management, 33*(1), 464–472. doi:10.1016/j.ijinfomgt.2013.01.001

Heeringa, W. (2004). Measuring Dialect Pronunciation Differences using Levenshtein Distance [Ph.D. thesis]. Rijksuniversiteit Groningen.

Hernández-Muñoz, J. M., Vercher, J. B., Muñoz, L., Galache, J. A., Presser, M., Hernández Gómez, L. A., & Pettersson, J. (2011). Smart Cities at the forefront of the future Internet, The Future Internet. *Lecture Notes in Computer Science*, *6656*, 447–462. doi:10.1007/978-3-642-20898-0_32

Hill, J., Horton, M., Kling, R., & Krishnamurthy, L. (2004). The platforms enabling wireless sensor networks. *Communications of the ACM*, *47*(6), 41–46. doi:10.1145/990680.990705

Hinamahgul, R. (2015). Cloud computing on the rise in Pakistan. *Thenews.com*. Retrieved on July 1, 2016 from http://www.thenews.com.pk/print/53809-cloud-computing-on-the-rise-in-pakistan

Holler, J., Tsiatsis, V., Mulligan, C., Avesand, S., Karnouskos, S., & Boyle, D. (2014). *From Machine-to-Machine to the Internet of Things: Introduction to a New Age of Intelligence*. Academic Press.

Honle, N., Kappeler, U. P., Nicklas, D., Schwarz, T., & Grossmann, M. (2005). *Benefits of Integrating Meta Data into a Context Model*. doi:10.1109/PERCOMW.2005.20

Hossain, M. S., Muhammad, G., Song, B., Hassan, M. M., Alelaiwi, A., & Alamri, A. (2015). Audio-Visual Emotion-Aware Cloud Gaming Framework. *Proceedings of the IEEE Transactions on Circuits and Systems for Video Technology* (pp. 2105-2118). Retrieved July 20, 2016 from http://ieeexplore.ieee.org/xpls/abs_all.jsp?arnumber=7122897

Hsu, C. H., Slagter, K. D., Chen, S. C., & Chung, Y. C. (2014). optimizing energy consumption with task consolidation in clouds. *Inform. Sci.*, *258*, 452–462. doi:10.1016/j.ins.2012.10.041

Huang, C., Hsu, C., Chen, D., & Cheni, K. (2014). Quantifying User Satisfaction in Mobile Cloud Games. *Proceeding of Workshop on Mobile Video* Delivery. Retrieved August 01, 2016 from http://ieeexplore.ieee.org/xpls/abs_all.jsp?arnumber=7122897

Huang, C., Hsu, C., Chen, D., & Cheni, K. (2014). Quantifying User Satisfaction in Mobile Cloud Games. *Proceedings of Workshop on Mobile Video Delivery*. Retrieved August 01, 2016 from http://ieeexplore.ieee.org/xpls/abs_all.jsp?arnumber=7122897

Hu, H., Wen, Y., Tat-Seng, C., & Li, X. (2014). Toward Scalable Systems for Big Data Analytics: A Technology Tutorial. *Practical Innovations: Open Solutions.*, *7*(1), 1–36.

Hummen, R., Shafagh, H., Raza, S., Voig, T., & Wehrle, K. (2014, June). Delegation-based Authentication and Authorization for the IP-based Internet of Things. *Proceedings of the 2014 Eleventh Annual IEEE International Conference on Sensing, Communication, and Networking (SECON)* (pp. 284-292). IEEE.

Indian Hobby Center. (n. d.). Avr-trainerboard. Retrieved from http://www.indianhobbycenter.com/product/avr-trainerboard/

International Telecommunications Union. (2005). ITU Internet Reports 2005: The Internet of Things Executive Summary.

Iotworm.com. (n. d.). Biggest challenges for the internet of things. Retrieved from http://iotworm.com/biggest-challenges-for-the-internet-of-things/

Jara, A. J., Zamora, M. A., & Skarmeta, A. F. (2009, August). HWSN6: hospital wireless sensor networks based on 6LoWPAN technology: mobility and fault tolerance management. *Proceedings of the International Conference on Computational Science and Engineering CSE'09* (Vol. 2, pp. 879-884). IEEE.

Jara, A. J., Zamora, M. A., & Skarmeta, A. F. (2010a). An initial approach to support mobility in hospital wireless sensor networks based on 6LoWPAN (HWSN6).

Jara, A. J., Zamora, M. A., & Skarmeta, A. F. (2010b, September). Intra-mobility for hospital wireless sensor networks based on 6LoWPAN. *Proceedings of the 2010 6th International Conference on Wireless and Mobile Communications (ICWMC)* (pp. 389-394). IEEE.

Jiawei, H., & Kamber, M. (2011). *Data Mining: Concepts and Techniques*. Morgan Kaufmann.

Jing, Q., Vasilakos, A. V., Wan, J., Lu, J., & Qiu, D. (2014). Security of the internet of things: Perspectives and challenges. *Wireless Networks, 20*(8), 2481–2501. doi:10.1007/s11276-014-0761-7

Jobidon, P. (2014). *Using big data to enhance e-commerce*. Retrieved 12 November 2015 from http://www.bpostinternational.com/en/content/using-big-data-enhance-e-commerce

Judge, S., Floyd, K., & Jeffs, T. (2014). Using mobile devices and apps to promote young children's learning. In K. L. Heider., & M. R. Jalongo (Eds.), Young children and families in the information age: Application of technology in early childhood (pp. 117-131). Netherland: Springer.

Juels, A. (2006). RFID security and privacy: A research survey. *IEEE Journal on Selected Areas in Communications, 24*(2), 381–394. doi:10.1109/JSAC.2005.861395

Kambourakis, G., Klaoudatou, E., & Gritzalis, S. (2007, April). Securing medical sensor environments: the codeblue framework case. *Proceedings of the Second International Conference on Availability, Reliability and Security ARES '07* (pp. 637-643). IEEE. doi:10.1109/ARES.2007.135

Kanoun, K., Ruggiero, M., Atienza, D., & Van Der Schaar, M. (2014). Low Power and Scalable Many-Core Architecture for Big-Data Stream Computing. Proceedings of the 2014 IEEE Computer Society Annual Symposium on VLSI (pp. 468–473). doi:10.1109/ISVLSI.2014.77

Karlof, C., Sastry, N., & Wagner, D. (2004, November). TinySec: a link layer security architecture for wireless sensor networks. *Proceedings of the 2nd international conference on Embedded networked sensor systems* (pp. 162-175). ACM. doi:10.1145/1031495.1031515

Katasonov, A., Kaykova, O., Khriyenko, O., Nikitin, S., & Terziyan, V. Y. (2008). Smart Semantic Middleware for the Internet of Things. Proceedings of the 5th International Conference on Informatics in Control, Automation and Robotics, Intelligent Control Systems and Optimization (pp. 169-178).

Kessler, B. (1995). Computational dialectology in Irish Gaelic. Proc. of the European ACL, Dublin (pp. 60–67). doi:10.3115/976973.976983

Ketchen, D. J. Jr, & Hult, G. T. M. (2007). Bridging organization theory and supply chain management: The case of best value supply chains. *Journal of Operations Management, 25*(2), 573–580. doi:10.1016/j.jom.2006.05.010

Khan, R. H., & Khan, J. Y. (2012a). Wide area PMU communication over a WiMAX network in the smart grid. *Proceedings of the IEEE International Conference on Smart Grid Communications (SmartGridComm)*, Tainan, Taiwan (pp. 187-192). doi:10.1109/SmartGridComm.2012.6485981

Khan, R. H., & Khan, J. Y. (2012b). A heterogeneous WiMAX-WLAN network for AMI communications in the smart grid. *Proceedings of the IEEE International Conference on Smart Grid Communications (SmartGridComm)*, Tainan, Taiwan (pp. 710-715). doi:10.1109/SmartGridComm.2012.6486070

Khorram, S., Koch, F. H., Van der Wiele, C. F., & Nelson, S. A. C. (2012). *Remote Sensing* (1st ed.). New York, NY, USA: Springer-Verlag; doi:10.1007/978-1-4614-3103-9

Kim, H. (2013). Mobile Games with an Efficient Scaling Scheme in the Cloud. *2013 International Conference on Information Science and Applications (ICISA)*, 1-3. Retrieved on August 09, 2016 from http://ieeexplore.ieee.org/xpls/abs_all.jsp?arnumber=6579356

Kim, H. (2013). Mobile Games with an Efficient Scaling Scheme in the Cloud. *Proceedings of the 2013 International Conference on Information Science and Applications (ICISA)*. Retrieved August 09, 2016 from http://ieeexplore.ieee.org/xpls/abs_all.jsp?arnumber=6579356

Kima, N., Chob, J., & Seob, E. (2014). Energy-credit scheduler: An energy-aware virtual machine scheduler for cloud systems. *Future Generation Computer Systems*, *32*(3), 128–137. doi:10.1016/j.future.2012.05.019

Koblitz, N. (1987). Elliptic curve cryptosystems. *Mathematics of Computation*, *48*(177), 203–209. doi:10.1090/S0025-5718-1987-0866109-5

Kolter, J. Z. & Maloof, M. A. (2007). Dynamic Weighted Majority: A New Ensemble Method for Drifting Concepts. *ACM Journal of Machine Learning Research*, (8), 2755-2790.

Kondrak, G. (2002). Algorithms for Language Reconstruction [Ph.D. thesis]. University of Toronto.

Koop, C. E., Mosher, R., Kun, L., Geiling, J., Grigg, E., Long, S., & Rosen, J. M. et al. (2008). Future delivery of health care: Cybercare. *IEEE Engineering in Medicine and Biology Magazine*, *27*(6), 29–38. doi:10.1109/MEMB.2008.929888 PMID:19004693

Kranen, P., Assent, I., Baldauf, C., & Seidl, T. (2011). The clustree: Indexing micro-clusters for anytime stream mining. *Knowledge and Information Systems*, *29*(2), 249–272. doi:10.1007/s10115-010-0342-8

Kumar, A. (2015) Internet of Things (IoT): Seven enterprise risks to consider. In *Internet of Things in the Enterprise* (pp. 13-23).

Lakshman, A., & Prashant, M. (2010). Cassandra: a decentralized structured storage system. *SIGOPS Oper. Syst. Rev.*, *44*(2). 35-40. doi:10.1145/1773912.1773922

Lam, C., & Warren, J. (2010). *Hadoop in action* (1st ed.). Greenwich: Manning Publications.

Laney, D. (2001). 3D data management: Controlling data volume, velocity and variety. Meta Group Inc Research Note.

Laney, D. (2012). The Importance of 'Big Data: A Definition. *Gartner*. Retrieved from https://www.gartner.com/doc/2057415/importance-big-data-definition

Laskowski, N. (2016). *Delving into an enterprise IoT initiative. Internet of Things in the Enterprise*. TechTarget.

Laver, J. (1994). *Principles of Phonetics*. Cambridge: Cambridge University Press. doi:10.1017/CBO9781139166621

Lawton, G. (2016). IoT Gateways Need Clear Security Framework. In IoT Poses New Problems for Developers (pp. 3-5).

Le Sueur, E., & Heiser, G. (2010). Dynamic voltage and frequency scaling: the laws of diminishing returns. *Proc. 2010 Int. Conf. Power-aware Comput. Syst.* (pp. 1–8).

Le, L. B., & Le-Ngoc, T. (2011). QoS provisioning for OFDMA-based wireless network infrastructure in smart grids. *Proceedings of the 24th Canadian Conference on Electrical and Computer Engineering (CCECE)*, Niagara Falls, Ontario, Canada (pp. 813-816). doi:10.1109/CCECE.2011.6030568

Leavitt, N. (2009, January). Is Cloud Computing Really Ready for Prime Time? *IEEE Computer*, *42*(1), 15–20. doi:10.1109/MC.2009.20

Lebart, L., & Rajman, M. (2000). Computing similarity. In R. Dale, H. Moisl, & H. Somers (Eds.), *Handbook of Natural Language Processing* (pp. 477–505). Basel: Dekker.

Lee & Whang. (2000). Information sharing in a supply chain. *Int. J. Manuf. Technol. Manag., 1*, 79–93.

Lee, S., Ryu, J., Min, K., Choi, W., & Won, J. (2000) Development and application of landslide susceptibility analysis techniques using geographic information system (GIS). *Proceedings of the IEEE International Geoscience and Remote Sensing Symposium (Vol. 1*, pp. 319-321).

Lee, W. (1994). Method and Apparatus for Detecting Direction and Speed using PIR Sensor. U.S. Patent 5291, 020.

Lee, H. L., Padmanabhan, V., & Whang, S. (1997a). The bullwhip effect in supply chains. Sloan Management Review, *38(3)*, 93–102.

Lee, H. L., Padmanabhan, V., & Whang, S. (1997b). Information distortion in a supply chain: The bullwhip effect. *Management Science, 43*(4), 546–558. doi:10.1287/mnsc.43.4.546

Leidner, D. E., & Jarvenpaa, S. L. (1995). The use of information technology to enhance management school education: A theoretical view. *Management Information Systems Quarterly, 19*(3), 265–291. doi:10.2307/249596

Leighon, T. (2009). Akamai and Cloud Computing: A Perspective from the Edge of the Cloud. White Paper. Akamai Technologies. Retrieved from http://www.essextec.com/assets/cloud/akamai/cloudcomputing- perspective-wp.pdf

Leppanen, T., Liu, M., Harjula, E., Ramalingam, A., Ylioja, J., Narhi, P., ... & Ojala, T. (2013). Mobile Agents for Integration of Internet of Things and Wireless Sensor Networks. *Proceedings of the IEEE International Conference on Systems, Man, and Cybernetics (SMC)* (pp. 14-21).

Levin, B. (1993). *English Verb Classes and Alternations: a Preliminary Investigation.* Chicago, London: University of Chicago Press.

Li, H., Han, Z., Lai, L., Qiu, R. C., & Yang, D. (2011). Efficient and reliable multiple access for advanced metering in future smart grid. *Proceedings of the IEEE International Conference on Smart Grid Communications (SmartGridComm),* Brussels, Belgium (pp. 440-444). doi:10.1109/SmartGridComm.2011.6102363

Li, J., Bao, Z., & Li, Z. (2015). Modeling Demand-Response Capability by Internet Data Centers Processing Batch Computing Jobs. *IEEE Transactions on Smart Grid, 6*(2), 737–774. doi:10.1109/TSG.2014.2363583

Linder, M., Galan, F., Chapman, C., Clayman, S., Henriksson, D., & Elmroth, E. (2010). The Cloud Supply Chain: A Framework for Information, Monitoring, Accounting and Billing. Retrieved from https://www.ee.ucl.ac.uk/~sclayman/docs/CloudComp2010.pdf

Li, S., Da Xu, L., & Wang, X. (2013). Compressed sensing signal and data acquisition in wireless sensor networks and internet of things. *IEEE Transactions on Industrial Informatics, 9*(4), 2177–2186. doi:10.1109/TII.2012.2189222

Liu, F., Narayanan, A., & Bai, Q. (2001). Real-Time Systems. Pearson education.

Lo, C.-H., & Ansari, N. (2012). The Progressive Smart Grid System from Both Power and Communications Aspects. *IEEE Communications Surveys and Tutorials, 14*(3), 799–821.

Lodha A (2016). Clinical Analytics – Transforming Clinical Development through Big Data. *Imperial Journal of Interdisciplinary Research, 2*(10).

Lodha, A. (2016). Big data analytics – Clinical integration and visualization.

Lodha, A. (2016). Analytics: An Intelligent Approach in Clinical Trail Management. *J. Clin. Trials*, *6*(05), e124. doi:10.4172/2167-0870.1000e124

Lodha, A. (2016). Globalization of Clinical Trials: Ethics and Conduct. *J. Biotechnol. Biomater.*, *6*(2), 229. doi:10.4172/2155-952X.1000229

Lopez, D., & Gunasekaran, M. (2015). Assessment of Vaccination Strategies Using Fuzzy Multi-criteria Decision Making. *Proceedings of the Fifth International Conference on Fuzzy and Neuro Computing (FANCCO-2015)* (pp. 195-208). Springer International Publishing.

Lopez, D., & Manogaran, G. (2016b). Big Data Architecture for Climate Change and Disease Dynamics. In *The Human Element of Big Data: Issues, Analytics, and Performance* (pp. 301-331). CRC Press. 10.1007/978-3-319-49736-5_7

Lopez, D., Gunasekaran, M., Murugan, B. S., Kaur, H., & Abbas, K. M. (2014, October). Spatial big data analytics of influenza epidemic in Vellore, India. *Proceedings of the 2014 IEEE International Conference on Big Data (Big Data)* (pp. 19-24). IEEE.

Lopez, D., & Sekaran, G. (2016a). Climate change and disease dynamics-A big data perspective. *International Journal of Infectious Diseases*, *45*, 23–24. doi:10.1016/j.ijid.2016.02.084

Lorincz, K., Malan, D. J., Fulford-Jones, T. R., Nawoj, A., Clavel, A., Shnayder, V., & Moulton, S. et al. (2004). Sensor networks for emergency response: Challenges and opportunities. *IEEE Pervasive Computing*, *3*(4), 16–23. doi:10.1109/MPRV.2004.18

Low, K. C. P., & Anshari, M. (2013). Incorporating social customer relationship management in negotiation. *International Journal of Electronic Customer Relationship Management*, *7*(3/4), 239–252. doi:10.1504/IJECRM.2013.060700

Lu, M. C., Tang, T. Y., Tsai, C. P., Wang, W. Y., & Li, I. H. (2011). Image-based landslide monitoring system. *Proceedings of the IEEE International Conference on System Science and Engineering (ICSSE)* (pp. 638-643).

Luce, P. A., & Pisoni, D. B. (1998). Recognizing spoken words: The neighborhood activation model. *Ear and Hearing*, *19*(1), 1–36. doi:10.1097/00003446-199802000-00001 PMID:9504270

Luo, X., Shen, B., Guo, X., Luo, G., & Wang, G. (2009). Human-Tracking using Ceiling Pyroelectric Infrared Sensors. *Proceedings of the IEEE International Conference on Control and Automation*, Christchurch, New Zealand (pp. 1716-1721).

Malan, D., Fulford-Jones, T., Welsh, M., & Moulton, S. (2004, April). Codeblue: An ad hoc sensor network infrastructure for emergency medical care. *Proceedings of the International workshop on wearable and implantable body sensor networks* (Vol. 5).

Manekar, A., & Pradeepini, G. (2015). A Review on Cloud-based Big Data Analytics. ICSES Journal on Computer Networks and Communication, 1(1). doi:10.1109/CICN.2015.160

Manogaran, G., Thota, C., Lopez, D., & Sundarasekar, R. (2017d). Big Data Security Intelligence for Healthcare Industry 4.0. In Cybersecurity for Industry 4.0 (pp. 103-126). Springer International Publishing.

Manogaran, G., Thota, C., Lopez, D., Vijayakumar, V., Abbas, K. M., & Sundarsekar, R. (2017a). Big data knowledge system in healthcare. In Internet of Things and Big Data Technologies in Next Generation Healthcare. Springer International Publishing.

Manogaran, G., & Lopez, D. (2016b). Health data analytics using scalable logistic regression with stochastic gradient descent. *International Journal of Advanced Intelligence Paradigms*, *9*(1), 1–18.

Manogaran, G., & Lopez, D. (2016c). A survey of big data architectures and machine learning algorithms in healthcare. *International Journal of Biomedical Engineering and Technology, 23*(4), 1–27.

Manogaran, G., & Lopez, D. (2017b). Disease surveillance system for big climate data processing and dengue transmission. *International Journal of Ambient Computing and Intelligence, 8*(1), 1–27.

Manogaran, G., & Lopez, D. (2017e). Spatial cumulative sum algorithm with big data analytics for climate change detection. *Computers & Electrical Engineering, 59*(5), 1–15. doi:10.1016/j.compeleceng.2017.04.006

Manogaran, G., Thota, C., & Kumar, M. V. (2016a). Meta Cloud Data Storage Architecture for Big Data Security in Cloud Computing. *Procedia Computer Science, 87*, 128–133. doi:10.1016/j.procs.2016.05.138

Manogaran, G., Thota, C., Lopez, D., Vijayakumar, V., Abbas, K. M., & Sundarsekar, R. (2017c). Big Data Knowledge System in Healthcare. In *Internet of Things and Big Data Technologies for Next Generation Healthcare* (pp. 133–157). Springer International Publishing.

March, V., Gu, Y., Leonardi, E., Goh, G., Kirchberg, M., & Lee, B. S. (2011). µcloud: Towards a new paradigm of rich mobile applications. *Procedia Computer Science, 5*, 618–624. doi:10.1016/j.procs.2011.07.080

Marinelli, E. (2009). Cloud Computing on Mobile Devices using MapReduce [Master Thesis Draft]. Computer Science Dept., Carnegie Mellon University (CMU).

Marx, V. (2013). Biology: The big challenges of big data. *Nature, 498*(7453), 255–260. doi:10.1038/498255a PMID:23765498

Mascolo, C. (2010). The power of mobile computing in a social era. *IEEE Internet Computing, 14*(6), 76–79. doi:10.1109/MIC.2010.150

Mata, F. J., Fuerst, W. L., & Barney, J. B. (1995). Information technology and sustained competitive advantage: A resource-based analysis. *Management Information Systems Quarterly, 19*(4), 487–505. doi:10.2307/249630

Mayer C.P. (2009). Security and Privacy Challenges in the Internet of Things. *Proceedings of the Workshops der Wissenschaftlichen Konferenz Kommunikation in Verteilten Systemen '09.*

McMahon, A., & McMahon, R. (2005). *Language Classification by the Numbers.* Oxford: Oxford University Press.

Meirong, T. I. A. N., & Xuedong, C. H. E. N. (2010). Application of Agent-based Web Mining in E-business. *Proceedings of the Second International Conference on Intelligent Human-Machine Systems and Cybernetics.*

Meng, X., & Chen, T. (2013) Event-driven communication for sampled-data control systems. *Proceedings of the Am. Control Conf. (ACC)* (Vol. 1, pp. 3002–3007).

Miller, G. A., & Nicely, P. E. (1955). An Analysis of Perceptual Confusions Among Some English Consonants. *The Journal of the Acoustical Society of America, 27*(2), 338–352. doi:10.1121/1.1907526

Mills, D. (1985). Network time protocol (NTP). Retrieved 24 May 2016 from https://tools.ietf.org/html/rfc958

Mircea, M., & Andreescu, A. (2011). Using Cloud Computing in Higher Education: A Strategy to Improve Agility. *Communications of the IBIMA.* Retrieved July 1, 2016 from http://www.ibimapublishing.com/journals/CIBIMA/cibima.html doi:10.5171/2011.875547

Moghavvemi, M., & Seng, L. C. (2004). Pyroelectric Infrared Sensor for Intruder Detection. *Proceedings of the IEEE Region Conference*, Tencon (pp. 656 – 659).

Mohanty, H. (2015). Big Data: An Introduction. In H. Mohanty, P. Bhuyan, & D. Chen (Eds.), Big Data (Vol. 11). India: Springer India. doi:10.1007/978-81-322-2494-5_1

Monczka, R. M., Petersen, K. J., Handfield, R. B., & Ragatz, G. L. (1998). Success factors in strategic supplier alliances: The buying company perspective. *Decision Sciences*, *29*(3), 553–577. doi:10.1111/j.1540-5915.1998.tb01354.x

Moosavi, S. R., Gia, T. N., Nigussie, E., Rahmani, A. M., Virtanen, S., Tenhunen, H., & Isoaho, J. (2016). End-to-end security scheme for mobility enabled healthcare Internet of Things. *Future Generation Computer Systems*, *64*, 108–124. doi:10.1016/j.future.2016.02.020

Morello, R., De Capua, C., Fabbiano, L., & Vacca, G. (2013, May 4-5). Image-Based Detection of Kayser-Fleischer Ring in Patient with Wilson Disease. *Proceedings of the IEEE 8th International Symposium on Medical Measurement and Applications*, Gatineau, Canada. doi:10.1109/MeMeA.2013.6549715

Mosavi, A., & Vaezipour, A. (2013). *Developing Effective Tools for Predictive Analytics and Informed Decisions* (tech. report). University of Tallinn.

Mukhopadhyay, A., Maulik, U., Bandyopadhyay, S., & Coello, C. A. C. (2014). A survey of multiobjective evolutionary algorithms for data mining: Part I. *IEEE Transactions on Evolutionary Computation*, *18*(1), 4–19. doi:10.1109/TEVC.2013.2290086

Myung, H. G., & Goodman, D. J. (2008). *Single Carrier FDMA: A New Air Interface for Long Term Evolution*. Chichester, UK: John Wiley and Sons. doi:10.1002/9780470758717

National Intelligence Council. (2008, April). Disruptive Civil Technologies — Six Technologies with Potential Impacts on US Interests Out to 2025 (Conference Report CR 2008–07). Retrieved from www.dni.gov/nic/NIC_home.html

Netimperative (2015). China digital trends in 2015: Huge shift to mobile as growth slows. Retrieved August 01, 2016 from http://www.netimperative.com/2015/09/china-digital-trends-in-2015-huge-shift-to-mobile-as-growth-slows/

Nielsen, A. (2013). What People Watch, Listen To and Buy. *Nielsen*. Retrieved from http://www.nielsen.com/us/en.html

Ning, H. N., Liu, H., & Yang, L. T. (2013). Cyber Entity Security in the Internet of Things. *Computer*, *46*(4), 46–53. doi:10.1109/MC.2013.74

Noetzel, A. S., & Selkow, S. M. (1999). An analysis of the general tree-editing problem. In D. Sankoff and J. Kruskal (Eds.), Time Warps, String Edits and Macromolecules: The Theory and Practice of Sequence Comparison (pp. 237–252).

Nordberg, H., Bhatia, K., Wang, K., & Wang, Z. (2013). Biopic: A hadoop-based analytic toolkit for large-scale sequence data. *Oxford Bioinformatics.*, *29*(33), 3014–3019. doi:10.1093/bioinformatics/btt528 PMID:24021384

ODriscoll, A., Daugelaite, J., & Sleator, R. D. (2013, October). Big Data, *Hadoop and Cloud Computing in Genomics. Journal of Biomedical Informatics*, *46*(5), 774–781. doi:10.1016/j.jbi.2013.07.001 PMID:23872175

Ohlhorst, F. J. (2012). *Big data analytics: turning big data into big money*. John Wiley & Sons. doi:10.1002/9781119205005

OnLive. (2016). Retrieved July 30, 2016 from http://onlive.com/

Osseiran, A., Monserrat, J., & Mohr, W. (2011). *Mobile and Wireless Communications for IMT-Advanced and Beyond*. Chichester, UK: John Wiley and Sons. doi:10.1002/9781119976431

OTOY. (2015). Retrieved on July 30, 2016 from http://www.home.otoy.com

P. S. Bradley, U. M. Fayyad, & C. Reina.(1998) Scaling clustering algorithms to large databases. *Proceedings of Knowledge Discovery and Data Mining* (pp. 9-15). AAAI Press.

Page, L., Brin, S., Motwani, R., & Winograd, T. (1998). *The PageRank Citation Ranking: Bring Order to the Web. Technical Report*. Stanford University.

Pan, F., & Sheng-guo, C. (2013). The Profiles and the Analysis of the Features on the Typical Landslides in the History of the Three Gorges Reservoir Area. *Proceedings of the IEEE International Conference on Intelligent System Design and Engineering Applications (ISDEA)* (pp. 1494-1497). doi:10.1109/ISDEA.2012.358

Papadimitriou, S., Sun, J., & Faloutsos, C. (2005). Streaming Pattern Discovery in Multiple TimeSeries. *Proceedings of 31ˢᵗ VLDB Conference*.

Patan, R., & Babu, M.R. (2015). A Study Analysis of Energy Issues in Big Data. *International J. Appl. Eng. Res.*, *10*(6), 15593–15609.

Perera, C., Jayaram, P.P., & Christwn, P. (2013). CSIRO Computational Informatics, Research school on Computer Science. arXiv:1312.6721v1 [cs.NI}

Perera, C., Zaslavsky, A., Christen, P., & Georgakopoulos, D. (2013). Context Aware Computing for The Internet of Things: A Survey. *IEEE Communications Surveys and Tutorials*, *16*(1), 414–454. doi:10.1109/SURV.2013.042313.00197

Perera, C., Zaslavsky, A., Christen, P., & Georgakopoulos, D. (2014). Sensing as a Service Model for Smart Cities Supported by Internet of Things. *Transactions on Emerging Telecommunications Technologies*, *25*(1), 81–93. doi:10.1002/ett.2704

Pérez, I. C., & Barbolla, A. M. B. (2014). *Exploring Major Architectural Aspects of the Web of Things*. Switzerland: Springer International.

Peters, S. (2013, January 15). *Tufts Center for the Study of Drug Development*. Retrieved September 24, 2016, from http://csdd.tufts.edu/news/complete_story/pr_ir_jan-feb_2013/

Petersen & Ragatz. (2005). Examination of collaborative planning effectiveness and supply chain performance. *J. Supply. Chain Manag.*, *41*, 14–25.

Piyare, R. (2013). Internet of Things: Ubiquitous Home Control and Monitoring System using Android based Smart Phone. *International Journal of Internet of Things*, *2*(1), 5–11.

Prabhakaran, V.P. (2016). IoT Security, Threats and Challenges. *HAKIN9 Magazine*.

Prerez, S. (2009). Why cloud computing is the future of mobile. Retrieved from http://www.readwriteweb.com

Pritchett, D. (2008). BASE: An Acid Alternative. *Queue*, *6*(3), 48-55. doi:10.1145/1394127.1394128

Purandare, P. (2008). Web Mining: A Key to Improve Business On Web. *Proceedings of the IADIS European Conference Data Mining*.

Purva, A., Bumanlag, J., Edelman, B., & Doetsch, U. (2011). *Spectrum Needs for Wireless Smart Meter Communications. Tech. Report*. Boulder: University of Colorado.

Raghupathi, W., & Raghupathi, V. (2014, February 7). Big data analytics in healthcare: Promise and potential. *Health Inf. Sci. Syst. Health Information Science and Systems*, *2*(1). doi:10.1186/2047-2501-2-3 PMID:25825667

Rahman, S., Majumder, M. A., Shaban, S. F., Rahman, N., Ahmed, M., Abdulrahman, K. B., & D'Souza, U. J. (2011). Physician participation in clinical research and trials: Issues and approaches. *AMEP Advances in Medical Education and Practice*, 85. doi:10.2147/amep.s14103

Rahmani, A. M., Thanigaivelan, N. K., Gia, T. N., Granados, J., Negash, B., Liljeberg, P., & Tenhunen, H. (2015, January). Smart e-health gateway: Bringing intelligence to internet-of-things based ubiquitous healthcare systems. *Proceedings of the 2015 12th Annual IEEE Consumer Communications and Networking Conference (CCNC)* (pp. 826-834). IEEE.

Rahul, M., & Shivaji, D. M. (2013). Cloud Based Technology In Higher Education: A Need of the Day. *ASM's International E-Journal of Ongoing Research in Management and IT.*

Rajasekhara Babu, M., Alok, A. J. B., & Bhatt, N. (2013). Automation Testing Software that Aid in Efficiency Increase of Regression Process. *Recent Patents Comput. Sci., 6*(2), 107–114. doi:10.2174/22132759113069990008

Rajasekhara Babu, M, & Krishna, P.V., and Khalid. (2013). A framework for power estimation and reduction in multi-core architectures using basic block approach. *Int. J. Commun. Networks Distrib. Syst., 10*(1), 40–51.

Rajgarhia, A., Stann, F., & Heidemann, J. (2004). Privacy-Sensitive Monitoring with a Mix of IR Sensors and Cameras. *Proceedings of 2nd International Workshop Sensor Actor Network Protocol Applications,* Boston, MA (pp. 21-29).

Raman, S. (2016). Analytics Proves Key To IoT. TechTarget.

Rao, A. P., Agarwal, S., Srinivas, K., & Rani, B. K. (2015). Learning Mechanism for RT Task Scheduling. *Proceedings of the 2015 IEEE International Conference On Computational Intelligence And Computing Research.*

Rao, A.P., Govardhan, A., & Pinagali, P. (2012, March). Scheduling different customer activities with sensing device. International Journal Advanced Information technology.

Ratasuk, R., Tolli, D., & Ghosh, A. (2010). Carrier Aggregation in LTE-Advanced. *Proceedings of the IEEE VTC Spring 2010* (pp. 1–5).

Ratner, B. (2011). *Statistical and machine-learning data mining: Techniques for better predictive modeling and analysis of big data* (2nd ed.). CRC Press Taylor and Francis Group. doi:10.1201/b11508

Redfearn, S. (2011, April 25). New data show number of principal investigators dropping 11% globally, and 20% in U.S. *CenterWatch News Online.* Retrieved September 24, 2016, from http://www.centerwatch.com/news-online/2011/04/25/new-data-show-number-of-principal-investigators-dropping-11-globally-and-20-in-us/#sthash.oLg4K7z5.dpbs

Rehman, M. S., & Sakr, M. F. (2010). Teaching the Cloud, Global Engineering Education. *Paper presented at the Learning Environments and Ecosystems in Engineering Education Conference.* Retrieved July 1, 2016 from https://www.researchgate.net/publication/224238671_Teaching_the_cloud_-_experiences_in_designing_and_teaching_an_undergraduate-level_course_in_cloud_computing_at_the_Carnegie_Mellon_University_in_Qatar

Reichle, R. H., Crow, W. T., Koster, R. D., Sharif, H., & Mahanama, S. P. P. (2008a). Contribution of soil moisture retrievals to land data assimilation products. *Geophysical Research Letters, 35*(1), L01404. doi:10.1029/2007GL031986

Rescorla, E., & Modadugu, N. (2012). Datagram transport layer security version 1.2.

Resnik, P. S. (1993). Selection and Information: A Class-Based Approach to Lexical Relationships [Ph.D. thesis]. University of Pennsylvania.

Rochwerger, B., Breitgand, D., Levy, E., Galis, A., Nagin, K., Llorente, I. M., & Galan, F. et al. (2010). The reservoir model and architecture for open federated cloud computing. *IBM Journal of Research and Development, 53*, 4–11.

Rodrigues, P., Gama, J., & Pedroso, J. (2006).ODAC: Hierarchical clustering of time series data streams. *Proceedings of the Sixth SIAM International Conference on Data Mining* (pp. 499-503). doi:10.1137/1.9781611972764.48

Rong, X. H., Chen, F., Deng, P., & Ma, S. L. (2011). A large-scale device collaboration mechanism. *Journal of Computer Research and Development, 48*(9), 1589–1596.

Rooth, M., Riezler, S., Prescher, D., Carroll, G., & Beil, F. (1999). Inducing an semantically annotated lexicon via em-based clustering. *Proceedings of the 37th Annual Meeting of the Association for Computational Linguistics*, Maryland. doi:10.3115/1034678.1034703

Rose, K. R., Eldridge, S., & Chapin, L. (2015). *The Internet of Things: An Overview understanding the Issues & Challenges of a more connected world.* In *IoT Society* (pp. 13–22).

Rosenthal, A., Mork, P., Li, M. H., Stanford, J., Koester, D., & Reynolds, P. (2010). Cloud Computing: A new business paradigm for biomedical information sharing. *Journal of Biomedical Informatics*, *43*(2), 342–353. doi:10.1016/j.jbi.2009.08.014 PMID:19715773

Ross, V. W. (2010). *Factors influencing the adoption of cloud computing by Decision making managers. (Capella University).* ProQuest Dissertations and Theses.

Roure, J., & Sanguesa, R. (1999). Incremental Methods for Bayesian Network Learning.

Rozados, I., & Tjahjono, B. (2014). Big Data Analytics in Supply Chain Management: Trends and Related Research. *Proceedings of the 6th International Conference on Operations and Supply Chain Management*, Bali. Retrieved from https://www.researchgate.net/publication/270506965_Big_Data_Analytics_in_Supply_Chain_Management_Trends_and_Related_Research

Sahin, F., & Robinson, E. P. (2002). Flow coordination and information sharing in supply chains: Review, implications, and directions for future research. *Decision Sciences*, *33*(4), 505–536. doi:10.1111/j.1540-5915.2002.tb01654.x

Saidhbi, S. (2012). A Cloud Computing Framework for Ethiopian Higher Education Institutions. *IOSR Journal of Computer Engineering*, *6*(6), 1-9. Retrieved July 1, 2016 from www.iosrjournals.org

Salem, M., Adinoyi, A., Rahman, M., Yanikomeroglu, H., Falconer, D., Kim, Y.-D., & Cheong, Y.-C. et al. (2010). An Overview of Radio Resource Management in Relay-Enhanced OFDMA-Based Networks. *IEEE Communications Surveys and Tutorials*, *12*(3), 422–438. doi:10.1109/SURV.2010.032210.00071

Sanaei, S. A. Z., Gani, A., & Khokhar, R. H. (2012). Tripod of requirements in horizontal heterogeneous mobile cloud computing. *Proceedings of the 1st International Conference on Computing, Information Systems, and Communications.*

Sang, Y., Shen, H., Inoguchi, Y., Tan, Y., & Xiong, N. (2006). Secure Data Aggregation in Wireless Sensor Networks: A Survey. Proceedings of the Seventh International Conference on Parallel and Distributed Computing, Applications and Technologies PDCAT '06 (pp. 315–320). doi:10.1109/PDCAT.2006.96

Saphanatutorial.com. (n. d.). Introduction to internet of things. Retrieved from http://saphanatutorial.com/introduction-to-internet-of-things-part-1/

Sayad, Y. O., Mousannif, H., & Le Page, M. (2015). *Crop Management Using BIG DATA.* IEEE.

Schaffers, H., Komninos, N., Pallot, M., Trousse, B., Nilsson, M., & Oliveira, A. (2011). Smart cities and the future internet: Towards cooperation frameworks for open innovation, The Future Internet. *Lecture Notes in Computer Science*, *6656*, 431–446. doi:10.1007/978-3-642-20898-0_31

Schulte im Walde, S. (2003). Experiments on the Automatic Induction of German Semantic Verb Classes [Ph.D. thesis]. *AIMS Report*, *9*(2).

Schumacher, A., Pireddu, L., Niemenmaa, M., Kallio, A., Korpelainen, E., Zanetti, G., & Heljanko, K. (2014). Simple and scalable scripting for large sequencing data sets in hadoop. *Bioinformatics (Oxford, England)*, *30*(1), 119–120. doi:10.1093/bioinformatics/btt601 PMID:24149054

Schutze, H. (1998). Automatic word sense discrimination. *Computational Linguistics, 24*(1), 97–123.

Semiconductor, O. N. (2011). Speeding up the Smart Grid: Technique for Delivering More Robust, Higher Data Rate Communications for Automatic Meter Reading (Tech. Report TND6018/D).

Shankar, M., Burchett, J. B., Hao, Q., Guenther, B. D., & Brady, D. J. (2006). Human-tracking systems using pyroelectric infrared detectors. *Optical Engineering, 45*(10), 106401–1, 106401–106410. doi:10.1117/1.2360948

Shen, W., Xu, Y., Xie, D., Zhang, T., & Johansson, A. (2011, September). Smart border routers for ehealthcare wireless sensor networks. *Proceedings of the 2011 7th International Conference on Wireless Communications, Networking and Mobile Computing (WiCOM)* (pp. 1-4). IEEE. doi:10.1109/wicom.2011.6040606

Shvachko, K., Kuang, H., Radia, S., & Chansler, R. (2010). The hadoop distributed file system. *Proceedings of IEEE 26th Symposium on Mass Storage Systems and Technologies.*

Sinnen, O., To, A., & Kaur, M. (2011). Contention-aware scheduling with task duplication. *Journal of Parallel and Distributed Computing, 71*(1), 77–86. doi:10.1016/j.jpdc.2010.10.004

Skourletopoulos, G., Mavromoustakis, C. X., Mastorakis, G., Rodrigues, J. J., Chatzimisios, P., & Batalla, J. M. (2015, December). A fluctuation-based modelling approach to quantification of the technical debt on mobile cloud-based service level. *Proceedings of the 2015 IEEE Globecom Workshops (GC Wkshps)* (pp. 1-6). IEEE.

Song, B., Choi, H., & Lee, H. S. (2008). Surveillance tracking system using passive infrared motion sensors in wireless sensor network. *Proc. of the International Conference on Information Networking ICOIN '08* (pp. 1–5). doi:10.1109/ICOIN.2008.4472790

Song, G., & Li, Y. (2005). Cross-Layer Optimization for OFDM Wireless Networks-Part I: Theoretical Framework. *IEEE Transactions on Wireless Communications, 4*(2), 614–624. doi:10.1109/TWC.2004.843065

Song, Y. (2013). Storage mining: Where it management meets big data analytics. *Proceedings of IEEE International Congress on Big Data*, New York, USA (pp. 421–422). doi:10.1109/BigData.Congress.2013.66

Spencer, B. (2013). Mobile users can't leave their phone alone for six minutes and check it up to 150 times a day. *Daily Mail*. Retrieved from http://www.dailymail.co.uk/news/article-2276752/Mobile-users-leave-phone-minutes-check-150-times-day.html

Stock, G. N., Greis, N. P., & Kasarda, J. D. (2000). Enterprise logistics and supply chain structure: The role of fit. *Journal of Operations Management, 18*(5), 531–547. doi:10.1016/S0272-6963(00)00035-8

Stonebraker, M., Madden, S., Abadi, D. J., Harizopoulos, S., Hachem, N., & Helland, P. (2007). The end of an architectural era: (it's time for a complete rewrite). Proceedings of the 33rd international conference on Very large data bases (VLDB '07) (pp. 1150-1160).

Strachan, D. (2012). *The best new travel technology*, Retrieved 18 September 2012 from http://www.telegraph.co.uk/travel/columnists/7534231/The-best-new-travel-technology.html

StreamMyGame. (2012). Retrieved August 01, 2016 from http://streammygame.com/smg/index.php

Street, W. N., & Kim, Y. A. (2001). Streaming Ensemble Algorithm (SEA) for large-scale classification. *Proceedings of the 7th ACM SIGKDD International Conference on Knowledge Discovery and Data Mining* (pp. 377-382).

Sullivan, J. (2004, April 1). *Subject Recruitment and Retention: Barriers to Success*. Retrieved September 24, 2016, from http://www.appliedclinicaltrialsonline.com/subject-recruitment-and-retention-barriers-success

Sun, D., Zhang, G., Yang, S., Zheng, W., Khan, S. U., & Li, K. (2015). Re-Stream: Real-time and energy-efficient resource scheduling in big data stream computing environments. *Information Science, 319*, 91-112.

Sun, D., Zhang, G., Zheng, W., & Li, K. (2015). *Key Technologies for Big Data Stream Computing. In Big Data* (pp. 193–214). Chapman and Hall/CRC.

SUPERGEN. (2012). *HiDEF (Highly Distributed Energy Futures)*. Smart Meters for Smart Grids. Briefing Paper.

Svinicki, M. D., & McKeachie, W. (2011). *Teaching Tips: Strategies, Research, and Theory for College and University teachers* (13th ed.). Belmont, CA: Wadsworth.

Swam, M. (2012). Sensor Mania! The Internet of Things Wearable Computing, Objective Metrics and the Quantified Self 2.0. *Journal of Sensor and Actuator Networks, 1*(3), 217–253. doi:10.3390/jsan1030217

Swann, J. (2013, January 18). Summary of NDA Approvals & Receipts, 1938 to the present. Retrieved September 24, 2016, fromhttp://www.fda.gov/aboutfda/whatwedo/history/productregulation/summaryofndaapprovalsreceipts1938tothepresent/default.htm

Sweeney, P. J., & Sweeney, P. J. Ii. (2005). *RFID for dummies*. Wiley Publishing, Inc.

Syed, N. A., Liu, H., & Sung, K. K. (1999). Handling concept drift in incremental learning with support vector machines. *Proceedings of the 5th ACM SIGKDD International Conference on Knowledge Discovery and Data Mining* (pp. 317-321). doi:10.1145/312129.312267

Syed, A., Gillela, K., & Venugopal, C. (2013). The future revolution on Big Data. *Future, 2*(6), 2446–2451.

Tam, V., Yi, A., Lam, E. Y., Chan, C., & Yuen, A. H. K. (2013). Using Cloud Computing and Mobile Devices to Facilitate Students Learning Through E-Learning Games. *Proceedings of the IEEE 13th International Conference on Advanced Learning Technologies* (pp. 471 – 472). Retrieved August 03, 2016 from http://ieeexplore.ieee.org/xpls/abs_all.jsp?arnumber=6601990

Tayade, D. (2014). Mobile Cloud Computing: Issues, Security, Advantages, Trends. *International Journal of Computer Science and Information Technologies, 5*(5), 6635-6639. Retrieved August 11, 2016 from http://citeseerx.ist.psu.edu/viewdoc/download?doi=10.1.1.660.8874&rep=rep1&type=pdf

Techquark.com. (n. d.). What is the Internet of things of things. Retrieved from http://www.techquark.com/2014/10/what-is-internet-of-things-iot.html

Thomason, S., & Kaufmann, T. (1988). *Language Contact, Creolization, and Genetic Linguistics*. Berkeley: University of California Press.

Thomas, R. W., Defee, C. C., Randall, W. S., & Williams, B. (2011). Assessing the managerial relevance of contemporary supply chain management research. *International Journal of Physical Distribution & Logistics Management, 41*(7), 655–667. doi:10.1108/09600031111154116

Thota, C., Manogaran, G., Lopez, D., & Vijayakumar, V. (2017). Big Data Security Framework for Distributed Cloud Data Centers. Proceedings of the Cybersecurity Breaches and Issues Surrounding Online Threat Protection (pp. 288-310). Hershey, PA: IGI Global. doi:10.4018/978-1-5225-1941-6.ch012

Thusoo, A. (2009). Hive- A warehousing solution over a map-reduce framework. *ACM Digital Library, 2*(2), 1626–1629.

Tibco. (2011). *Spotfire Analytics – Transforming Clinical Development*. Retrieved from http://spotfire.tibco.com/assets/blt9ebddf0e420042ec/spotfire-clinical-development.pdf

Tilak, S., Abu-Ghazaleh, N., & Heinzelman, W. (2002). A taxonomy of wireless micro-sensor network models. *ACM Mobile Computing and Communications Review, 6*(2), 28–36. doi:10.1145/565702.565708

Tiwari, K.P., & Dewangan, K.K. (2015). Introduction to Internet and its Challenges. *International Journal of Research in Engineering, Science and Technologies- Circuit Branches, 1*(2), 26-34.

Tory, M., & Moller, T. (2004). Rethinking Visualization: A High-Level Taxonomy. *Proceedings of the IEEE Symposium on Information Visualization* INFOVIS '04 (pp. 151–158). doi:10.1109/INFVIS.2004.59

Trifu, M. R., & Ivan, M. L. (2014). Big Data: present and future. *Database Systems Journal, 5*(1), 32-41. Retrieved from http://www.dbjournal.ro/archive/15/15_4.pdf

Tsai, C.-W., Lai, C.-F., & Vasilakos, A. V. (2014). Future internet of things: Open issues and challenges. *Wireless Networks, 20*(8), 2201–2217. doi:10.1007/s11276-014-0731-0

Tufts University. (2008, January/February). Growing protocol design complexity stresses investigators, volunteers (Rep. No. Volume 10 Number 1). Retrieved September 15, 2016, from http://csdd.tufts.edu/files/uploads/jan-feb_impact_report_summary.pdf

Turner, V., Gantz, J.F., Reinsel, D., & Minton, S. (2014, April). The Digital Universe of Opportunities: Rich Data and the Increasing Value of the Internet of Things. Report from IDC for EMC.

Uckelmann, D., Harrison, M., & Michahelles, F. (Eds.). (2011). *Architecting the Internet of Things.* Springer.

Uckelmann, D., Harrison, M., & Michahelles, F. (2011). *Architecting the Internet of Things.* Springer. doi:10.1007/978-3-642-19157-2

Udelhoven, T. (2013). Big data in Environmental Remote Sensing Challenges and Chances. *Proceedings of the UniGR Workshop on Big Data Challenges and Opportunities.*

Uma, S., Mudinuri, K. M., Repetski, S., Venkataraman, G., Che, A., Brian, T., . . . Stephens, R. S. (2013). Knowledge and Theme Discovery across Very Large Biological Data Sets Using Distributed Queries: A Prototype Combining Unstructured and Structured Data. Retrieved from http://journals.plos.org/plosone/article?id=10.1371/journal.pone.0080503

Umair, S., Muneer, U., Zahoor, M. N., & Malik, A. W. (2015). Mobile computing: issues and challenges. *Paper presented at the 12th International Conference on High-capacity Optical Networks and Enabling/Emerging Technologies,* Islamabad Pakistan. Retrieved July 6, 2016 from http://ieeexplore.ieee.org/xpls/abs_all.jsp?arnumber=7395438

van Coetsem, F. (1988). *Loan Phonology and the Two Transfer Types in Language Contact.* Dordrech: Foris Publications.

Vendler, Z. (1967). *Linguistics in Philosophy.* Ithaca, NY: Cornell University Press.

Verma, J. P., Patel, B., & Patel, A. (2015). Big Data Analysis: Recommendation System with Hadoop Framework. *Proceedings of the 2015 IEEE Int. Conf. Comput. Intell. Commun. Technol.* (pp. 92–97). doi:10.1109/CICT.2015.86

Vermesan, O., & Friess, P. (2014). Internet of Things– From Research and Innovation to Market Deployment. River Publishers.

Vermesan, O., & Friess, P. (2013). *Internet of Things- Converging Technologies for Smart Environments and Integrated Ecosystems.* River Publishers.

Viceconti, M., Henney, A., & Morley-Fletcher, E. (2016, January). In silico clinical trials: How computer simulation will transform the biomedical industry. *International Journal of Clinical Trials.* doi:10.18203/2349-3259.ijct20161408

Vilajosana, I., Llosa, J., Martinez, B., Domingo-Prieto, M., Angles, A., & Vilajosana, X. (2013, June). A. Angles, and X. Vilajosana, "Bootstrapping smart cities through a self-sustainable model based on big data flows. *IEEE Communications Magazine, 51*(6), 128–134. doi:10.1109/MCOM.2013.6525605

Vitevitch, M. S., & Luce, P. A. (1999). Probabilistic Phonotactics and Neighborhood Activation in Spoken Word Recognition. *Journal of Memory and Language, 40*(3), 374–408. doi:10.1006/jmla.1998.2618

Wagner, A. (2004). Learning Thematic Role Relations for Lexical Semantic Nets [Ph.D. thesis]. Universitat Tubingen.

Wallgren, A. (2016). *How is IoT changing software development? Cloud Expo conference, Javits Center*. New York: Published by TechTarget IoT Agenda.

Wang, C., Rayan, I. A., & Schwan, K. (2012). Faster, larger, easier: reining real-time big data processing in cloud. *Proceedings of the Posters and Demo Track, Middleware '12* (pp. 4:1–4:2). New York: ACM. doi:10.1145/2405153.2405157

Want, R., Schilit, B. N., & Jenson, S. (2015, January). Enabling the Internet of Things. *Computer, 48*(1), 28–35. Retrieved from http://parallelanddistributedsystems.weebly.com/uploads/7/7/0/3/77031663/enabling_the_internet_of_things.pdf doi:10.1109/MC.2015.12

Websiteoptimization.com. (2017, March 30). Webpage Analyzer (Web Page Speed Analysis). Retrieved from www.websiteoptimization.com

Wegener, D., Mock, M., Adranale, D., & Wrobel, S. (2009). Toolkit-based High-Performance Data Mining of Large Data on MapReduce Clusters. *Proc. Int'l Conf. Data Mining Workshops (ICDMW'09)* (pp. 296-301). doi:10.1109/ICDMW.2009.34

Welbourne, E., Battle, L., Cole, G., Gould, K., Rector, K., Raymer, S., & Borriello, G. et al. (2009). Building the Internet of Things Using RFID The RFID Ecosystem Experience. *IEEE Internet Computing, 13*(3), 48–55. doi:10.1109/MIC.2009.52

Weng, Q. (2011). *Advances in Environmental Remote Sensing: Sensors, Algorithms, and Applications*. Boca Raton, FL, USA: CRC Press. doi:10.1201/b10599

White, T. (2019). Hadoop, the Definitive Guide. O Reilly Media. Retrieved on July 1, 2016 from https://www.iteblog.com/downloads/OReilly.Hadoop.The.Definitive.Guide.4th.Edition.2015.3.pdf

Wikipedia. (2015, November 2). Hot swapping. Retrieved 2 November 2015 from https://en.wikipedia.org/wiki/Hot_swapping#References

Wikipedia. (2015, November 20). Round-robin scheduling. Retrieved 20 November 2015 from https://en.wikipedia.org/wiki/Round-robin_scheduling

Wikipedia. (2016, February 25). Storm (event processor). Retrieved 25 February 2016 from https://en.wikipedia.org/w/index.php?title=Storm_(event_processor)&redirect=no

Wikipedia. (2016, February 7). Storm (software). Retrieved 7 February 2016 from https://en.wikipedia.org/wiki/Storm_(software)

Wikispaces. (2015). Interactive or Online Processing. Retrieved 5 November 2015) from http://dis-dpcs.wikispaces.com/3.3.5+Batch,+Online+%26+real+time+Processing

Wyld, D. C. (2009). Moving to the cloud: An Introduction to Cloud Computing in Government. IBM Center for The Business of Government. Retrieved July 1, 2016 from http://faculty.cbpp.uaa.alaska.edu/afgjp/padm601%20fall%202010/Moving%20to%20the%20Cloud.pdf

Xu, J., Chen, Z., Tang, J., & Su, S. (2014). T-Storm: Traffic-aware Online Scheduling in Storm. *Proceedings of the IEEE Int. Conf. Distrib. Comput. Syst.* (pp. 535-544). doi:10.1109/ICDCS.2014.61

Xu, Y., Yang, S., Tang, Y., Gao, Y., & Du Q. (2010). Study and application of landslide disaster refinement forecast system in district level based on GIS. *Proceedings of the IEEE International Conference on Geoinformatics* (pp. 1-4). doi:10.1109/GEOINFORMATICS.2010.5567657

Xu, L., & Beamon, B. M. (2006). Supply chain coordination and cooperation mechanisms: An attribute based approach. *J. Suppl. Chain Manag.*, *42*(1), 4–12. doi:10.1111/j.1745-493X.2006.04201002.x

Xu, Y., Li, K., He, L., & Truong, T. K. (2013). A DAG scheduling scheme on heterogeneous computing systems using double molecular structure-based chemical reaction optimization. *Journal of Parallel and Distributed Computing*, *73*(9), 1306–1322. doi:10.1016/j.jpdc.2013.05.005

Yaacoub, E.E., & Dawy, Z. (2012). Resource Allocation in Uplink OFDMA Wireless Systems: Optimal Solutions and Practical Implementations. IEEE press.

Yang, W., Wang, M., & Shi, P. (2013). Using MODIS NDVI Time Series to Identify Geographic Patterns of Landslides in Vegetated Regions. *IEEE Geoscience and Remote Sensing Letters*, *10*(4), 707–710. doi:10.1109/LGRS.2012.2219576

Yarowsky, D. (1995). Unsupervised word sense disambiguation rivaling supervised methods. *Proceedings of 33rd Annual Meeting of the Association for Computational Linguistics*, Cambridge, MA (pp. 189–196). doi:10.3115/981658.981684

Yun, J., & Song, M. H. (2014). Detecting Direction of Movement using Pyroelectric Infrared Sensors. *IEEE Sensors Journal*, *14*(5), 1482–1489. doi:10.1109/JSEN.2013.2296601

Yu, Y., & Wang, X. (2015). World Cup 2014 in the Twitter World: A big data analysis of sentiments in U.S. sports fans tweets. *Computers in Human Behavior*, *48*, 392–400. doi:10.1016/j.chb.2015.01.075

Zaharia, M., Das, T., Li, H., Hunter, T., Shenker, S., & Stoica, I. (2013). Discretized streams: Fault-tolerant streaming computation at scale. *Proceedings of the Twenty-Fourth ACM Symposium on Operating Systems Principles* (pp. 423–438). doi:10.1145/2517349.2522737

Zamith, M., Joselli, M., Clua, E. W. G., Montenegro, A., Leal-Toledo, R. C. P., Valente, L., & Feijo, B. (2011). A Distributed Architecture for Mobile Digital Games Based on Cloud Computing. *Proceedings of the 2011 Brazilian Symposium on Games and Digital Entertainment (SBGAMES)* (pp. 79-88). Retrieved August 02, 2016 from http://ieeexplore.ieee.org/xpls/abs_all.jsp?arnumber=6363221

Zamith, M., Joselli, M., Esteban, W. G. C., Montenegro, A., & Regina, C. P. Leal-Toledo; Luis Valente; Bruno Feijó (2011). A Distributed Architecture for Mobile Digital Games Based on Cloud Computing. *Proceedings of the 2011 Brazilian Symposium on Games and Digital Entertainment (SBGAMES)* (pp. 79-88). Retrieved August 02, 2016 from http://ieeexplore.ieee.org/xpls/abs_all.jsp?arnumber=6363221

Zappi, P., Farella, E., & Benini, L. (2007). Enhancing the Spatial Resolution of Presence Detection in a PIR based Wireless Surveillance Network. Proceedings of Advanced Video and Signal Based Surveillance, London, UK (pp. 295-300). doi:10.1109/AVSS.2007.4425326

Zappi, P., Farella, E., & Benini, L. (2008). Pyroelectric Infrared Sensors based Distance Estimation. *Proceedings of the 7th IEEE Sensors Conference*, Lecce, Italy (Vol. 8, pp. 716-719).

Zappi, P., Farella, E., & Benini, L. (2010). Tracking motion direction and distance with pyroelectric IR sensors. *IEEE Sensors Journal*, *10*(9), 1486–1494. doi:10.1109/JSEN.2009.2039792

Zaslavsky, A. (2013). Internet of things and ubiquitous sensing. Computing Now. Retrieved from https://www.computer.org/web/computingnow/archive/september2013

Zaslavsky, A., Perera, C., & Georgakopoulos, D. (2012). Sensing as a Service and Big Data. *Proceedings of the International Conference on Advances in Cloud Computing (ACC '12)*, Bangalore, India.

Zhang, H., Chen, G., Ooi, B. C., Kian-Lee, T., & Zhang, M. (2015). In-Memory Big Data Management and Processing: A Survey. *IEEE Transactions on Knowledge and Data Engineering, 27*(7), 1920–1948. doi:10.1109/TKDE.2015.2427795

Zhang, H., Wei, X., Zou, T., Li, Z., & Yang, G. (2014). Agriculture big data: Research status, challenges and countermeasures. *Proceedings of Computer and Computing Technologies in Agriculture, China* (pp. 137–143).

Zhang, T., Ramakrishnan, R., & Livn, M. (1997). BIRCH: A new data clustering algorithm and its applications. *Data Mining and Knowledge Discovery, 1*(2), 141–182. doi:10.1023/A:1009783824328

Zheng, D.E., & Carter, W.A. (2015). Leveraging the Internet of Things for a More Efficient and Effective Military. CSIS Strategic Technologies Program.

Zheng, K., Yang, Z., Zhang, K., Chatzimisios, P., Yang, K., & Xiang, W. (2016). Big data-driven optimization for mobile networks toward 5G. *IEEE Network, 30*(1), 44–51. doi:10.1109/MNET.2016.7389830

Zheng, Y. (Ed.), *Encyclopedia of mobile phone behavior*. Hershey, PA: IGI Global.

Zhou, F., Cao, F., Qian, W., & Jin, C. (2008). Tracking clusters in evolving data streams over sliding windows. *Knowledge and Information Systems, 15*(2), 181–214. doi:10.1007/s10115-007-0070-x

Zhou, H., & Benton, W. C. Jr. (2007). Supply chain practice and information sharing. *Journal of Operations Management, 25*(6), 1348–1365. doi:10.1016/j.jom.2007.01.009

Zhuravlev, S., Saez, J. C., Blagodurov, S., Fedorova, A., & Prieto, M. (2013). Survey of Energy-Cognizant Scheduling Techniques. *IEEE Transactions on Parallel and Distributed Systems, 24*(7), 1447–1464. doi:10.1109/TPDS.2012.20

Zhu, X. M., & Lu, P. Z. (2009, May). Multi-dimensional scheduling for real-time tasks on heterogeneous clusters. *Journal of Computer Science and Technology, 24*(3), 434–446. doi:10.1007/s11390-009-9235-2

Zikopoulos, P., Parasuraman, K., Deutsch, T., Giles, J., & Corrigan, D. (2012). *Harness the power of big data The IBM big data platform*. McGraw Hill Professional.

Zong, Z., Manzanares, A., Ruan, X., & Qin, X. (2011). EAD and PEBD: Two energy-aware duplication scheduling algorithms for parallel tasks on homogeneous clusters. *IEEE Trans. Comput., 60*(3), 360–374.

Zorzi, M., Gluhak, A., Lange, S., & Bassi, A. (2010). *From Todays Intranet of Things to a Future Internet of Things:* A Wireless- and Mobility-Related View. *IEEE Wireless Communication, 17*(6), 43–51. doi:10.1109/MWC.2010.5675777

About the Contributors

A.V. Krishna Prasad working as a Professor in Department of Computer Science and Engineering at KL University. He completed his Ph.D. in Computer Science from Sri Venkateswara University, Tirupati in 2012. He is an Editorial Board Member and Reviewer for several International Journals. He published several papers in national and international journals. His Interested Research areas are Mining, Big Data and Analytics.

* * *

Jawahar A has obtained his B.Tech in Electrical and Electronics Engineering from Jawaharlal Nehru Technological University Kakinada, Andhra Pradesh in 2012 and M.Tech. in Power System Control and Automation from Jawaharlal Nehru Technological University Kakinada, Andhra Pradesh in 2014. He worked as Project Fellow in Central Power Research Institute, Bangalore. He is currently working as Senior Research Fellow in Naval Research Board Project.

Faizan Ahmed is a MS student at Department of Computing, National University of Sciences and Technology-SEECS, Islamabad, Pakistan.

Muhammad Anshari is researcher and information system's practitioner. He received his BMIS (Hons) from International Islamic University Malaysia, his Master of IT from James Cook University Australia, and his PhD program at Universiti Brunei Darussalam.

Syamimi Ariff Lim is currently a lecturer teaching in ICT related area in the School of Business and Economics, Universiti Brunei Darussalam. She was the Director of e-Government Innovation Centre (eG.InC) from 2011-2016. She graduated with a PhD from Brunel Business School, Brunel University in 2009. Her research interests are in the area of ICT, e-Commerce, and other digital platforms.

Syed Hassan Askari is a MS student at Department of Computing, National University of Sciences and Technology-SEECS, Islamabad, Pakistan.

M. Rajasekhara Babu is a senior faculty member at School of Computing Science and Engineering, VIT University. He obtained his B.Tech. in ECE from SV University, Tirupathi, A.P and M.Tech. in C.S.E. from NIT Calicut, Kerala. He took his Ph.D. in CSE from VIT University, Vellore, Tamil Nadu, India. He was instrumental in establishing Intel Multi-Core Architecture Research Laboratory in collaboration with Intel, India at VIT University. He produced more than 75 international/national publications and authored 3 books in the area of computer architecture, compiler design and grid computing. He edited 5 volumes of 3 international conferences proceedings and published by Allied, Macmillan and Springer Publishers. Dr. RajaBabu has served in various prestigious positions as Division Leader (TCS & LT), Program Manager, etc., in VIT University. Currently, Dr. M Rajababu is working in the area of energy-aware applications for Internet of Things (IoT) and high-performance applications for Multi-Core Architectures.

Peyakunta Bhargavi, is working as Assistant Professor in the Department of Computer Science, Sri Padmavathi Mahila Visvavidyalayam (SPMVV), Tirupati. Received her Ph.D. from Sri Padmavati Women's University, Tirupati. She has 18 years of professional experience. She is member in IEEE, CSI, ISTE, IASCIT, IAENG and, MEACSE. Associate fellow member in AP Science Congress Association. Her areas of interest are Data mining, Soft Computing, Cloud Computing and Big Data Analytics.

Hallah Shahid Butt is a MS student at Department of Computing, National University of Sciences and Technology-SEECS, Islamabad, Pakistan.

Krishnaveer Abhishek Challa (b. 1991) is currently working as Soft Skills Trainer cum Faculty at Department of Foreign Languages, Andhra University. He is pursuing PhD from Department of Linguistics, Andhra University. He is also the Secretary of Linguistics Research Society and Honorary CEO of Tao Educare. He worked as Assistant Professor of English at Gayatri Vidya Parishad College for Degree & PG Courses (A), Visakhapatnam, India. He worked as Guest Faculty at Andhra University College of Engineering (A). He received MA in English Language & Literature from Adikavi Nannaya University and Masters in Journalism and Mass Communications from Andhra University. He qualified State Eligibility Test (SET) for Lectureship/Assistant Professorship. His specialization is International Communication. He also completed Masters in Philosophy, Hindi, Economics, Linguistics and Computer Science. He did his Bachelor of Arts in Economics, Political Science & Special English from Andhra University. He also completed Bachelor of Library & Information Science (BLiSc) from Dr. B.R. Ambedkar Open University. He did P.G. Diplomas in Management, English Language & Linguistics, Communication Skills, Functional English, English Language Teaching, Translation, Environmental Studies and Social Exclusion and Inclusive Policy. He did Diplomas in French, German, Functional Arabic and Yoga. He authored 40 books and published 75 Research Articles, Poetry and Book reviews in reputed Journals, Edited Volumes and Newspapers and Seminar Proceedings. He presented his research papers in numerous Seminars and was the resource person for many Workshops. He was selected as a student at Blekinge Tekniska Hogskola (BTH), Sweden and completed many courses. He won first prize in National Level Debate Competition on 'Green Manufacturing'. He acted and directed many Short Films and Documentaries and won an award.

Amardeep Das is working as an Assistant Professor in the Department of IT at C. V. Raman College of Engineering, Bhubaneswar, India. He received M. Tech. degree from BPUT, Rourkela, India and B. Tech. degree from BPUT, Rourkela, India in CSE. He has published few papers in reputed journals and conferences. He acted as reviewers in many reputed journals and conferences.

Prasant Kumar Dash is presently working in the department of Computer Science and Engineering of C. V. Raman College of Engineering, Bhubaneswar, Odisha, India. He is continuing a PhD. in the department of Computer Science and Engineering of SUIIT, Burla, Odisha, India. He has received the Master's degree (M.Tech(CSE)) from Biju Pattanaik University of Technology, Rourkela, Odisha in the year 2014.And also, he has completed MCA from Veer Surendra Sai University of Technology, Burla, Odisha, India in the year 2009. He has published some research papers in the national and international journals in the field of Wireless Sensor Network. Now, he is working in a different area like queuing technique, congestion control of different layers of the network (WSN, UWSN).

Harry Foxwell is an Associate Professor at the Volgenau School of Engineering, George Mason University, in Fairfax, Virginia. His earlier career includes serving as Principal System Engineer for the Oracle Corporation's Public Sector Division.

Sadaf Jalil is a MS student at Department of Computing, National University of Sciences and Technology-SEECS, Islamabad, Pakistan.

Singaraju Jyothi is a Professor in Computer Science. She worked as Director, University Computer Centre, Head, Dept. of Computer Science, Head (I/C), Dept. of Computer Science and Engineering, BOS Chairperson, BOS member and so on. She has 25 years teaching experience and 30 years' research experience. 9 Ph.D., 7 M.Phil were awarded and 8 Ph.D. scholars are being guided under her supervision. She is senior member of IEEE & IACSIT, fellow of RSS, ISCA & SSARSC, member of ACM, IET & IAENG and life member of CSI, ISTE and ISCA. More than 80 papers published in International and National Journals and 60 papers presented in International and National conferences. 8 books were authored and edited by her. She has conducted 2 national and 2 international conferences. She has completed one UGC major Project and she is handling one DBT major project and to be handled two more DBT projects. Her areas of interest in Image Processing, Soft Computing, Data Mining, Bioinformatics and Hyperspectra.

A. Kalyan has completed his B.Tech in 2001 and an M.Tech in the year 2004. Has been actively teaching for more than 11 years and has worked with various prestigious institutions.

Anvita Karara is a Life Science Professional with expertise in Clinical Trial Design and modeling. She pursued her Masters in Biotechnology and Management from Carnegie Mellon University, USA. She has worked prior in this space with leading bio-pharmaceutical companies such as Genentech (a Roche company) and Onyx Pharmaceutical (an Amgen subsidiary).

Safdar Abbas Khan is an assistant professor at School of Electrical Engineering and Computer Sciences (SEECS) at National University of Sciences and Technology (NUST) Islamabad, Pakistan. He completed his doctoral thesis with specialization in computer science from the University of Paris, France in 2011. By training he is a mathematician. He completed his master's in mathematics with Gold Medal from Quaid-i-Azam University, Islamabad, Pakistan. He is the author of a few publications in renowned international journals. His areas of research and interest include the application of mathematics to various fields of engineering and technology.

Akhil Khare was awarded his Bachelors and Masters of Technology Degree from RGTU Bhopal in Information Technology, PhD from JNU in Computer Science and Engineering. His areas of interest are Computer Network, Software Engineering and Multimedia System. He has 13years' experience in teaching and research. He has published more than 100 research papers in journals and conferences. He has also guided 20 postgraduate students. He is a recognized Ph.D. Supervisor for various Universities in India and presently guiding 03 Ph.D. scholars. He also authored 03 books and have 04 Patents and 10 copyrights.

Ankit Lodha is Analytics Operations Lead in Clinical Application & Analytical Services (CAAS) at Amgen. Within Amgen he has worked on R&D and Commercial Analytics. Before this positon, he has provided strategic consulting services, supporting the analytics, data reporting, and data management needs of senior leadership at AstraZeneca and Pfizer. He holds a Bachelors in Biotechnology Engineering from Dr. D.Y. Patil University, Masters in Business of Bioscience from Keck Graduate Institute and MBA from Redlands University – School of Business.

Daphne Lopez is a Professor in the School of Information Technology and Engineering, Vellore Institute of Technology University. Her research spans the fields of grid and cloud computing, spatial and temporal data mining and big data. She has a vast experience in teaching and industry. She is the author/ co–author of papers in conferences, book chapters and journals. She serves as a reviewer in journals and conference proceedings. Prior to this, she has worked in the software industry as a consultant in data warehouse and business intelligence. She is a member of International Society for Infectious Diseases.

Nagaraju Mamillapally is presently working in Adarsh Degree & PG College as Head of the Department in Computer Science. He completed Master's Degree in Computer Science from Osmania University and Master's Degree in Technology from JNTUH and having 12 years of teaching experience. His area of interest in research is Cloud Computing, Big Data, Web Mining and IoT. Presently he is doing research in specific areas like Big Data Analysis, Website Quality Assurance and Internet of Things.

Gunasekaran Manogaran is currently pursuing PhD in the School of Information Technology and Engineering, Vellore Institute of Technology University. He received his B.E. and M.Tech from Anna University and Vellore Institute of Technology University respectively. He has worked as a Research Assistant for a project on Spatial Data Mining funded by Indian Council of Medical Research, Government of India. He published peer-reviewed journals/conferences/book chapters including International Journal of Infectious Diseases (Impact Factor 1.859), IEEE International Conference on Big Data, USA (paper acceptance rate: 18.5%), The Human Element of Big Data: Issues, Analytics, and Performance, CRC (In Press) and Handbook of Research on Cybersecurity and Online Threat Protection, IGI Global (In Press). His current research interests include Data Mining, Big Data Analytics and Health Informatics. He got an award for young investigator from India and Southeast Asia by Bill & Melinda Gates Foundation. He is a life time member of International Society for Infectious Diseases.

Brojo Kishore Mishra is an Associate Professor in the Department of Information Technology and IQAC Coordinator of C. V. Raman College of Engineering, Bhubaneswar. Now he is the Regional Student Coordinator for Computer Society of India (CSI), Region - IV. He has received his Ph.D (Computer Science) from Berhampur University in 2012 and has supervised more than 10 M. Tech theses in the area of Data/ Opinion Mining, Soft Computing applications and Security. Dr. Mishra has published more than 30 research papers in international journals and conference proceedings and 05 invited book chapters. Dr. Mishra has chaired various international conferences and he has been a member of numerous international program committees of workshops and conferences in the area of Computer Science. He serves as Guest Editor in IJRSDA, IJKDB and IJACR special issue journals and an editorial board member of many international journals. He was associated with a CSI funded research project as a Principal Investigator. He was the Jury Coordination Committee Member of All IEEE Young Engineers' Humanitarian Challenge (AIYEHUM 2015) project competition, organized by IEEE Region 10 (Asia pacific) and IEEE Day 2015 & 2016 Ambassador for IEEE Kolkata section. He is a life member of ISTE, CSI, and member of IEEE, ACM, IAENG, UACEE, and ACCS.

Nishchol Mishra was born in Vidisha, India, in 1977. He received the B.E. degree in Computer Science & Engineering from the Barkatullah University, Bhopal, India, in 2000, and the M.Tech. and Ph.D. degrees in Computer Science & Engineering from Rajiv Gandhi Proudyogiki Vishwavidyalaya (RGPV), Bhopal, India, in 2003 and 2014, respectively. His current research interests include Multimedia data mining, Big data analytics, Social Media analytics, IoT and Cyber Forensics. He is a Life Member of the Indian Society for Technical Education (ISTE) and Computer Society of India (CSI).

Trivikram Mulukutla is working as senior lecturer in Adarsh Degree & PG College in Department of Computer Science. He completed a Master's Degree in Computer Applications from Osmania University and Master's Degree in Technology from Allahabad Agricultural University and having 20 years of teaching experience. He is also pursuing Ph.D in Computer Science at Rayalaseema University, Kurnool. His area of interest is Web Mining and Internet of Things.

Rizwan Patan is a Teaching Cum Research Associate at School of Computer Science and Engineering, VIT University. Received the B.Tech. And M.Tech. Degrees in Computer Science and Engineering from the JNTU-A University in Andhra Pradesh, India in 2012 and 2014, respectively. Present doing Ph.D. in Computer Sciences and Engineering from the VIT University in Tamil Nadu, India. He is Edited and authored 1 Book and 8 International/National publications and 3 International/National conference proceedings. His research interests include Big Data, Real-Time Data Processing, Soft Computing, Fault Tolerance, And High Performance Computing.

M. K. Priyan is currently pursuing a PhD in the Vellore Institute of Technology University. He received my Bachelor of Engineering and Master of Engineering degree from Anna University and Vellore Institute of Technology University, respectively. His current research interests include Big Data Analytics, Internet of Things, Internet of Everything, Internet of Vehicles in Healthcare. He is the author/ co-author of papers in international journals and conferences.

P. Raja Rajeswari is working as a professor in the Department of computer science and engineering at KL University. He has 16 years of work experience.

P. Venkateswara Rao is a Professor in Audisankara college of Engineering and Technology, Gudur. His Research area is Data Mining and Neural Networks. He has published many papers in various reputed journals, national and international conferences.

Varsha Sharma is an Assistant Professor at School of IT, Rajiv Gandhi Proudyogiki Vishwavidyalaya (RGPV), Bhopal. She received the degree of B.E in Computer Science & Engineering from RGPV in 2003. She completed her M.Tech and Ph.D in Computer Science & Engineering from RGPV in 2007 and 2013 respectively. Her current research interest is in Wireless Networks, Big Data and IoT.

Pallavi Shrivastava is working at Matrusri Engineering College, Saidabad, Hyderabad, India as an Assistant Professor, ECE Dept. her areas of interest are image processing and Multimedia System. She has three Intellectual property rights (IPR) and more than Thirty research publications in various journals and conferences.

G. Sreedhar is working as an Associate Professor in the Department of Computer Science, Rashtiya Sanskrit Vidyapeetha (Deemed University), Tirupati, India since 2001. G. Sreedhar received his Ph.D in Computer Science and Technology from Sri Krishnadevaraya University, Anantapur, India in the year 2011. He has over 15 years of Experience in Teaching and Research in the field of Computer Science. He published more than 15 research papers related to web engineering in reputed international journals. He published 4 books from reputed international publications and he presented more than 15 research papers in various national and international conferences. He handled research projects in computer science funded by University Grants Commission, Government of India. He is a member in various professional bodies like academic council, board of studies and editorial board member in various international journals in the field of computer science, Information Technology and other related fields. He has proven knowledge in the field of Computer Science and allied research areas.

Vadlamudi Sucharita is working as an Associate professor in K L University. Her research area is DataMining and Neural Networks. Presently, she is working towards Big Data Analytics and cloud computing.

Revathi Sundarasekar is a professor in the School of Information Technology and Engineering, Vellore Institute of Technology University. Her research spans the fields of grid and cloud computing, spatial and temporal data mining, and Big Data. She has vast experience in teaching and industry. She is the author/coauthor of papers in conferences, book chapters, and journals. She serves as a reviewer in journals and conference proceedings. Prior to this, she worked in the software industry as a consultant in data warehouse and business intelligence. She is a member of the International Society for Infectious Diseases.

Kallam Suresh received his Bachelor and Master degree from Jawaharlal Nehru Technological University, Hyderabad and Ph.D. from VIT University, Vellore, Tamilnadu. He is currently working as Assistant Professor, Department of I.T, AITS, Rajampet, A.P, India. Previously he worked as Foreign Faculty in East China University of Technology, ECIT Nanchang Campus, Jiangxi-330013, P.R.China and Visiting Faculty for Jiangxi Normal University, P.R. China. He has published more than 20 national and International conference papers and 9 international journals and one Book published. He received best paper award in 2005 and Got First prize in National Paper Presentation in 2008. His field of interest is Internet of Things, Big Data, and High Performance Computing.

Marcus Tanque is a highly-regarded technology strategist and an author with proven skills in business/data analytics, corporate security/engineering strategies, policies. He also has vested expertise in artificial intelligence, cyber security practices, governance, enterprise infrastructure & management and diverse IT consulting practices. Dr. Tanque has a repertoire of technical competencies in assorted consultative functions for the government, public and private sectors. His natural entrepreneurial flair coupled with unparalleled contributions to academic, federal, and industry customers is of significance. Dr. Tanque has been supporting mission-critical business and technology projects: IT engineering, program/project management, systems security, machine learning, cyber security operations, artificial intelligence, big data analytics, information & communications technology as well as cloud-based solutions. Dr. Tanque holds a Ph.D. in Information Technology with a dual specialization in Information Assurance and Security as well as a Masters in Information Systems Engineering.

Chandu Thota is currently working as Technology Analyst in the Infosys Ltd., India. He received his MCA from Jawaharlal Nehru Technological University, Hyderabad. He Qualified UGC-NET (Computer Science and Applications) exam which has been conducted by University Grants Commission (UGC), HRD Ministry, Government of India. He published peer-reviewed conferences/book chapters including Handbook of Research on Cybersecurity and Online Threat Protection, IGI Global (In Press). Currently he is working on projects with Java, J2EE, Cloud Computing and Infosys Finacle technologies. His current research interests include Cloud Computing, Security, Big Data and IoT.

Sajid Umair was born in Nowshera KPK, Pakistan in 1992. He has a matric degree from Govt. high school A.C Center Nowshera and FSc (Computer Science) degree from Pakistan degree collage Nowshera. He received the B.S. degree in computer science from IBMS, The University of Agriculture Peshawar, Pakistan, in 2013, and got a silver medal in his B.S. degree, and is currently pursuing M.S. in computer science from School of Electrical Engineering and Computer Science (SEECS), National University of Sciences and Technology (NUST), Islamabad Pakistan. His current research work includes Computer Science with Video Processing, Mobile Journalism, Digital image processing and Mobile Cloud Computing. He is also a member of High Performance Computing (HPC) Lab and Excellence for Mobile Computing (EMC) Lab at SEECS NUST. His research papers are also published on the topics of Mobile Cloud Computing, Artificial Neural Networks, Support Vector Machine, and Mobile Journalism. He is also a chief commissioner award holder in scouting. He is the nephew of senior Anchorperson/Journalist Javed Iqbal and Grandchild of great Pashto poet Samandar Khan Samandar.

R. Varatharajan received his B.E., M.E. and Ph.D. degrees all in Electronics and Communication Engineering from Anna University and Bharath University, India. His main area of research activity is Medical Image processing, Wireless Networks and VLSI Physical Design. He has served as a reviewer for Springer, Inderscience and Elsevier journals. He has published many research articles in refereed journals. He is a member of IEEE, IACSIT, IAENG, SCIEI and ISTE wireless research group. He has been serving as Organizing Chair and Program Chair of several International conferences and in the Program Committees of several International conferences. Currently he is working as an Associate professor in the Department of Electronics and Communication Engineering at Sri Ramanujar Engineering College, Chennai, India.

Elias Yaacoub received the B.E. degree in Electrical Engineering from the Lebanese University in 2002, the M.E. degree in Computer and Communications Engineering from the American University of Beirut (AUB) in 2005, and the PhD degree in Electrical and Computer Engineering from AUB in 2010. He worked as a Research Assistant in the American University of Beirut from 2004 to 2005, and in the Munich University of Technology in Spring 2005. From 2005 to 2007, he worked as a Telecommunications Engineer with Dar Al-Handasah, Shair and Partners. From November 2010 till December 2014, he worked as a Research Scientist / R&D Expert at the Qatar Mobility Innovations Center (QMIC). Afterwards, he joined Strategic Decisions Group (SDG) where he worked as a Consultant till February 2016. He is currently an Associate Professor at the Arab Open University (AOU). His research interests include Wireless Communications, Resource Allocation in Wireless Networks, Intercell Interference Mitigation Techniques, Antenna Theory, Sensor Networks, and Bioinformatics.

Index

Purchase Print, E-Book, or Print + E-Book

IGI Global books can now be purchased from three unique pricing formats:
Print Only, E-Book Only, or Print + E-Book. Shipping fees apply.

www.igi-global.com

Recommended Reference Books

ISBN: 978-1-4666-9834-5
© 2016; 314 pp.
List Price: $195

ISBN: 978-1-4666-9770-6
© 2016; 485 pp.
List Price: $200

ISBN: 978-1-4666-6539-2
© 2015; 2,388 pp.
List Price: $2,435

ISBN: 978-1-4666-9466-8
© 2016; 2,418 pp.
List Price: $2,300

ISBN: 978-1-4666-9572-6
© 2016; 854 pp.
List Price: $465

ISBN: 978-1-5225-0058-2
© 2016; 1,015 pp.
List Price: $465

Looking for free content, product updates, news, and special offers?
Join IGI Global's mailing list today and start enjoying exclusive perks sent only to IGI Global members.
Add your name to the list at **www.igi-global.com/newsletters**.

Publishing Information Science and Technology Research Since 1988

www.igi-global.com Sign up at www.igi-global.com/newsletters f facebook.com/igiglobal t twitter.com/igiglobal

Stay Current on the Latest Emerging Research Developments

Become an IGI Global Reviewer for Authored Book Projects

 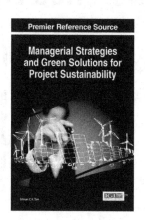  

The overall success of an authored book project is dependent on quality and timely reviews.

In this competitive age of scholarly publishing, constructive and timely feedback significantly decreases the turnaround time of manuscripts from submission to acceptance, allowing the publication and discovery of progressive research at a much more expeditious rate. Several IGI Global authored book projects are currently seeking highly qualified experts in the field to fill vacancies on their respective editorial review boards:

Applications may be sent to:
development@igi-global.com

Applicants must have a doctorate (or an equivalent degree) as well as publishing and reviewing experience. Reviewers are asked to write reviews in a timely, collegial, and constructive manner. All reviewers will begin their role on an ad-hoc basis for a period of one year, and upon successful completion of this term can be considered for full editorial review board status, with the potential for a subsequent promotion to Associate Editor.

If you have a colleague that may be interested in this opportunity, we encourage you to share this information with them.

www.igi-global.com

InfoSci®-Books

A Database for Progressive Information Science and Technology Research

Maximize Your Library's Book Collection!

Invest in IGI Global's InfoSci®-Books database and gain access to hundreds of reference books at a fraction of their individual list price.

The InfoSci®-Books database offers unlimited simultaneous users the ability to precisely return search results through more than 75,000 full-text chapters from nearly 3,400 reference books in the following academic research areas:

Business & Management Information Science & Technology • Computer Science & Information Technology
Educational Science & Technology • Engineering Science & Technology • Environmental Science & Technology
Government Science & Technology • Library Information Science & Technology • Media & Communication Science & Technology
Medical, Healthcare & Life Science & Technology • Security & Forensic Science & Technology • Social Sciences & Online Behavior

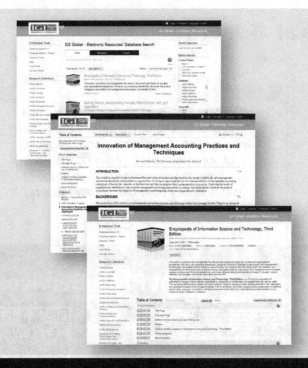

Peer-Reviewed Content:
• Cutting-edge research
• No embargoes
• Scholarly and professional
• Interdisciplinary

Award-Winning Platform:
• Unlimited simultaneous users
• Full-text in XML and PDF
• Advanced search engine
• No DRM

Librarian-Friendly:
• Free MARC records
• Discovery services
• COUNTER4/SUSHI compliant
• Training available

To find out more or request a free trial, visit:
www.igi-global.com/eresources

IGI Global
DISSEMINATOR OF KNOWLEDGE
www.igi-global.com

www.igi-global.com

IGI Global Proudly Partners with

Enhance Your Manuscript with
eContent Pro's Professional and Academic
Copy Editing Service

Additional Services

Expert Translation

eContent Pro Translation provides professional
translation services across key languages
around the world. Our expert translators will
work to provide a clear-cut translation of your
document, while maintaining your original
meaning and ensuring that your document is
accurately and professionally translated.

Professional Proofreading

eContent Pro Proofreading provides fast,
high-quality, affordable proofreading that
will optimize the accuracy and readability
of your document, ensuring that its
contents are communicated in the
clearest way possible to your readers.

IGI Global Authors Save 20% on eContent Pro's Services!

Scan the QR Code to Receive Your 20% Discount

The 20% discount is applied directly to your eContent Pro shopping cart when placing
an order through IGI Global's referral link. Use the QR code to access this referral link.
eContent Pro has the right to end or modify any promotion at any time.

Email: customerservice@econtentpro.com

econtentpro.com

Become an IRMA Member

Members of the **Information Resources Management Association (IRMA)** understand the importance of community within their field of study. The Information Resources Management Association is an ideal venue through which professionals, students, and academicians can convene and share the latest industry innovations and scholarly research that is changing the field of information science and technology. Become a member today and enjoy the benefits of membership as well as the opportunity to collaborate and network with fellow experts in the field.

IRMA Membership Benefits:

- **One FREE Journal Subscription**
- **30% Off Additional Journal Subscriptions**
- **20% Off Book Purchases**
- Updates on the latest events and research on Information Resources Management through the IRMA-L listserv.
- Updates on new open access and downloadable content added to Research IRM.
- A copy of the Information Technology Management Newsletter twice a year.
- A certificate of membership.

IRMA Membership $195

Scan code or visit **irma-international.org** and begin by selecting your free journal subscription.

Membership is good for one full year.

www.irma-international.org

www.igi-global.com

5% Pre-Pub Discount

Order through www.igi-global.com with **Free Standard Shipping**.

The Premier Reference for Computer Science & Information Technology

Encyclopedia of

Information Science and Technology

Fourth Edition

Mehdi Khosrow-Pour   Volume I

100% Original Content
Contains 705 new, peer-reviewed articles covering over 80 categories in 11 subject areas

Diverse Contributions
More than 1,00 experts from 74 unique countries contributed their specialized knowledge

Easy Navigation
Includes two tables of content and a comprehensive index in each volume for the user's convenience

Highly-Cited
Embraces a complete list of references and additional reading sections to allow for further research

Coming Soon to:

InfoSci®-Books

Encyclopedia of Information Science and Technology Fourth Edition

A Comprehensive 10-Volume Set

Mehdi Khosrow-Pour, D.B.A. (Information Resources Management Association, USA)
ISBN: 978-1-5225-2255-3; © 2018; Pg: 7,500; Release Date: July 31, 2017

For a limited time, <u>receive the complimentary e-books for the First, Second, and Third editions</u> with the purchase of the *Encyclopedia of Information Science and Technology, Fourth Edition* e-book.**

The **Encyclopedia of Information Science and Technology, Fourth Edition** is a 10-volume set which includes 705 original and previously unpublished research articles covering a full range of perspectives, applications, and techniques contributed by thousands of experts and researchers from around the globe. This authoritative encyclopedia is an all-encompassing, well-established reference source that is ideally designed to disseminate the most forward-thinking and diverse research findings. With critical perspectives on the impact of information science management and new technologies in modern settings, including but not limited to computer science, education, healthcare, government, engineering, business, and natural and physical sciences, it is a pivotal and relevant source of knowledge that will benefit every professional within the field of information science and technology and is an invaluable addition to every academic and corporate library.

Scan for Online Bookstore

5% Pre-Pub Discount Pricing*

Hardcover: **$5,410**
Org. Price: US $5,695

E-Book: **$5,410**
Org. Price: US $5,695

Hardcover + E-Book: **$6,550**
Org. Price: US $6,895

Both E-Book Prices Include:
• *Encyclopedia of Information Science and Technology, First Edition E-Book*
• *Encyclopedia of Information Science and Technology, Second Edition E-Book*
• *Encyclopedia of Information Science and Technology, Third Edition E-Book*

* 5% pre-publication discount plus free standard shipping is good through one month after publication date and cannot be combined with any other discount offer, with the exception of the free first, second, and third edition's e-book offer.

** Purchase the Encyclopedia of Information Science and Technology, Fourth Edition e-book and receive the first, second, and third e-book editions for free. Offer is only valid with purchase of the fourth edition's e-book. Offer expires January 1, 2018.

Recommend this Title to Your Institution's Library: www.igi-global.com/books

www.igi-global.com/infosci-ondemand

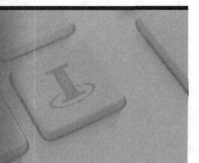

InfoSci®-OnDemand

Continuously updated with new material on a weekly basis, InfoSci®-OnDemand offers the ability to search through thousands of quality full-text research papers. Users can narrow each search by identifying key topic areas of interest, then display a complete listing of relevant papers, and purchase materials specific to their research needs.

Comprehensive Service

- Over 81,600+ journal articles, book chapters, and case studies.

- All content is downloadable in PDF format and can be stored locally for future use.

No Subscription Fees

- One time fee of $37.50 per PDF download.

Instant Access

- Receive a download link immediately after order completion!

Database Platform Features:

- Comprehensive Pay-Per-View Service
- Written by Prominent International Experts/Scholars
- Precise Search and Retrieval
- Updated With New Material on a Weekly Basis
- Immediate Access to Full-Text PDFs
- No Subscription Needed
- Purchased Research Can Be Stored Locally for Future Use

"It really provides an excellent entry into the research literature of the field. It presents a manageable number of highly relevant sources on topics of interest to a wide range of researchers. The sources are scholarly, but also accessible to 'practitioners'."

- Lisa Stimatz, MLS, University of North Carolina at Chapel Hill, USA

"It is an excellent and well designed database which will facilitate research, publication and teaching. It is a very very useful tool to have."

- George Ditsa, PhD, University of Wollongong, Australia

"I have accessed the database and find it to be a valuable tool to the IT/IS community. I found valuable articles meeting my search criteria 95% of the time."

- Lynda Louis, Xavier University of Louisiana, USA

Recommended for use by researchers who wish to immediately download PDFs of individual chapters or articles.

www.igi-global.com/e-resources/infosci-ondemand

www.igi-global.com

Printed in the United States
by Bookmasters

Printed in the United States
By Bookmasters